W9-CZN-466

LABOR AND EMPLOYMENT

RELATIONS ASSOCIATION SERIES

INEQUALITY, UNCERTAINTY, AND OPPORTUNITY

The Varied and Growing Role of Finance in Labor Relations

Edited By
Christian E. Weller

First Edition
ISBN 978-0-913447-10-9

LABOR AND EMPLOYMENT RELATIONS ASSOCIATION SERIES
Proceedings of the Annual Meeting (published electronically beginning in 2009)
Annual Research Volume (published in the summer/fall)
LERA Online Membership Directory (updated daily, member/subscriber access only)
LERA Newsletter (published electronically 3–4 times a year)
Perspectives on Work (published once a year in the summer/fall)
Perspectives on Work Online Companion (published twice a year as a supplement)

Information regarding membership, subscriptions, meetings, publications, and general affairs of the LERA can be found at the Association website at www.leraweb.org. Members can make changes to their member records, including contact information, affiliations, and preferences, by accessing the online directory at the website or by contacting the LERA national office.

LABOR AND EMPLOYMENT RELATIONS ASSOCIATION
University of Illinois at Urbana-Champaign
School of Labor and Employment Relations
121 Labor and Employment Relations Building
504 East Armory Ave., MC-504
Champaign, IL 61820
Telephone: 217/333-0072   Fax: 217/265-5130
Websites: www.leraweb.org
E-mail: leraoffice@illinois.edu

CONTENTS

Introduction

CHRISTIAN E. WELLER
University of Massachusetts Boston
and
Center for American Progress

OVERVIEW

Finance has grown in many respects in developed economies over the past three decades to the extent that financial measures and goods and services have become a pervasive part of modern market economies.

As a start, financial services and employment in financial institutions make up an increasing share of employment. And nonfinancial businesses increasingly prioritize short-term performance measures to satisfy financial markets that have grown not only in size but also in importance. Moreover, households have seen a rise in risk exposure as financial markets, goods and services, and financial performance measures started to dominate. Households increasingly have to weather financial markets on their own, for instance, as they save for retirement. These large-scale trends have direct implications for labor relations at every level of the economy. The rising importance of financial markets has translated into increasing economic and labor market instability around the globe. Typical boom and bust cycles in financial markets have had larger effects on economic and job growth than in the past.

Second, the way businesses operate has fundamentally changed as nonfinancial businesses increasingly adhere to short-term financial measures to satisfy those who finance their operations. And third, some individuals have seen their economic circumstances improve, in rare instances quite heftily, if they could find ways to benefit from the growing importance of finance. Many others, however, saw their economic security sharply erode as labor market and financial market risk exposure for households grew.

What does this all mean? Understanding the myriad ways in which the growth of finance can impact the way we work can give us better insights into the causes of and potential solutions to addressing economic instability and income and wealth inequality, for instance, by creating more and better economic opportunities for many, not just a few. All chapters in this book touch on two or three of the main themes—instability, inequality, and opportunity (or lack thereof).

This research volume gives readers a sense of the complex and pervasive link between finance and labor relations. It addresses key connections between finance and labor relations at every level of the economy: the macroeconomy, industries, firm, and households. It also discusses the role of a variety of financial products, such as individual retirement savings plans, stock options, private equity investments, and consumer credit, in shaping the increasingly tight relationship between finance and labor relations.

This volume further provides a sense of the dual nature of finance in labor relations—the growing risks to and potential opportunities for economic security—when discussing employee ownership, socially responsible investing, and income diversification. It also illustrates that the growing influence of finance on labor relations is not limited to the United State but plays out in different ways in other parts of the world.

Finally, many chapters draw important policy lessons from research, demonstrating that the relationship between finance and labor relations and the consequences of this relationship can change. In other words, this research volume covers a lot of important ground and serves as an entry point to scholars, teachers, activists, and neutrals interested in learning more about the link between finance and labor relations.

I should note that our understanding of the complex nature of the growing role of finance in labor relations is still evolving as new financial products become available, different parts of the economy adopt new financial services, and regulations introduced in the aftermath of the financial crisis of 2007 through 2009 take shape. Several chapters hence address emerging topics that will likely need further research by interested scholars. This applies in varying degrees to Sara Bernardo's chapter on the link between household debt and labor market uncertainty; to Janet Boguslaw and Alexander Kaufman's chapter on targeted investments such as socially responsible investing and pension fund activism; and to the work of Hina Sheikh, Stephen Lerner, and Rita Berlofa on organizing financial service workers in the United States and Brazil—as well as to my own chapter, co-authored with Jeffrey Wenger, on the need for and lack of income diversification for vulnerable households.

Other chapters, in comparison, are more definitive: they are the culmination of long-standing research projects, often spanning decades of the lead researchers' expertise. Examples here include William Lazonick's chapter on the changing nature of labor amid new managerial orientations, Rosemary Batt and Eileen Appelbaum's work on private equity; Joseph Blasi, Richard Freeman, and Douglas Kruse's research on employee ownership; and Edward Wolff's insights on the link between individual retirement savings and wealth inequality. Accordingly, this research volume gives readers a sense of the tremendous work that scholars have already undertaken to get a handle on how finance affects labor relations as well as on the many emerging and still-developing research questions.

I have organized this research volume in the following way: The first two chapters address the macroeconomic aspects of the link between finance and labor relations. The next three chapters deal with the connection between the growing role of finance and labor relations at the industry level and are followed by three chapters that examine the link between finance and labor relations at the firm level. The final three chapters address how the changing landscape impacts individuals.

SECTION AND CHAPTER DESCRIPTIONS

As explained previously, I grouped the chapters by the level of the economy that constitutes the primary unit of analysis of the respective chapters. Other organizing principles—such as arranging chapters by whether they primarily focus on uncertainty, inequality, or opportunity—proved more difficult to do because many chapters cover more than one of these three themes.

Table 1 offers a cursory look at the various aspects of each chapter. It shows the level of the economy that serves as the primary focus of the chapter; the main themes of each chapter as they relate to the volume's three themes of instability, inequality, and opportunity; each chapter's geographic coverage; and whether the chapter contains detailed policy implications, including alternative policy proposals or more limited policy lessons.

Macroeconomic Level

The first section, on the macroeconomic effects of the link between finance and labor relations, consists of two chapters. The chapter by Teresa Ghilarducci and Joelle Saad-Lessler presents evidence that the gradual replacement of defined benefit (DB) pensions with individual defined contribution (DC) savings plans—a key aspect of tying individual fortunes to financial market outcomes—has chipped away at the stabilizing effect of DB pensions during economic recessions.

Next, Joel Cutcher-Gershenfeld, Dan Brooks, Noel Cowell, Christos Ioannou, Martin Mulloy, Danny Roberts, Tanzia Saunders, and Søren Viemose show that adherence to financial market measures in macroeconomic adjustments has severely eroded labor protections in a number of countries such as Denmark, Greece, Jamaica, and the United States.

Industry Level

The second section consists of three chapters that address a number of key issues at the industry level. Janet Boguslaw and Alexander Kaufman discuss the potential and substantial limitations of targeted financial investment strategies such as socially responsible investing to influence economic outcomes in nonfinancial corporations.

TABLE 1
Summary Descriptions of Research Volume Chapters

Chapter	Authors	Main focus	Economic level	Theme	Geographic coverage	Policy implications
1	Ghilarducci and Saad-Lessler	Economic stability during recessions	Macroeconomy	Instability and inequality	United States	Detailed policy implications
2	Cutcher-Gershenfeld, Brooks, Cowell, Ioannou, Mulloy, Roberts, Saunders, and Viemose	Economic adjustments after crises in Denmark, Greece, Jamaica, and the United States	Macroeconomy	Instability, inequality, and opportunity	Denmark, Greece, Jamaica, and the United States	Limited policy implications
3	Boguslaw and Kaufman	Targeted investments to affect finance's role in nonfinancial corporations	Industry (nonfinancial corporations)	Inequality and opportunity	United States	Limited policy implications
4	Dörre	Growing prioritization of financial goals over other metrics in German industries	Industry (German metal and electronics)	Inequality and opportunity	Germany	Limited policy implications
5	Sheikh, Lerner, and Berlofa	Organizing bank workers in Brazil and the United States	Industry (financial services)	Inequality and opportunity	Brazil and the United States	Detailed policy implications
6	Lazonick	Growth of stock options, declining innovation, and rising inequality	Firm (management compensation and labor relations)	Instability, inequality, and opportunity	United States	Detailed policy implications

TABLE 1 (continued)
Summary Descriptions of Research Volume Chapters

Chapter	Authors	Main focus	Economic level	Theme	Geographic coverage	Policy implications
7	Batt and Appelbaum	Private equity investments and their impact on job creation and worker compensation	Firm (financial investment)	Inequality and opportunity	United States	Detailed policy implications
8	Blasi, Freeman, and Kruse	Employee stock ownership	Firm (employee compensation tied to financial markets)	Inequality and opportunity	United States	Detailed policy implications
9	Wolff	Changing retirement savings, wealth inequality, and retirement income security	Household (wealth)	Inequality and opportunity	United States	Limited policy implications
10	Bernardo	Labor market insecurity and household indebtedness	Household (debt)	Instability and inequality	United States	Limited policy implications
11	Weller and Wenger	The need and potential for income diversification	Household (income)	Inequality and opportunity	United States	Detailed policy implications

Klaus Dörre then presents an overview of the development of new management models that prioritize short-term financial metrics over other goals in the German metal and electronics industries. He argues that such a prioritization is not preordained but rather is dependent on key social institutions, including collective bargaining, that policy can weaken or strengthen.

Hina Sheikh, Stephen Lerner, and Rita Berlofa take a closer look at organizing in the financial services sector in the United States, where few workers belong to unions or are covered by collective bargaining agreements, and in Brazil, where many workers are union members and benefit from collective bargaining agreements. They argue that Brazil's bank workers can maintain their collective bargaining agreements only if they do not compete with U.S. workers, who are not covered by such agreements, and that the future of unions in key industries in this globalized industry depends on international coordination between labor organizations.

Firm Level

The third section of this research volume investigates how particular financial arrangements shape labor relations at the firm level. William Lazonick discusses how changes in managerial incentives, especially the growing emphasis on performance-based compensation in the form of stock options, has altered corporate priorities, reduced investments, and lowered innovation while increasing the economic insecurity and income inequality faced by workers.

Rosemary Batt and Eileen Appelbaum then tackle the complexities of private equity investments in U.S. firms and the implications of those investments for job creation and wages. They argue that such investments have the potential to save jobs in failing firms. The potential benefits, though, are often overstated, in their view, because of a lack of accountability by private equity investors to a firm's stakeholders or are simply unknown because private equity investments lack transparency.

Joseph Blasi, Richard Freeman, and Douglas Kruse present evidence on the effect of employee stock ownership on labor relations. They find that firms with broad-based employee stock ownership plans tend to generate more goodwill among workers and greater trust between employees and employers, and reduce worker turnover.

Household Level

The final section of this research volume examines the implications of the growing link between finance and labor relations on household economic security. Edward Wolff summarizes detailed data on household wealth and traces the rise of wealth inequality in part to the replacement of DB pensions with DC savings plans. The growth of individual savings that have taken the place of DB pensions has brought increasing retirement income insecurity—that is, present labor market challenges following from substantial changes in the way workers are compensated can have long-lasting effects on the economic security of households.

Sara Bernardo considers the existing evidence on how rising labor market risks that followed from the increasingly short-term financial market orientation of many employers intersect with rising household debt. She argues that there is some evidence of a vicious cycle by which rising labor market risks increase household indebtedness and that this indebtedness increases the cost of job loss (i.e., economic insecurity rises more sharply and lasts longer than in the past because households are more in debt).

Finally, my chapter co-authored with Jeffrey Wenger considers the need for greater income diversification in an era of rising labor market uncertainty and income inequality, the potential for such income diversification as financial products have become more pervasive, the persistent lack of income diversification for many households, and the policy lessons to bolster both public and private income-support mechanisms.

CONCLUSION

This research volume covers a lot of ground on a variety of issues related to the growing link between finance and labor relations. I hope readers find it to be a helpful introduction to the existing research on a complex and growing array of issues. It is my further hope, and that of the chapter authors, that this research volume can serve as a useful tool in both teaching and shaping research agendas.

Chapter 1

How 401(k) Plans Make Recessions Worse

Teresa Ghilarducci
Joelle Saad-Lessler
The New School for Social Research

THE GREAT RECESSION AND AUTOMATIC STABILIZERS

The Great Recession of 2008–2009, the worst recession since the Great Depression (1929–1937), reduced national wealth by 10%, or $15 trillion, in 2008.[1] The gap between actual real gross domestic product (GDP) and potential output fell precipitously in 2009 by $504 billion. And because of the decline in household and business spending, millions of workers lost their jobs. Between December 2007 and December 2009, employment fell by 5.7%—a loss of 8.3 million jobs—and the unemployment rate peaked at 10%.

Because of job, income, and wealth losses, consumers spent dramatically less in every major expenditure category (except for health care)[2] from 2007 to 2010, and almost 39% of households experienced job loss, an underwater mortgage, or other significant declines in wealth (Hurd and Rohwedder 2010). To help mitigate the effects of the recession, the U.S. federal government spent $700 billion for a number of substantial, one-time, and stimulus programs.[3] Meanwhile, built-in automatic stabilizers "did their thing" by injecting billions of dollars into the spending stream of the economy. Traditional automatic stabilizers such as unemployment insurance (UI), the Temporary Assistance for Needy Families (TANF) program, the Supplemental Nutritional Assistance Program (SNAP), and the program with the largest effect—the progressive tax system (i.e., the average marginal tax rate shrinks as more people fall into the lower brackets)—helped the Great Recession avoid becoming a colossal depression.

Overlooked in this retelling is the role of nontraditional automatic stabilizers: Social Security's Old-Age and Survivors Insurance (OASI), Social Security Disability Insurance (SSDI), and Medicare. People use these programs in recessions as income and life-style support, and the taxes used to finance those programs reduce spending in expansions (Thompson and Smeeding 2013). Annuity-based retirement accounts backed by government programs also helped the economy while financial market–based retirement programs, such as 401(k)-type programs, hurt the economy.

Five government automatic stabilizers—progressive income taxes, UI, OASI, SSDI, and Medicare—reduced the number of jobs lost in 2009 by a low of 81,456 and a high of 967,506—the range depends on which marginal propensity to consume is used. Because 401(k) plans work in the opposite, destabilizing direction, the number of jobs lost in 2009 was greater; the estimates of jobs lost because of 401(k) plans range from 36,236 to 119,735.

This chapter discusses how the macroeconomy was destabilized by 401(k) plans and how many jobs were lost because of those plans, using updated assumptions and parameters from Okun's law. Okun's law stipulates that a 1% increase in the difference between the current size of the economy and what it could be (the gap between actual and potential GDP) causes the unemployment rate to drop by 0.45 percentage points (Ball, Leigh, and Loungani 2013). OASI, SSDI, UI, Medicare, and federal taxes temper the output gap's effect on unemployment by injecting more net household spending in recessions and dampening spending in expansions. Those programs are automatic stabilizers. In contrast, 401(k) plans and other financial market–based retirement accounts have a destabilizing effect; the reductions in wealth and income in recessions cause less spending and more induced labor supply than would otherwise be (measuring the labor supply effects of the programs are outside the scope of this chapter).

The Great Recession reduced the value of some retirement assets but not others. Over half of households own individual retirement accounts (IRAs), 401(k)s, and 401(k)-type accounts, and the values of those accounts fell by an average of 14% in 2008, with wealthy households losing the most (VanDerhei 2009). Middle-class and lower-income households, whose current and future retirement income wealth derives primarily from OASI, SSDI, defined benefit pension plans, and Medicare, lost almost nothing in the 2008–2009 recession (Gustman, Steinmeier, and Tabatabai 2011; Thompson and Smeeding 2013).

Also, Federal Reserve economists Peterman and Sommer (2014) found that Social Security programs reduced the exposure of households to the wealth shock of the Great Recession.

The microeconomy of worker and retiree households experienced the Great Recession very differently depending on how much of their retirement income and expected retirement income came from a promised stream of income from Social Security programs and from traditional pensions—and how much of their retirement wealth relied on financial market–based assets.

The macroeconomy also benefited from government-based retirement assets and suffered, like households suffered, from having retirement income depend on financial market–based assets: 401(k) plans whose value depended on flows, dividends, and capital gains from stocks, bonds, and other financial assets. In short, the existence of 401(k) plans and other financial market–based retirement wealth—whose values fluctuate with the business cycle—made the last recession deeper and caused slightly more unemployment than would have happened otherwise if 401(k) plans had not existed.

During a recession, the output gap increases the unemployment rate, but the unemployment rate would have been higher without the traditional and untraditional automatic stabilizers. The bundled positive effect of the six programs [OASI, SSDI, UI, Medicare, 401(k) plans, and income taxes] on reducing unemployment is larger when the effect of 401(k) plans is eliminated. For example, during the recession in 2009, the five government-based automatic stabilizers together reduced the effects that declining GDP had on unemployment from 2.26 to 1.55 percentage points (Table 1a, line 4, columns 2 and 4) in the presence of the 401(k) consumption effect, and from 2.18 to 1.55 (Table 1a, line 4, columns 2 and 3) in its absence, assuming a marginal propensity to consume (MPC) of 0.9.[4]

If, however, we assume an MPC of 0.09, the five government automatic stabilizers together reduced the effects that declining GDP had on unemployment from 1.63 to 1.55 (Table 1b, line 4, columns 3 and 4) in the presence of the 401(k) consumption effect, and from 1.60 to 1.55 (Table 1b, line 4, columns 2 and 3) in its absence. Without 401(k) plans, the mitigation effect of traditional automatic stabilizer programs (progressive income taxes and UI) and nontraditional old-age programs—OASI, SSDI, and Medicare—would have been larger.

When we translate these changes in the unemployment rate into numbers of jobs lost,[5] we find that the five government automatic stabilizers together dampened the effect of a rising output gap, reducing the number of jobs lost in 2009 by 81,456—from 2,470,370 to 2,388,914 (Table 2a, line 4, columns 3 and 4)—assuming an MPC of 0.09, and by 967,506—from 3,356,420 to 2,388,914 (Table 2b, line 4, columns 3 and 4)—assuming an MPC of 0.9, in the absence of 401(k) plans. But in the presence of 401(k) plans, the number of jobs lost in 2009 was greater by 36,236 (Table 2a, line 4, column 6), assuming an MPC of 0.09, and by 119,735 (Table 2b, line 4, column 6), assuming an MPC of 0.9.

SOCIAL SECURITY, 401(k) PLANS, AND AGGREGATE DEMAND

Most U.S. workers and employers are required to participate in the Social Security system. In addition, approximately 50% of workers have employers who voluntarily provide private retirement plans that come in two types: defined benefit (DB) and 401(k) type, which is a defined contribution

TABLE 1a

Estimated Unemployment Rate Change If Specific Business Cycle–Related Programs Were Not Embedded in the Economy (using complete data, including post-recession years,[6] assuming a marginal propensity to consume [MPC] of 0.9)

Year	Predicted unemployment rate change (% points) based on Okun's law	Predicted unemployment rate change (% points) based on Okun's law, absent consumption effects of OASI, SSDI, UI, Medicare, taxes, and 401(k) plans	Predicted unemployment rate change (% points) based on Okun's law, absent consumption effects of OASI, SSDI, UI, Medicare, and taxes, but including the consumption effect of 401(k) plans
2006	−0.32	−0.45	−0.46
2007	−0.22	−0.30	−0.31
2008	0.47	0.66	0.68
2009	1.55	2.18	2.26
2010	−0.69	−0.98	−1.01
2011	−0.22	−0.31	−0.32
2012	−0.51	−0.71	−0.73
2013	−0.07	−0.09	−0.09

TABLE 1b

Estimated Unemployment Rate Change If Specific Business Cycle–Related Programs Were Not Embedded in the Economy (using complete data, including post-recession years,[6] assuming a marginal propensity to consume [MPC] of 0.09)

Year	Predicted unemployment rate change (% points) based on Okun's law	Predicted unemployment rate change (% points) based on Okun's law, absent consumption effects of OASI, SSDI, UI, Medicare, taxes, and 401(k) plans	Predicted unemployment rate change (% points) based on Okun's law, absent consumption effects of OASI, SSDI, UI, Medicare, and taxes, but including the consumption effect of 401(k) plans
2006	−0.32	−0.33	−0.34
2007	−0.22	−0.22	−0.23
2008	0.47	0.49	0.49
2009	1.55	1.60	1.63
2010	−0.69	−0.72	−0.73
2011	−0.22	−0.23	−0.23
2012	−0.51	−0.52	−0.53
2013	−0.07	−0.07	−0.07

TABLE 2a
Number of People Unemployed If Specific Business Cycle–Related Programs Were Not Embedded in the Economy (using complete data, including post-recession years,[7] assuming a marginal propensity to consume [MPC] of 0.09)

Year	Total number of unemployed	Predicted change in unemployment, in number of jobs lost, based on Okun's law (holding the labor force constant)	Predicted change in unemployment, in number of jobs lost, based on Okun's law (holding the labor force constant)	Predicted change in unemployment, in number of jobs lost, based on Okun's law (holding the labor force constant), absent consumption effects of OASI, SSDI, UI, Medicare, and taxes, but including the consumption effect of 401(k) plans	Differential effect of 401(k) plans on unemployment, in number of jobs lost
2006	7,001,000	(486,872)	(503,651)	(510,807)	(7,156)
2007	7,077,000	(332,319)	(344,213)	(349,078)	(4,865)
2008	8,925,000	728,652	751,661	762,451	10,790
2009	14,265,000	2,388,914	2,470,370	2,506,606	36,236
2010	14,825,000	(1,066,956)	(1,102,946)	(1,119,238)	(16,292)
2011	13,748,000	(343,364)	(355,222)	(360,374)	(5,152)
2012	12,506,000	(783,243)	(808,747)	(820,432)	(11,685)
2013	11,460,000	(102,790)	(106,108)	(107,577)	(1,469)

TABLE 2b

Number of People Unemployed If Specific Business Cycle–Related Programs Were Not Embedded in the Economy (using complete data, including post-recession years,[7] assuming a marginal propensity to consume [MPC] of 0.9)

Year	Total number of unemployed	Predicted change in unemployment, in number of jobs lost, based on Okun's law (holding the labor force constant)	Predicted change in unemployment, in number of jobs lost, based on Okun's law (holding the labor force constant)	Predicted change in unemployment, in number of jobs lost, based on Okun's law (holding the labor force constant), absent consumption effects of OASI, SSDI, UI, Medicare, and taxes, but including the consumption effect of 401(k) plans	Differential effect of 401(k) plans on unemployment, in number of jobs lost
2006	7,001,000	(486,872)	(677,445)	(700,740)	(23,295)
2007	7,077,000	(332,319)	(462,114)	(477,878)	(15,765)
2008	8,925,000	728,652	1,013,418	1,048,460	35,041
2009	14,265,000	2,388,914	3,356,420	3,476,155	119,735
2010	14,825,000	(1,066,956)	(1,502,673)	(1,556,904)	(54,231)
2011	13,748,000	(343,364)	(481,168)	(498,182)	(17,014)
2012	12,506,000	(783,243)	(1,093,589)	(1,131,939)	(38,350)
2013	11,460,000	(102,790)	(141,831)	(146,628)	(4,797)

(DC) plan. Most workers with DB plans also have a DC plan. Most workers with DC plans do not have a DB plan. One reason OASI works as an automatic stabilizer is its size and scope. OASI is a universal defined benefit plan (93% of workers participate in OASI; most others are state and local public employees who have similarly structured plans). All OASI benefits are paid out as an annuity. The monthly pension amount is based on years of credited service and a career average salary indexed for inflation. In contrast, DC plans are individual retirement accounts in which workers (and often employers) voluntarily contribute to the plan; the balance of the fund depends on total contributions, investment performance, and fees. The investment vehicle in 401(k) plans is chosen by the employer, though the portfolio mix is chosen by the employee [most of the assets in IRAs come from 401(k) plans].

Traditional and Nontraditional Automatic Stabilization

Automatic stabilizers are government or private-market programs that are (1) permanently installed, (2) well defined in their main provisions and purposes, and (3) reliably linked to cyclically sensitive criteria so that the programs' effects operate quickly without government decisions (Auerbach and Feenberg 2000; Egle 1952). Automatic stabilizers should produce budget deficits during slumps and surpluses during upswings—expanding the economy's stock of cash in slumps and reducing the cash stocks in expansions—and lowering the public's demand for cash during slumps while raising the demand for cash during expansions. In fact, an automatic stabilizer is effective because it begins its compensatory effect without waiting for new policy decisions or the recognition of changes in the cycle.

Fortunately, developed nations had automatic stabilizers in place during the recession, which quickly boosted household consumption when workers lost their jobs, wages stagnated, and other sources of income dried up. The surprising and aggressive nature of the downturn prompted many critics of government policy to reconsider the fiscal role of government and social insurance (Rajan 2010).[8]

The Three Channels by Which Retirement Plans Act as Automatic Stabilizers

When an economy goes into a contraction, income from work and income and asset values from accounts tied to the financial markets either fall or the increases become smaller. These income effects induce workers to reduce spending and delay retiring, while retirees are induced to return to the labor market. These wealth, income, and labor effects make recessions worse.

If an economy depends on financialized retirement accounts—accounts whose values depend directly and immediately on financial markets—the values of the accounts are pro-cyclical: they increase when the economy is expanding and decrease when the economy is contracting. This means that households with financial market–based retirement accounts are less likely to spend and more likely to work, or seek work, in recessions, causing unemployment to rise and making recessions worse. Thus, the retirement income security system affects the macroeconomy through three channels: income, wealth, and labor market channels.

The first channel is the income effect; the level and change in retirement income affects household consumption immediately and directly through the income effect. The second channel is the wealth effect; changes in the level of retirement wealth can cause a family to feel wealthy or poor, which affects their immediate spending and saving decisions. The third channel is how the level and changes in retirement income and antici-pated retirement income affect household labor market decisions. For example, in recessions, workers and retirees who depend on retirement income that is based on the financial markets are likely to experience retirement wealth losses. The retirement income and wealth loss means older workers are less likely to voluntarily retire and retirees are more likely to go back to work or seek work during recessions precisely when employ-ers do not need workers. In expansions, the reverse happens with equally perverse results; workers feel wealthy as their 401(k) balances increase so they may retire earlier than they planned and spend more on houses and consumer items than they otherwise would, helping to fuel inflation and a labor shortage.

Whereas financial market–based retirement plans destabilize the macroeconomy, guaranteed retirement accounts—whose values are immune to financial market fluctuations—have an opposite, stabilizing, effect over the business cycle. OASI and annuities from DB plans do not affect spending and job creation by causing workers and retirees to slow down spending and increase work effort in recessions. DB and OASI income is stable over the business cycle because the values of these accounts for retirees are not tied to the financial system. An economy might be in recession, but falling asset values do not reduce retirement wealth, income, and consumption—and workers with DB plans retire or stay retired (Hermes 2006; Maestas 2004). Therefore, a retirement income security system that depends on more, rather than less, secure retirement wealth and income—retirement income that smooths out income over the business cycle—would help stabilize the macroeconomy.

Ghilarducci, Saad-Lessler, and Fisher (2012) showed that OASI, DB plans, and 401(k) flows changed over the business cycle. When recessions hit, the OASI system took in smaller contributions and paid out more benefits, which kept consumption relatively stable over the business cycle. OASI is countercyclical and helps stabilize the economy during a recession. In contrast, net flows from 401(k) plans were positive over the business cycle and continue to be four years after the recession. As stock market prices increase, wealth increases and workers consume more—bidding up prices and retiring earlier—which worsens an already tight labor market. Conversely, when asset prices in 401(k) retirement accounts fell, older workers stayed longer in the labor market (Norris 2014). Workers and retirees relying on financial market–based retirement accounts saved more as they experienced a decrease in their wealth balances (Peterman and Sommer 2014; Pounder 2009).

Darby and Melitz (2008) found for countries in the Organisation for Economic Co-operation and Development (OECD) that retirement programs act like nontraditional automatic stabilizers. They estimate that a $1 increase in actual output relative to "full employment" (potential) output leads to 13.5 cents less in social spending, with retirement income programs like the OASI system in the United States, on average, contributing a third to that social spending. We extended Darby and Melitz's work by distinguishing between types of retirement programs—DC and DB types. We found that four years later, the countercyclical effect of OASI was even stronger and the destabilizing effects of 401(k) plans were worse.

METHODOLOGY AND DATA

We use Darby and Melitz's (2008) specifications and identify the inflows and outflows from each program in terms of levels and shares of GDP. The "shares" analysis describes how absolute changes in expenditures or benefits (outflows) and taxes or contributions (inflows) trend over time, as a percentage of GDP.

The output gap is the ratio of realized to potential GDP for the analysis in shares and the difference between realized GDP and potential GDP for the analysis in levels. Potential GDP is estimated as the trend component of actual GDP after applying a Hodrick–Prescott filter (Hodrick and Prescott 1997), a widely used technique to disaggregate short-term fluctuations and longer cycles.

Equation 1 defines the change in the size of different programs (measured by net flows as shares of the U.S. economy) as dependent on changes in the output gap and other controls. Equation 2 defines changes in the absolute level of net flows of a program as reliant on changes in the absolute size of the output gap and other factors. When the elasticity coefficient of the output gap is positive, an increase in the output gap leads to an increase in the level and GDP share of program flows.

We control for omitted variable bias by controlling for changes in the age profile of the population by adding the fraction of the population between 25 and 54 years of age and the fraction of the population age 65 or over (W_i).

$$\Delta \left(\frac{x_{it}}{Y_t^{Nominal}} \right) = \alpha + \beta_i \Delta \left(\frac{Y_t^{Real}}{Y_t^{Potential}} \right) + \gamma_i Z_{it} + \lambda_i W_t + \varepsilon_{it} \qquad (1)$$

$$\Delta x_{it} = \alpha_i + \beta_i \Delta \left(Y_t^{Real} - Y_t^{Potential} \right) + \gamma_i Z_{it} + \lambda_i W_t + \varepsilon_{it} \qquad (2)$$

In the equations, i denotes the inflow/outflow component of each plan, t denotes time, x is the specific program, Y is GDP, and Z includes the lag of the dependent variable, both in levels and in differences.

The coefficient of interest in both sets of specifications is β. In the shares equation (Equation 1), β is the percentage point change in the GDP share of inflows/outflows for every 1 percentage point increase in the difference between realized and potential output. Therefore, if β is positive, the relevant program's share of inflows and outflows (measured as a share of GDP) increases with GDP growth. Alternatively, if β is negative, the program's GDP share of inflows/outflows shrinks as output grows. In the levels analysis (Equation 2), the β coefficient describes what happens to the relevant program's level of inflows/outflows when output increases by $1.

Outflows from the programs add income and cause an income effect in the economy, whereas inflows into the programs reduce income. The net effect on the economy is the impact on outflows minus inflows. If the net impact of the program is positive, an increase in the output gap leads to a net increase in income to households. This implies a positive feedback into the economy when it is already growing. As a result, we are left with amplified and destabilizing cyclical economic swings. On the other hand, if the net impact of the program is negative, an increase in the output gap results in the relevant program's reducing household income. This counteracts and reduces the effect of the output gap, and then we consider the program to be an automatic stabilizer. Results yield the automatic stabilization properties of the various retirement institutions and the government programs. The size of the stabilization effect of government programs provides a benchmark to compare the economically significant impacts of 401(k) plans and the Social Security system.

Endogeneity in these automatic stabilization regressions is a problem because changes in the output gap lead to changes in automatic stabilizer program levels and shares (which is the very purpose of automatic stabilization programs), and those very changes feed back to affect the output gap (the ordinary least squares estimation would yield a biased β coefficient).

Indeed, the Wu–Hausman test of endogeneity test indicates that endogeneity is present. Therefore, we use instrumental variables in a two-stage least squares estimation. The instrumental variables are real gross business investment and the change in exports because those variables affect output but are not affected by automatic stabilizer programs.[9]

Data on Flows

We used data on inflows and outflows for OASI, 401(k) retirement accounts, SSDI, UI, Medicare, and federal income tax collections. Data for OASI, SSDI, and Medicare come from the Social Security Administration; the U.S. Department of Labor reports UI benefits. Information on 401(k) plans is available from the Department of Labor's Form 5500 data, and information on federal income taxes, nominal and real GDP, and real gross business investment comes from the Bureau of Economic Analysis (BEA).

Finally, we calculate the proportion of the population between the ages of 25 and 54 and the fraction age 65 or over using data from the U.S. Current Population Survey (CPS). All data are annual and national, with the data range starting in 1971 and ending in 2012 for OASI, SSDI, Medicare, and taxes. The data range for 401(k) plans is 1984 through 2011, and the data range for unemployment insurance is 1972 through 2012 (the appendix contains detailed information on these sources. We use annual data because that is what is available for 401(k) plans and OASI. We are not aware of the availability of quarterly data for these programs).

In the period ending in 2012, federal income taxes constituted the largest source of inflows into the government's coffers, with tax collections making up an average of 8% of GDP over all time periods. The second largest inflow source was OASI, at about 4% of GDP, followed by Medicare at 2%. About 1% of GDP is made up of 401(k), while disability insurance inflows weigh in at 0.6%, and unemployment insurance inflows represent a diminutive 0.3% of GDP. Given the size of inflows from these programs, we expect Medicare, OASI, and 401(k) plans to have a significant impact on the macroeconomy, but size is not all that matters. Sensitivity to the business cycle also matters. Though Medicare is large, we don't expect the demand for Medicare services to be as sensitive to the business cycle as Social Security benefit receipts are. But Medicare taxes are tied to payroll—2.9% of payroll—so Medicare premiums are sensitive to the business cycle, as are FICA deductions for Old-Age, Survivors, and Disability Insurance (OASDI), at 12.4% of payroll. Table 3 summarizes the relative size of the six programs in the economy.

TABLE 3
Average Shares of Traditional and Nontraditional
Stabilizers from 1971–2012 and 1984–2011

Retirement Programs That Vary Over the Business Cycle	
Social Security (FICA) taxes' share of GDP	3.9%
401(k) contributions' share of GDP	1.3%
SSDI inflow share	0.6%
Medicare inflow share	1.2%
Traditional Automatic Stabilizers	
Unemployment insurance inflow share	0.3%
Federal income tax collection share	7.8%

RESULTS: SOCIAL SECURITY PROGRAMS STABILIZE, 401(k) PLANS DESTABILIZE

Before the Great Recession, every 1 percentage point increase in the GDP output gap resulted in a contraction of net spending from OASI, SSDI, UI, Medicare, and taxes, which had a stabilizing, calming effect on the economy. Net flows from those programs were decreasing by 0.34 percentage points in the expansion. In contrast, net flows from 401(k) plans increased by 0.05 percentage points. OASI, SSDI, UI, Medicare, and federal personal income taxes acted as automatic stabilizers, while 401(k) plans had a destabilizing effect.

After the 2009 recession, automatic stabilizer effects of the government programs became stronger, with every 1 percentage point increase in the GDP output gap resulting in reduced net flows from the stabilizing programs by 0.43 percentage points. But the destabilizing effects of 401(k) plans were reduced, with net flows from 401(k) plans increasing by 0.02 percentage points for every 1 percentage point increase in the output gap (Table 4).

Examining the impact of the programs in terms of levels, in the pre-2008 data, for every $1 increase in real GDP, net flows from the various government programs shrank by 45 cents, which tempered the expansion. These stabilizing effects were weakened by the effect of net flows from 401(k) plans, which increased by 5 cents. In other words, 401(k) plans reduced the automatic stabilization impact of government programs by 11% measured in levels and 15% measured in shares before the recession.

TABLE 4
Net Impact of a Change in the Output Gap for Each Program

Program	Before the recession		After the recession	
	In shares	In levels	In shares	In levels
OASI	−0.03	−0.05	−0.02	−0.07
401(k)	0.05	0.05	0.02	0.03
UI	−0.06	−0.06	−0.07	−0.07
SSDI	−0.01	0	−0.01	−0.01
Medicare	−0.03	0	−0.01	−0.01
Federal income tax collections	−0.21	−0.34	−0.32	−0.45
OASI, UI, SSDI, Medicare, taxes	−0.34	−0.45	−0.43	−0.61
401(k)	0.05	0.05	0.02	0.03

Using years after the recession, the effects of a $1 increase in real GDP were a 61 cent reduction in net flows from government programs, while net flows from 401(k) plans grew by 3 cents. In other words, 401(k) plans reduced the automatic stabilization impact of government programs by 5% in levels and shares. The results are in Table 4.

Are the Results the Same in an Expansion?
The impact of the change in the economy (the output gap) is not the same when GDP is increasing relative to full employment compared with when GDP is decreasing. We identify the asymmetry by creating a dummy variable that takes on a value of 1 when the economy is in recession and 0 otherwise (see Ghilarducci, Saad-Lessler, and Fisher 2012). We interact this recession dummy with the change in the output gap and add the interaction term to the specification. When the output gap is positive (indicating an expansion), the impact of an increase in the output gap is the coefficient on the change in the output gap. When the output gap is negative (indicating a recession), the impact of an increase in the output gap is the coefficient on the change in the output gap plus the coefficient on the interaction term.

Using all data years in our sample, we find significant asymmetrical effects of a change in the output gap for disability inflows and tax collections when measured in shares. The progressive tax system and disability program have more powerful effects in recessions than in expansions. We think the disability program has a much greater stabilizing impact in recessions than in expansions because potential disability participants—who are most likely older and perhaps marginally disabled—are highly sensitive to the prospects of being laid off or not finding work. The progressive tax system may not have such a large effect in downturns because low-income people, already in low brackets, are more likely to lose income through job loss or a reduction in hours. In the upturns, more people get jobs and pay taxes and more income moves up into higher marginal tax brackets.

CONCLUSIONS

Making retirement plans depend on financial markets by expanding 401(k) plans could worsen recessions and change labor relations by building in forces that keep long-term unemployment higher than it would be, especially for older workers. We find that 401(k) plans reduce the automatic stabilization impact of government programs by 11% measured in levels and to 15% measured in shares. Including the period after the Great Recession, 401(k) plans reduce the automatic stabilization impact of government programs by 5%. These results highlight a significant destabilizing problem with 401(k) retirement plans, and with any retirement system dependent on financial markets because of feedback on spending through the wealth and income effect.

The OASI system (and to a lesser extent SSDI and Medicare), along with progressive income taxes and unemployment insurance, functions as an automatic stabilizer by increasing spending more than would have occurred and lessening the increase in unemployment than would have otherwise occurred. At the same time, 401(k) plans exacerbated the decline in spending caused by the fall in output, making recessions worse.

California passed the Secure Choice Pension Plan in 2012 in an effort to secure retirement income for California workers. Seven state legislatures have also passed bills to create or study the creation of retirement savings vehicles for workers in their states. These savings vehicles would be funded with regular employee contributions and pay out a stream of income in the form of an annuity (Bradford 2014; U.S. GAO 2009). Five other states are considering similar legislation.

These efforts to create secure retirement accounts for all workers could have major unintended positive effects on the macroeconomy. The pension plans would help protect state economies from reduced state spending when recessions hit and would avoid forcing layoffs and cuts in social services just when they are needed the most.

APPENDIX: HOW WE TRANSLATED CHANGES IN UNEMPLOYMENT INTO NUMBER OF JOBS LOST

We observe the change in the output gap that happened every year. This change in the output gap includes all changes in consumption that happened in response to the initial change as a result of flows from government programs and 401(k) plans.

The change in unemployment is the Okun's law estimate of changes in the unemployment rate caused by the change in the output gap. Using an Okun's law estimate of −0.45, the change in the unemployment rate = (dlnY − dlnYpotential)*−0.45. This is the baseline unemployment effect constructed from Okun's law.

To identify what the unemployment rate effect would have been in the absence of government programs and 401(k) plans, we have estimates from our regressions of what happens to flows from various programs in response to a $1 change in the output gap. We apply to these estimates an MPC estimate and an assumed average tax rate of 20.7% and obtain estimated consumption responses of various programs to a $1 change in the output gap. We multiply these estimated consumption responses by the actual change in the output gap to obtain the actual change in consumption from the various programs in response to the change in the output gap (we acknowledge that this is subject to double counting—we are using changes in the output gap, which include the consumption effect, to calculate the consumption effect—and we welcome alternative suggestions to avoid this double counting).

Next, we construct estimates of what the output gap would have been without the consumption effects of the various programs by subtracting the consumption response caused by (1) all government programs and 401(k) plans and (2) all government plans without the effect of 401(k) plans. From these estimates, we construct the implied change in the unemployment rate that ensues with and without the consumption response from specific programs.

We then multiply the change in the unemployment rate by the labor force, assuming no change in the labor force, to obtain the number of jobs lost. Finally, we compare the change in the number of unemployed people when we take into account all government programs with and without 401(k) plans to arrive at the differential impact of 401(k) plans on unemployment.

Our data for these calculations are derived from the following sources:

- 401(k) Data: Yearly, 1984–2007. Form 5500 Data, Department of Labor, Table E20 (http://1.usa.gov/ 1AqSBtb)
- Old-Age and Survivors Insurance (OASI) Program, Disability Insurance (DI), and Medicare Data: Yearly, 1971–2009; Social Security Administration (http://1.usa.gov/1AqSQEI)
- Unemployment Insurance Data: Yearly, 1971–2009. Department of Labor Unemployment Insurance Chartbook (http://1.usa.gov/1BGNSmy)
- Federal Income Taxes, Nominal and Real Gross Domestic Product, and Gross Business Investment: Yearly 1971–2009; National Income Accounts of the United States (http://1.usa.gov/1bapk0a)

TABLE A1

Estimated Impact of a Change in the Output Gap on Changes in the GDP
Shares of Program Outflows/Inflows, Using Pre-Recession Data Only

Program outflows/inflows	Coefficient	H_0 p-value	H_2 p-value	R^2	F-value
OASI inflows	−0.030**	0.003	0.583	0.5713	9.85963
OASI outflows	−0.062**	0.001	0.398	0.5151	10.1956
401(k) inflows	0.017**	0.195			
401(k) outflows	0.069**	0.004	0.139	0.4478	15.5133
DB inflows	−0.022	0.438			
DB outflows	−0.008**	0.808			
Unemployment insurance inflows	0.010**	0.523			
Unemployment insurance outflows	−0.053**	0.005	0.496	0.5591	11.3406
Disability insurance inflows	−0.004	0.949			
Disability insurance outflows	−0.012**	0.000	0.813	0.5683	10.1078
Medicare inflows	0.002	0.654			
Medicare outflows	−0.031**	0.073	0.176	0.6355	12.181
Federal income tax collections	0.205**	0.000	0.024	0.5659	10.2016

TABLE A2
Estimated Impact of a Change in the Output Gap on Changes in the GDP
Levels of Program Outflows/Inflows, Using Pre-Recession Data Only

Program outflows/inflows	Coefficient	H_0 p-value	H_2 p-value	R^2	F-value
OASI inflows	0.049**	0.644			
OASI outflows	−0.029*	0.019	0.236	0.79	66.402
401(k) inflows	0.054**	0.000	0.866	0.5168	5.04646
401(k) outflows	0.100**	0.003	0.351	0.5239	6.48358
DB inflows	−0.026	0.312			
DB outflows	0.009	0.749			
Unemployment insurance inflows	0.011**	0.220			
Unemployment insurance outflows	−0.049**	0.000	0.345	0.6804	20.4693
Disability insurance inflows	0.003	0.436			
Disability insurance outflows	−0.006	0.001	0.765	0.8209	60.7673
Medicare inflows	0.030	0.419			
Medicare outflows	−0.008	0.306			
Federal income tax collections	0.342**	0.002	0.608	0.7689	49.8166

TABLE A3
Estimated Impact of a Change in the Output Gap on Changes in the GDP
Shares of Program Outflows/Inflows, Using Data (Including Post-Recession Years)

Program outflows/inflows	Coefficient	H_0 p-value	H_2 p-value	R^2	F-value
OASI inflows	−0.022**	0.02	0.46	0.46	13.11
OASI outflows	−0.039**				
401(k) inflows	0.048**	0.02	0.76	0.74	29.03
401(k) outflows	0.067**				
DB inflows	−0.020*				
DB outflows	−0.010**				
Unemployment insurance inflows	0.011**				
Unemployment insurance outflows	−0.063**	0.00	0.24	0.59	6.02
Disability insurance inflows	−0.008*				
Disability insurance outflows	−0.012**	0.01	0.73	0.44	16.22
Medicare inflows	−0.001				
Medicare outflows	−0.013**				
Federal income tax collections	0.318**	0.00	0.56	0.48	14.55

TABLE A4
Estimated Impact of a Change in the Output Gap on Changes in the GDP
Levels of Program Outflows/Inflows, Using Data (Including Post-Recession Years)

Program outflows/inflows	Coefficient	H_0 p-value	H_2 p-value	R^2	F-value
OASI inflows	0.037**				
OASI outflows	–0.033**	0.05	0.79	0.70	40.89
401(k) inflows	0.066**	0.01	0.55	0.87	373.81
401(k) outflows	0.096**				
DB inflows	–0.036*	0.04	0.72	0.73	207.52
DB outflows	–0.001				
Unemployment insurance inflows	0.008**	0.04	0.77	0.71	58.13
Unemployment insurance outflows	–0.058**	0.00	0.47	0.79	40.53
Disability insurance inflows	–0.002				
Disability insurance outflows	–0.008**	0.00	0.87	0.71	80.73
Medicare inflows	0.013**				
Medicare outflows	–0.006				
Federal income tax collections	0.450**	0.00	0.52	0.76	92.38

ENDNOTES

[1] Between 2007 and 2010, inflation-adjusted median net worth of families in the Federal Reserve Board's Survey of Consumer Finances fell by 38.8%, while mean net worth dropped 14.7% (authors' calculations).

[2] "Hard Times: How the Economic Slowdown Has Changed Consumer Spending in America," *The Economist* (http://econ.st/1xpxNkN).

[3] The Troubled Asset Relief Program (TARP); the American Recovery and Reinvestment Act (ARRA); expanded TANF, SNAP, UI, and the Earned Income Tax Credit (EITC); and infrastructure projects.

[4] The effect of the different government programs, as well as 401(k) plans, on consumption depends on the value we assign to the marginal propensity to consume (MPC). A number of studies have attempted to pin down the value of the MPC (e.g., Carroll, Slacalek, Tokuoka, and White 2015), and the results fall in a wide range, from a low of 0.09 (Pounder 2009) to a high of 0.9 per dollar (Agarwal and Qian 2013).

[5] For details on the calculations done to translate changes in unemployment into numbers of jobs lost with and without the impacts of different programs, please refer to the appendix.

[6] The numbers in Tables 1a and 1b were calculated using Okun's law, which stipulates that every 1% increase in the output gap leads to a 0.45 percentage point decrease in the

unemployment rate. We multiplied the percentage point change in the output gap each year by –0.45 to get the effect on the unemployment rate pursuant to the effect of all government programs. So, in 2006, the unemployment rate was 4.608. That included the effects of all government programs, which were responsible for a –0.0033 percentage point change in the unemployment rate. In other words, without the impact of government programs, the unemployment rate would have been 4.608 + 0.0033 = 4.6113. Other columns in the tables reflect what the effects on the unemployment rate would have been if only a subset of the government programs were in place.

[7] The percentage point changes in the unemployment rate from Tables 1a and 1b were converted into numbers of jobs created or lost by multiplying the unemployment rate changes (divided by 100) by the labor force.

[8] "[S]ocial transfers, in particular the rather generous systems of unemployment insurance in Europe, play[ed] a key role in the stabilization of disposable incomes and explain a large part of the difference in automatic stabilizers between Europe and the US" (Dolls, Fuest, and Peichl 2010).

[9] The validity of the instruments is verified by conducting a Sargan–Hansen over-identification test and by comparing the partial R-squared of the first-stage regression. The instrument is highly correlated with the endogenous variable and the F-value associated with the instruments; therefore, these are adequate instruments. Time series data raise concern about serial correlation. Our specifications look at changes in flows on changes in independent variables, but because we use differenced data, the impact of serial correlation is likely to be negligible. We calculate heteroscedasticity and auto correlation robust standard errors (HAC) using Newey–West techniques. Therefore, our estimates correct for the presence of any serial correlation and for heteroscedasticity.

REFERENCES

Agarwal, S. and W. Qian. 2013. "Consumption and Debt Response to Unanticipated Shocks: Evidence from a Natural Experiment in Singapore." *American Economic Review*, Vol. 104, no. 12, pp. 4205–4230 (http://bit.ly/1SCDc4E).

Auerbach, A., and D. Feenberg. 2000. "The Significance of Federal Taxes as Automatic Stabilizers." *Journal of Economic Perspectives*, Vol. 14, no. 3, pp. 37–56.

Ball, L.M., D. Leigh, and P. Loungani. 2013. *Okun's Law: Fit at Fifty?* NBER Working Paper 18668. Cambridge, MA: National Bureau of Economic Research (http://bit.ly/1Cj07uX).

Bradford, Hazel. 2014 (May 12). "States Pushing to Offer Retirement Accounts to Private Sector Workers." *Pensions & Investments* (http://bit.ly/1G8C6pt).

Carroll, C.D., J. Slacalek, K. Tokuoka, and M.N. White. 2015 (Mar. 6). *The Distribution of Wealth and the Marginal Propensity to Consume* (http://bit.ly/1DL9ghC).

Darby, J., and J. Melitz. 2008. "Social Spending and Automatic Stabilizers in the OECD." *Economic Policy*, Vol. 23, no. 56, pp. 716–756.

Dolls, M., C. Fuest, and A. Peichl. 2010. "Automatic Stabilisers and the Economic Crisis in Europe and the US." Vox—CEPR's Policy Portal (http://bit.ly/1Cj1jyp).

Egle, W.G. 1952. *Economic Stabilization*. Cincinnati: University of Cincinnati Press.

Ghilarducci, T., J. Saad-Lessler, and E. Fisher. 2012. "The Macroeconomic Stabilisation Effects of Social Security and 401(k) Plans." *Cambridge Journal of Economics*, Vol. 36, no. 1, pp. 237–251.

Gustman, A., T. Steinmeier, and N. Tabatabai. 2011. *How Did the Recession of 2007–2009 Affect the Wealth and Retirement of the Near Retirement Age Population in the Health and Retirement Study?* NBER Working Paper 17547. Cambridge, MA: National Bureau of Economic Research.

Hermes, S. 2006. "What Role Do Financial and Health Constraints Play in Partial Retirement?" Labor and Employment Relations Association Series, *Proceedings of the 58th Annual Meeting.* Boston, Jan. 6–8, 2006.

Hodrick, R., and E. Prescott. 1997. "Postwar U.S. Business Cycles: An Empirical Investigation." *Journal of Money, Credit, and Banking*, Vol. 29, no. 1, pp. 1–16.

Hurd, M.D., and S. Rohwedder. 2010. *Effects of the Financial Crisis and Great Recession on American Households.* NBER Working Paper 16407. Cambridge, MA: National Bureau of Economic Research.

Maestas, N. 2004. *Back to Work: Expectations and Realizations of Work After Retirement.* Retirement Research Center Working Paper #2004-085. Ann Arbor: University of Michigan.

Norris, F. 2014 (May 13). "Older Workers Cling to Their Jobs: Crowding Out the Younger." *New York Times*, p. B3.

Peterman, W.B., and K. Sommer. 2014. *How Well Did Social Security Mitigate the Effects of the Great Recession?* Finance and Economics Discussion Series, Divisions of Research & Statistics and Monetary Affairs. Washington, DC: Federal Reserve Board of the United States.

Pounder, L. 2009. *Consumption Response to Expected Future Income.* International Finance Discussion Papers, 2009-971. Washington, DC: Federal Reserve Board of the United States.

Rajan, R. 2010. *Fault Lines: How Hidden Fractures Still Threaten the World Economy.* Princeton, NJ: Princeton University Press.

Thompson, J., and T. Smeeding. 2013. *Inequality and Poverty in the United States: The Aftermath of the Great Recession.* Finance and Economics Discussion Series, Divisions of Research & Statistics and Monetary Affairs. Washington, DC: Federal Reserve Board of the United States.

U.S. Government Accountability Office (U.S. GAO). 2009 (Jul.). *Private Pensions: Alternative Approaches Could Address Retirement Risks Faced by Workers but Pose Trade-Offs* (http://1.usa.gov/1Lfv4Gb).

VanDerhei, J. 2009 (Feb.). *The Impact of the Recent Financial Crisis on 401(k) Account Balances.* EBRI Issue Brief No. 326. Washington, DC: Employee Benefit Research Institute.

CHAPTER 2

Financialization, Collective Bargaining, and the Public Interest

JOEL CUTCHER-GERSHENFELD
University of Illinois at Urbana-Champaign

DAN BROOKS
United Auto Workers (retired)

NOEL COWELL
University of the West Indies (Jamaica)

CHRISTOS A. IOANNOU
Organization for Mediation and Arbitration (Greece)

MARTIN MULLOY
Ford Motor Company (retired)

DANNY ROBERTS
University of the West Indies (Jamaica)

TANZIA S. SAUNDERS
University of the West Indies (Jamaica)

SØREN VIEMOSE
Kalovig Center (Denmark)

INTRODUCTION

The system of collective bargaining has long been defined as centered on three actors—labor, management, and government (Dunlop 1958). This configuration was appropriate for many decades in many nations, where collective bargaining operated at the intersection of labor markets and product or service markets. Economists characterized the demand for labor as a "derived demand," based first on the demand for products or services. Productivity gains enabled growth in the product or service markets, which then enabled wage gains in labor markets. In the 21st century, however, the growing importance of financial markets is changing the calculus in multiple ways; our focus is on the impacts of financial markets on collective bargaining. At stake are not just the interests of labor and management—but also society.

Ideally, financial markets are relatively neutral actors in employment relations—holding firms and even nations accountable when financial models are not sustainable and rewarding them when there is financial stability and growth. As we document here, however, the operation of financial markets can depart from the ideal with forms of agency that add complexity to the employment relationship and that don't always serve society's interests. When these markets are unstable, such as occurred with the subprime crisis in the United States or in the meltdown of the Greek economy, the actions by financial organizations and institutions actively intrude in product and service markets, as well as labor markets. Financial markets operate across national boundaries in ways that can compromise the sovereignty of nations, so this increased degree of agency has substantial implications. The term "financialization" is used in this chapter to characterize this increased salience of financial markets and increased agency on the part of financial organizations and institutions in society.

In this chapter, we explore the impact of financialization on collective bargaining by considering three countries' cases. First, we present the case of Greece—perhaps the most highly visible intersection of financial pressures and collective bargaining dynamics, with public sector collective bargaining being the primary focus. As is implied in the section on Greece, the changes are near mythic in their scale and scope.

Second, we turn to the case of Jamaica, which has not been in the public spotlight to the same degree as Greece, but represents a case in which the International Monetary Fund (IMF) and the World Bank have become formal fourth actors in the collective bargaining process (along with labor, management, and government) in response to the country's heavy indebtedness.

Third, in the U.S. case, we examine the collapse and bail out of the U.S. auto industry, with the many complex financial dynamics that interweave with what has historically been a private, decentralized system of collective bargaining. Turning to the public sector in the United States, we document how fiscal crises in the public sector have served to erode collective bargaining rights in fundamental ways.

The historical developments, case examples, and survey data presented from these three countries are intended to be illustrative not definitive. In each case, more comprehensive analysis is necessary. Still, the information assembled does point out dynamics that are vivid and consequential. In *The Transformation of American Industrial Relations*, Kochan, Katz, and McKersie (1986) identified the importance of alignment at the workplace, collective bargaining, and strategic levels as a requirement for transformative change in the U.S. industrial relations system.

Financial markets introduce dynamics at the strategic level of the system, which have implications—as we document here—for the collective bargaining level. In all cases, the implications represent greater complications for labor and management, as well as increased difficulty in achieving the alignment needed for productive transformation into "high road" economies, combining good jobs and high performance in expanding ways.

In each country's case, the write-up is by co-authors with direct experience in that country's context, drawing on a mix of primary and secondary sources. In the Greek and Jamaican cases, British spelling is used where specific laws or initiatives are named.

A limitation of case studies is, of course, that they are hard to generalize to other cases. A further limitation of country cases is that the full diversity of practices in a given country cannot be fully summarized in a multi-country write-up. On the other hand, the advantage of these three countries' cases is that they illuminate new dynamics and can be generative of new theory. Some initial thoughts along those lines are included with the conclusion.

The public interest is included as a focus in this chapter, in addition to the interests of labor and management. Government is traditionally seen as representing the public interest in labor–management relations (aside from its role as the employer in the public sector). While this continues to be an important consideration, the degree to which the public sees collective bargaining as serving its interests can be complicated when financial dynamics drive a focus of government on cost cutting more than service delivery or assurances of checks and balances in society. This set of dynamics will be considered in these cases.

Ultimately, a fundamental question is raised: If collective bargaining is a valued social institution for balancing the interests of labor, management, and the public, what mechanisms should be considered for taking into account the interests of financial institutions as a fourth institutional actor? What mechanisms, if any, provide a check and balance for labor, management, and the public when dealing with financial dynamics? More broadly, what theories might span the interplay of labor markets, product or service markets, and capital markets? How do we connect theory and practice in this new, more complex context? We suggest here that financialization in these cases may be advancing the short-term interests for financial organizations and institutions, with only limited checks and balances available to other stakeholders in society.

GREECE

Greece is a prominent case in which the impact of financialization on collective bargaining processes and outcomes has been extensive. Greece provides a case of complete overhauling of the system for collective bargaining in both the public and the private sectors, under the main influence of the financial markets.

The impact of financial markets and of the financial and public debt crisis of 2009 on Greek collective bargaining institutions, processes, and outcomes can be summed up by recourse to Greek mythology: it is a case of bargaining institutions and processes reaching, because of financialization, the unavoidable stage of being between the twin terrors of sirens Scylla and Charybdis. In this modern Greek Odyssey, Scylla pounced and recast private sector collective bargaining institutions, processes, and outcomes; and Charybdis swallowed the pre-existing system of collective bargaining in the public sector, completely dragging collective bargaining out of the public sector. Today, the national system of collective labor relations in Greece is radically changed in both private and public sectors.

The Economic Fundamentals and Financialization

The role of financial markets in the collective bargaining developments is twofold. It is the financialization built up before the crisis that drove Greece and its bargaining institutions and processes—reaching the unavoidable stage of being between Scylla and Charybdis—and having to suffer both evils. The Greek economy from 2008 through 2013 contracted by 23% of gross domestic product (GDP), and unemployment tripled from 8.5% to 27.3%; in other words, one quarter of GDP and one fifth of jobs were lost. The nose-diving GDP has been critical for Greece's debt sustainability. The government debt, despite the 2012 restructuring, was in 2013 at €319 billion and soared to 175.1% of GDP, resulting in heavy exposure and heavy regulation by financial markets. But this exposure and overregulation has been a repercussion of the nose-diving GDP, and both the numerator and the denominator should be explained by referring to the buildup of a large structural imbalance between the tradables and the nontradables sectors of the Greek economy (Ioannou and Ioannou 2013).

When Greece became a member of the euro currency area, in 2000, its sector of internationally tradable goods and services corresponded to only 25% of its GDP, the lowest ratio in the EU-15 at the time. Greece also had the lowest productivity of the industry sector in the EU-15. Even before joining a currency system that was not optimal for Greece (that is, the Eurozone), the Greek balance of trade and the current account both presented significant deficits (in 2000 at −9.5% and −11.2% of the GDP, respectively).

After its first decade in the Eurozone, and despite average annual nominal GDP growth of 4%, the Greek economy began collapsing in 2009. By that time, the tradables sector had shrunk to 20.5% of GDP, and the balance of trade and the current account both presented significant deterioration (at −14.9% and −15.7% of the GDP, respectively). Indeed, during that decade, excessive public (but also private) borrowing, with very low (German) interest rates, was overcompensating for the chronic and increasing inability of the tradables sector to provide to the economy the liquidity of the common European currency that was necessary to sustain high inflation and a hypertrophic consumption pattern.

In Greek mythology, the Sirens were dangerous yet beautiful creatures who sang enchanting songs to lure sailors to their deaths by shipwreck on the rocky coast of their island. Public (and private) overborrowing can be likened to the Sirens, luring a country to the dangers to financialization. It is noteworthy that from 2000 to 2009, while GDP per capita in Greece rose from €12,600 to €20,700, government debt per capita soared faster, from €12,896 to €26,509. And this happened via the Sirens of financialization. Hence, during Greece's first decade in the Eurozone, there were insufficient productivity gains to have enabled growth in product or service markets, which then could have enabled wage gains in labor markets. Excessive financialization bolstered the illusion of growth and inflation, while at the same time it undermined further the productive capacity of the economy.

In this context, collective bargaining (operating at the intersection of labor markets and product/service markets), along with wage formation in both the private and the public sectors, became the victim of modern Sirens: steadily increasing public and private borrowing from abroad, under the illusion by both lenders and borrowers that a member of the European Economic and Monetary Union could not go bankrupt or risk insolvency. The visibility of capital markets in relation to the sectoral balance between tradables and nontradables, and, indeed, both private and public sector collective bargaining, was quite low before the crisis—but was of key importance.

When, at the end of 2009, the overborrowing became evident and unsustainable, the Greek crisis developed as a volatile process by which the relative prices of nontradables to tradables readjusted in line with fundamentals—all under the pressure of unstable financial markets. In that sense, Greece is a prominent case in which exposure to financial markets introduced adverse dynamics at the strategic level of the productive system, with massive implications for collective bargaining institutions and processes.

After the crisis, a fourth actor, which played an increasingly key role in the decade before the crisis, became dominant in the traditional triangle of employment regulation among government, labor, and management: the financial markets and the institutional creditors. The center of gravity of the public interest, as represented by the government in coalitions and consultation/bargaining with labor and management, was lost. During the crisis, there was no room for social dialogue in the public sector, and it had failed or produced only marginal results in the private sector (ILO 2012; Ioannou 2012; Patra 2012). In fact, social dialogue had failed even in the economic boom and financialization period (1993 through 2008) for both private and public sectors, resulting in waves of strikes, court appeals, International Labour Organization missions, politicization, and significant changes in the political landscape.

The Scale and Scope of Change

Let us first focus on the public sector, which since 2010 has been at the center of three processes:

- A major fiscal consolidation to reduce primary expenditures in the public sector as a percentage of GDP—from 48.3% in 2009 to 40.4% in 2013 and to 35.6% in 2015.

- Widespread reform of public management, affecting central administration, local government, health services, pensions and social security, and every segment of the Greek public sector.

- A massive privatization program incorporating all public sector utilities, rail and road transport, airports and seaports, gaming, and public sector real estate assets. This program was estimated at €50 billion in 2010 and downsized to €25 billion in 2012 (13% of the 2012 GDP). The downsizing was the result of the "balance sheet recession" (the collapse of most asset prices).

Public sector cutbacks and structural reforms in public sector employment relations have been central to the fate of the nation. Pay levels and pay formation procedures, employment levels and status, and collective and individual employment relations have been subject to successive centralized emergency measures and interventions (Ioannou 2013) instituted by the troika of the European Commission, the European Central Bank, and the International Monetary Fund and adopted by the national government and Parliament.

The impact of this dramatic state retrenchment and reform has made Greece an experiment in "testing the limits," even more than the "Mother of All Budgets" in New Zealand in 1991 (Starke 2008). Public sector employment relations had an impact on 20.7% of the labor force (which in 2008 was the public sector share of total employment). Public sector employment in Greece grew to 20.7% from 19.3% in 2000, compared with an average of 15% in countries belonging to the Organisation for Economic Co-operation and Development. In Greece, civil servants had no formal right to collective bargaining for wages and were able to shape wage policy only by informal means of collective action and consultation. Civil servants could be members of unions, which did provide other representational services.

Workers employed in general government, who accounted for 7.9% of total employment (an increase from 6.9% in 2000), had no formal collective bargaining rights, either. Their pay and working conditions were changed by the emergency measures. The changes also applied to what are termed "private law employees" working in general government institutions and public sector corporations for whom collective agreements and collective bargaining in public sector corporations had been annulled. Likewise, workers employed in public corporations, who accounted for 12.8% of total employment in 2008 (up from 12.5% in 2000), saw their status change in both procedural and essential terms. Although they were the most unionized segments of the economy, and most active in collective bargaining, those workers lost the right to bargain and had their public sector employment relations relegated to that of the private sector. Those changes were part of the adjustment program for the reform of the Greek public administration, which also included a 20% reduction in public sector employment—a target for decrease in general government employment by 150,000 by 2015.

Fiscal consolidation has been the main driver for the restructuring and elimination of bargaining rights—because of government debt reaching €329 billion in 2010 at 148.3% of GDP (Eurostat 2014). Before the 2009–2010 crisis, the issues regarding the public sector in Greece had been mainly questions of efficiency not of size. The financial dynamics drove the government to focus on cost cutting more than service delivery.

While Charybdis resulted in abolishment of collective bargaining rights and processes for public sector and in a centralized pay policy, Scylla caused a vast decentralization of collective bargaining in the private sector, a huge reduction in collective bargaining coverage, and a further move away from collective employment relations. These actions represent a paradigm change in Greek wage formation and employment relations (Ioannou 2014). Before the crisis (prior to 2010, the collective bargaining framework was provided by legislation passed in 1990), private sector collective bargaining took place at national, industry, and company levels. The national general collective agreement—referred to by its Greek initials, EGSSE—set the national minimum wage. Bargaining for better pay and working conditions occurred first at industry/occupation levels and then at company levels.

However, changes introduced after the 2010 crisis and the provision of IMF and EU financial support fundamentally changed the bargaining structure and processes. In February 2012, the government cut the minimum wage by 22% for workers age 25 and above and by 32% for workers under age 25. In November 2012, new legislation moved the authority to set the national minimum wage from EGSSE to the ministerial council. In 2015, that authority was given to the Ministry of Labor but with the requirement that employers and unions be consulted. However, the new coalition government elected in the January 2015 plans to reverse to this pre-existing system.

The hierarchy of agreements changed, introducing much greater flexibility at the company level. Before the change, bargaining at the company level was allowed only to improve national and industry-level agreements. After the change, company negotiators were permitted to agree to worse conditions than those set at national industry/occupation level.

Moreover, under legislation introduced in 2011, worker representatives no longer were required to belong to a union; instead, "associations of persons" were given the right to sign company-level collective agreements, provided that 60% of the employees belong to the association. In parallel, the possibility of extending industry/occupation-level agreements to employers who had not signed those agreements was frozen until the end of the adjustment program period (currently 2016).

The terms under which employers and unions have access to arbitration and mediation also changed in ways that weakened the position of the unions. In 2010, arbitration was restricted to setting minimum wages. In 2012, access to arbitration was possible only if both sides—unions and employers—agreed to it (Ioannou 2012). However, the High Court ruled as unconstitutional (in decision 2307/2014, published in July 2014) the requirement for mutual consent of the parties before arbitration could begin. The arbitration system is due to be amended and will revert to the arrangements that applied prior to February 2012, under which its jurisdiction was not restricted and recourse to it was unilateral (Ioannou 2014).

Implications for Collective Bargaining

It is now clear that these fundamental changes (despite the return of the right to arbitration) transformed both the bargaining structures and the bargaining outcomes. From 200 industrial/occupational collective agreements through which labor relations were regulated in Greece in 2000 through 2010, fewer than 20 still existed in 2013. Conversely, company-level agreements soared from 227 in 2010 to 976 in 2012, and another 409 were added in 2013. The evidence suggests that from 2011 through 2013, company-level bargaining and most of the agreements signed by the "associations of persons" were used to rapidly increase the use of decentralized collective bargaining for the purpose of implementing wage cuts in all sectors (Ioannou and Papadimitriou 2013).

This paradigm change affected the scope of collective bargaining in Greece. It is estimated that collective bargaining coverage from the late 1990s until the crisis began was 65%. The current estimate is much lower—approximately 10%. Before the crisis, the Greek Mediation and Arbitration Service estimated that 22% of all employees were union members (the database on Institutional Characteristics of Trade Unions, Wage Setting, State Intervention and Social Pacts put union density in Greece in 2011 at a slightly higher 25.4% [ICTWSS 2013]). Those numbers were much higher in the public and state-owned sectors. But during the crisis, the most unionized areas of the public sector—the public utilities in which employees have high levels of union membership—were excluded from collective bargaining. At the same time, one fifth of private sector jobs were lost, along with their union members and representatives in collective bargaining (Ioannou 2014).

These radical shifts in collective bargaining toward decentralization and away from collective employment relations to individual employment relations and contracts were seen by the European Commission, the European Central Bank, and the International Monetary Fund troika and the adjustment program as a means to implement "internal devaluation" (Ioannou 2012) to allow Greece to realign wages and recover the competitiveness it lost over its first decade in the Eurozone.

In terms of unit labor costs, the effective exchange rate for Greece was forecast to fall by 21.6% between 2009 and 2014. By the end of 2014, Greece had broadly regained its 1995 labor cost competitiveness position relative to the Eurozone (European Commission 2014). The key driver for this change has been the predominance of financial markets and institutional creditors over an economy and society that have weakened their productive and institutional capacity in response to the call of the Sirens of financialization, well before the global crisis (2007–2008), the Greek public debt crisis (2009–2010), and the crisis of confidence in the euro (2011).

In hindsight, we might say that the public interest in government–labor–management relations lies with a strong tradables sector and strong employment relations system in that sector acting as the driver of the national system. In the Greek case, unregulated financialization produced a modern Odyssey, with the Sirens of financialization that lured government, management, and labor with promises of riches (financialization and overborrowing were considered means of sustainable growth). Ultimately, however, financialization proved to be the Scylla and Charybdis that ended the traditional collective bargaining system in Greece. Despite that the new coalition government (elected in January 2015) seeks its reinstatement, it cannot be easily restored by legal means alone because it depends also on structural and real economy factors that have been seriously affected by the repercussions of financialization.

JAMAICA

The story of financialization in Jamaica is one of a deepening relationship between the country and the IMF/World Bank over a period of nearly 40 years during which the country has suffered secular economic decline punctuated by its own internal financial crises. It is, in addition, the story of a small, open, and vulnerable economy that continues to be ravaged by economic challenges.

Jamaica's economic policy can be roughly divided into four broad phases. The first took place between 1977 and 1979. During that brief and tumultuous period, the democratic socialist government of Prime Minister Michael Manley tentatively, reluctantly, and sometimes clandestinely, embraced the IMF in the face of burgeoning foreign debt and rapidly dwindling net international reserves. The second phase (1980 through 1989) began with an open and enthusiastic embrace of the economic policies of the IMF by Prime Minister Edward Seaga's government. By the middle of the 1980s, however, there was emerging estrangement, skepticism, and more grudging compliance with the prescriptions of the IMF (Thorburn and Morris 2008). In the third phase, Jamaica temporarily severed relationships with the IMF. Significantly, however, during the 1990s, the country entered into a period of deepened economic liberalization, while courting international creditors and maintaining alignment with the "Washington Consensus" suite of policies (Williamson 1993, 2004). The final phase began in 2013, when Jamaica finalized negotiations on a four-year program of balance of payment support, known as an Extended Fund Facility, with the IMF.

Collective bargaining in Jamaica operates in the context of these key macroeconomic phases, which must be reviewed in more detail to fully appreciate the context.

Jamaica Meets the IMF

Toward the end of Prime Minister Michael Manley's first term in office in 1976, in the face of a looming economic crisis, heightening ideological tensions, and public opinion heavily stacked against relations with the IMF, the Jamaican government approached the Fund for balance of payment support. Because Manley was a democratic socialist, his move was a surprise to many, and the negotiations were shrouded in secrecy, taking place in the country's north coast travel mecca, with an IMF team dressed as tourists (Witter 2012)! The negotiations concluded with the Fund identifying a standard range of closely interrelated weaknesses in the Jamaican economy and following up with a standard range of policy prescriptions.

The impact on collective bargaining was immediate. To counteract wage inflation and an over-regulated labor market, the IMF prescribed a seemingly contradictory mix of quantitative wage restrictions and labor market deregulation (Richards, Rapley, and King 2009; Witter 2012). The original wage guidelines sought to restrict wage increases to between 10% and 15% of the wage fund. However, in the context of rising prices (inflation was 27%, 17%, and 10% in 1974, 1975, and 1976, respectively, and would be 11% in 1977 and 35% in 1978) and declining economic growth, trade unions openly opposed the wage guidelines. In the face of early evidence that the guidelines were being flouted, the government introduced legislative amendments that made it illegal for the country's arbitral body to support the granting of wage increases that were inconsistent with the prescribed restraints. The amendments were promulgated by Parliament as expression of the "national interest" (Cowell 1992).

Trade unions, however, remained strident and vocal in their opposition, and collective labor agreements were expanded to include a range of so-called nontax allowances. So, at least until this practice was curtailed by explicit amendments to income tax legislation in the late 1990s, employers under pressure from trade unions exploited a loophole in the IMF-inspired statutory wage restrictions. While wage increases were subject to review by the state's arbitration tribunal, perks and allowances were not. For a while, therefore, the parties were able to increase worker take-home pay while maintaining the fiction of adherence to the wage guidelines.

A Period of Growth

A few months before losing the general elections of 1980, the Manley government, facing both internal (social and political) and external pressure, parted company with the IMF over differences in policy direction. The new prime minister, Edward Seaga, renewed the relationship soon after coming to power. His regime was widely thought to have been aligned with the Washington Consensus, as was illustrated by the layoff of some 30,000 public sector employees (Spaulding 2013). Despite a significant decline in the bauxite/alumina industry (a major foreign exchange earner) and other challenges (such as a crippling natural disaster, Hurricane Gilbert, in 1988), the country began to show evidence of growth by 1986. This expansion continued until 1990 at a rate of approximately 5% a year. At the same time, however, Stone (1989) noted that the share of wages and salaries (relative to gross profits) declined significantly as a share of GDP.

The decade of the 1980s was one of deepening estrangement between the government and the national trade union movement—significant because it was a government led by a political party (the Jamaican Labour Party) that had deep trade unions roots and that even now continues to maintain close trade union links. As a result, Seaga faced strong opposition from organized labor, and this opposition culminated in a general strike in 1985. In stark contrast to a tradition of dialogue with the trade union movement, the Seaga government reacted by terminating the employment of several hundred public employees. A fear of further reprisals effectively muted the trade union movement, taking the edge off union militancy. Still, as a result of widespread social discontent, the Seaga government was removed from power in 1989.

The Interregnum
Judging by its public rhetoric, the new government led by Michael Manley in a second term as prime minister from 1989 until 1992 was almost indistinguishable from the market-led government that it replaced. Yet it was a government of contradictions. Under the administration of a new prime minister, P.J. Patterson, Jamaica severed relations with the IMF in 1992. Nevertheless, it inaugurated a policy of economic liberalization leading to massive inflation and a dramatic increase in government borrowing from both local and international sources. The result was that a decade later, by the end of March 2002, the country's debt-to-GDP ratio had climbed to 133% of GDP, of which domestic debt accounted for 88% (Thompson 2002). During that period, the economy suffered a major financial crisis that set the tone not only for a return to the IMF but to many aspects of employment relations, including the character of collective bargaining that was to take place thereafter.

The factors precipitating the virtual insolvency of the financial system and the failure of almost all of the country's indigenous financial institutions are hotly debated. What is beyond dispute, however, is that the period was characterized by initial liberalization of the exchange rate, which led to currency devaluations and high rates of inflation in an economy that, then as now, is highly dependent on imports. To contain the inflation and protect the exchange rate, the government advanced an aggressive monetary policy dominated by high interest rates. In the context of a financial sector that was, to say the least, insufficiently regulated, the result was a drift away from productive activity in favor of high-yielding government paper (Clarke 2011). In an effort to salvage the situation, the government set up the Financial Sector Adjustment Company (FINSAC) toward the end of 1996. FINSAC assumed control of 13 of the island's indigenous financial institutions and their more than 200 subsidiaries and associated companies.

During that period, the government began to engage in dialogue with the national trade union movement with a view to rationalizing the public sector labor climate and setting a tone for improved relations within the private sector. Central to this process was an effort to limit the power of trade unions to play off one government department against the other, by shifting from the traditionally decentralized to a more centralized approach to collective bargaining. In November 2003, private sector unions and employers entered into the Partnership for Progress, which also included university scholars and key nongovernmental organizations. The following year saw a more dramatic move, in the form of what is now seen as a historic Memorandum of Understanding between the trade union confederation and the government of Jamaica in 2004. These forms of social dialogue and partnership were "designed to build trust and seek consensus on issues of national importance, with the objective of promoting a climate which [would] foster sustained economic growth, equity and social justice for the benefit of the widest cross-section of the Jamaican people" (Collister 2005).

A key element of this Memorandum of Understanding was the preservation of public sector employment levels, which had seen a reversal of the policy of the 1980s and, by the end of 2003, represented some 12% of the employed labor force (Taylor 2013). In return, public sector employees agreed to a wage freeze, while the government set additional targets to contain inflation and ensure economic growth.

Two more Memoranda of Understanding were signed—in 2006 and 2008—with annual inflation hovering around 8% or 9% during those years. The first Memorandum of Understanding called for a 20% cap on the public sector wage fund for the period 2006 through 2008. In return, the government again promised to contain inflation and grow the economy. The third Memorandum of Understanding with the national trade unions further entrenched the shift toward centralized bargaining. The process, however, was far from smooth. Several major unions stayed away from the initial signing, and it was only in December 2009 that the nurses' union (after a bitter and acrimonious public education campaign) agreed to the same terms as the other unions (Jamaica Information Service 2009). These Memoranda of Understanding had to overcome considerable challenges. As Kavan Gayle, president of the Bustamante Industrial Trade Union, commented at the time: "Employers don't trust trade unions, trade unions don't trust employers, and nobody don't trust the government but we are going to start an element of trust" (Rose 2009).

Return to the IMF

Just over two years following another change of government in September 2007, Jamaica signaled its return to the IMF with a 27-month Stand-By Arrangement (SBA). The SBA lasted for less than one year, however, because in the run-up to elections in December 2011, the government breached performance targets, including the central government wage-to-GDP ratio. In the meantime, the country had become one of the most indebted in the world, with public debt amounting to some 140% of GDP. Just prior to signing the most recent (April 2013) agreement with the

IMF, Jamaica was spending approximately 55% of its national budget on debt servicing. Another 25% went into wages and salaries for public sector workers (McIntosh 2013; Wint 2013).

Discussion with the IMF continued under the new government and, at the beginning of April 2013, the government emerged from the most protracted negotiations in the history of its relationship with that institution. As on previous occasions, the agreement with the IMF called for a policy of wage restraint. The government, as a "prior condition" for balance of payment support, managed to convince the unions that represented more than 80% of the public sector workforce to agree to additional wage restraints for the years 2013 through 2015, which was intended to facilitate a reduction in public sector wages from 10.9% of GDP to 9% by March 2016.

One of the key elements of the present agreement is the extent to which it is managed by the private sector. As part of the monitoring and implementation process, the government has set up an Economic Programme Oversight Committee (EPOC). This 11-person committee includes the chief executives of four of the largest financial institutions, one of whom (along with the governor of the Bank of Jamaica) is the co-chair and chief spokesperson. The embattled trade union movement is represented by two people: one, a career trade unionist and general secretary of the Jamaica Association of Local Government Officers; and the other, an outspoken journalist who routinely comments on economic issues (*Jamaica Gleaner* 2015).

In 2013, a national labor–management summit was hosted by the Hugh Lawson Shearer Trade Union Education Institute and the Mona School of Business of Management of the University of the West Indies, Mona, with support from the government of Jamaica. Figure 1 presents the results of a survey distributed to 229 labor and management leaders in advance of the summit. Fifty-one people responded (for a response rate of 22%), with 51% of the responses from labor, 22% of the responses from management, and 28% of the responses from neutrals or others. Caution is urged in interpreting these results because they are cross-sectional and from a relatively small sample of labor and management leaders. Nevertheless, in a context marked by a dearth of empirical research, they represent a rare glimpse of the views held by the employment relations community about a crucial area of public policy such as the quality of public services, the public interest, and spending restraint.

All parties see the future potential as great compared with the present, though neutrals are more restrained than the representatives from labor and management. Labor is more positive than management about the current levels of quality in the delivery of public service and the current degree to which the public interest is taken into account. Management is more

FIGURE 1
Perceptions of Jamaican Labor and Management
Leaders and Neutrals About the Current State and Future
Potential for Public Services, Public Interest, and Spending Restraint

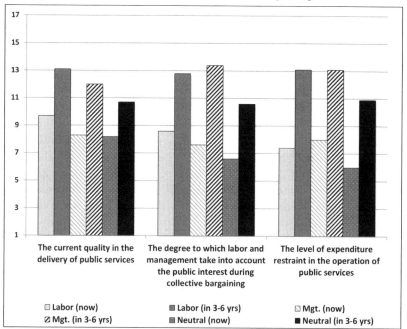

Note: Means are based on scale of 1–17, with 1 = very negative and 17 = very positive for the first item (delivery of public services) and 1= very ineffective and 17 = very effective for the other two items.

positive than labor about the current level of expenditure restraint. In both cases, however, labor's and management's assessments of the current situation are around the mid-point on the scale—which is not a positive assessment from either side.

The Jamaican Outcome

Following the first set of IMF agreements in the 1970s, three Jamaican economists concluded that the agreements had resulted in declines in the quality and range of social services, reduced purchasing power, chronic rise in unemployment, and a generally lower standard of living (Girvan, Bernal, and Hughes 1980). The period of the 1980s saw economic growth—but few tangible benefits for labor, which, particularly after the failed general strike of 1985, had languished in the face of the "huge toll in human suffering" flowing from "over hasty reforms of the IMF" (Prime Minister Edward Seaga, cited in Thorburn and Morris

2008:23). The period between the mid-1980s and 1990s was marked by trade liberalization, inflation, and massive distension, followed by a collapse of the financial sector and the hollowing out of the real economy. After presiding over a period of high interest rates that resulted in a massive shift of resources into the hands of the financial elite, the Jamaican government proceeded to invest a significant proportion of national output (present and future) in an attempt to stave off the collapse of the financial sector.

At the beginning of the country's long and arduous journey with the IMF, the national trade union movement was at its peak. In power was a pro-labor government, headed by the most charismatic and the last of three consecutive prime ministers to have emerged from the trade union movement. Forty years since its birth, free decentralized collective bargaining had become institutionalized.

The entry of the IMF added a fourth party to the traditional tripartite system of labor governance. During the 1970s, the IMF's influence was felt primarily through the introduction of the "national interest clause" in the Labour Relations and Industrial Disputes Act. The 1980s saw free-market liberalization and globalization as the government adopted an arm's length approach to collective bargaining. During the 1990s, even though the IMF was absent, the policies of the Washington Consensus remained while government set out on a policy of wage containment through social dialogue.

The current phase marks the maturation of this process of social dialogue and a consolidation of the policy of wage restraint. Central to this process has been a series of Memoranda of Understanding. Those agreements have had basic characteristics in common, including (1) recognition of a parlous state of economy, (2) preservation of public sector jobs, (3) wage restraint, and (4) a framework for the conduct of good industrial relations practice in the public sector (e.g., disclosure of information, openness, transparency, mutual respect). The IMF is an accepted fourth actor in the system, though so far that model has not yet delivered improved outcomes for labor, management, or the nation.

UNITED STATES

The United States' recession, beginning in late 2006 in certain sectors of the economy and impacting the full society in 2008, increased the visibility of capital markets in relation to both private and public sector collective bargaining. In the process, the important role of the public interest in labor–management relations was highlighted. In some ways, these newly visible connections represent positive developments, while in other ways they reveal stress and limitations in the institutions.

The Ford–UAW Case

The U.S. auto industry faced economic pressures in advance of the broader collapse of the U.S. economy. In 2006, for example, the Ford Motor Company lost $17 billion and began a two-year process of voluntary separations and retirements that would reduce the hourly workforce from over 100,000 to under 50,000. Although the financial pressures facing Ford were comparable to those facing its primary domestic competitors, GM and Chrysler, Ford was able in 2009 to avoid bankruptcy and turn down the offer of a federal bailout package. By 2010, Ford celebrated leadership in global quality, and by 2013 its profits were approximately $9 billion, with hourly workers receiving profit-sharing checks of over $8,500 each (Cutcher-Gershenfeld, Brooks, and Mulloy 2015).

The role of financial markets in this story are many. First, Ford's ability to not take the federal money rested, in part, on a strategic decision prior to the recession to establish a line of credit for $23 billion—mortgaging the entire business including the Ford oval (that is, the brand itself). Ford's competitors were critical of the move at the time, but they had not anticipated how debilitating financial swings could be in today's economy.

Second, the 2007 auto negotiations featured the establishment of Voluntary Employee Benefit Associations (VEBAs) with General Motors, Chrysler, and Ford that used a combination of cash and stock to take all liability for retiree benefits off the books of the auto firms and onto the UAW, which instantly (through the VEBA) became the largest private purchaser of health care services in the U.S. economy. This move was instrumental in improving the credit ratings of the auto companies—in the case of Ford improving all the way from junk bond status in 2006 to investment grade in 2011. Achieving investment-grade status was highly consequential, saving Ford an estimated half a billion dollars per quarter in interest payments.

Third, even though Ford didn't take the government bailout, it did support this dramatic intervention of the U.S. government in the industry because the collapse of either of its competitors would have devastating implications for the supply base—potentially bringing down all companies in the industry. In that sense, the financial crisis in the economy led the auto industry into new and complex financial arrangements. The UAW, for example, was both a negotiator with the federal government as a representative of the workforce being asked to make concessions as part of the bankruptcy and a creditor holding considerable stock in all three companies as a result of the VEBA agreement.

Importantly, the UAW was able to prevent the more severe imposed reduction in wages for newly hired workers that was being advocated by the U.S. Congress. By first negotiating with Ford in 2009, rather than with U.S. government representatives on behalf of GM and Chrysler, the UAW was able to achieve an agreement for a reduction that was sufficient for recovery—but no more. This additional check and balance in the system protected standards of living and tax revenues in many communities to a greater degree than would have happened otherwise.

The result of these and related developments is that decision making within the auto companies and within the UAW now takes into account capital markets in expanded ways. In particular, the parties have to more explicitly mitigate the additional volatility that characterizes capital markets.

Public Sector Developments

In the case of public sector labor relations in the United States, the intrusion of capital markets into collective bargaining has been even further reaching than in the auto industry. During the last quarter of the 20th century, the trend had been primarily toward expanded collective bargaining rights for public sector workers. By the mid-1990s, at least some public sector workers had some bargaining rights in 40 of the 50 states. Beginning in 2009 and continuing for the next five years, there have been challenges to public sector collective bargaining rights in at least 14 states. Over 550 bills were introduced in state legislatures challenging aspects of public sector collective bargaining, with changes in 13 states: Arizona, Idaho, Indiana, Michigan, Montana, New Hampshire , Ohio, Oklahoma, South Carolina, Tennessee, Utah, Wisconsin, and Wyoming. The changes in Ohio were introduced and subsequently reversed. Debates continue in many of these and other states (Cutcher-Gershenfeld and Rubenstein 2013).

In all of the cases where there were challenges to public sector collective bargaining rights, the stated motivation for the challenges involved the need for increased fiscal constraint. This was in the context of state budgets that were experiencing shortfalls that had not been seen since the recession of the early 1980s or, in some cases, not since the Great Depression of the 1930s. In this regard, the collapse of capital markets brought massive instability to public sector finances, and public sector collective bargaining frequently became the casualty.

In a survey of public sector labor and management representatives in Wisconsin, the implications of the changes are highly visible (Cutcher-Gershenfeld et al. 2013). Wisconsin was one of the first states to establish collective bargaining rights for public sector workers (a half century ago), and it made some of the farthest-reaching changes—removing bargaining rights for all but police and fire public sector workers on February 11, 2011. A survey was sent to 1,577 union and management leaders in spring 2013, with responses received from 445 people. The survey was distributed through the Wisconsin Employment Relations Commission and local chapters of the Labor and Employment Relations Association. The number of responses from management (69.5%) were three times the responses from labor (23.0%), with the balance from neutrals and others (7.5%). The lower response rate from union leaders is not a surprise because many were facing the elimination of their roles and there was skepticism by some about participating in any survey on these issues. The responses were distributed across all parts of the public sector, including police (29.2%), fire (27.0%), public transit (5.2%), K–12 education (39.6%), higher education (4.7%), municipal government (43.6%), and state government (4.7%). The results are reported for labor and management separately.

Although it was a cross-sectional survey, respondents were asked to look back and describe how they remembered things were three years earlier (before the change in the law), how things were at the time of the survey, and how they anticipated things would be three years in the future. As Figure 2 indicates, the views of labor and management looking back were highly similar with regard to dispute resolution and their workplace being a great place to work. Looking at the present and looking ahead, however, the opinions become increasingly divergent.

When looking back, the views of labor and management are similar, but they are not highly favorable. In retrospect, there was room for improvement, but the current situation holds little prospect for such improvement.

As illustrated in Figure 3, the divergence is not nearly as strong when it comes to the public interest. Management sees itself as more committed than it sees labor, and labor sees itself as more committed than management is. Interestingly, both groups project deterioration in the commitment of their counterpart—and even modest deterioration in their own commitment. The picture that emerges is one of divergence and contested terrain.

These data suggest that any mechanisms for collective governance in the workplace will have to span increasingly divergent views and experiences.

Although financial factors drove the challenges to public sector collective bargaining rights, the economic recovery is beginning to generate budget surpluses in many of the states that presented economic justifications for the erosion of representation rights. So far, however, there has not been a return of collective bargaining rights. Wages have long been seen by economists as "sticky" downward—that is, wage increases happen easily as economic conditions improve, but wage decreases happen with more difficulty as economic conditions deteriorate. Now we see a reverse

FIGURE 2

Wisconsin Labor and Management Representative Opinions: "Great Place to Work" and "Dispute Resolution"

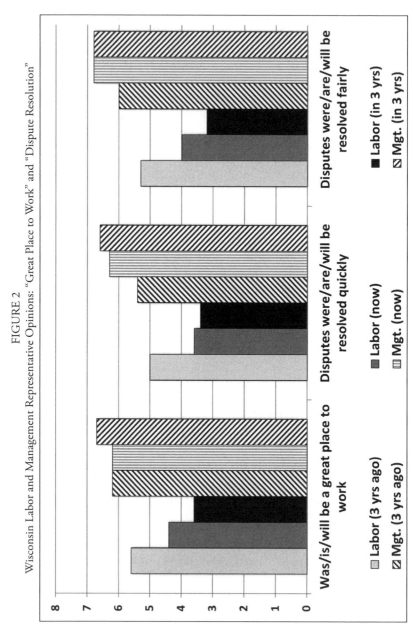

Note: Mean results presented are based on a scale from 0 (never) to 8 (continuous).

FIGURE 3

Wisconsin Labor and Management Representative Opinions: "Quality and Efficiency of Public Services"

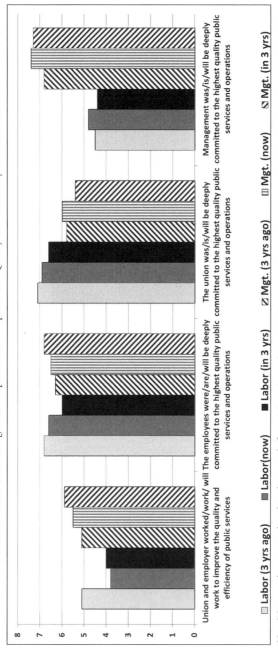

Note: Mean results presented are based on a scale from 0 (never) to 8 (continuous).

case, where collective bargaining rights may be removed with comparative ease in a crisis but are difficult to re-establish when the crisis is over. This situation suggests that disruptions associated with financial factors in the public sector are not part of the normal ebb and flow of power that was intended to be channeled by the institutions of collective bargaining. In the case of the auto industry in the United States, there has been more of a check and balance possible, with the role of financial institutions serving as an exogenous shock to the system, with a ratcheting down of wages and benefits but not a fundamental change in the institutional arrangements.

In the long run, there may be a return of some of the lost collective bargaining rights in the public sector, but these developments suggest that the "strategic" level of the Kochan, Katz, and McKersie (1986) model needs to be expanded to incorporate fundamental challenges to the very existence of a system of industrial relations.

CONCLUSION

This chapter contains a selective review of developments in three countries. As such, caution is urged in generalizing from the material presented. Still, patterns are evident from these examples that suggest certain aspects of capital markets have had and will continue to have profound implications for the institutions of collective bargaining.

In the cases of Greece and Jamaica, we see how financial institutional arrangements, including the European Economic and Monetary Union, the World Bank, and the International Monetary Fund can all be direct actors in the collective bargaining process. While the dynamics do involve negotiation, the bargaining reflects considerable power imbalance. The result, on one hand, is agreements that are largely imposed on labor and management. On the other hand, as with any imposed agreement, there is also a poor record of compliance. More recent developments in both countries have taken a somewhat more problem-solving approach, though there are still continuing stresses and uncertainties in each case. If financial organizations and institutions are to be formal actors in a system of labor and employment relations, there needs to be better mechanisms to facilitate the surfacing of interests and the generation of options that take these interests into account.

In the case of the United States, we see the disruption of long-established arrangements, including the erosion or elimination of U.S. public sector bargaining rights in a number of states—motivated by economic crisis. At the same time, in the case of the UAW and Ford in the United States, we see adoption of a more problem-solving approach to negotiations and results that directly address major financial pressures on the parties. The United States is certainly a less extreme case than either Greece or Jamaica, though it, too, is remarkable how quickly collective bargaining rights in the United States have been eroded in some public sector jurisdictions and how slowly they are returning now that the crisis has been abated.

Beyond the United States, there are many other countries where the impact of financialization has been far more limited. Consider what may be the nation that is the model of highly collaborative collective bargaining, led by the parties—Denmark. The norms of private resolution of labor–management issues in Denmark date back to the September Compromise of 1899, and they continue to function well. For example, even with severe financial pressures facing Scandinavian Airlines in 2009, 39 unions and nine distinct business entities spanning three countries (Denmark, Norway, and Sweden) were able to agree to a problem-solving, interest-based approach to bargaining that addressed the financial issues and preserved the overall institutional structure.

These basic principles of negotiations in Denmark have been under heavy pressure and still are. But the general understanding between the parties that they have to work together to overcome the economic crisis to maintain jobs continues to build on the robust foundation of the old September Compromise. Similarly, the nation's doctors are unionized and they, too, were able to use problem-solving tools and methods to address important financial and service-delivery challenges in the health care system. Denmark did experience an unprecedented four-week lockout of public school teachers in 2013. Although financial issues were a factor in that negotiation, the government's decision to lock out the teachers was more out of frustration with entrenched positions than an effort to impose a new financial regime.

During their biannual labor contract negotiations, unions and managers in Denmark have worked together to "handle" the economic crisis. The unions have generally shifted from more traditional issues to more innovative issues, such as occupational health, education, equal opportunities, and corporate social responsibility. The current understanding is that wages and other traditional issues, though still important, have to be of lower priority as long as "we are losing jobs." In this sense, the experience in Denmark reminds us that not all nations are experiencing the intrusion of financialization into collective bargaining—so caution is required when generalizing from the three cases included here.

Implications

First, it is clear that existing institutional arrangements are not designed to support social dialogue in the context of an extreme fiscal crisis. In some respects, these situations need action more than dialogue. At the same time, there is a great risk of unilateral action that over-reaches or otherwise misses the mark. In the U.S. case, the mix of public and private negotiations (with GM and Chrysler negotiating with the federal government, on the one hand, and Ford negotiating privately, on the other) provided an appropriate check and balance. There is also the risk of poor compliance with the imposed agreement, which was the case at various times in Jamaica.

Second, it is clear that the relationships among financial markets, product or service markets, and labor markets are incompletely understood and that the implications for collective bargaining are considerable. Shifts in product or service markets can drive concessions or growth in labor markets. This situation can be handled by the established institutions of labor and employment relations. Shifts in financial markets can provide pretext for eliminating collective bargaining altogether, which happened in various degrees in all three countries. That was not something contemplated by the labor and employment relations institutions.

Third, and finally, there is not much evidence of resilience in the institutions at the extreme—once collective bargaining is undermined, it is not easily re-established. It seems that if you want to maintain the bargaining system and the institutions during financialization of the social dialogue, you have to negotiate that issue in itself—that is, negotiate agreements on how to negotiate when the very institutions are on the table.

The public interest is in institutional arrangements that simultaneously ensure growth in what are termed "good jobs" and high performance (whether in the delivery of public services or the generation of private value). Government is not necessarily a protector of this public interest. When government and financial institutions (national and international) act in unilateral ways to avert financial collapse or to mitigate deteriorating financial conditions, there are many nations that do not have well-established mechanisms in place to fully take into account the interests of all stakeholders or to revisit the unilateral actions once conditions improve.

While the three cases presented here are distinct in many ways, they have in common the shocking ease with which established institutional arrangements of labor and employment relations have been set aside. The challenge for labor, management, and society, is to fashion institutional arrangements that take into account the interests of financial actors, as well as labor, management, and government, in ways that lead all parties to adjust to future crises within the bounds of agreed-upon "rules of the game." Ultimately, such a system should provide forms of stability that will be rewarded by the financial markets as they deliver on the promise of good jobs and high performance.

REFERENCES

Clarke, C. 2011. "The Tragic Folly of FINSAC." *Jamaica Gleaner* (http://bit.ly/1Fp3vqa).

Collister, Keith. 2005. "A Fragile or Failed State?" *The Sunday Gleaner.*

Cowell, N.M. 1992. *A Summary of Test Cases in Jamaican Labour Law.* Kingston: Joint Trade Unions Research Development Centre.

Cutcher-Gershenfeld, J., D. Brooks, and M. Mulloy. 2015. *Inside the Ford–UAW Transformation: Pivotal Events in Creating Value and Delivering Results.* Cambridge, MA: MIT Press.

Cutcher-Gershenfeld, J., N. Carpenter, L. Hunter, T. Kochan, and C. Olson. 2013. "Summit Dialogue." 2013 Wisconsin Public Sector Labor & Employment Relations Conference, Madison, WI, May 2.

Cutcher-Gershenfeld, J., and S. Rubinstein. 2013. "Innovation and Transformation in Public Sector Employment Relations: Future Prospects on a Contested Terrain." *Ohio State Journal on Dispute Resolution*, Vol. 28, no. 2, pp. 107–144.

Dunlop, John Thomas. 1958. *Industrial Relations Systems.* New York: Henry Holt and Company.

European Commission. 2014. *The Second Economic Adjustment Programme for Greece, Fourth Review—April 2014, European Economy 2014.* Occasional Papers 192.

Eurostat. 2014 (Apr. 23). "Provision of Deficit and Debt Data for 2013—First Notification." Eurostat News Release, Euroindicators 64/2014.

Girvan, Norman, Richard Bernal, and Wesley Hughes. 1980. *The IMF and the Third World: The Case of Jamaica 1974–1980.* Kingston: Ian Randle.

ICTWSS. 2013 (Apr.). Database on Institutional Characteristics of Trade Unions, Wage Setting, State Intervention and Social Pacts in 34 Countries Between 1960 and 2012. Compiled by Jelle Visser, Amsterdam Institute for Advanced Labour Studies, University of Amsterdam, Version 4 (http://www.uva-aias.net/207).

International Labour Office (ILO). 2012. *Report on the High Level Mission to Greece.* Athens, September 19–23, 2011.

Ioannou, C. 2012. "Recasting Greek Industrial Relations: Internal Devaluation in Light of the Economic Crisis and European Integration." *International Journal of Comparative Labour Law and Industrial Relations*, Vol. 28, no. 2, pp. 199–222.

Ioannou, C. 2013. "Greek Public Service Employment Relations: A Gordian Knot in the Era of Sovereign Default." *European Journal of Industrial Relations*, Vol. 19, no. 4, pp. 295–308.

Ioannou, C. 2014. *Paradigm Change in Wage Formation and Greek Industrial Relations* (mimeo).

Ioannou, C., and C. Papadimitriou. 2013. *Collective Bargaining in Greece in 2011 and 2012: Tendencies, Disruption and Prospects* (in Greek). Athens: Organization for Mediation and Arbitration (http://bit.ly/1Fp7qTY).

Ioannou, D., and C. Ioannou. 2013. "Greece: Victim of Austerity or of a Dutch Disease?" *Foreign Affairs, The Hellenic Edition*, no. 18, pp. 40–54 (in Greek; English summary available at http://bit.ly/1DF8xsy).

Jamaica Gleaner. 2015. *Meet the Members of the EPOC* (http://bit.ly/1EALznk).

Jamaica Information Service. 2009 (Dec. 2). "Gov't to Pay Nurses Over $430m in Wage Increase" (http://bit.ly/1EAKETT).

Kochan, T., H. Katz, and R. McKersie. 1986. *The Transformation of American Industrial Relations*. New York: Basic Books.

McIntosh, Douglas. 2013. "PIOJ Head Says Multi-Billion Projects Will Contribute to Growth Projections." Jamaica Information Service (http://bit.ly/1Ew31PA).

Patra, E. 2012 (Feb.). *Social Dialogue and Collective Bargaining in Times of Crisis: The Case of Greece*. ILO Working Paper No. 468702. Geneva: International Labour Office.

Richards, L., J. Rapley, and D. King. 2009. *Jamaica and the IMF: Addressing the Issues*. Kingston: Caribbean Policy Research Institute (http://bit.ly/1Fp8Vl7).

Rose, D. 2009 (Mar. 13). "Red Stripe HR Director Takes on BoJ Governor." *Jamaica Gleaner* (http://bit.ly/1EAKZGb).

Spaulding, Gary. 2013. "When Seaga Swung the Axe." *The Gleaner* (http://bit.ly/1FiaYXD).

Starke, P. 2008. *Radical Welfare State Retrenchment: A Comparative Analysis*. Basingstoke, UK: Palgrave Macmillan.

Stone, C. 1989. *Politics Versus Economics: The 1989 Elections in Jamaica*. Kingston: Heinemann Publishers.

Taylor, Orville. 2013 (Mar. 10). "MOU IV: What Will the Workers Get?" *The Gleaner* (http://bit.ly/1Ew39yG).

Thompson, M. 2002 (Apr. 18). "Paying Dearly for the FINSAC Debt." *Jamaica Gleaner*.

Thorburn, D., and D.M. Morris. 2008. *Jamaica's Foreign Policy: Making the Economic Development Link*. Kingston: The Jamaican Economy Project (http://bit.ly/1FpbbbZ).

Williamson, J. 1993. Democracy and the "Washington Consensus." *World Development*, Vol. 21, no. 8, pp. 1329–1336.

Williamson, J. 2004 (Jan. 13). *The Washington Consensus as Policy Prescription for Development*. Lecture, "Practitioners of Development" Series. Washington, DC: World Bank (http://bit.ly/1FpcLe7).

Wint, Alvin. 2013 (Apr. 19). "The Jamaican Economy and Prospects for the Future." *Jamaica Observer* (http://bit.ly/1DF9bWR). Witter, M. 2012 (Jul. 8). "Lessons from the IMF Experiences." *Jamaica Gleaner* (http://bit.ly/1FpcZlr).

CHAPTER 3

Gaining Traction:
Socially Responsible Investments,
Targeted Markets, Sustainable Impacts

JANET BOGUSLAW
Brandeis University

ALEXANDER B. KAUFMAN
Washington, D.C.

INTRODUCTION

The past 30 years have seen a proliferation of financial products and services and an increase in individually invested savings. These changes have increased the awareness of households about their material involvement with financial markets. Many investors, at both the individual and institutional levels, are also increasingly aware of the social consequences that arise from the allocation of these investments. Investors who make allocation choices that consider social outcomes and seek to align their investments with their values are called socially responsible investors, and the investments they make are called socially responsible investments (SRI).

The term "socially responsible investment" refers specifically to an investment strategy designed to achieve normatively desirable outcomes in addition to a positive return on investment (ROI). A related concept, pension activism (PA), is a pension fund's use of its holdings to promote the contributor's interests in addition to achieving a positive ROI. Pension activism is almost always associated with union pensions. The ideas are related because both activities use the financial mechanisms of investment as the means for attaining their goals; in many, but not all, cases there is an overlap in SRI and PA objectives to improve environmental, social, and labor outcomes.

In theory, SRI and PA offer a means of social influence via use of the financial system. At the heart of SRI is the idea that industry can be democratized: if industry is collectively owned, it can be collectively operated, at least in theory. The current legal structure of Western capitalism gives individual investors partial ownership of "publicly owned" institutions. As owners, labor and social activists, as well as ordinary citizens, may theoretically direct these institutions and circumvent—or supplement—organizing and politics as a means of affecting institutional change. Citizens may exercise their right to vote on corporate, as well as government, behavior. Given the expanding influence of the financial industry and the growing number of individuals who personally manage retirement funds, such as 401(k)s and direct stock purchases, SRI and PA offer a powerful means to directly influence private institutional practices by affecting the flow and behavior of capital (Jones 1980).

Although large potential exists, SRI and PA face such high barriers to implementation that social scientists have yet to rigorously observe systemic effects of either SRI or PA. No comprehensive formal model of SRI or PA exists, but we may roughly expect these investment strategies to operate in similar if not identical ways. Scattered empirical evidence seems to indicate that PA has yet to be successfully implemented on a large scale. Empirical evidence on the direct impacts of SRI is mixed and lacks quantitative rigor. However, a boom in public, academic, and private interest in SRI indicates widespread belief in the growing power of SRI as well as PA, despite the decline in managed pensions.

Evidence of a systematic market impact of SRI has yet to be found, though there is some positive preliminary evidence. Growth in SRI and associated efforts to push for greater corporate accountability and transparency should produce means to evaluate the efficacy of SRI in the coming decade. Where there have been successful instances of SRI, environmental and social issues have generally been the focus, with labor interests limited to a handful of successful SRI initiatives. Labor relations are important but not a leading priority among socially responsible investors. Some corporate governance issues, such as executive compensation and shareholder rights plans, align with labor interests and are gaining more traction. Labor relations are overwhelmingly focused on overseas labor standards such as working conditions and safety (Proffitt and Spicer 2006). Almost all SRI investments that specifically screen for labor relationship are pension owned, indicating little interest outside of the labor movement itself.

In this chapter, we first provide an overview of SRI and PA activities in the United States and abroad over the past half century, including the relationship between labor and investment. Historical and qualitative information is presented first and is the primary means offered to explain the general effects of SRI and PA. Next, we outline in greater detail the theoretical and limited quantitative empirical research on SRI and PA and comment on the structural and legal impediments to SRI and PA efficacy. Finally, we present a number of qualitative examples of labor outcomes that resulted from PA and SRI and attempt to synthesize conclusions about the impacts and future of SRI and PA and their implications for labor.

The Context and Emergence of SRI and PA

The vast majority of money invested as SRI resides in securities (i.e., stocks and bonds). In the United States, the relative size of pension funds has steadily decreased over the past 20 years as employers have shifted the risks associated with retirement investments onto individuals (Hardin 2014). This trend represents a serious decline in the potential of PA, though most pension funds were never involved in PA to begin with.

In place of pension funds, defined contribution plans have become the standard way of saving for retirement. Defined contribution plans include 401(k) accounts and IRAs, through which the employee defers income into a long-term savings account. Use of these products has increased as employers have shifted away from pension funds. Though the past decade has seen retirement saving decrease by incidence and in the aggregate, the use of defined contribution plans is still increasing as pension participation shrinks. This trend is less pronounced in Europe but is present nonetheless (Peters 2010). Efforts to structure these contribution plans as "opt-out" rather than "opt-in" is one effort to increase the level and regularity of contributions.

These trends mean that an individual's deferred income (retirement savings) represents a shrinking, but still sizeable, proportion of the market. Though less investment is collectively owned—decreasing the potential of PA affecting the entire market—the same shift that hurts PA may actually increase the prevalence and market power of SRI.

The discretionary options of individual retirement accounts often include the option to invest in SRI. Whereas effective PA requires collective action and majority support from employees—and imposes severe legal restrictions on managers—socially responsible individual retirement funds mostly circumvent these necessities. It is likely that the growth of such funds and the increasingly simple process of SRI have driven the increase in SRI over the last decade (Sparks 2002).

Socially Responsible Investing

The philosophy behind socially responsible investment is for the investor to induce socially positive behavior (or discourage the opposite) through the decision to provide, withhold, or withdraw investment (Statman 2000). This idea has been present in American culture dating back to the middle of the 18th century when the Religious Society of Friends, also known as the Quakers, prohibited its members from involvement in the slave trade (Knoll 2002). Today, SRI is an umbrella term that may refer to any investment strategy that considers environmental, social, or governmental (ESG) consequences of the financial investment (Magalhães 2013).

Many strategies fit the definition of SRI, but they can be broadly grouped under the labels of *impact investment*, *screening*, and *management*.

Impact investment actively directs funds toward projects that are expected to have a positive social externality (or avoid a common negative externality). For instance, a venture capitalist might invest in a particularly union-friendly construction company to promote union-friendly policies within an industrial sector and therefore be considered an impact investor. Impact investing is meant to produce positive social outcomes that would not occur without the investment (Brest and Born 2013).[1]

Screening encompasses the refusal of initial investment or withdrawal of investment on a similar ESG basis (often referred to as "divestment"). Most socially responsible mutual funds screen out investments that fail to meet particular benchmarks of social responsibility (Sparks 2002). A widely known example of divestment was the movement to withdraw investments from South Africa in the 1980s, which was designed to create economic pressure to abolish the system of racial segregation known as apartheid.

The managerial approach to SRI, called "activist" by some, includes activities such as shareholder engagement, shareholder activism, and promotion of corporate social responsibility (CSR), among others. For example, a stockholder who files a shareholder resolution that binds management to permit labor organizing would be practicing managerial SRI (Blackburn 2007).

Figure 1 provides examples of the broad range of criteria that may enter into these investment decisions and related institutional practices. In all cases, SRI is still an investment and is designed to achieve a return on the original investment as well as promote a social goal. Individuals or institutions that lend or make "investments" *without* the expectation of a return on the initial investment, such as nonprofit student loan lenders that do not recover the full cost of loans, may be considered charitable organizations rather than socially responsible investors.

Pension Activism

Pension activism is a closely related concept. It uses most of the same financial mechanisms as SRI but advances particular interests of the pension holders. Pension activism does not always fall under the socially responsible label because labor goals may be socially neutral or favor one SRI priority over another. Pension activism is usually associated with government and union pensions, although, theoretically, any interest group with a large enough financial position could be influential. A handful of private pension funds have played an activist role.

For the sake of specificity, we begin with an overview of pension activism by looking at American union pension funds in the past half century. A secular, structured approach to activist investing emerged in the 1950s amid the American post-war unionization movement when unions

FIGURE 1
Commonly Used SRI Criteria

Negative Screens	Positive Screens
Alcohol	Human rights
Tobacco	Labor relations
Gambling	Employment/equality
Defense/weapons	Environment
Animal testing	Proxy voting

Criteria can include labor issues about

- Child labor
- Workers forced into compulsory labor
- Fair living wages, rights to free association/collective bargaining
- Equal opportunity and nondiscriminatory treatment
- Gender diversity in executive positions
- Safe work environments
- Health and lifestyle benefits provided to employees

Source: Adapted from Fung, Law, and Yau (2010).

recognized that their pension funds could be used as an economic tool for advancing the interests of organized labor (Paul and Harbrecht 1959). In the 1980s, the AFL-CIO recommended unions exercise pension activism, in which unions used the financial power of their pension funds to exert leverage and encourage investment favorable to labor (Freeman 1985). The modern ideas behind this union policy can be traced to Rifkin and Barber's *The North Will Rise Again*, which described a plan for labor to regain political and economic strength via the economic power of pension funds (Rifkin and Barber 1978).

In 1981, the AFL-CIO issued a directive to use union pension funds:

> To increase employment … [and] to advance social purposes such as workers' housing and health centers. To improve the ability of workers to exercise their rights as share-holders in a coordinated fashion. To exclude from union pension plan investment portfolios companies whose policies are hostile to workers' rights. (Freeman 1985)

Even at the time, there were significant barriers to implementation. The 1974 Employee Retirement Income Security Act (ERISA) had already placed severe constraints on such investment strategies by legally obligating pension fund managers to maximize return while minimizing risk (Lamon 1976). In light of this legal barrier to allocative flexibility, most pension funds pursued shareholder activism, the form of SRI in which the investor (in this case the pension fund) is actively involved with the business and operations management (Fung, Hebb, and Rogers 2001). It took a number of years for unions to begin coordinating their efforts, but by the mid-1990s, labor pensions were a leader in the field of shareholder activism, with pension funds submitting resolutions and organizing support for shareholder proposals (religious investors, for their own moral purposes, also became leaders in shareholder activism at the same time) (Sjöström 2008). Pension activism tends to focus on corporate governance issues, including persuading management to recognize union activity, preventing anti-union management from becoming entrenched, and assisting striking unions.

Pension funds have also been able to exert targeted managerial influence without filing shareholder resolutions. In some instances, a pension fund's legal stake in a company was enough to command the attention and to direct behavior of management without filing a resolution—given the implicit legal and financial threat associated with ownership. Perhaps the most famous instance of such pension activism was that of the United Steelworkers, who in 1997 helped end a strike by exerting influence on the company through pension fund ownership (Marens 2004).

Pension activism in the 21st century focuses more on impact investment than on management. The AFL-CIO Housing Investment Trust, an investment fund chartered in the 1980s to promote socially responsible and labor interests through construction investments, is the largest domestic pension fund targeting labor-friendly investments. The fund increased its holdings from a value of $500 million in 1992 to approximately $4.2 billion in 2013 and claims to have generated 70,000 union jobs (AFL-CIO Housing Investment Trust, no date). The other large, labor-friendly private equity fund is the Multi-Employer Property Trust. Together these funds hold just over $10 billion, and while they have been successful at creating jobs as well as earning normal returns, they represent only a drop in the $16 trillion dollar bucket of domestic pension funds (Towers Watson 2013).

While such an investment strategy has proven successful on a small scale, no formal analysis has explored the market effects of such investments. It is not clear whether this type of investment promotes activity that would not otherwise occur, or whether these impact funds have crowded out other similar investment in the housing market. For these reasons, some scholars question whether the gains of shareholder activism and impact investing are economically significant or just politically symbolic (Fung, Hebb, and Rogers 2001).

While it is clear that instances of pension activism have helped resolve labor disputes, funded projects that use unionized labor, and contributed to building affordable housing and producing other social goods, there is little in the way of empirically documented market effect. These strategies have generally been insufficient to increase the size or power of domestic unions in the face of other anti-labor forces by themselves (Marens 2004). The success of impact investing and PA has thus been limited to specific interventions and targeted investments.

The role of labor pension funds in Canada also bears mention. Until 2013, between 40% and 50% of all Canadian venture capital was invested through Labour Sponsored Investment Funds (LSIFs). These funds were originally established to harness union resources to promote economic growth in certain Canadian regions. However, these funds should not be considered true PA because they do not specifically target or require union- or labor-friendly businesses, nor do they require the use of union money. Instead, they require only union sponsorship, which essentially requires a union to appoint the fund management. These funds have become widespread in Canada because they receive sizeable tax credits. They were never explicitly intended to promote labor's interests (instead they were supposed to instigate economic growth) and have reportedly suffered from poor organizational management, with below-market returns and high management fees (Anderson and Tian 2003). A key study to take on the question of impact found that there was little tangible social impact from these funds (Olson 2006).

The primary understanding that has emerged from the LSIFs is that union discretion in appointment of fund managers is not sufficient to advance labor goals nor to induce management to engage in effective (or any) PA. It seems, by comparison, that active management strategies—such as those employed by the Housing Investment Trust—are more likely to affect social outcomes than simply appointing "labor-friendly" managers.

The Scope of Socially Responsible Investing

Scenarios such as pension fund intervention on behalf of striking workers are clearly pension activism and are conceptually distinct from the general concept of SRI. With respect to shareholder resolutions, however, pension activism overlaps with the SRI label. Most SRI shareholder resolutions related to "employment issues" are partially or fully filed by union or public pension funds. Such activism should thus be understood to exist within the context of SRI as well as PA.

In contrast to pension activism, the scale and scope of socially responsible investments have expanded in the past decade. Socially responsible investments may include labor interests, but they may also include environmental and social goals. Large growth has been seen in the market for SRI over the past decade, though growth seems to have been driven primarily by concerns about environmental sustainability (US SIF 2012), as discussed later in this chapter. Because of the loose definition of socially responsible investment, it is difficult to determine the magnitude of existing SRI. Global estimates range from as much as $8 trillion[2] to a conservative $400 billion (PRI Initiative 2013). Based on estimates of total global managed assets of $79.8 trillion, there may be as much as 11% of global assets under management committed to responsible investing, or there may be as little as 1% (Langley 2010), depending on who is estimating and how SRI is being defined. As discussed later in this chapter, the ambiguity of definition has important consequences for the consideration of impact.

The concept of SRI has become internationally relevant with the United Nations Principles for Responsible Investment (PRI) initiative. An international network of investors, PRI works to enroll signatories who agree to incorporate responsible investment criteria into their decision making and ownership practices. PRI aspires to function at the international level by contributing to the development of a more sustainable and responsible global financial system. Specifically, PRI advocates for

> an approach to investment that explicitly acknowledges the relevance to the investor of environmental, social, and governance (ESG) factors, and the long-term health and stability of the market as a whole. It recognizes that the generation of long-term sustainable returns is dependent on stable, well-functioning and well-governed social, environmental, and economic systems. It is driven by a growing recognition in the financial community that effective research, analysis, and evaluation of ESG issues is a fundamental part of assessing the value and performance over the medium and longer term, and that this analysis should inform asset allocation, stock selection, portfolio construction, shareholder engagement, and voting. (PRI Initiative 2014)

The PRI initiative has been signed by hundreds of investor groups and represents the start of a cultural shift toward recognizing the moral and financial implications of investment allocation, as well as the power investors have to implement sustainable and ethical investment strategies. Much of this commitment is discretionary, however, since the United Nations lacks means of credible enforcement.

Many foundations rely on shareholder advocacy coalitions to promote diverse SRI goals. For example, As You Sow represents investor clients in engagements with corporate executives on environmental and human rights issues. Others draw on investor collaborations to have impacts of scale and focus (US SIF 2014). The Coalition of Immokalee Workers (CIW) demonstrates the way investor pressure can affect the market. In 1993, the Coalition of Immokalee Workers (CIW), a community-based farmworkers organization based in Immokalee, Florida, representing over 4,000 farmworkers, organized to increase tomato harvester wages by one cent per pound picked and to establish a third-party mechanism for monitoring worker complaints of abuse. Investors such as the Needmor Fund joined other concerned investors in co-filing several resolutions at Yum! Brands, Taco Bell's parent company, with large minority shareowner support for resolutions and ongoing efforts by investors to engage Yum! over these issues (Korten 2009). The company agreed to a settlement with the Immokalee Workers in 2005, and major buyers signed an agreement with CIW to ensure safe, healthy working conditions and a sustainable living wage for tomato harvesters.

By 2009, CIW had used similar organizing and shareholder pressure to induce Taco Bell, McDonald's, Burger King, Subway, and Whole Foods to sign the agreement (Korten 2009). The agreement developed and instituted a code of conduct that improved wages and increased workplace protections, including minimum wage guarantees and a zero-tolerance policy on child labor. By 2010, it was extended as the CIW's Fair Food principles—including a strict code of conduct, a cooperative complaint resolution system, a participatory health and safety program, and a worker-to-worker education process—to over 90% of the Florida tomato industry (CIW 2013).

Standards for SRI, including social priorities and the rigor of enforcement, are varied, which makes estimating compliance difficult. Funds that undertake only basic screening usually rule out investments in alcohol-, tobacco-, and gambling-related industries and comprise the majority of SRI. Most investors do not screen for impact, although the number of managers who proactively select for desirable human rights, labor relations, and employment quality is rising. Industry experts estimate that only 1% to 2% percent of global assets under management are managed under issue-specific social screens or impact strategies (Geczy, Stambaugh, and Levin 2003). Until recently, the majority of SRI investments were made by European pension funds, many of which were actively involved with ESG concerns before the recent surge in public awareness related to SRI (Crifo and Mottis 2013).

The total SRI assets under actively responsible[3] management have grown dramatically. The US SIF has estimated that SRI assets in the United States have grown from $2.7 trillion in 2007 to $3.7 trillion in 2012 (Figure 2). A number of factors drive this growth, but above-average

FIGURE 2

Sustainable and Responsible Investing in the United States, 1995–2012

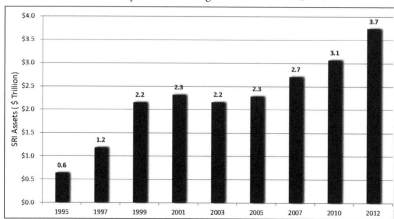

Source: Adapted from US SIF (2012).

returns to SRI are not among them. This growth means that demand for these investments is rising; investors are learning about, or becoming convinced of, the purported social impacts and financial security of SRI, and hence are allocating more funds toward SRI.

A burgeoning interest in sustainable business and an increased awareness of the power of financial markets after the great recession may explain increased demand for responsible asset management. At the same time, money managers are recognizing the marketing value of SRI. Some of the growth in SRI strategies may be attributable to changes made by asset managers to bring their strategies under the SRI umbrella (US SIF 2012) and to managers adopting SRI practices as a means of attracting investment (Becht, Franks, Mayer, and Rossi 2010).

Exclusion (by screening) of companies that have unsustainable or otherwise socially irregular impacts is by far the largest segment of the SRI market, covering between 80% and 90%[4] of all responsibly managed assets. Within all types of SRI funds, it is difficult to determine the market share[5] of different SRI priorities because there is little standardization among investment groups. Sustainability appears to be of paramount importance, with human rights and corporate governance as the second and third leading priorities (US SIF 2012).

The expansion of SRI strategies may also be a result of the increasing accessibility of information, enabling precise social targeting. There are only a few instances of independently established SRI criteria; most new funds borrow or mimic their social strategy from a few original institutions that were among the first to establish themselves in this market. This is similar to the pattern of growth by entrepreneurial technology firms, a pattern that suggests SRI strategies significantly alter the institutional logic of financial practitioners who undertake them (Arjalies 2010).

The growth of SRI overturned previously established notions of valuation and allocation and surprised many investors who doubted SRI could ever become as widespread or successful as it is today (Bengtsson 2008). Nevertheless, the academic evidence available suggests that the economic impact of SRI has been limited and the social movements driving SRI are not yet able to prioritize in ways that produce large-scale, targeted economic impact.

THEORIES OF SRI PROCESS AND IMPACT
A fully developed theoretical framework of socially responsible investment does not exist. Informal theories for the causal mechanism (i.e., how socially responsible investment causes social change) span a wide spectrum of ideas. While some theories of SRI, such as the ideas behind impact investing, are relatively clear, the details of precisely how portfolio screening leads to social change are murky at best.

Impact Investing
In some cases, SRI may be thought of as having a direct impact; SRI may induce a positive (possibly deliberate) externality resulting from a socially responsible business strategy or from the development of alternative, socially responsible technology. For instance, an SRI investor might target air pollution by investing in either a company that produces highly efficient engines (a particular business strategy) or a company that produces electric engines (an alternative solution).

The idea of direct impact undergirds the philosophy of impact investing and, to some extent, managerial action. In theory, individual investors need only to direct their funds (and managers) toward investments that will produce desired social outcomes. The theory behind impact investing, in which an investor who recognizes the need for a social outcome allocates investment toward a project that meets such an end (Jackson 2013), is relatively simple and well documented (Renneboog and Szilagyi, no date). Impact investing is the most theoretically simple type of SRI, but is often the most complicated to implement, and is, possibly for that reason, the least common form of SRI.

Managerial Control
In theory, public owners of firms have some managerial discretion. In almost all Western economies, management in public firms is legally

required to act on any shareholder resolution that is approved by a majority of shareholders. However, owing to informational problems between investors and firms—and to the collective action problem of organizing shareholders—it is not entirely clear that shareholder activism affects firm behavior. When investors are multiple steps removed from firm management, which is almost universally the case, they may lack the information and managerial proximity to effect internal corporate change (Bebchuk 2005; Hoffman 1996).

The basic shareholder activism model works like this: An activist investor holding at least one share of stock in a public company is legally entitled to file a "shareholder resolution," which, if adopted, provides a directive to the firm's management. All shareholders may vote on whether the resolution should be adopted, and votes are allocated in proportion to ownership stake (Gillan and Starks 2007).

The current U.S. legal structure actively undermines the shareholder resolution process. Filing deadlines allow management to void resolutions. Laws that define fiduciary "duty," or responsibility for maximizing income, were implemented to protect investors, but they limit the scale and ambition of SRI decisions. "Reasonable" implementation and burden modification laws provide loopholes for companies to escape shareholder directives that are legally mandated (Ryan and Wiggins 2004). Firms also have stronger legal representation than activists and further oppose campaigns by responsible investors by providing alternative information to shareholders (Opler and Sokobin 1995).

The single biggest barrier to effective and widespread shareholder activism is the shareholder voting system. A resolution must be supported by more than 50% of ownership, but management is *legally charged with allocating votes that are not cast*. Management will, almost by definition, vote against any shareholder resolution that makes it to a vote. Thus, every uncast vote is functionally a vote against the shareholder proposal (Bebchuk 2005). The vast majority of shareholders do not vote in such resolutions, which makes it extremely difficult for shareholders to garner the support needed to influence management decisions.

Market Effects

SRI may also function by exerting financial pressure on an entire market. It may be the case that firms that are not specifically targeted for screening, positive investment, or managerial control can still be induced to behave in a socially desirable way by the actions of investors. When individuals or pension funds place retirement savings in SRI funds, they may be implicitly assuming that there are market effects from such investments. The sentiment that SRI will be effective "if enough people do it" reflects the idea that SRI can affect markets, as does the logic of divestment.

The theory of "market effects" is a basic story of supply and demand. Theoretically, a sufficiently large group of investors can affect a firm's cost of capital—which can also be thought of as the price firms pay for investment—by decreasing the supply of capital available to irresponsible firms. This decrease in supply, and subsequent price increase, would either drive irresponsible firms out of the market or force firms to establish responsible practices to obtain capital at a lower cost (Heinkel, Kraus, and Zechner 2001; Statman 2000).

To affect the market, investors must affect the cost of capital for socially responsible firms. This may occur if

- Investors target socially responsible firms because responsible corporate behavior produces (and simultaneously signals) otherwise unobserved value;

- Investors prefer not to invest in irresponsible firms and thus screen out such firms, decreasing the supply of "irresponsible" capital; or

- Investors prefer to invest in firms that will have a positive social impact, increasing the supply and lowering the cost of "responsible" capital.

Screening essentially encompasses the second and third mechanisms simultaneously because money *not* invested in irresponsible companies is invested in responsible ones. Given that investors also prefer low risk and high returns, the magnitude of effects from mechanisms 2 and 3 will depend on the magnitude of the trade-off, if it exists, between preferences for SRI and returns (Haigh and Hazelton 2004; Statman 2000).

There is no convincing reason to believe that socially responsible investments will have significantly higher returns than the market overall. Likewise, there is little evidence that "socially responsible behavior" represents a competitive advantage for firms, although there is significant reason to believe that it could represent a competitive disadvantage in the short term, though if consumer preferences change toward responsibility, such behavior could have potential longer-term payoffs. In today's world, corporate reputation and workplace desirability may increase a firm's value, but costs associated with changing methods of production, and the trade-off between labor costs and growth (from reinvestment), are probably larger by several orders of magnitude (Reinhardt et al. 2008). The empirical evidence, described later, supports the theory that SRI funds do not outperform the market[6] (Cortez, Silva, and Areal 2012).

This viability of the supply and demand mechanisms (the second and third items in the bullet list at the top of this page) is controversial. If markets are truly efficient, the cost of capital will not be affected by investor preferences. In such a world, the cost of capital (which will be reflected in stock prices) is determined by the underlying value of the firm, not by supply and demand. In this efficient world, when responsible investors do not invest in irresponsible firms, other investors swoop in and provide capital at the same cost. This scenario also implies that SRI strategies do not maximize returns because SRI funds abandon investments that others are willing to make.

There is ample evidence, however, that markets are not (informationally) efficient in this way (Shiller 1981) and that investor demand can and does affect the price of capital (Gompers and Metrick 2001). Accordingly, there is reason to believe that a sufficiently large amount of market "pressure" from investors can affect the market. The amount that would need to be withheld or divested is an unresolved and empirical question, as discussed in the following section.

EMPIRICAL EVIDENCE

There is no consensus on results of empirical research that seeks to quantify the systematic social effects of SRI or pension activism. Measuring social outcomes is an extremely difficult undertaking. Impact investing (and withholding strategies) face heterogeneity of SRI standards, small scales (relative to the market), uncertainty over implementation, and difficulty in describing counterfactual investment strategies. These factors all limit the identification of causal impact resulting from investment decisions on both social and (investment) market outcomes. To put it simply, there is too little SRI and too little standardization to effectively measure how these investments influence the issues or the organizations targeted. A lack of theoretical structure for the impact of SRI further hinders the design of such empirical tests. With this caveat in mind, there is some limited empirical evidence available that examines the efficacy of SRI.

Impact Investing

Theories of SRI market effects enable us to interpret a wide range of empirical results. We begin with evidence on the market effects of impact investing, which are particularly difficult to assess because impact investing represents only a small and emerging market. Estimates of the size of the impact investing market have ranged from $8 billion to $50 billion (JP Morgan 2010).

While there is evidence that this market is growing rapidly, impact strategies remain almost unique to each investor, and there is no direct evidence of marketwide impacts. The potential of such strategies may be reflected in the fact that many large institutions in the United States and the European Union have recently begun reporting on impact investing (Brest and Born 2013). Recent and optimistic estimates suggest it is plausible for impact investing to grow to represent 1% of estimated professionally managed global assets over the next ten years, creating a market of over $500 billion (Freireich and Fulton 2009). There is little way to measure the true effect of impact investments, though case studies offer qualitative evidence that this type of SRI can be effective in achieving modest social goals on a small scale (Parthenon Group 2010).

Screening

There is some reason to believe that portfolio screening does have a market effect. Investors seem to exhibit a growing preference for socially responsible investments. Assets managed in funds with explicit commitments to SRI have increased by almost 500% in the past 20 years in the United States and almost 900% in the European Union over the same period (EuroSIF 2012). Furthermore, returns to SRI are not systematically lower than returns on traditional investment; therefore, it does not appear that investors are making a "trade-off" when they invest in SRI funds, or at least it seems the trade-off is small enough to go undetected (Renneboog and Szilagyi, no date).[7] To the extent that SRI has a similar return on investment to traditional investments, SRI strategies should become more common and will result in increasing market pressure on firms to act responsibly.

Empirical evidence on the market effects of SRI is limited, and most of the literature is concerned with a single instance of global divestment (in South Africa).[8] The divestment campaign produced a discernible but economically negligible market effect (Posnikoff 1997; Teoh, Welch, and Wazzan 1999). These analyses do not consider the political effects of the South African divestment. There are instances of widespread discussion and attention related to issues of improving labor practices for individual corporations; however, changes in corporate practice have been driven primarily through pressure on corporate reputation and risk, not from strategic social investment practices. In theory, both political and economic forces may work in tandem.

The most revealing work on the effect of SRI screening comes from a study by Chava (2014) that shows limited and indirect evidence that firms facing environmental scrutiny have a higher cost of capital. Though more research is needed, this finding provides preliminary evidence that screening is indeed working as theorized—that SRI is making "irresponsible" behavior more expensive. This is the first study that tests for the capital market effect of SRI, and much more work is needed to draw any strong conclusions. Other work that indirectly tests for the effect of screening on capital costs has shown weak (insignificant) results in the expected direction, which fits with the premise that screening would be effective on a larger scale (Curran and Moran 2007).

The final link between the investor and social change comes when a firm actually changes behavior in response to higher costs. A survey of more than 60 companies conducted by Oekom Research (2013) identified specific measures or actions taken in response to demands or inquiries that they could trace back directly to the SRI market. Most of the measures relate to the collection of data and reporting. Other areas that were affected include supply chain management, human rights, and sustainability. Corporate governance, climate change, and water management practices were also changed by SRI, though less often. The report provides some basic evidence that SRI is—somehow—changing firm behavior, though the exact mechanism is not entirely clear.

At the level of individual corporations, inquiries alone from SRI investors and rating firms are driving changes in corporate practices. It would appear that simply raising the question of responsible practices and making inquiries public is often enough to spur at least symbolic action from firms. Though such inquiries do not seem to drive substantial policy changes, they do show that corporations are concerned about the material impacts of their reputations (Oekom Research 2013).

Screening and Returns on Investment

Although there is a large body of work on the returns to SRI, it would be a mistake to evaluate the effectiveness of screening based only on the abnormal returns to SRI portfolios. When markets are not fully efficient, as described previously, it is not clear how effective SRI will manifest with respect to stock prices. It is probably true that when SRI investors screen out certain options, there is some movement toward equilibrium whereby new investors move in to replace old investors in irresponsible firms. To the extent this substitution occurs (and that extent may be very small), we expect a penalty to the returns on SRI. Though there is no conclusive evidence on the subject, the literature seems to indicate that, if anything, there is a small, marginally significant drop in returns for SRI.

At the same time, academics have also observed that socially positive corporate behavior, documented in the literature on corporate social responsibility (CSR), actually increases a firm's value (Flammer 2013). Empirical observations indicating a negative or neutral return to SRI but also indicating positive returns to CSR present something of a paradox (Lobe and Walkshäusl 2011). If positive social behavior really is valuable, why don't we observe a higher market value for SRI stocks?

Scholtens and Dam (no date) provide a reasonable theoretical explanation. Their argument is based on the assumption that some investors and companies prefer to limit socially negative externalities. These investors and firms derive value from limiting negative externalities and thus responsible firms will lower levels of production (to limit the negative externality) and achieve below-average stock market returns because of below-average growth in production. It also implies that responsible firms will have higher returns on capital because those firms will stop production before marginal costs appear to match marginal revenue.[9] Thus, it appears that higher returns on capital, coupled with lower levels of output, can explain why CSR produces higher-than-average returns for a company— but SRI produces either average- or below-average returns.

This idea is not as radical as it may seem initially. Firms that can quantify the costs of negative externalities and that are willing to include these costs in their overall production decisions exist today. The largest barriers to such responsible behavior may well be a firm's awareness and measurement of social outcomes, not its willingness to respond. Most importantly, this theory of SRI shows that we cannot determine true effects of SRI simply on the basis of abnormal stock returns, be they positive or negative.

Shareholder Activism

There is slightly more empirical evidence with respect to shareholder activism. Karpoff (1998) found that shareholder activism had a small and limited effect on corporate governance in the 1990s. Barber (2007) estimates that shareholder activism by the California Public Employees' Retirement System (CalPERS) pension fund created $3.1 billion in value between 1992 and 2005, suggesting that shareholder activism can affect a firm's behavior and decisions. However, despite a smattering of successful shareholder interventions, the majority of shareholder activism is unsuccessful and changes that are implemented are generally tweaks rather than paradigm shifts. Sjöström (2008) conducted a meta-analysis of case studies and empirical research on shareholder activism and found that most studies conclude that shareholder activism had a small impact, if any, over the past 20 years and that shareholder activism, when successful, tends to produce small changes within a managerial paradigm, as opposed to large-scale institutional change.

Sjöström (2008) also has findings relevant to the relationship between SRI and labor. He found that "the main contribution of union financial activism over the last 20 years has not mainly been to organized labour." Agrawal (2012) provides strong evidence[10] that unions attempt to affect labor relations in private firms through shareholder activism. However, the empirical evidence relating SRI to labor outcomes is limited to a minimal number of case studies and surveys. Additional evidence comes from a study done by Waring and Edwards (2008), who examined interviews and case studies of SRI activity in Australia. They found that managers of SRI funds exert a disproportionate influence on the behavior of companies they are invested in by providing guidance on socially responsible action and by threatening their social reputation. The authors further conclude that the scope of impact is limited by the relatively heterodox practice of activist investing and that the effect of activism and associated threat is limited by return on investment concerns.

The United Nations' Principles for Responsible Investment (PRI) Initiative also provides case studies and reports on a range of SRI activities.[11] Case studies of socially responsible private equity investments, all of which use management strategies to effect change, demonstrate targeted efforts to improve a single or several aspects of a business model, most often related to the environment. One of these reports on firms practicing responsible investment in infrastructure assets shows that labor relations are not a priority for more than half of the surveyed firms. While other United Nations' case studies profile the actions of socially responsible investors in hedge funds and financial companies, the extent to which stated commitments represent a tangible commitment to invest differently, as opposed to a possible marketing approach to target a specific class of investors, is not clear.

Additional case studies of labor-targeted investments show several pension funds specifically investing in projects that employ unionized labor, but few of these funds have been successful in creating a measurable social impact while realizing sound financial gains. In some cases, investors can direct investment toward domestic and unionized labor without sacrificing a return (Croft 2009). This activity is limited to a small number of investors and represents under $100 billion in investment. It is likely that growth of such labor-friendly capital management is constrained by the complexity of a "double bottom line" and the relative lack of incentives for investment professionals to undertake such an issue.

Even in cases of shareholder activism in which investors attempt to raise returns, as opposed to affect social outcomes, there is mixed evidence about whether activism can affect corporate behavior. While the legal structure of ownership is designed to allow activist investors to align management priorities with their own, this research shows that even when shareholder resolutions are accepted, they rarely (if ever) have a strong impact on firms' behavior, despite legal requirements (Gillan and Starks 2007). More active forms of management, however, including private communication and pressure tactics, appear to be highly effective at altering managerial behavior to produce higher financial returns (Becht, Franks, Mayer, and Rossi 2010). Whether such actions would also be effective to produce social outcomes has not been researched.

Despite the scarcity of actual data, socially responsible investment, in its many forms, is actively pursued across a wide range of investors (Table 1). Individuals today are more financially aware of and responsible for decisions about their investments—in many cases having the option of lobbying for the option to invest their 401(k) retirement plans in socially responsible funds. Organizations such as labor unions or religious organizations

TABLE 1
The Range of Investment Models

Type of investors	Type of investments	Examples
Individuals	Mutual funds, retirement 401(k)s	*Calvert Group*—Uses SRI approaches such as strategic engagement and shareholder advocacy to encourage positive change in companies, both to establish certain commitments and to encourage concrete progress.
		Domini—Universal human dignity and diversity are among long-term investment objectives. Works to ensure that they become objectives of the corporations in which they invest.
Organizations (labor groups, religious groups)	Pension funds, faith-based mutual funds	*AFL-CIO Housing Investment Trust*—Focuses on labor investment goals that range from job development to creation of affordable housing and strong neighborhoods.
		GuideStone (church fund)—Managed according to Christian values to benefit those who have served the Baptist Church.
Philanthropies	Impact investments	*Rockefeller Foundation's Impact Investing Fund*—Supplied $38 million to accelerate investments to improve the lives of the poor or vulnerable.
		Acumen Fund—Raises charitable donations to make long-term debt or equity investments in early-state companies, providing reliable and affordable access to opportunities for low-income populations.
Government	Social impact bonds	*Utah*—Funds early childhood education.
		Massachusetts—Focuses on reducing recidivism among juvenile offenders.

increasingly invest in pensions and mutual funds designed to have broad impact. Philanthropic foundations, such as The Rockefeller Foundation, are pursuing impact investing to advance social aims that create sustained and scalable change in new directions. Additionally, government is increasingly using social impact bonds (SIBs) to create incentives and financial matches to advance public interests, an activity many consider a variation on SRI.[12]

New Metrics for Assessment

It is unlikely that a theoretical model will be able to provide a conclusive answer about how SRI impacts markets and social outcomes. The answers to these questions depend on major unresolved questions in finance, such as market efficiency and an investor's relationship to the firm. Quantitative empirical work may reveal direct evidence of impacts from socially responsible investment strategies.

A number of firms have recently begun developing and marketing social performance metrics. These metrics include newly standardized but otherwise conventional assessments of social performance, as well as new methods for measuring social impact. This measurement includes collection and reporting of internal data and consumer or stakeholder data, all of which may be collected by survey or reflected in financial outcomes. While many of these metrics are still based on qualitative assessments, new reporting of old metrics—including employee wages, benefits, protections, and organizing rights for the purpose of social impact analysis—may lead to new studies (Soyka and Bateman 2012).

POSITIVE IMPACTS OF SRI AND PA ON LABOR AND EMPLOYMENT PRACTICES

Socially responsible investment and pension activism are still relatively new mechanisms for increasing control over capital and redirecting its societal impacts. Although the evidence is still lean, the breadth of their reach, potential impact, and ability to produce solid returns on investment while advancing broad social interests suggests that it is simply a question of organization, management, and time before conclusive evidence can be produced. Additional examples of this potential at the level of the firm, across broad sectors, and addressing diverse issues are emerging and warrant some brief exposure here.

Investments to Spur Specific Changes in Corporate Policy

Equal Employment Opportunity
Numerous resolutions have been advanced asking companies to pledge not to discriminate against employees based on their sexual orientation—and have been withdrawn when the companies agree to expand their

nondiscrimination policies to include that guarantee. For example, in 2013 the Swift Foundation and the Wallace Global Fund co-filed a resolution asking East West Bancorp to "amend its written equal employment opportunity policy to explicitly prohibit discrimination based on sexual orientation and gender identity or expression." Walden Asset Management served as the lead filer; other co-filers included Tides (a public foundation) and Trillium Asset Management. The filers withdrew the resolution when East West Bancorp agreed to modify its policies (US SIF 2014).

Rights and Property of Indigenous People
In May 2009, Calvert Investments announced that its Calvert Social Index Fund would sell its shares in Weyerhaeuser Company because the company no longer met the criteria outlined in its indigenous peoples' rights policy. Calvert had been in talks with Weyerhaeuser since 2003 over its policies addressing indigenous peoples' rights and had pointed to some progress, but it was not enough to allay Calvert's strong concerns about the company's influence on treaty implementation negotiations between Grassy Narrows First Nation and the Province of Ontario. It is reported that Weyerhaeuser put pressure on the Province of Ontario to conclude or circumvent the negotiations so that the company could regain access to timber from the Whiskey Jack Forest (DeSimone, Trone, and Panek 2010).

Investments to Spur Community Impact in Housing and Jobs

Economically Targeted Investments
Economically targeted investments (ETIs) are public pension investment strategies that target initiatives such as the creation of affordable housing and jobs. For example, since 1981 the New York City's United Federation of Teachers pension fund has invested about 2% of its retirement funds in creating affordable housing and jobs in New York City neighborhoods and has achieved solid returns. As of 2012, it had earned market rate returns of 5.80% for one year, 6.64% for five years, 5.83% for ten years, and 8.82% since inception.

The retirement system has invested $209 million in the AFL-CIO Housing Investment Trust, which has a joint mission of providing affordable housing and creating union jobs. Since January 2002, the trust's investments have provided employment for up to 3,000 union workers in developing or rehabilitating more than 21,800 units of affordable multi-family housing in New York City. Among its investments is $134 million for capital improvements at the Penn South Cooperative Apartments in Midtown, which will create 600 union construction jobs over the next 20 years and enable it to keep its 2,820 units affordable. This ETI requires that all contractors follow a responsible contractor policy, which includes the payment of fair wages and benefits to workers. Also participating in this initiative are the city's other four retirement systems for public employees—the New York City Employee Retirement System, the Board of Education Retirement System of the City of New York, the New York City Police Pension Fund, and the New York City Fire Department Pension Fund (UFT 2013).

Mortgage-Backed Community Investments

Mortgage-backed community investments such as the AFL-CIO Investment Trust Corporation, which operates the Housing Investment Trust (HIT) and the Building Investment Trust (BIT), are the best-known examples of PA. HIT is a fixed-income fund specializing in mortgage-backed securities insured or guaranteed by the U.S. federal government or government-sponsored enterprises. Since inception, it has made commitments of over $5 billion in projects and estimates that those projects have created 50,000 union jobs and provided financing for more than 80,000 units of housing. BIT is a $2.6 billion pooled real estate fund serving over 150 union-related pension fund beneficiaries. Since 1988, it has helped finance over 158 projects, yielding more than 10,000 units of multifamily housing and commercial real estate. BIT estimates its projects have created 7,800 jobs (Croft 2009).

Investments Driven Through Collaboration to Impact Corporate or Community Practices and Employment Outcomes

Jointly Managed Pension Funds

The Union Labor Life Insurance Company (Ullico) is an example of a jointly managed trust fund designed to invest in worker-friendly, job-producing construction projects and industries. According to Ullico, from 1995 to the end of the third quarter of 2006, it had invested $16.1 billion in 219 projects, creating 162,000 jobs. Its investment in Newport News Shipbuilding's double-hull project in the 1990s provided work for 12,000 steel workers over a 28-month period, and a pre-hire agreement guaranteed jobs for 150 members of the Seafarers International Union. Ullico exited the investment, recovering 100% of invested capital plus an internal rate of return of 20.4% (Croft 2009).

Coalitions of Shareholders and Other Institutional Investors' Networks

These groups advance specific management goals. The Thirty Percent Coalition, for example, represents institutional investors, senior business executives, board members, corporate governance experts, and senior business executives who seek to achieve greater gender diversity on the boards of U.S. publicly traded companies. The coalition's goal is for women to hold at least 30% of all board directorships at public companies by 2015, up from about 13% in 2014. In February 2013, the coalition launched a letter campaign to major listed companies that did not have female representation on their boards, urging them to make greater efforts to increase board diversity. The signatories represented approximately $1.2 trillion in assets under management. Institutional investors have filed shareholder resolutions or engaged in other follow-on activities with the companies that have not responded to the letter (US SIF 2014).

Missions and values have guided the development of SRI and PA investment priorities and policies in areas that impact employment and labor practices. Some investors have chosen to invest in community development to support job and affordable housing creation. Others have ensured that proxy votes are used and have filed shareholder resolutions directly or through investor coalitions on issues of particular interest. As the SRI industry expands, so do the resources available for active participation in developing mission-related investment strategies, identifying specific investment opportunities, forecasting financial performance, and taking the lead on shareholder engagement opportunities. There are strong indications that SRI and PA can have significant impacts on labor practices when labor's interests and strategy are clearly defined.

CONCLUSIONS

Given the relative size and heterogeneity of SRI, the true impacts will be observable only with expansion of SRI assets and the standardization of SRI criteria. While socially responsible investors must act in good faith for now, emerging evidence shows a tangible economic and political effect from SRI. The positive social impact of such investments may take a long time to uncover, but the evidence that does exist provides individual and institutional investors with some assurance of their impact and solid support for alternative management strategies.

Labor pension funds in particular stand to benefit from recent quantitative evidence showing normal (market rate) returns to SRI because managers are required to justify their actions as prudent, which would prohibit accepting lower returns. Evidence that particular investment strategies can impact labor relations and practices, or evidence of the impact of labor-friendly private equity, could provide a legal basis and political support among union members for increased pension activism, though it is largely missing from the academic and business literature. Beyond legal restrictions, the inherent conflict between labor costs and profit maximization remains an unresolved problem within SRI, and it is probably the largest barrier to the growth of labor-friendly investments. There is also growing tension between labor and environmental interests that may cause competition within SRI portfolios. This could potentially lead certain groups to actively oppose the SRI principles of the others.

As the role of financial products and services in society increases, so too does the social power of the owners of capital. As more workers actively engage in managing their capital and retirement funds through direct investments, the role of the individual—not just the broker—becomes ever more powerful in shaping corporate behavior and impacts. There are still significant legal, informational, and structural economic incentives that need to change or be circumvented so that SRI or PA can have a significant economic and social impact. But the SRI movement is still in its infancy and is gaining traction as improved technology and awareness make it appear more feasible and more credible. As SRI grows, it has the potential to enable ordinary people and institutional investors to have positive impacts on behalf of those who otherwise have little control over the resources that govern their well-being.

ENDNOTES

[1] Positive investment—the purchase of stock or allocation of capital to an organization deemed socially valuable—is not considered impact investing and is better understood as a form of screening. See discussion later in the chapter.

[2] This figure is the estimated total for assets managed by signatories of the United Nations Principles of Responsible Investment (PRI Initiative 2013).

[3] Meaning that managers incorporate ESG information or screen out socially irresponsible firms when making investment decisions.

[4] By value.

[5] Market share of SRI priorities can be understood as the extent to which SRI is targeted toward a specific social goal.

[6] There is a large body of evidence showing that firms which undertake corporate social responsibility (CSR) activities have higher returns on investment than companies that do not (Flammer 2013; Margolis, Elfenbein, and Walsh 2007). CSR is philosophically related to—but functionally different from—SRI, and the two behaviors should not be confused. If CSR-practicing firms outperform traditional firms, it may be tempting to conclude that the same will be true of firms that are considered SRI. Such a conclusion would be incorrect; a fully consistent explanation for this paradox is offered by Scholtens and Dam (no date) and discussed later in the chapter.

[7] The vast majority of scholarship and attention surrounding SRI focuses on the expected returns of SRI portfolios. Nevertheless, if SRI fails to affect the cost of capital, there may be no link between the SRI investor and social outcomes. Thus, market-level returns to SRI should be understood as necessary but not sufficient for producing social change.

[8] The case of Western institutional divestment from South Africa stands as the single largest move toward a socially responsible investment strategy, which was both large and homogeneous enough in its aims to evaluate quantitatively.

[9] Actually, the firms do produce at optimal levels, but they incorporate the social cost of the negative externality into the production function. Returns on capital investment

appear to be higher because the firms do not count the social cost as a cost of production on their balance sheet.

[10] Including over 500 labor-related shareholder resolutions in his sample.

[11] The studies, available at http://www.unpri.org/publications, are as follows:

- *Responsible Investment and Hedge Funds: A Discussion Paper* (2012): http://bit.ly/1JUAVwo

- *Principles for Responsible Investment in Farmland: A Compendium of Case Studies* (2011): http://bit.ly/1vfhb3y

- *Responsible Investment in Infrastructure: A Compendium of Case Studies* (2011): http://bit.ly/1JUCuuf

- *Responsible Investment in Private Equity: Case Studies* (2011): http://bit.ly/1JUCZ7B

[12] In an SIB agreement, the government sets a specific, measurable outcome that it wants achieved in a population and promises to pay an external organization—sometimes called an intermediary—if and only if the organization accomplishes the outcome. SIBs are one example of what the Obama administration calls "Pay for Success" financing.

REFERENCES

AFL-CIO Housing Investment Trust. No date. *Socially Responsible Investing* (http://bit.ly/1EULaOo).

Agrawal, A.K. 2012. "Corporate Governance Objectives of Labor Union Shareholders: Evidence from Proxy Voting." *Review of Financial Studies*, Vol. 25, no. 1, pp. 187–226. doi: 10.2307/41302016

Anderson, S., and Y. Tian. 2003. "Incentive Fees, Valuation and Performance of Labour Sponsored Investment Funds." *Canadian Investment Review*, Vol. 16. no. 3, pp. 20–27.

Arjalies, D.-L. 2010. "A Social Movement Perspective on Finance: How Socially Responsible Investment Mattered." *Journal of Business Ethics*, Vol. 92, no. 1, pp. 57–78. doi: 10.1007/s10551-010-0634-7

Barber, B.M. 2007. "Monitoring the Monitor: Evaluating CalPERS' Activism." *The Journal of Investing*, Vol. 16, no. 4, pp. 66–80. doi: 10.3905/joi.2007.698965

Bebchuk, L. 2005. "The Case for Increasing Shareholder Power." *Harvard Law Review*, Special Issue, Vol. 118, no. 3, pp. 833–914 (http://bit.ly/1Do2El9).

Becht, M., J. Franks, C. Mayer, and S. Rossi. 2010. "Returns to Shareholder Activism: Evidence from a Clinical Study of the Hermes UK Focus Fund." *Review of Financial Studies*, Vol. 22, no. 8, pp. 3093–3129.

Bengtsson, E. 2008. "A History of Scandinavian Socially Responsible Investing." *Journal of Business Ethics*, Vol. 82, no. 4, pp. 969–983.

Blackburn, W.R. 2007. *The Sustainability Handbook: The Complete Management Guide to Achieving Social, Economic and Environmental Responsibility*. Washington, DC: Environmental Law Institute.

Brest, P., and K. Born. 2013. "Up for Debate: When Can Impact Investing Create Real Impact?" *Stanford Social Innovation Review*, Fall (http://bit.ly/18Cs9G7).

Chava, S. 2014. *Socially Responsible Investing and Expected Stock Returns*. Atlanta: College of Management, Georgia Institute for Technology.

Coalition of Immokalee Workers (CIW). 2013. "Historic Breakthrough in Florida's Tomato Fields." Press release (http://bit.ly/18Svl02).

Cortez, M.C., F. Silva, and N. Areal. 2012. "Socially Responsible Investing in the Global Market: The Performance of US and European Funds." *International Journal of Finance & Economics*, Vol. 17, no. 3, pp. 254–271.

Crifo, P., and N. Mottis. 2013. "Socially Responsible Investment in France." *Business and Society*, September, pp. 1–18. doi: 10.1177/0007650313500216

Croft, T. 2009. *Helping Workers' Capital Work Harder: A Report on Global Economically Targeted Investment.* Vancouver: Global Unions Committee on Workers' Capital.

Curran, M., and D. Moran. 2007. "Impact of the FTSE4Good Index on Firm Price: An Event Study." *Journal of Environmental Management*, Vol. 82, no. 4, pp. 529–537.

DeSimone, P., D. Trone, and S. Panek. 2010. *Creating a Sustainable World: A Guide to Responsible Stewardship of American Indian Assets.* Washington, DC: Social Investment Forum.

European Sustainable and Responsible Investment Forum (EuroSIF). 2012. *European SRI Study.* Brussels: EuroSIF.

Flammer, C. 2013. *Does Corporate Social Responsibility Lead to Superior Financial Performance? A Regression Discontinuity Approach.* Cambridge, MA: MIT Sloan School of Management.

Freeman, R.B. 1985. "Unions, Pensions, and Union Pension Funds." In D.A. Wise, ed., *Pensions, Labor, and Individual Choice.* Chicago: University of Chicago Press, pp. 89–122.

Freireich, J., and K. Fulton. 2009. *Investing for Social and Environmental Impact: A Design for Catalyzing an Emerging Industry.* San Francisco: Monitor Institute.

Fung, A., T. Hebb, and J. Rogers, eds. 2001. *Working Capital: The Power of Labor's Pensions.* Ithaca, NY: Cornell University Press.

Fung, H.-G., S.A. Law, and J. Yau. 2010. *Socially Responsible Investment in a Global Environment.* Cheltenham, UK: Edward Elgar.

Geczy, C.C., R.F. Stambaugh, and D. Levin. 2003. *Investing in Socially Responsible Mutual Funds.* Philadelphia: The Rodney L. White Center for Financial Research, University of Pennsylvania.

Gillan, S., and L.T. Starks. 2007. "The Evolution of Shareholder Activism in the United States." *Journal of Applied Corporate Finance*, Vol. 19, no. 1, pp. 5–73.

Gompers, P.A., and A. Metrick. 2001. "Institutional Investors and Equity Prices." *The Quarterly Journal of Economics*, Vol. 116, no. 1, pp. 229–259.

Haigh, M., and J. Hazelton. 2004. "Financial Markets: A Tool for Social Responsibility." *Journal of Business Ethics*, Vol. 52, no. 1, pp. 59–71.

Hardin, C. 2014. "Neoliberal Temporality: Time-Sense and the Shift from Pensions to 401(k)s." *American Quarterly*, Vol. 66, no. 1, pp. 95–118.

Heinkel, R., A. Kraus, and J. Zechner. 2001. "The Effect of Green Investment on Corporate Behavior." *Journal of Financial and Quantitative Analysis*, Vol. 36, no. 4, pp. 431–449.

Hoffman, A.J. 1996. "The Strategic Response to Investor Activism." *Sloan Management Review*, Vol. 37, no. 2, pp. 51–64.

Jackson, E.T. 2013. "Interrogating the Theory of Change: Evaluating Impact Investing Where It Matters Most." *Journal of Sustainable Finance and Investment*, Vol. 3, no. 2, pp. 95–110.

Jones, T.M. 1980. *Corporate Social Responsibility Revisited, Redefined*. California Management Review, Vol. 22, no. 3, p. 59.

J.P. Morgan. 2010. *Impact Investments: An Emerging Asset Class*. New York: J.P. Morgan (http://1.usa.gov/1EUGqIx).

Karpoff, J.M. 1998. *The Impact of Shareholder Activism on Target Companies: A Survey of Empirical Findings* (4th ed.). Chicago: George J. Stigler Center for the Study of the Economy and the State, University of Chicago.

Knoll, M.S. 2002. "Ethical Screening in Modern Financial Markets: The Conflicting Claims Underlying Socially Responsible Investment." *The Business Lawyer*, Vol. 57, February, pp. 681–726.

Korten, A.E. 2009. *Change Philanthropy: Candid Stories of Foundations Maximizing Results Through Social Justice*. San Francisco: Jossey-Bass, pp. 58–63.

Lamon, H.V. 1976. "Professional Money Mangers: Fiduciary Responsibility Under ERISA." *Real Property, Probate and Trust Journal*, Vol. 11, no. 3, pp. 519–556.

Langley, Paul. 2010. "The Ethical Investor, Embodied Economies, and International Political Economy." In R. Abdelal, M. Blyth, and C. Parsons, eds., *Constructing the International Economy*. Ithaca, NY: Cornell University Press, pp. 211–240.

Lobe, S., and C. Walkshäusl. 2011 (May 9). *Vice vs. Virtue Investing Around the World*. Social Science Research Network (http://bit.ly/1EUI5Os).

Magalhães, P.A. 2013. *Sustainability in the Financial Value Chain*. Master's thesis. Vrije Universiteit Brussel (http://bit.ly/18Ctgpa).

Marens, R. 2004. "Waiting for the North to Rise: Revisiting Barber and Rifkin after a Generation of Union Financial Activism in the U.S." *Journal of Business Ethics*, Vol. 52, no. 1, pp. 109–123.

Margolis, J.D., H.A. Elfenbein, and J.P. Walsh. 2007. *Does It Pay to Be Good? A Meta-Analysis and Redirection of Research on the Relationship Between Corporate Social and Financial Performance*. Cambridge, MA: Harvard Kennedy School.

Oekom Research. 2013. *The Impact of SRI: An Empirical Analysis of the Impact of Socially Responsible Investments on Companies*. Munich: Oekom Research (http://bit.ly/18CsTLl).

Olson, D.G. 2006. "Fair Exchange: Providing Citizens with Equity Managed by a Community Trust, in Return for Government Subsidies or Tax Breaks to Business." *Cornell Journal of Law and Public Policy*, Vol. 15, no. 2, pp. 106–243.

Opler, T.C., and J. Sokobin. 1995. *Does Coordinated Institutional Activism Work? An Analysis of the Activities of the Council of Institutional Investors*. Columbus: Fisher College of Business, The Ohio State University.

Parthenon Group. 2010. *Investing for Impact: Case Studies Across Asset Classes*. Bridges Ventures, The Parthenon Group, and the Global Impact Investing Network (http://bit.ly/18CtE7b).

Paul, P., and S.J. Harbrecht. 1959. *Pension Funds and Economic Power* (1st ed.). New York: The 20th Century Fund.

Peters, J. 2010. "The Rise of Finance and the Decline of Organised Labour in the Advanced Capitalist Countries." *New Political Economy*, Vol. 16, no. 1, pp. 73–99.

Posnikoff, J.F. 1997. "Disinvestment from South Africa: They Did Well by Doing Good." *Contemporary Economic Policy*, Vol. 15, no. 21, pp. 78–86. doi: 10.1111/j.1465-7287.1997.tb00456.x

PRI Initiative. 2013. *PRI Annual Report 2013* (http://bit.ly/1CgrA02).

PRI Initiative. 2014. "About the PRI Initiative"(http://bit.ly/18CtKf7).

Proffitt, W.T., and A. Spicer. 2006. "Shaping the Shareholder Activism Agenda: Institutional Investors and Global Social Issues." *Strategic Organization*, Vol. 4, no. 2, pp. 165–190.

Reinhardt, F.L., R.N. Stavins, and R.H.K. Vietor. 2008 (May). *Corporate Social Responsibility Through an Economic Lens*. NBER Working Paper Series. Cambridge, MA: National Bureau of Economic Research (http://bit.ly/1EUKb0O).

Renneboog, L., and P.G. Szilagyi. No date. *The Success and Relevance of Shareholder Activism through Proxy Proposals*. Center Discussion Paper Series No. 2009-65: Bruxelles, Belgium: European Corporate Governance Institute.

Rifkin, J., and R. Barber. 1978. *The North Will Rise Again: Pensions, Politics and Power in the 1980's*. Boston: Beacon Press.

Ryan, H.E., and R.A. Wiggins. 2004. "Who Is in Whose Pocket? Director Compensation, Board Independence, and Barriers to Effective Monitoring." *Journal of Financial Economics*, Vol. 73, no. 3, pp. 497–524.

Scholtens, B., and L. Dam. No date. *Towards a Theory of Responsible Investing*. Groningen, Netherlands: University of Groningen Department of Economics, Econometrics and Finance (http://bit.ly/18CtZH0).

Shiller, R.J. 1981. "The Use of Volatility Measures in Assessing Market Efficiency." *The Journal of Finance*, Vol. 36, no. 2, pp. 291–304.

Sjöström, E. 2008. "Shareholder Activism for Corporate Social Responsibility: What Do We Know?" *Sustainable Development*, Vol. 16, no. 3, pp. 141–154.

Soyka, P.A., and M.E. Bateman. 2012. *Finding Common Ground on the Metrics That Matter*. New York: The Investor Responsibility Research Center Institute.

Sparks, R. 2002. *Socially Responsible Investment: A Global Revolution*. West Sussex, UK: Wiley.

Statman, M. 2000. "Socially Responsible Mutual Funds." *Financial Analysts Journal*, Vol. 56, no. 3, pp. 30–39.

Teoh, S.H., I. Welch, and C.P. Wazzan. 1999. "The Effect of Socially Activist Investment Policies on the Financial Markets: Evidence from the South African Boycott." *Journal of Business*, Vol. 72, no. 1, pp. 35–89.

Towers Watson. 2013. *Global Pension Assets Study*. towerswatson.com (http://bit.ly/164lv9M).

United Federation of Teachers (UFT). 2013. "Pension Fund Does Well by Doing Good." (http://bit.ly/1EUJjt9).

United States Forum for Sustainable and Responsible Investment (US SIF). 2012. *2012 Report on Sustainable and Responsible Investing Trends in the United States*. Washington, DC: US SIF Foundation.

United States Forum for Sustainable and Responsible Investment (US SIF). 2014. *Unleashing the Potential of US Foundation Endowments: Using Responsible Investment to Strengthen Endowment Oversight and Enhance Impact*. Washington, DC: US SIF Foundation (http://bit.ly/1EUNIMt).

Waring, D.P., and D.T. Edwards. 2008. "Socially Responsible Investment: Explaining Its Uneven Development and Human Resource Management Consequences." *Corporate Governance: An International Review*, Vol. 16, no. 3, pp. 135–145. doi: 10.1111/ j.1467-8683.2008.00676.x

Beyond Shareholder Value? The Impact of Capital Market–Oriented Business Management on Labor Relations in Germany

Klaus Dörre

Friedrich-Schiller-Universität Jena

INTRODUCTION

Since the global economic crisis of 2007–2009, Germany has managed to avoid significant job losses. Unemployment and underemployment declined, while employment reached record highs, even though (or maybe precisely *because*) the country's trade unions remained relatively strong and worker codetermination fairly robust. The German model of social capitalism, as it seems, is witnessing an unexpected renaissance. This comes as a paradox, though, because Germany's economic and political elites, through a combination of coincidence, political will, and "productive failure," have subjected the institutions of the German model to a form of creative destruction in recent years. I argue, however, that this destruction went only so far. Residual elements of social capitalism continue to exist and help mitigate the destructive force of the finance-driven *Landnahme*.[1]

This chapter applies and tests this argument by examining the relationship between capital market–oriented corporate management and labor relations in the German metal and electronics industry. I discuss the case of shareholder value–oriented management of companies to illustrate how internal financialization[2] helps introduce a gradual change in structures of codetermination and labor relations. But I also show that opposing forces simultaneously emerged, which helped develop an amalgam of hybrid management systems. This chapter first outlines characteristics of social capitalism and labor relations in the metal and electronics industry in Germany. It then touches on the rhetoric and reality of capital market–oriented business management, outlines its phases of implementation, examines the impact on organized labor relations, and discusses changes in the wake of the crisis of 2007–2009 to formulate some concluding remarks.

INDUSTRY AND LABOR RELATIONS IN GERMAN CAPITALISM

The neo-institutionalist literature (Crouch and Streeck 1997; Hall and Soskice 2001; Beyer 2003; Berghahn and Vitols 2006) depicts West German social capitalism as an example of a capitalist society in which corporate actors can orient the pursuit of profits toward the long term, thus balancing profit seeking with the interests of organized labor (Shonfield 1964; Albert 1992). Key to this balance was diversified, high-quality production in market niches that could support relatively high wages. Production occurred in the context of key institutions, including central banks, dual vocational education and training[3], and a distinct system of German labor relations—companywide collective bargaining agreements, sector-specific wages for different regions, and flexible adjustment at the shop-floor level (Streeck 1997; Abelshauser 2005; Hassel 2006). The class struggle was fought at the industry level, while individual companies saw a more or less vigorous representation of interests that ensured a cooperative and flexible adjustment of wage standards to the respective local conditions (Kotthoff 1994; Müller-Jentsch 2008).

It was accepted that wage norms have priority over in-house agreements, leading to a "convoy" effect. Militant workforces at large companies could push through agreements in benchmark settlements in labor conflicts, which would then also go into effect for less well-organized workers (Dörre 2010). The state provided negotiating parties with only a legal framework, and labor and management could draw on a comprehensive set of labor laws. Questions arose during the 1990s whether this dual system of interest representation by works councils on the enterprise level and wage regulation on the industry level could survive in a globalized world. Social capitalism had to fight for its survival pressured by problems resulting from German reunification and economic globalization. It was widely held that traditionalist German economic culture with all of its collectivist traditions would ultimately be unable to resist the temptations of the American individualist challenge. For instance, Wolfgang Streeck claimed that the "deregulating tendency of globalization" is threatening to produce the "perverse outcome" in which the "less productive Anglo-American model of capitalism may replace the more efficient 'Rhenish model'" (1997: 51–53).

From this perspective, it must seem only natural that German social capitalism was fundamentally reformed after 2000. The Social Democratic–Green Party government (1998–2005) in particular oversaw several reforms introducing elements of competition into the social security systems, partially privatizing the protection against social risks, liberalizing access to financial markets, weakening labor market protections, and promoting atypical and often precarious forms of employment (Streeck 2009;

Gumbrell-McCormick 2011; Lehndorff 2012; Holst and Dörre 2013). The hope that corporatist regulation of interests could adapt to the reconfigured framework by building social compromise based on a supply side orientation (i.e., the shared concern about enterprise competitiveness) was abandoned following the failure of the Alliance for Labor and Competitiveness, comprised of the government, trade unions, and employers' federation (Heinze 2006). Changes in the system of collective bargaining, which at least for a while could have been interpreted as a kind of "coordinated decentralization" embedded in corporatist arrangements (Rehder 2003), in reality meant a weakening of labor unions (Brinkmann et al. 2008; Gumbrell-McCormick and Hyman 2013; Urban 2013). At the same time, the capacity for tripartite deals that mobilized support from trade unions for government projects was severely reduced after the politics of the "Agenda 2010"[4] had alienated trade unions and their membership.

Yet there has been no all-out assault on trade unions, the collective bargaining system, or structures of codetermination in Germany. Rather, the erosion of organized industrial relations took place through incremental reforms (Dörre 2011b). These reforms nevertheless amount to radical changes in the system of German labor relations, even though they were obscured by the existence of formally intact institutions. Trade union affiliation in former West Germany was at about 35% of all workers in 1980, but it declined to around 18% for all of Germany by 2013 (Friedrich-Ebert-Stiftung 2014:6). As a result of this erosion of trade union organizational power, the incentive to organize among corporations also waned. Many employers' associations introduced a form of membership that was no longer tied to compliance with collective bargaining agreements (Haipeter 2011a:13). As a result, trade unions are confronted with the loss of their negotiating counterpart in some sectors.

In general, compliance with collective bargaining agreements has been on the decline. Between 1995 and 2010, the share of companies committed to collective bargaining agreements in West Germany has decreased from 54% to 34%. In East Germany, the same period witnessed a drop from 28% of companies to 17% (Helfen 2011). The outsourcing of corporate service divisions intensifies this process because it helps to circumvent wage norms. The proportion of companies in industry-related support services committed to collective bargaining agreements is about 14% in West Germany and 18% in East Germany (Ellguth and Kohaut 2011; Helfen 2011). This erosion of collective bargaining fosters low-wage competition and a fragmentation of collective bargaining, characterized by undercutting and outbidding. Small trade unions in certain professional branches where occupational groups possess high primary power (pilots, doctors, locomotive engineers, air traffic controllers, etc.) may manage to achieve demands that the conglomerate trade unions (Ver.di, IG Metall, IG BCE) can only dream of. Conversely, small splinter unions in poorly organized sectors such as temporary labor have long accepted labor contracts that offer wages of less than €5 an hour. In sum, the lack of compliance with collective bargaining agreements has contributed to the erosion of the organizational and institutional power of wage earners.[5]

LANDNAHME: THE SELECTIVE EXPROPRIATION OF WAGE EARNERS' SOCIAL ASSETS

We call these changes in organized labor relations *Landnahme*—a selective expropriation of social assets of wage earners (Dörre 2009, 2011a). The key argument of capitalist *Landnahme* is that capitalism cannot reproduce exclusively from within. It requires the utilization and exploitation of noncapitalist milieus that it encounters outside and within certain not (yet) commercialized sectors of capitalist societies. Recent versions of this theory suggest that the "exterior" of the capitalist mode of production can be actively created (Harvey 2005:140). The chain of *Landnahmen* is thus potentially endless. The "blasting apart of purely economic regularities through political action" (Arendt 2006:335) can and must repeat itself constantly on an ever-expanding scale to allow for new *Landnahmen* that help capitalism reproduce. The finance-capitalist *Landnahme*, which has engulfed major capitalist economies since the 1980s, creates an "exterior" through recommodification and social exclusion (decommodification). Employees are released from the protections of the welfare state and in some cases driven out of the production process altogether, only to be reintegrated under precarious conditions that eliminate some social and participatory rights of a "social citizen" in German capitalism (Castel 2005).

The targets of finance-capitalist *Landnahmen* include institutions, forms of social organization, and social rules. The codetermined, negotiated enterprise and organized labor relations thus become targets. Policies of (re)commodification in business and throughout society lead to fewer social assets and a more selective distribution of the remaining goods. Social assets refer to "assets to maintain one's existence," which the welfare state provides to those who previously had no such assets. These are the equivalent of social security provisions (eligibility for pensions, health care, wage norms, etc.) (Castel 2005). *Landnahme* then means that the protective shield of the welfare state is being peeled away layer by layer. The result is a rising number of precariously employed workers (low-wage workers, temporary workers, special-order contractors, fixed-term and marginally employed, single self-employed, involuntary part-timers, "multi-jobbers"). They are exposed to an above-average risk of poverty and unemployment and are disadvantaged in terms of participatory rights, occupational safety, health insurance, and pension benefits (Brinkmann et al. 2006; Castel and Dörre 2009).

The competition-driven *Landnahme*, however, occurs at different speeds because it is modified and influenced by field-specific and sector-specific countermovements. Trade unions, for example, still have their strongholds in manufacturing—and Germany relies more heavily on its manufacturing sector than other countries do. With a share of 22.4% of total gross value production (GVP) in Germany in 2012, the country's industrial base is still relatively broad (Deutsche Bank 2013:1–5) and has remained stable since the onset of the global economic crisis. Moreover, with a share of 30.5% of the European Union's GVP, Germany is by far the most important European industrial nation. Mechanical engineering and automotive industries are the centerpiece of German manufacturing, with each accounting for about 16% of industrial GVP in 2011. Both sectors are characterized by their high export ratios, specifically 62% and 64% of goods produced, respectively, in 2012.

These industries are deeply anchored in Germany. Many companies look back on long traditions and cooperate closely with established suppliers, equipment dealers, and research institutions. The technology-intensive sectors employ about 40% of all industrial workers (Deutsche Bank 2013). These firms enjoy good international standing, even though they are often medium size and family owned (Berghahn 1986; Amable 2003; Quack 2006). German manufacturing has hence adapted to the growing demand from Asia, particularly China. German-made products are often necessary for the process of catching up economically and are highly desired by an emerging Chinese middle class, making it possible "to increase industrial value creation in Germany, although it remains a high-wage location" (Deutsche Bank 2013:7).

Furthermore, the trend toward shifting production abroad waned in Germany despite relatively high labor costs, with an average of almost €37 per hour compared with €10 in the Czech Republic and €6.65 in Poland (Deutsche Bank 2013:6). Approximately 25% of German firms reported shifting production abroad from the mid-1990s to the early 2000s, but only about 15% of firms in 2006 indicated that they had shifted production abroad over the preceding two years, and this percentage dropped to only 11% by 2010–2011 (Fraunhofer ISI 2013). In 2003, 87% of companies that relocated their production stated that the main reason was lower wage costs abroad; by 2012, this percentage had dropped to 71%.

Generally, the labor cost share in manufacturing has decreased and eventually fallen below 20% (Deutsche Bank 2013:13). Manufacturing's stability and export capacity allows for codetermination and labor relations to remain comparatively stable within the organizational sector of IG Metall (Industrial Union of Metalworkers). While employees in other sectors had to accept above-average losses, those in the manufacturing export economy have managed to maintain their earnings or even to increase them (Hauptmann and Schmerer 2012).

However, other strongholds of trade union organizational power also witnessed profound changes, some of which can be traced to financialization. The market for corporate management that emerged in the wake of the Schröder government's (1998–2005) financial market reforms destroyed the old networks of corporate Germany, in which banks and nonfinancial corporations supported one another with industrial policy proposals (Windolf 2013). Since then, Germany has become a preferred market for foreign direct investment (FDI). Between 2008 and 2012, the number of foreign investment projects in Germany rose from 390 to 624 (Ernst and Young 2013). The FDI inflow caused changes in ownership of manufacturing companies. The share of foreign stock investments in 24 Deutscher Aktien Index companies was 45% in 2005 and rose to about 57% by 2012 (Bundesbank 2012; Ernst and Young 2013). The old networks of corporate Germany have consequently been replaced with transnational networks of corporate control in which financial market actors play a greater role than in the past. The altered ownership relations and the internationalization of firms have contributed to the transition to capital market–oriented forms of corporate management, which engulfed both the German metal and electronics industry as well as the entire industrial sector in a series of waves.

WHAT IS SHAREHOLDER VALUE AND WHAT IS IT GOOD FOR?

The term "shareholder value management" often refers to short-term–oriented management and profit maximization prioritization over other goals (Fligstein 2001; Crouch 2011). Yet, according to its proponents, strengthening corporate owners' interests is supposed to solve the principal-agent problem, whereby corporate managers (agents) do not always operate in the interest of owners (principals). An orientation toward the interests of capital market investors is supposed to increase efficiency by limiting the tendency of top management to develop autonomous interests (Rappaport 1986). A strict orientation toward the interests of shareholders instead is meant to effectively rein in the opportunism of a strategically competent management that tends to pursue its particular interests to the detriment of the company, thus eliminating the supposed competitive distortions created by a socially responsible entrepreneur (Friedman 1982:165).

The Efficiency Myth: Logical Problems of Financialized Control

This claim of higher efficiency contains a fundamental logical flaw (Dörre and Brinkmann 2005). Owner orientation amounts to gradually eliminating the forms of codeterminative decision making that had developed organically in codetermined enterprises over time and subordinating them, in the name of liquidity, to an external control based on narrow individual self-interest (Berle and Means 1997 [1932]; Aglietta and Rebérioux 2004). Enterprises with negotiated worker codetermination in a capitalism of coordinated markets ideally achieve an approximation of equilibrium between the interests of various stakeholders, while simultaneously executing the internalization of social compromise. But one of the main assumptions of shareholder value proponents is that mechanisms for social compromise in enterprises with codetermination are too cumbersome and complex to survive in globalized capitalism. A stricter orientation of corporate management toward shareholder interests supposedly raises corporate efficiency and profits, ultimately benefiting all parties involved.

The equation of shareholder orientation with economic efficiency relies on an irresolvable corporate control problem. With regard to the coordinating activity of corporate management, shareholders and capital market actors remain outsiders. Owners can evaluate management activities only from an outside perspective and only after the fact, basing their financial decisions on prolonged trends and on forecasts rather than actual knowledge about corporate operations. A strategically capable management can harness this uncertainty as a source of power because of its insider knowledge (Crozier and Friedberg 1993). However, to the same extent that owner orientation results in the abandonment of mechanisms of internal compromise, the influence of insiders who could actually correct this autonomization of management interests diminishes (Fligstein 2001:168–169). The guiding principle of efficient corporate management via shareholder value ends up so unstable that it can never be realized in a pure form (Berle 1963:28).

Confronted with conditions of uncertainty and the relative autonomization of the financial sector, it makes perfect sense for the management of world market–oriented corporations to bring their strategic operations in line with the rates of return enjoyed by market leaders. In an economy in which companies become commodities and serve as investment objects for excess capital, liquidity becomes a strategic objective for top management. The shareholder value form of corporate management leads to an "accumulation regime of the owners of assets" (Aglietta 2000:66) or of a finance capitalism (Windolf 2005b).

Corporations need to maintain liquidity to acquire external assets and to protect against hostile takeovers. Companies therefore set revenue targets broken down for decentralized units. Ideally, this process ensures that each decentralized unit is subjected to strict financial control. Financial operations can be monitored from a corporate headquarters that insists solely on short-term financial performance criteria. This drives companies to "achieve the highest (and quickest) possible capital accumulation at the stock market exchanges," and the ubiquitous threat of "replacing the management or being bought out" suffices to exert pressure on the costs of labor and the employees again and again "without considering in the least any future developments" (Aglietta 2000:50). Shareholder value management consequently represents a "rationality myth" (Deutschman 1997). The pressure applied by institutional investors structures the interaction of key actors within and outside of corporations. Capital market–oriented management then becomes a transfer mechanism of finance-capitalist *Landnahmen*.

Shareholder Value: Transfer Mechanism of a New *Landnahme*

The *modus operandi* of such a *Landnahme* encompasses a wide range of transfer mechanisms, which include shareholder value orientation. The shareholder value regime is one link between the demands of rapidly changing markets, the yield expectations of owners, and the companies' profit maximization goals on one hand, and the organization of the enterprise, production, and the labor force on the other hand. A distinction must be made between the guiding principle of shareholder value, its practical realization, and the impact that this regime has on social rules and regulations.

The guiding principle prioritizes profits as *the* central benchmark of corporate management over other performance criteria. Shareholder value management establishes a minimum profitability, which in turn should be achieved (or rather, guaranteed) by the optimal application of internal and external tools of flexibilization (Paul 2012:197). Corporate earnings and profits derived therefrom do not appear as the result of economic performances actually delivered in the real economy. Rather, they are declared as binding targets as indices and in budgeting. These benchmarks are then assigned to decentralized corporate units. The key parameter of control is the economic value added as control criterion to make the minimum profitability visible.

However, the practical implementation of this guiding principle occurs in enterprises that can be understood as deeply hierarchized fields of power (Bourdieu 1998). At each level, special interests, power constellations, and rules of the game exist that cannot be fundamentally altered overnight through a new corporate management system. The interests of corporate headquarters contrast with those of a corporation's individual departments, whose interests in turn also differ from those of the management of individual production units. The various filters that exist within the management hierarchy are already sufficient to prevent any new corporate management system from taking root in its pure form.

It is likely that any new form of management will undergo significant modifications during its practical implementation, leading to highly contradictory impacts. More-established management systems are combined with new elements and reshaped (hybridization). This holds true in part for the effects of shareholder value management on market-restricting social rules, resulting in a gradual shift of management systems (Streeck 2009: 240) felt within and underneath what from the outside appear to be robust, healthy institutions. The "negotiated enterprise" and all it entails—internal labor markets, cultures of codetermination, labor regulations, and wage-related laws—still exists. Yet in the daily experience of a large proportion of the workforce, its institutions and regulations are gradually losing their protective functions.

PHASES OF IMPLEMENTATION

If we use the heuristics of mutually interwoven, relatively autonomous fields of power in a corporation, it becomes clear that shareholder value management as a set of binding principles, instruments, and practices does not operate the same way in each enterprise. More accurate is the notion of a guiding principle that is modified during implementation and changes continually. This process is accurately illustrated by the individual stages of adoption and implementation of the shareholder value concept in world market–oriented corporations.

The first phase (1990 to about 1997) included the implementation of elements of a flexible mode of production.[6] At that point, there were already enterprises operating according to the shareholder value doctrine, but they were usually subsidiaries of larger corporations located abroad. Decisive changes occurred at the corporate and shop-floor levels (Sauer 2013). The microeconomic goal of flexible labor rested on a break-even point established so firmly that even strong economic fluctuations could be absorbed without ever becoming unprofitable. Staff represented the crucial flexibilization potential, which was instrumental in keeping a mode of production functional and marked by very lean buffers with respect to time, material, and personnel. Competition among enterprise units was the key incentive for continual efforts toward rationalization and cost cutting. Flexible enterprise organization hence actively involved employees in rationalization processes.

The adoption of the shareholder value doctrine spread to broader layers of world market–oriented companies during the second phase (between 1997 and 2002).[7] Its characteristic feature is evaluation of the operative results of single company units through capital market benchmarks. This narrows down the range for the modernization of labor organization.

Under pressure from a management culture geared to short-term results, only the politically unproblematic is practiced. Experiments with participatory group work—for instance, allowing a wide scope of activities and some leeway for worker participation—are on the defensive. Still, the shareholder regime does imply some dynamic changes. It aids in breaking up fossilized hierarchies and management structures, restructuring fields of business and revealing otherwise hidden cost drivers. Through performance-related remuneration, not only top management but entire hierarchies down to the third or fourth level are obligated to meet forecasted returns or earnings, or specified profit targets. This transition to value-oriented management is often accompanied by changes in the corporate and shop-floor management. Highly distinct management practices are brought together by the idea of shareholder value. These practices range from management via target costs (headquarters only prescribes the price of the final product, while the organization of production is left entirely to the individual units) to combinations of tight profit control and detailed specifications for production concepts. Shareholder value and internal financialization do not merely replace previous systems of management, but synchronize them.

In the third phase (2002–2006), the rule-changing power of the new control regime fully unfolds.[8] With the implementation of the shareholder value regime, the issue is no longer profitability alone. Instead, the securing of pre-defined minimum returns (or rather, minimum profits) represents an essential management objective. This approach draws even the plants and corporate subsidiaries that had previously been operating at a profit into the disastrous spiral of competition between production sites. Plant segmentation, outsourcing, and outplacement contribute to the loss of binding companywide bodies of rules and regulations and contractual relationships.

This is one of many examples of the gradual but ultimately rule-changing power of the shareholder value regime. Codetermination and collective agreements formally remain in effect, but works councils and shop-floor management are virtually forced into coalitions of competition. Their supposed common adversaries—corporate headquarters or institutional investors—are quite frequently located outside their country's national borders. A permanent situation of competition among and between employees, even within their own company, erodes and undermines the protective function of collective bargaining agreements. Beneath the still existent, formally intact, institutional cloak, an "exterior" is emerging—a social reality that is markedly distinct from the ideal of social capitalism (Höpner 2003). This reality is illustrated by the changes in shop-floor labor relations that have taken place over the years.

IMPACTS ON LABOR RELATIONS

Change can be identified at two levels: first, the altered control mode in financialized enterprises and, second, the undermining of collective bargaining by means of decentral competitiveness pacts and corresponding changes in codetermination structures.[9]

Dilemmas of Market-Centered Control

Financialized corporate and shop-floor organization is characterized by some specific dilemmas of control and command. Financial control as well as production planning and scheduling (PPS) must be harmonized, various "egos" in different departments and centers must be kept in check, management functions must be coordinated, and executive personnel and staff must be committed to company and performance goals.

IT-supported attempts to obtain performance data as comprehensive as possible are one possible remedy for this dilemma. Operational accounting based on electronic data acquisition and processing lays the foundations for productivity and efficiency calculations by management. However, the criteria used to extract large quantities of data have a selective effect. Often, this produces a false objectivity that obscures the rigidity of decentralized company organization induced by competition and the social preconditions for the goings-on of production. Electronic control is thus ultimately an insufficient management instrument. The same is more or less true for internal transfer prices and tracking systems.

Many firms therefore add earnings target agreements to their electronic control, encompassing all of the company's departments (Sauer 2013:7–26). Unrealistic earnings targets, however, can have counterproductive effects. Superiors thus have an interest in formulating realistic targets together with those under their authority. This arrangement leads to a wide array of individualized negotiations, agreements, and quasi-contracts that could never function without a minimum of consensual practices. Here we encounter one of the paradoxes of in-house market regulation and financialization. All attempts to expose operational performances to evaluation by price create the need for integration, which precisely does *not* rest on relations of economic exchange but on communication (Minssen 1999; Brinkmann 2011; Sauer 2013:53–56).[10]

Various efforts to cope with this dilemma of flexible corporate and enterprise organization amount to a gradual transformation of Fordist corporate bureaucracies. This transformation does not entail the replacement of direct administrative forms by indirect hegemonic (Glißmann and Peters 2001) or "monistic" (Revelli 1999) forms of rule. Indeed, it was the Fordist factory itself that usually functioned hegemonically and indirectly (Aglietta 1979; Boyer and Durand 1997). In post-Fordist operative and corporate organizations, the contents and forms of hegemony formation are subject to change. Operative restructuring takes place in companies in which the overhaul of regulations from the Fordist era (i.e., those designed to limit the market) is high on the agenda. Management's hegemonic capacity results mainly from the political mobilization of economic imperatives and practical constraints.

Hierarchy and bureaucratic organization by no means disappear. Instead, the management endowed with the competency to make decisions uses the "diffuse power" of the market (Mann 1994) to discipline workforces and their representatives. Enterprises and workforces are expected to expand and contract with market conditions. Strategic and operational decentralization allows for retention of some partly autonomous segments (plants, profit or cost centers, "mini-factories," business units) in a state of permanent competition (Hirsch-Kreinsen 1995:427; Sauer and Döhl 1996:46). The resulting economic insecurity brought forth by all these activities becomes the source of power for management rule by means of budgeting, investment allocation, and resource allocation.

The functioning of the market-centered management mode includes the reification of coercion and the anonymization of dominance. When "the market" prescribes the targets, the responsibility of managers and owners seems marginal. The career-boosting rotation common among managerial elites means that corporate rule literally ceases to have a face. A market-centered control mode emerges that affects the power balance between interest groups within the company. The "simple" conflict between workers' wages and corporate profits is gradually replaced by the "tripolar contradiction between interest rates, profits and wages" (Altvater and Mahnkopf 1996:26).

Unlike authoritarian power, the diffuse power of the market does not work according to a master–slave principle. Its effect is founded on indeterminacy; it articulates itself in abstract and anonymous forms. It frequently appears as a constraint that seems inescapable. The management hierarchy does not vanish, but rather it harnesses the abstract market power to obscure its own influence. This "faceless" rule is extremely difficult to perceive by those being ruled, although it does not always function perfectly. In such fragile structures, which remain reliant on social integration to minimize disruptions, there is no automatic tendency toward flexibilization or increasing management's power.

Despite the undeniable growth of power asymmetries, pressure from world market competition cannot be seamlessly transferred to the bottom ranks of individual corporations. Real or simulated competitive situations can be used by top management to bring workforces and their organized interest representation to heel, but the weapon of permanent competition between different production sites is a double-edged sword. Permanent competition undermines the social coherence of in-house compromise formation. Especially in those cases in which conflict-minimizing cooperation for a long time served as an important productivity factor, the introduction of permanent competition can easily become an open-ended program for destruction with uncertain outcomes.

Thus, management relies on voluntary consensus on the part of those ruled, on argumentative reasoning, and therefore on consensus-building measures. Management of flexible corporate bureaucracies is a series of complicated balancing acts. Management is continually challenged to find an appropriate mix between centralism and decentralism, heteronomy, and self-determination, and exclusive decision-making power of the head-quarters and participative inclusion of employees. Members of the organization must develop work methods and behavioral codes that stabilize fragile cooperation.

Many companies are hence now witnessing the emergence of an entire complex of quasi-institutions such as learning centers, quality and problem-solving groups, continuous improvement process campaigns, workplace training, and advanced training measures. By conveying competencies for participating in production-related issues, these tools become integral to hegemonic rule within the workplace. The implementation of new codes of conduct is possible only if new management principles are conveyed in a manner that is not exclusively top-down, but instead is complemented by recourse to producers' knowledge in a bottom-up manner (Dörre 2001; Dörre and Brinkmann 2005; Brinkmann 2011; Sauer 2013).

Irrespective of all these differentiations, a new manager type emerges unlike the type socialized in the fading Rhenish capitalism and its negotiating procedures. The new type of manager is a profit manager responsible for financial calculations (Dörre 2002). This type of manager was still relatively young during the phase of implementation. His or her entire energy and loyalty are devoted to the (regional or national) production location, yet only for as long as the position lasts. The rhetoric of participation is a natural element of the behavioral repertoire of the new managers. However, they no longer associate participation-oriented social techniques with an idea of social partnership stemming from fundamental ethical–political convictions. Although they may well enter into compromises, the give and take that was for so long common in the "negotiated enterprise" is alien to them. Instead, they embody a new, competition-centered "spirit of capitalism" (Boltanski and Chiapello 2003). They thus occupy the zones of controlled autonomy within corporate organization in a different way than the socially committed type.

The frictions between the financial logic and the operative world of production may still persist; nevertheless, profit managers often lack the understanding—and the standing—to leverage the new logic of production within their respective workplaces (Dörre 2001). The capacity of the intermediate operative management to participate in an in-house collective will that would be capable of correcting the arbitrariness of upper-level management with decision-making power over strategic matters is waning.

Competitiveness Pacts as the Standard Form of Regulation

Labor relations consequently integrate the corresponding protagonists and institutions into the maelstrom of competitive restructuring. The shop-floor actors initially adhere to established procedures. They preserve procedural rules and safeguard established scopes of action. However, workplace exchange relations that correspond to a pattern of "cooperative problem-solving" (Kotthoff 1994; Müller-Jentsch 1994) by no means are an adequate indicator of regulatory stability. Changes after all first appear at the level of in-house political compromise building. Cohesion policy throughout the era of social capitalism consisted of the fundamental belief that the social integration of workers and the social harmony resulting from it represented the essential lever for improving and increasing economic performance (Hirsch and Roth 1986; Streeck 1997; Aglietta 2000). In the restructured organization, social integration and worker participation are considered legitimate only to the extent that they serve to increase competitiveness. This inversion of priorities shapes exchange relations between actors.

Under expanding Fordism, the object of negotiation was the decoupling of wage labor from market risks. The social model of the German employee is a historical product of these exchange relations. This model epitomized the predominantly male wage laborer endowed with social rights, participating in productivity increases, and integrated into standard employment forms for the rest of his life. In the era of the financialized regime, by contrast, negotiations revolve around the extent to which the fate of employees is linked to market risks. As the case of temporary employment guarantees shows, the issue at stake is how much insecurity and uncertainty workers can and should tolerate. Social exchange in finance capitalism thus means bidding farewell to the traditional employee status.

This recoupling of workers to market risks has advanced the most among the growing number of low-wage workers, temporary and agency workers, the dependent self-employed, subcontractors, and the marginally employed who, together with part-time employees, constitute almost one third of all employment relationships today (Bosch and Weinkopf 2007; Weinkopf 2010; Rhein 2013; Statistisches Bundesamt 2013). Yet even the remaining core corporate workforces cannot escape recommodification. Local competitiveness pacts, for instance, that operate in a gray area between wage agreements and labor law, have become the standard form of corporate regulation (Haipeter 2011b). They represent the contractual form in which the recommodification of labor power is accomplished. Workplace policies promoting worker concessions under the motto of "more flexibility in wages, working hours and working conditions in exchange for limited employment guarantees" have created a web of partly formal, partly informal agreements that stand in a tension-filled relationship toward the collectively agreed-upon compromise formulas (Dörre 2002:400–406; Bispinck 2005; Streeck 2009:38–45). According to this optimistic reading, "in-house alliances" represent successful adaptation to altered conditions of competition. Market orthodoxy (e.g., Sinn 2005) argues for a radical decentralization of collective bargaining and labor relations. From an institutionalist perspective, one can reply that the flexibilization of labor could in fact be achieved within the given frame constituted by labor law, industry-wide wage agreements, and codetermination.

But this is only half of the story. After all, collective bargaining agreements have already been disabled or damaged in many areas, particularly with regard to performance control and working hours. The "negotiated" or "controlled" decentralization of contractual relationships, which often cannot clearly be distinguished from "wild" deregulation, shows that the regulatory hierarchy within German industrial relations has begun to shift irreversibly. Even in their organizational strongholds like the automotive industry, trade unions today are forced to accept multimillion-euro "cost-cutting packages," the burden of which is placed exclusively on employees. As a result of such in-house company pacts, the function of collective bargaining is changing. Industry-wide wage agreements today often define only a wage *ceiling*. Negotiations in the individual companies then revolve around the degree of deviation downward in terms of wages and or upward in terms of working hours (Bispinck 2005; Dörre and Röttger 2006; Bispinck 2011; Behruzi 2013).

The quality of these in-house, site-specific competitiveness pacts varies. Deals that involve the renouncement of any possibility of company relocation in return for unpaid additional labor in the guise of an extension of weekly working hours is worlds apart from the "Volkswagen Deal" that ties deviations from in-house wage agreements to the creation of new jobs

(Schumann 2006). To concede that such decentralized site-specific pacts may in some cases bear a sort of temporary stabilizing function is not to regard them as the optimal form of exchange regulation in the post-Fordist era. It may well be the case that representatives of organized labor show considerable faith in company employment pacts, which they in turn hope will pay off in better times (Kotthoff 1998). However, the anonymous mode of rule in flexible enterprises makes it questionable whether such a trust bonus still has any addressee inside management. It thus makes little sense to interpret site-specific pacts as general evidence of successful flexibility or as an expression of a "cooperative modernization" of the German model (Haipeter 2011b).

Actors in industrial relations are creating new interdependencies among regulatory institutions. The source of the dynamic is in-house compromise finding, which for employees often entails pushing back on their interests. The discrepancy between workplace activity and trade union policy is widening: the trade unions are being pushed onto the defensive even in their strongholds, and in-house labor–capital coalitions, once the embodiment of German capitalism (Fligstein 2001), become alliances dominated by capital.

For some time, it seemed as if a type of coexistence between finance capitalism and codetermination structures could actually be arranged, but the pinpricks against codetermination have probably increased. Companies use the legal form of Europa AG ("Europe, Inc.") to circumvent unwanted codetermination structures in their own enterprises. Strategically competent management is paying less and less attention to wage earners' power (Arbeitskreis Strategic Unionism 2013), as reflected in codetermination regulations. Even well-organized workforces in the few remaining trade union strongholds (e.g., automotive corporations such as Volkswagen and Opel) have been subjected to repeated competitiveness pacts that reduce staff (Behruzi 2013).

Some companies have even seen the decoupling of profitability and employment security. That often means additional jobs are created only in exchange for significant concessions on the part of organized labor. A textbook example of this dynamic is the Braunschweig Volkswagen plant, where shop committee representatives agreed to construction of an additional factory building employing 2,000 new workers while accepting wage levels significantly below the Volkswagen standard.

CRISIS AND SHAREHOLDER VALUE: A CASE STUDY

As argued so far, the term "shareholder value management" stood for a conceptual idea that functioned as a guiding principle and that could be combined with varying practices over time. Although the actual forms of implementation varied, the guiding principle was presented as the only available option of corporate governance in an age of globalization. Yet after the crisis of 2007–2009, many of the measures that for a long time were seen as necessary adaptations to the imperatives of globalized financial markets appear in an altogether different light. One-sided returns-oriented and cost-oriented management strategies led to the emergence of companies that required extensive government support to survive the crisis. The relationship between political elites and trade union leadership groups changed again during the global crisis (Dörre and Schmalz 2013; critically: Schwarz-Kocher 2014).

The door to elite deals incorporating trade union leadership groups has surprisingly reopened. The so-called crisis corporatism (Urban 2010, 2013) was successful in Germany, particularly in manufacturing. The global economic disaster led to a differentiation among political and economic elites. Political elites were surprised by the outbreak of the crisis and were looking for allies in their crisis management. The fear of losing positions of power and the uncertainty caused by the failure of market-orthodox policy advisors drove parts of the weakened political class to once again cooperate closely with organized labor. German trade unions, especially IG Metall mastered the crisis management with downright virtuosity. By resorting to relatively conventional measures such as prolonged short-time work and temporary payments for scrapping older vehicles, it was possible to largely secure the employment of core workforces. This cooperation paid off for German trade unions, which noticed broad public support during wage negotiations for the first time in a long while.

In an economy in which state-funded rescue packages, prolonged short-time work, and scrappage programs are necessary to cushion against the worst effects of a crisis, the shareholder regime should presumably lose its claim to legitimacy. Yet this is not the case to any significant extent. One reason is the self-transformations of the regime itself, which in some enterprises had been set in motion long before the crisis. Our initial research in selected firms and corporations underscores these points.[11] In the case of a former utility vehicle manufacturer that has transformed into an internal supplier of another automobile corporation in recent years, the guiding principle of shareholder value has been increasingly sidelined as a legitimation strategy beginning as early as 2006, largely because of a change in the corporation's executive board. The new management distanced itself from their predecessors' shareholder value orientation and announced a new "philosophy." Tasks and responsibilities that had once been delegated downward were recentralized, which in turn caused the centralized structure that had been associated with the corporation's internal financialization to be partially abandoned. Department managers may still be responsible for profit and loss (P&L), and their salaries may still be tied to net operating profit after tax, but decentralized decision making has been noticeably reduced. Corporate headquarters exercises its control through budgets and human resource planning; production planning (and scheduling—PPS) is centralized at the level of divisional management. This example of human resource policy demonstrates the loss of autonomy of shop-floor management: even before the crisis, permanent hires had to be approved by headquarters not by shop-floor management. The reduction of flexible employment became the last resort of management during the crisis.

Several systems overlap on the shop floor: the central steering by the corporation itself, the management of the departments within each division, and the management at the level of individual plants or factories. Department heads thus are confronted with three overlapping management systems that intersect at the P&L responsibility of the department manager—framed by budget control and human resource planning. They must reconcile the capital market–oriented goals of company management with goals based on production. Consequently, there is no coherent system of management that encompasses all levels of the company hierarchy within the plant. The transfer mechanism by which the capital-market orientation of corporate management influences production is constituted by budget control, human resource planning, and the continuous gathering of operational data in the guise of so-called key performance indicators.

This example highlights a gradual shift in corporate management. Even though shareholder value's worth as an ideological backdrop for justifying management strategies is declining and yielding to new "management trends," some elements of capital market–oriented corporate management are being inscribed even more vigorously into certain business procedures. The crucial levers for this process are budget control and centralized human resource planning. Though department heads may have P&L responsibility, they are nevertheless controlled by headquarters via its control over the budget. Budgeting also affects personnel costs, which in turn exerts pressure on employees and their representatives. When increasing production, companies resort to hiring temporary workers because those workers can be booked as material expenses (Holst, Nachtwey, and Dörre 2009). Our case study shows that many such corporations operate under the guiding assumption that a fixed proportion of the workforce should stay flexible. Thus, companies could quickly ablate excess personnel in moments of crisis.

So what we find in the surveyed company undergoing a crisis is a capital market–oriented, highly flexible, short term–oriented management form devoid of the semantics of shareholder value. The substance of the control regime oriented toward short-term profit and earnings targets, however, lives on. Indeed, earnings targets have little weight during a crisis, but little has changed with regard to the short-term orientation of management. Results are still assessed at very short intervals. Throughout the crisis thus far, the main slogan seems to be "protect the result!" To increase liquidity and prevent the outflow of financial resources, all departments are subject to assessment for potential cost cutting, which subsequently may threaten production. The temporary shutdown of machines to cut down on electricity use increases the risk of malfunction as does the postponement of necessary investments. The self-assertion and persistence of an orientation toward the capital market—even and particularly *during* the current crisis situation—in corporate management show that long-term production interests must yield to short-term liquidity interests.

The pressure on employees and their representatives does not ease. There is an ongoing "flexibility contest" in which workers' willingness to adjust and adapt has become management's decisive resource. Some of the excess employees are assigned to select departments of the company that, owing to the centrally enforced cutback on agency and temporary workers, now in fact have a need for additional personnel. For those departments with a surplus of workers, this in-house shifting of staff is quite lucrative because it reduces labor costs in the short term and thus improves quarterly results.

The various forms of flexibilization enacted internally usually place significant strain on workers. But departments able to demand and implement these flexibilizations gain a meaningful in-house competitive advantage vis-à-vis other departments. The flexibility of the workforce has a positive effect in the short term because employment is ensured. In the long run, however, there is a danger of different company sites, and thereby the employees involved, out-competing one another in terms of performance standards.

Moreover, there are several indicators that, in some plants, the crisis was used to intensify output demanded from employees so as to make the best possible use of short-time labor arrangements. For individual production sites, this meant externalizing some production costs, while, for the employees, it involved an intensification of work performance and workload.

CAPITAL MARKET–ORIENTED MANAGEMENT AND PRECARITY

The example illustrates how capital market–oriented forms of management can have an impact with or without the semantics of shareholder value. Capital market–oriented tracking systems are just one form of control, which can function only in combination with other management systems. The outcome is an amalgam of highly diverse modes of management. Yet all of them must deal with the unpredictability of volatile markets that has become ubiquitous. Management increasingly must react to market fluctuations and anticipate them as far in advance as possible with respect to investments, production volumes, and employment and working conditions. The unpredictability of the markets becomes the object of planning itself, while the "speculation on the future" (Holst 2012) becomes the main indicator for measuring the flexibility of the production system and employment. The aim of keeping profit margins stable in volatile markets is pursued via instruments that have long been known.

Correspondingly, personnel planning is guided by the median line of an average capacity utilization. Upward and downward sales fluctuations are to be cushioned by flexible staffing. Permanent employment, in comparison, becomes an investment that binds capital for decades. Head counts—planning specifications for employment equivalents—and strict budgeting represent the main levers to restrict such investments. If the management of decentralized units cannot meet production targets based on the full-time equivalents allocated to it, it is left with the option of hiring some form of external flexible labor, as is the case in the state-of-the-art BMW plant in Leipzig. Apart from the temporary workers are the permanent de facto temporary workers employed by subcontractors whose services are purchased via special-order contracts; these permanent de facto temps are in turn to be distinguished from the temps working for the same subcontractor but who are hired only for a limited period.

Grouped around the core workforces of end-producers in a structure resembling concentric circles are varying precarious forms of employment—the wages, standards of security, and quality of work of which decrease the greater the distance to the core workforces (Dörre 2012; Holst 2013). Tripartite crisis management has changed very little about this trend. Before the crisis, IG Metall had focused its energies on the problem of increased strategic use of temporary labor by capital and management. It successfully managed to organize temporary workers and forced many employers to promise improvements to precariously employed workers. The crisis changed this picture dramatically. In the metal and electronics industry, tens of thousands of temporary workers and fixed-term subcontractors were laid off. Only very few sites saw any noteworthy trade union resistance.

As workforce surveys show (Dörre, Holst, and Matuschek 2013), this approach corresponded to the orientations of many members of the core workforce. The core workforces expressed feelings of class solidarity throughout the crisis, albeit predominantly within the confines of their own company and among others engaged in similar forms of employment. In a representative survey at a large car manufacturer with around 6,000 employees and a union density of 90% among manual and white-collar workers, my colleagues and I found empirical evidence for this exclusive solidarity. The highest levels of agreement with the statement, "A society in which everybody is kept safe cannot survive in the long run," were found among workers and white-collar staff close to production (52%); office clerks were the group who showed most disagreement. This result seems at odds with the opposition to past labor market reforms, which was strongest on the shop floor. But it is the same group of workers and white-collar staff close to the production process who are most strongly in favor (54%) of exerting more pressure on the unemployed (Dörre, Holst, and Matuschek 2013:223).

Trade union efforts on behalf of the core workforces have heightened the recognition unions receive within workplaces and from the public. In 2011, IG Metall registered—for the first time in two decades—an upward trend in membership figures and has exhibited significant growth ever since. This trend can be observed particularly among young members, temporary workers, and the eastern administrative divisions (Grosser 2012; IG Metall 2012, 2013). In eastern Germany in particular, where union traditions and institutions are relatively weak, a whole series of new works councils were founded; main grievances often included bad pay and criticism of paternalistic structures in the company's executive leadership (Schmalz, Hinz et al. 2013). Requests for assistance in establishing works councils after the crisis came from the same companies that seemed to be impenetrable fortresses for the trade unions before. In other regions and companies, collective bargaining and direct participation of the unions rank and file in company-related decision making hint at the chances of a renewal of the organizational power of trade unions.

This success, however, comes with a price. The record labor-force participation resulted from an increase in employment levels, including in the metal and electronics industry, which to a large extent relies on precarious employment (Schröder and Urban 2014). Labor market divisions have been further cemented in the wake of the crisis (Lehndorff 2012; Holst and Dörre 2013). The crisis management of the large industrial unions was successful primarily for permanent employees in export industries. By comparison, no similar gains were made in the less-organized service sectors with a high proportion of female employees. Should this tendency continue in the future, a prolonged fragmentation of collective interests is inevitable. Trade unions would no longer act as intermediary organizations representing the interests of all wage earners; they would merely be the mediators of an exclusive solidarity among a few well-represented groups.

So far, this has not been a dominant trend encompassing all trade unions to the same degree. Rather, one can observe a new phase of organizational learning within the unions that runs counter to the spontaneous tendency toward exclusive solidarity. Precarization made it back onto the trade unions' agenda (e.g., in the form of wage agreements in the metal industry in which some wage increases and improvements for temporary workers were achieved (Urban 2013; Wetzel 2013). These sector-specific agreements solve neither the problem of temporary employment nor that of precarity—at least not entirely—but they prove that the tendency toward exclusive solidarity is not predetermined. The way that permanent employees and precarized groups relate to one another depends heavily on the alternatives for action they are offered by works council representatives and trade unions. Frequently, it is unconventional practices, mobilizations, and strikes, as well as interest-driven policies coupled directly with rank-and-file participation, that allow for effective crisis management and moves toward inclusive solidarity (Dribbusch 2011; Schmalz, Hinz et al. 2013).

SOME CONCLUSIONS

In summary, my findings are contradictory. Since the 1980s, German labor relations and the manufacturing industry in general have fallen prey to a trend toward fragmentation and decentralization of regulations and interest-driven policies—a trend that is exacerbated by finance-capitalist transfer mechanisms. Not least because of the difficulty in precisely identifying the indirect effects of finance capitalism (Windolf 2005a) on labor relations, a controversial debate exists about the extent of the changes and their exact causes.[12]

The *Landnahme* argument contributes to this debate by demonstrating the comprehensive effects of financialization on corporate governance and labor relations. Finance-capitalist *Landnahme* implies that the social order of capitalist societies changes. The basic rule of social capitalism, according to which a just distribution of productivity gains and the provision of social goods to wage earners have a productive effect, is gradually being invalidated. Its place is being taken by a new basic rule that states that social goods are to be provided only to the extent required for the promotion of economic competitiveness.

A capitalism that used to draw its strength from social cohesion has become a competitive society that selectively accommodates the propertyless classes internally only insofar as it tries to link the interests of these classes to the pursuit of economic dominance and export strength. This process occurs in a field-specific manner, without any kind of master plan or homogeneous strategic subject. Finance capitalism's scope of possibility, however, makes it possible that essential elements of the competition-centered basic rule are extended to social fields and organizations that cannot as such, or only through numerous mediations, be reached by financial market actors. This occurs via adaptation, implementation, and application of finance-capitalist principles in domains and organizations that indeed follow—in some cases drastically—different regulatory systems and rationality principles.

This is precisely the case in German manufacturing and its labor relations. It is by no means only joint stock corporations that resort to the finance-capitalist toolbox. A family-owned business such as the supply firm Schaeffler, for example, attempted to gain control over its larger competitor Conti in the form of a credit-financed takeover and ended up at the mercy of the lending institution involved (Hinz and Woschnack 2013). Export-oriented industrial enterprises usually operate within markets in which capital market–oriented companies define minimum profitability. Credit institutions determine transparency rules for small and medium-size enterprises lacking equity, thus forcing rigid benchmark systems and reporting duties on these companies. Contracts with executive personnel that are limited in time and bound to a proof of profitable balance long ago started to appear outside large joint stock corporations. And the application of the principle of competition can be felt even within fields in the social economy and the educational sectors, the organization of which (at least in theory) knows no profit orientation (Dörre and Neis 2010; Dörre and Haubner 2012).

Even within the export economy, the result of the finance-capitalist *Landnahme* is never the simple replacement of one social reality with another. Social capitalism and its negotiated enterprises do not disappear. They continue to exist as a subdominant, coevolutionary tendency. Capital market–oriented management in Germany is based, at least in those companies with codetermination structures, on "negotiated shareholder value" (Vitols 2003). Yet the specific type and content of the negotiation are determined by a new hierarchy of objectives and action corridors that are based on a finance-capitalist exploitation of the social sphere. As a result, hybrid management systems and organizational forms emerge that, when taken together, through combination, overlapping, partial overhaul, and modification, do in fact produce a new social reality—that is to say, qualitatively, which allows the social capitalism of the Fordist era to continue to exist merely as an empty institutional shell (Streeck 2009, 2013).

The competition-driven *Landnahme* of social assets functions not simply via a *fait accompli* that leaves the actors of organized labor relations with no choice but to acquiesce. Taking the implementation and modification of capital market–oriented management as an example, it proves that there is substantial room to maneuver. This leeway results from countermovements, from "land concessions" (i.e., the opposite of the *Landnahme*), which feed off at least three sources. These source include, first, intrinsic contradictions and paradoxes of finance-capitalist transfer mechanisms. On its downside, shareholder value management produces, as has been shown, an increased demand for communicative and consensus-based practices, which do not neatly match a principle of competition that has taken on a life of its own.

Second are systemic dysfunctionalities, as was made most evident in the global crisis of 2007–2009. Over the long term, such crises and their consequences undermine the legitimacy of finance-capitalist practices. In the enterprises my colleagues and I have studied, we found that majorities of surveyed workers and employees, as well as large portions of executive management, already doubted that the finance-capitalist economy is viable over the long term (Dörre, Happ, and Matuschek 2013).[13]

Third, such losses in legitimation can result in recalcitrant practices that may culminate in a renewal of the organizational power of trade unions and the revitalization of their conflict and mobilization capacity. Meanwhile, numerous indicators hint that such a process of renewal is already under way, especially in the manufacturing sector (Dribbusch 2011; Urban 2013; Wetzel 2013). Even deviations from a collective bargaining agreement, usually the starting point for undermining collective standards at the industry level, can become the starting point of a revitalization of trade union agency if they allow for new forms of member participation, as was realized over the course of the IG Metall campaign, "Besser statt billiger" ("Better, not cheaper") (Lehndorff 2011). During that campaign, acceptance of competitiveness pacts was tied to innovation measures in the workplace and hinged on a vote by the union's rank and file. Moreover, the crisis management in the metal sector from 2007 through 2009 was successful only because of the intervention of works councils and trade unions that took action against layoff plans by executive management (Schmalz, Hinz et al. 2013; Schwarz-Kocher 2014). In that context, it is beyond doubt that codetermination, collective bargaining, and labor law continue to represent an important source of institutional power for wage earners.

None of this indicates a return to the old social capitalism. The strong position of Germany and its manufacturing in the world economy since the crisis has been used to combine a selective social cohesion *internally* with a strictly competition-centered policy of domination *externally*. The expansionist ideology legitimating the external *Landnahme* feeds more on myth than on the social reality of capitalist restructuring. It is the myth of successful labor market and social reforms that defines the guiding principle to which European neighbors are expected to subscribe. According to the credo of the German economic elite, Europe must become one large, export-oriented domestic economy. However, the German model and its manufacturing sector cannot be copied, let alone generalized at the level of the European domestic market.

The admirers of the German model often miss the fact that the finance-driven *Landnahme* has changed the social architecture of markets, management, and organization to a degree that makes the simple transfer and generalization of compromises and institutions that originated in social capitalism impossible. The technical, organizational, and politico-cultural restructuring of this production model has progressed so far that a return to previous conditions is utterly impossible. What remains constant is the high degree of instability and proneness to crisis of the finance-capitalist regime. The shareholder value doctrine corresponds to the utopia of a pure market society. That this negative utopia, if followed to its logical conclusion, has a destructive impact on society has already been demonstrated quite impressively by Karl Polanyi (1978). Despite such experiences, it seems obvious that it takes time for societies to move toward "self-defense." Without a revitalization of combative trade unions that adapt to new conditions instead of mourning the passing of social capitalism, a democratic "self-defense" will hardly be possible (Offe 2013; Streeck 2013). That the German labor relations model still provides a relatively favorable framework is a lesson that key actors within and beyond Germany's borders still need to learn.

ACKNOWLEDGMENTS

I am grateful to Jan-Peter Herrmann, Loren Balhorn, Florian Butollo, Christian Weller, Manfred Füchtenkötter, and Hans Rackwitz for their support in the finalization of this article.

ENDNOTES

[1] *Landnahme* literally means land grabbing, land appropriation, or territorial gain. It refers to the internal and external capitalist expansion (explained in more detail in this chapter). I use the German term *Landnahme* throughout the chapter because there is no exact translation.

[2] I define financialization as the introduction of tight profit control and its implementation via indicatorized tracking systems and target agreements (different: Krippner 2011).

[3] This system of professional training in Germany combines on-the-job training and vocational education.

[4] The Agenda 2010 was a comprehensive reform agenda drawn up by the government of Gerhard Schröder in 2003. It included the previously mentioned reform complexes.

[5] I distinguish between wage earners' structural power, which may result from a certain position in the labor market or the production process; organizational power, which is based on a formal association in unions and political organizations; and institutionally constituted power in the form of law, wage standards, codetermination, etc. (Wright 2000; Silver 2003; Dörre 2011b:8–48).

⁶ Cf. Dörre 2001, 2002:37–214. That study was based on multiple surveys conducted in 36 enterprises in the metal and electronics industry as well as the IT sector. It consists of expert interviews and topic-centered interviews with members of executive boards (n = 73), intermediate and lower management and specialists (n = 163), employees (n = 163), and members of works councils (n = 106), as well as with trade unionists, representatives of employers' associations, and politicians (n = 1,144; Dörre 2002:35).

⁷ Cf. Dörre 2002:345–379.

⁸ This discussion is based on a study conducted from 2001 through 2005 in the regions of Nuremberg, Dortmund, and Chemnitz. The empirical substance consists of 163 topic-centered interviews with trade unionists, members of works councils, managers, local politicians, and representatives of regional networks. In addition, my colleague and I included participant observations (21), transfer and feedback workshops (9), and company case studies (Dörre and Röttger 2006:141–172). The study included 23 enterprises in the metal and electronics industry as well as the IT sector.

⁹ This discussion is based on Dörre 2001, 2002. Another study dealt with the role of members of works councils from the metal and electronics industry with a view to regional politics and civil society. The surveyed regions included Kiel/Neumünster, Hannover, Braunschweig, Jena, eastern Brandenburg, and Zwickau. The research consisted of expert surveys in the different regions (n = 71), a qualitative survey of shop stewards (n = 83), and a standardized survey of members of works councils (n = 407; Candeias, Dörre, and Röttger 2009).

¹⁰ Thus, Sennett's conjecture that software would suffice to establish control in organizations managed along targets—and that it results in a dramatic concentration of power over the employees (Sennett 1998)—does not bear up against empirical inspection.

¹¹ The following discussion is based on research in 12 companies. The study deals, with, among other things, the effects of capital market–oriented management on the use of temporary labor. The empirical data are made up of 83 topic-centered interviews with company and trade unions experts in the metal and electronics industry (Holst, Nachtwey, and Dörre 2009). They also include research conducted in an electronics company in East Germany (n = 456, 2007–2008) and in a southern German automaker. The study comprised three standardized surveys (production-related staff, n = 1,442; clerks, n = 618; executive staff, n = 262), conducted in 2010 and 2011, as well as three qualitative surveys, the first of which was conducted in 2009, involving 59 employees; and the second and third in 2012 with 35 and 6 respondents, respectively (cf. Dörre, Happ, and Matuschek 2013:277–280).

¹² For instance, there is a debate about whether or not finance capitalism competitiveness pacts are exclusive to joint stock corporations (Beyer 2009; Faust, Bahnmüller, and Fisecker 2011; Kraemer 2012).

¹³ On the basis of a cluster analysis, four different patterns of consciousness can be distinguished within the studied car manufacturing plant, which again can be divided into two main clusters. We refer to these main clusters as "the critics" (roughly 42%) and "the moderates" (roughly 58%). Starting from a markedly dichotomic concept of society, the critics formulate a harsh critique of contemporary capitalism, addressing power imbalances and distributional injustice in particular. The moderates, as a group, oscillate between a certainly less pronounced critique and a more or less affirmative view of society. My colleagues and I have not been able to identify a cluster to which we could ascribe the respondents who strongly defend contemporary capitalism's competition regime. The critics

are divided into two subgroups: the "system critics" and the "competitive individuals." Although the system critics develop an inclusive concept of society as a result of their social critique, competitive individuals articulate a desire for dissociation that bears considerable potential for exclusion. The other main cluster of moderates is divided into the subgroups of the "competitive corporatists" and the "affirmatives." Competitive corporatists are in some aspects similar to competitive individualists. However, despite a harsher critique of capitalism, the potential for exclusion, which is far more visible in the competitive individualists, seems to be less pronounced in the competitive corporatists. The workers belonging to the cluster of "affirmatives" may also voice a strong critique in some instances; their concept of society is markedly more positive and their critique not nearly as fundamental. The cluster analysis itself is based on a standardized survey of autoworkers (n = 1,442) who were employed at a plant with a total staff of 6,000 workers in 2010 (Dörre, Holst, and Matuschek 2013:198).

REFERENCES

Abelshauser, Werner. 2005. "Die Wirtschaft des deutschen Kaiserreichs: Ein Treibhaus nachindustrieller Institutionen." In Paul Windolf, ed., *Finanzmarkt-Kapitalismus: Analysen zum Wandel von Produktionsregimen*. Wiesbaden: VS Verlag für Sozialwissenschaften, pp. 172–195.

Aglietta, Michel. 1979. *A Theory of Capitalist Regulation: The US Experience*. London: Verso.

Aglietta, Michel. 2000. *Ein neues Akkumulationsregime: Die Akkumulationstheorie auf dem Prüfstand*. Hamburg: VSA.

Aglietta, Michel, and Antoine Rebérioux. 2004. *Dérives du capitalisme financier*. Paris: Michel.

Albert, Michel. 1992. *Kapitalismus contra Kapitalismus*. Frankfurt am Main: Campus.

Altvater, Elmar, and Birgit Mahnkopf. 1996. *Grenzen der Globalisierung*. Münster: Westfälisches Dampfboot.

Amable, Bruno. 2003. *The Diversity of Modern Capitalism*. Oxford: Oxford University Press.

Arbeitskreis Strategic Unionism. 2013. "Jenaer Machtressourcenansatz 2.0." In Stefan Schmalz and Klaus Dörre, eds., *Comeback der Gewerkschaften? Machtressourcen, innovative Praktiken, internationale Perspektiven*. Frankfurt am Main/New York: Campus, pp. 345–375.

Arendt, Hannah. 2006. *Elemente und Ursprünge totalitärer Herrschaft: Antisemitismus, Imperialismus, totale Herrschaft*. München: Piper.

Behruzi, Daniel. 2013. "Kurzlebige Kooperation: Betriebliche Handlungsstrategien in der Krise." In Stefan Schmalz and Klaus Dörre, eds., *Comeback der Gewerkschaften? Machtressourcen, innovative Praktiken, internationale Perspektiven*. Frankfurt am Main/New York: Campus, pp. 148–160.

Berghahn, Volker. 1986. *The Americanisation of West German Industry: 1945–1973*. Cambridge: Cambridge University Press.

Berghahn, Volker, and Sigurd Vitols, eds. 2006. *Gibt es einen deutschen Kapitalismus? Tradition und globale Perspektiven der sozialen Marktwirtschaft*. Frankfurt am Main/New York: Campus.

Berle, Adolf. 1963. *The American Economic Republic*. New York: Harcourt.

Berle, Adolf, and Gardiner Means. 1997 (1932). *The Modern Corporation and Private Property*. New Brunswick, NJ: Harcourt, Brace and World.

Beyer, Jürgen, ed. 2003. *Vom Zukunfts- zum Auslaufmodell? Die deutsche Wirtschaftsordnung im Wandel*. Wiesbaden: Westdeutscher Verlag.

Beyer, Jürgen. 2009. "Varietät verspielt? Zur Nivellierung der nationalen Differenzen des Kapitalismus durch globale Finanzmärkte." In Jens Beckert and Christoph Deutschmann, eds., *Wirtschaftssoziologie*. Wiesbaden: VS Verlag für Sozialwissenschaften, pp. 305–325.

Bispinck, Reinhard. 2005. "Tarifstandards unter Druck: Tarifpolitischer Jahresbericht 2004." *WSI Mitteilungen*, Vol. 58, no. 2, pp. 59–68.

Bispinck, Reinhard, ed. 2011. *Zwischen "Beschäftigungswunder" und "Lohndumping"? Tarifpolitik in und nach der Krise*. Hamburg: VSA.

Boltanski, Luc, and Ève Chiapello. 2003. *Der neue Geist des Kapitalismus*. Konstanz: UVK.

Bosch, Gerhard, and Claudia Weinkopf, eds. 2007. *Arbeiten für wenig Geld: Niedriglohnbeschäftigung in Deutschland*. Frankfurt am Main/New York: Campus.

Bourdieu, Pierre. 1998. "Das ökonomische Feld." In Margareta Steinrücke, Pierre Bourdieu, and Franz Schultheis, eds., *Der Einzige und sein Eigenheim*. Hamburg: VSA, pp. 162–204.

Boyer, Robert, and Jean-Pierre Durand. 1997. *After Fordism*. London: Macmillan.

Brinkmann, Ulrich. 2011. *Die unsichtbare Faust des Marktes: Betriebliche Kontrolle und Koordination im Finanzmarktkapitalismus*. Berlin: Edition Sigma.

Brinkmann, Ulrich, Hae-Lin Choi, Richard Detje, Klaus Dörre, Hajo Holst, Serhat Karakayali, and Catharina Schmalstieg. 2008. *Strategic Unionism: Aus der Krise zur Erneuerung?* Wiesbaden: VS Verlag für Sozialwissenschaften.

Brinkmann, Ulrich, Klaus Dörre, Silke Röbenack, Klaus Kraemer, and Frederic Speidel. 2006. *Prekäre Arbeit: Ursachen, Ausmaß, soziale Folgen und subjektive Verarbeitungsformen unsicherer Beschäftigungsverhältnisse*. Bonn: Friedrich-Ebert-Stiftung.

Bundesbank. 2012. *Bilanz der Direktinvestitionen für Deutschland 1990/1995–2011/2012*. (http://www.bundesbank.de).

Candeias, Mario, Klaus Dörre, and Bernd Röttger. 2009. "Betriebsräte in lokalen Zivilgesellschaften." *Industrielle Beziehungen*, Vol. 16, no. 2, pp. 186–187.

Castel, Robert. 2005. *Die Stärkung des Sozialen: Leben im neuen Wohlfahrtsstaat*. Hamburg: Hamburger Edition.

Castel, Robert, and Klaus Dörre, eds. 2009. *Prekarität, Abstieg, Ausgrenzung: Die soziale Frage am Beginn des 21. Jahrhunderts*. Frankfurt am Main/New York: Campus.

Crouch, Colin. 2011. *Das befremdliche Überleben des Neoliberalismus*. Berlin: Suhrkamp.

Crouch, Colin, and Wolfgang Streeck, eds. 1997. *Political Economy of Modern Capitalism: Mapping Convergence and Diversity*. London: Sage.

Crozier, Michel, and Erhard Friedberg. 1993. *Die Zwänge kollektiven Handelns: Über Macht und Organisation*. Hain: Beltz Athenäum.

Deutsche Bank. 2013. *Re-Industrialisierung Europas: Anspruch und Wirklichkeit: EU Monitor*. Frankfurt am Main: DB Research.

Deutschmann, Christoph. 1997. "Die Mythenspirale. Eine wissenssoziologische Interpretation industrieller Rationalisierung." *Soziale Welt*, Vol. 48, no. 1, pp. 55–70.

Dörre, Klaus. 2001. "Das deutsche Produktionsmodell unter dem Druck des Shareholder Value." *Kölner Zeitschrift für Soziologie und Sozialpsychologie*, Vol. 4, pp. 675–704.

Dörre, Klaus. 2002. *Kampf um Beteiligung: Arbeit, Partizipation und industrielle Beziehungen im flexiblen Kapitalismus*. Wiesbaden: Westdeutscher Verlag.

Dörre, Klaus. 2009. "Die neue *Landnahme*: Dynamiken und Grenzen des Finanzmarktkapitalismus." In Klaus Dörre, Stephan Lessenich, and Hartmut Rosa, eds., *Soziologie – Kapitalismus – Kritik: Eine Debatte*. Frankfurt am Main: Suhrkamp, pp. 21–86.

Dörre, Klaus. 2010. "Überbetriebliche Regulierung von Arbeitsbeziehungen." In Fritz Böhle, Günter Voß, and Günther Wachtler, eds., *Handbuch Arbeitssoziologie*. Wiesbaden: VS Verlag für Sozialwissenschaften, pp. 873–912.

Dörre, Klaus. 2011a. "Capitalism, *Landnahme* and Social Time Regimes: An Outline." *Time and Society*, Vol. 20, no. 1, pp. 69–93.

Dörre, Klaus. 2011b. "Functional Changes in the Trade Unions: From Intermediary to Fractal Organization?" *International Journal of Action Research*, Vol. 7, no. 1, pp. 8–48.

Dörre, Klaus. 2012. "Krise des Shareholder Value? Kapitalmarktorientierte Steuerung als Wettkampfsystem." In Klaus Kraemer and Sebastian Nessel, eds., *Entfesselte Finanzmärkte: Soziologische Analysen des modernen Kapitalismus*. Frankfurt am Main/New York: Campus, pp. 121–143.

Dörre, Klaus, and Ulrich Brinkmann. 2005. "Finanzmarkt-Kapitalismus: Triebkraft eines flexiblen Produktionsmodells." In Paul Windolf, ed., *Finanzmarkt-Kapitalismus: Analysen zum Wandel von Produktionsregimen*. Wiesbaden: VS Verlag für Sozialwissenschaften, pp. 85–116.

Dörre, Klaus, Anja Happ, and Ingo Matuschek, eds. 2013. *Das Gesellschaftsbild der LohnarbeiterInnen: Soziologische Untersuchungen in ost- und westdeutschen Industriegebieten*. Hamburg: VSA.

Dörre, Klaus, and Tine Haubner. 2012. "*Landnahme* durch Bewährungsproben: Ein Konzept für die Arbeitssoziologie." In Klaus Dörre, Dieter Sauer, and Volker Wittke, eds., *Kapitalismustheorie und Arbeit: Neue Ansätze soziologischer Kritik*. Frankfurt am Main/New York: Campus, pp. 63–108.

Dörre, Klaus, Hajo Holst, and Ingo Matuschek. 2013. "Zwischen Firmenbewusstsein und Wachstumskritik. Subjektive Grenzen kapitalistischer *Landnahmen*." In Klaus Dörre, Anja Happ, and Ingo Matuschek, eds., *Das Gesellschaftsbild der LohnarbeiterInnen: Soziologische Untersuchungen in ost- und westdeutschen Industriegebieten*. Hamburg: VSA, pp. 198–261.

Dörre, Klaus, and Matthias Neis. 2010. *Das Dilemma der unternehmerischen Universität: Hochschulen zwischen Wissensproduktion und Marktzwang*. Berlin: Edition Sigma.

Dörre, Klaus, and Bernd Röttger, eds. 2006. *Im Schatten der Globalisierung: Strukturpolitik, Netzwerke und Gewerkschaften in altindustriellen Regionen*. Wiesbaden: VS Verlag für Sozialwissenschaften.

Dörre, Klaus, and Stefan Schmalz. 2013. "Einleitung. Comeback der Gewerkschaften? Eine machtsoziologische Forschungsperspektive." In Stefan Schmalz and Klaus Dörre, eds., *Comeback der Gewerkschaften? Machtressourcen, innovative Praktiken, internationale Perspektiven*. Frankfurt am Main/New York: Campus, pp. 13–38.

Dribbusch, Heiner. 2011. "Organisieren am Konflikt: Zum Verhältnis von Streik und Mitgliederentwicklung." In Thomas Haipeter and Klaus Dörre, eds., *Gewerkschaftliche Modernisierung*. Wiesbaden: VS Verlag für Sozialwissenschaften, pp. 231–263.

Ellguth, Peter, and Susanne Kohaut. 2011. "Tarifbindung und betriebliche Interessen-vertretung: Aktuelle Ergebnisse aus dem IAB Betriebspanel 2010." *WSI-Mitteilungen*, Vol. 64, no. 5, pp. 242–247.

Ernst and Young. 2013. *Standort Deutschland: Erfolg und Verantwortung*. Berlin: Ernst and Young, Growing Beyond.

Faust, Michael, Reinhard Bahnmüller, and Christiane Fisecker. 2011. *Das kapitalmarkt-orientierte Unternehmen: Externe Erwartungen, Unternehmenspolitik, Personalwesen und Mitbestimmung*. Berlin: Edition Sigma.

Fligstein, Neil. 2001. *The Architecture of Markets: An Economic Sociology of Twenty-First-Century Capitalist Societies*. Princeton: Princeton University Press.

Fraunhofer ISI. 2013. *Globale Produktion von einer starken Heimatbasis aus. Modernisierung der Produktion*. Karlsruhe: Fraunhofer ISI.

Friedman, Milton. 1982. *Capitalism and Freedom*. Chicago: University of Chicago Press.

Friedrich-Ebert-Stiftung (FES). 2014. *Die DGB-Gewerkschaften seit der Krise. Entwick-lungen, Herausforderungen, Strategien*. Heiner Dribbusch and Peter Birke. Berlin: FES.

Glißmann, Wilfried, and Klaus Peters. 2001. *Mehr Druck durch mehr Freiheit: Die neue Autonomie in der Arbeit und ihre paradoxen Folgen*. Hamburg: VSA.

Grosser, Dietmar. 2012. *IG Metall Thüringen hat mehr Mitglieder*. Thüringer Allgemeine vom 27.01.2012: 4.

Gumbrell-McCormick, Rebecca. 2011. "European Trade Unions and 'Atypical' Workers." *Industrial Relations Journal*, Vol. 42, no. 3, pp. 293–310.

Gumbrell-McCormick, Rebecca, and Richard Hyman. 2013. *Trade Unions in Western Europe: Hard Times, Hard Choices*. Oxford: Oxford University Press.

Haipeter, Thomas. 2011a. "Einleitung: Interessensvertretungen, Krise und Modernisierung—über alte und neue Leitbilder." In Thomas Haipeter and Klaus Dörre, eds., *Gewerkschaftliche Modernisierung*. Wiesbaden: VS Verlag für Sozialwissenschaften, pp. 7–28.

Haipeter, Thomas. 2011b. "Tarifabweichungen, Betriebsräte und Gewerkschaften-Modernisierungschancen in lokalen Konflikten." In Thomas Haipeter and Klaus Dörre, eds., *Gewerkschaftliche Modernisierung*. Wiesbaden: VS Verlag für Sozialwissenschaften, pp. 31–60.

Hall, Peter, and David Soskice. 2001. *Varieties of Capitalism: The Institutional Foundations of Comparative Advantage*. Oxford: Oxford University Press.

Harvey, David. 2005. *Der neue Imperialismus*. Hamburg: VSA.

Hassel, Anke. 2006. "Die Schwächen des 'deutschen Kapitalismus.'" In Volker Berghahn and Sigurd Vitols, eds., *Gibt es einen deutschen Kapitalismus? Tradition und globale Perspektiven der sozialen Marktwirtschaft*. Frankfurt am Main/New York: Campus, pp. 200–214.

Hauptmann, Andreas, and Hans-Jörg Schmerer. 2012. "Lohnentwicklung im Verarbeitenden Gewerbe: Wer profitiert vom deutschen Exportboom?" *IAB Kurzberichte. Aktuelle Analysen aus dem Institut für Arbeitsmarkt- und Berufsforschung*, Vol. 22, no. 20. Nürnberg.

Heinze, Rolf G. 2006. *Wandel wider Willen: Deutschland auf der Suche nach neuer Prosperität*. Wiesbaden: VS Verlag für Sozialwissenschaften.

Helfen, Markus. 2011. "Tarifpolitische Parallelwelten." *Mitbestimmung*, Vol. 57, no. 7–8, pp. 20–23.

Hinz, Sarah, and Daniela Woschnack. 2013. "Der Fall Schaeffler: Die widersprüchliche Entstehung einer Mitbestimmungskultur." In Stefan Schmalz and Klaus Dörre, eds., *Comeback der Gewerkschaften? Machtressourcen, innovative Praktiken, internationale Perspektiven.* Frankfurt am Main/New York: Campus, pp. 161–174.

Hirsch, Joachim, and Roland Roth. 1986. *Das neue Gesicht des Kapitalismus: Vom Fordismus zum Post-Fordismus.* Hamburg: VSA.

Hirsch-Kreinsen, Hartmut. 1995. "Dezentralisierung: Unternehmen zwischen Stabilität und Desintegration." *Zeitschrift für Soziologie*, Vol. 24, no. 6, pp. 422–435.

Holst, Hajo. 2012. "Die Konjunktur der Flexibilität—zu den Temporalstrukturen im Gegenwartskapitalismus." In Klaus Dörre, Dieter Sauer, and Volker Wittke, eds., *Kapitalismustheorie und Arbeit: Neue Ansätze soziologischer Kritik.* Frankfurt am Main/New York: Campus, pp. 222–239.

Holst, Hajo. 2013. "'Commodifying Institutions'—Vertical Disintegration and Institutional Change in German Labour Relations." *Work, Employment and Society*, Vol. 28, no. 1, pp. 3–20.

Holst, Hajo, and Klaus Dörre. 2013. "The Revival of the German Model? De-standardization of Employment and Work and the New Labour Market Regime." In Max Koch and Martin Fritz, eds., *Non-Standard Employment in Europe: Paradigms, Prevalence and Policy Responses.* Basingstoke, UK: Palgrave Macmillan, pp. 132–149.

Holst, Hajo, Oliver Nachtwey, and Klaus Dörre. 2009. *Funktionswandel von Leiharbeit: Neue Nutzungsstrategien und ihre arbeits- und mitbestimmungspolitischen Folgen.* Frankfurt am Main: Otto-Brenner-Stiftung.

Höpner, Martin. 2003. *Wer beherrscht die Unternehmen? Shareholder Value, Managementherrschaft und Mitbestimmung.* Frankfurt am Main/New York: Campus.

IG Metall. 2012. Auf einem sehr guten Weg. Interview mit Detlef Wetzel vom 23.01.2012. (http://bit.ly/1C3t6jz).

IG Metall. 2013. Interne Statistik zur Mitgliederentwicklung: Frankfurt a.M.

Kotthoff, Hermann. 1994. *Betriebsräte und Bürgerstatus: Wandel und Kontinuität betrieblicher Mitbestimmung.* München/Mering: Hampp.

Kotthoff, Hermann. 1998. "Mitbestimmung in Zeiten interessenspolitischer Rückschritte. Betriebsräte zwischen Beteiligungsofferten und 'gnadenlosem Kostensenkungsdiktat.'" *Industrielle Beziehungen*, Vol. 5, no. 1, pp. 76–100.

Kraemer, Klaus. 2012. "Ideen, Interessen und Institutionen: Welchen Beitrag kann die Soziologie zur Analyse moderner Finanzmärkte leisten?" In Klaus Kraemer and Sebastian Nessel, eds., *Entfesselte Finanzmärkte: Soziologische Analysen des modernen Kapitalismus.* Frankfurt am Main/New York: Campus, pp. 25–62.

Krippner, Greta R. 2011. *Capitalizing on Crisis: The Political Origins of the Rise of Finance.* Cambridge, MA: Harvard University Press.

Lehndorff, Steffen. 2011. "'Besser statt billiger' als Türöffner zur Stärkung der Gewerkschaft? Anregungen aus einer gewerkschaftlichen Innovationskampagne für die 'Trade union revitalisation studies.'" In Thomas Haipeter and Klaus Dörre, eds., *Gewerkschaftliche Modernisierung.* Wiesbaden: VS Verlag für Sozialwissenschaften, pp. 86–112.

Lehndorff, Steffen, ed. 2012. *A Triumph of Failed Ideas: European Models of Capitalism in the Crisis.* Brussels: European Trade Union Institute.

Mann, Michael. 1994. *Geschichte der Macht: Erster Band. Von den Anfängen bis zur griechischen Antike.* Frankfurt am Main/New York: Campus.

Minssen, Heiner. 1999. "Direkte Partizipation contra Mitbestimmung? Herausforderungen durch diskursive Koordinierung." In Walther Müller-Jentsch, ed., *Konfliktpartnerschaft.* München/Mering: Hampp, pp. 129–156.

Müller-Jentsch, Walther. 1994. "Über Produktivkräfte und Bürgerrechte." In Niels Beckenbach and Werner van Treeck, eds., *Umbrüche gesellschaftlicher Arbeit.* Göttingen: Schwartz, pp. 643–661.

Müller-Jentsch, Walther. 2008. "Gewerkschaften als intermediäre Organisationen." In Walther Müller-Jentsch, ed., *Arbeit und Bürgerstatus: Studien zur sozialen und industriellen Demokratie.* Wiesbaden: VS Verlag für Sozialwissenschaften, pp. 51–78.

Offe, Claus. 2013. "Europa in der Falle." *Blätter für deutsche und internationale Politik,* Vol. 2013, no. 1, pp. 67–80.

Paul, Axel T. 2012. "Crisis? What Crisis? Zur Logik der Spekulation oder Warum die Hypotheken-Krise lehrt, dass die nächste Krise kommt." In Klaus Kraemer and Sebastian Nessel, eds., *Entfesselte Finanzmärkte: Soziologische Analysen des modernen Kapitalismus.* Frankfurt am Main/New York: Campus, pp. 181–200.

Polanyi, Karl. 1978. *The Great Transformation. Politische und ökonomische Ursprünge von Gesellschaften und Wirtschaftssystemen.* Frankfurt am Main: Suhrkamp.

Quack, Sigrid. 2006. "Die transnationalen Ursprünge des 'deutschen Kapitalismus.'" In Volker Berghahn and Sigurd Vitols, eds., *Gibt es einen deutschen Kapitalismus? Tradition und globale Perspektiven der sozialen Marktwirtschaft.* Frankfurt am Main/New York: Campus, pp. 63–85.

Rappaport, Alfred. 1986. *Creating Shareholder Value.* New York: Free Press.

Rehder, Britta. 2003. *Betriebliche Bündnisse für Arbeit in Deutschland. Mitbestimmung und Flächentarif im Wandel.* Frankfurt am Main: Campus.

Revelli, Marco. 1999. *Die gesellschaftliche Linke: Jenseits der Zivilisation der Arbeit.* Münster: Westfälisches Dampfboot.

Rhein, Thomas. 2013. "Erwerbseinkommen: Deutsche Geringverdiener im europäischen Vergleich." *IAB Kurzberichte. Aktuelle Analysen aus dem Institut für Arbeitsmarkt- und Berufsforschung,* no. 15.

Sauer, Dieter. 2013. *Die organisatorische Revolution: Umbrüche in der Arbeitswelt—Ursachen, Auswirkungen und arbeitspolitische Antworten.* Hamburg: VSA.

Sauer, Dieter, and Volker Döhl. 1996. "Die Auflösung des Unternehmens? Entwicklungstendenzen der Unternehmensreorganisation in den 90er Jahren." In Institut für Sozialwissenschaftliche Forschung e.V. ISF München, Institut für Sozialforschung (IfS) an der Universität Frankfurt am Main, Internationales Institut für Empirische Sozialökonomie gGmbH (INIFES), and Soziologisches Forschungsinstitut an der Universität Göttingen e.V. (SOFI), eds., *Jahrbuch Sozialwissenschaftliche Technikberichterstattung 1996: Schwerpunkt Reorganisation.* Berlin: Edition Sigma, pp. 19–76.

Schmalz, Stefan, Sarah Hinz, Daniela Woschnack, Dennis Schwetje, and Benjamin Paul. 2013. "IG Metall mit Rückenwind: Zum wachsenden Engagement der Beschäftigten." In Stefan Schmalz and Klaus Dörre, eds., *Comeback der Gewerkschaften? Machtressourcen, innovative Praktiken, internationale Perspektiven.* Frankfurt am Main/New York: Campus, pp. 255–270.

Schröder, Lothar, and Hans-Jürgen Urban, eds. 2014. *Gute Arbeit. Profile prekärer Arbeit—Arbeitspolitik von unten.* Frankfurt am Main: Bund-Verlag.

Schumann, Michael, ed. 2006. *VW Auto 5000: ein neues Produktionskonzept: Die deutsche Antwort auf den Toyota-Weg*. *Eine Veröffentlichung des Soziologischen Forschungsinstituts an der Universität Göttingen (SOFI)*. Hamburg: VSA.

Schwarz-Kocher, Martin. 2014. "Wettbewerbskorporatismus oder neue Machtressource? Gewerkschaftliche Betriebspolitik im Spannungsfeld der Korporatismuskritik." *Sozialer Fortschritt*, Vol. 63, no. 1–2, pp. 13–21.

Sennett, Richard. 1998. *Der flexible Mensch: Die Kultur des neuen Kapitalismus*. Berlin: Berlin Verlag.

Shonfield, Andrew. 1964. *Modern Capitalism*. Oxford: Oxford University Press.

Silver, Beverly J. 2003. *Forces of Labor: Workers' Movements and Globalization since 1870*. Cambridge: Cambridge University Press.

Sinn, Hans-Werner. 2005. *Ist Deutschland noch zu retten?* Berlin: Ullstein.

Statistisches Bundesamt (DeStatis). 2013. *Datenreport 2013: Ein Sozialbericht für die Bundesrepublik Deutschland*. Bonn: BPB.

Streeck, Wolfgang. 1997. "German Capitalism: Does It Exist? Can It Survive?" In Colin Crouch and Wolfgang Streeck, eds., *Political Economy of Modern Capitalism: Mapping Convergence and Diversity*. London: Sage, pp. 33–54.

Streeck, Wolfgang. 2009. *Re-Forming Capitalism: Institutional Change in the German Political Economy*. Oxford/New York: Oxford University Press.

Streeck, Wolfgang. 2013. *Gekaufte Zeit: Die vertagte Krise des demokratischen Kapitalismus*. Berlin: Suhrkamp.

Urban, Hans-Jürgen. 2010. "Wohlfahrtsstaat und Gewerkschaftsmacht im Finanzmarkt-Kapitalismus: Der Fall Deutschland." *WSI-Mitteilungen*, Vol. 63, no. 9, pp. 443–450.

Urban, Hans-Jürgen. 2013. "Gewerkschaftsstrategien in der Krise: Zur Handlungsfähigkeit der Gewerkschaften im Gegenwartskapitalismus." In Stefan Schmalz and Klaus Dörre, eds., *Comeback der Gewerkschaften? Machtressourcen, innovative Praktiken, internationale Perspektiven*. Frankfurt am Main/New York: Campus, pp. 269–289.

Vitols, Sigurd. 2003. "Verhandelter Shareholder Value: Die deutsche Variante einer angloamerkianischen Praxis." In Jürgen Beyer, ed., *Vom Zukunfts- zum Auslaufmodell?: Die deutsche Wirtschaftsordnung im Wandel*. Wiesbaden: Westdeutscher Verlag, pp. 133–154.

Weinkopf, Claudia. 2010. "Warum Deutschland einen gesetzlichen Mindestlohn braucht." *Vorgänge. Zeitschrift für Bürgerrechte und Gesellschaftspolitik 191*, Vol. 49, no. 3, pp. 38–49.

Wetzel, Detlef, ed. 2013. *Organizing: Die Veränderung der gewerkschaftlichen Praxis durch das Prinzip Beteiligung*. Hamburg: VSA.

Windolf, Paul, ed. 2005a. *Finanzmarkt-Kapitalismus: Analysen zum Wandel von Produktionsregimen*. Wiesbaden: VS Verlag für Sozialwissenschaften.

Windolf, Paul. 2005b. "Was ist Finanzmarkt-Kapitalismus?" In Paul Windolf, ed., *Finanzmarkt-Kapitalismus: Analysen zum Wandel von Produktionsregimen*. Wiesbaden: VS Verlag für Sozialwissenschaften, pp. 20–57.

Windolf, Paul. 2013. "Institutionelle Eigentümer im Finanzmarkt-Kapitalismus." In Bernhard Emunds and Wolf-Gero Reichert, eds., *Den Geldschleier lüften! Perspektiven auf die monetäre Ordnung in der Krise*. Marburg: Metropolis, pp. 207–229.

Wright, Eric O. 2000. "Working Class Power, Capitalist Class Interests, and Class Compromise." *American Journal of Sociology*, Vol. 105, no. 4, pp. 957–1002.

CHAPTER 5

Organizing the U.S. Financial Sector: Industry Reform and Raising Labor Standards Through Transnational Alliances

HINA SHEIKH
Community Coalition

STEPHEN LERNER
Georgetown University

RITA BERLOFA
Sindicato dos Bancários de São Paulo, Osasco e Região

INTRODUCTION

In the United States, there is now a greater concentration of wealth and power in the hands of Wall Street and big banks than before the financial collapse of 2008. The financialization of the economy has left municipalities, school boards, and other government entities trapped in exploding interest swaps and toxic loans. Forty million people have $1.3 trillion in student debt, and nearly ten million people are still trapped in underwater mortgages. Despite these circumstances, the financial industry's dominance of the economy continues and grows.

Bank workers, had they been unionized, could have played a crucial rule in holding the financial industry accountable and even calling attention to industry practices that led to the Great Recession. Unionized bank workers, who do not fear termination, could have exposed and resisted sales practices and sales goals based on selling toxic products to consumers as a condition of employment. Bank workers, like nurses in a hospital, could become the front line in advocating and bargaining for the best service and products for consumers. Unionized bank workers in the United States, like bank workers in other countries, could play a leading role in demanding stricter regulations and oversight of the financial sector.

There is a need and opportunity in the financial sector to organize to improve conditions for workers and to challenge the practices that have crippled the United States economy. This need requires a different kind of organizing campaign whose goal is to achieve transformative social and economic change.

This chapter aims to demonstrate that through transnational alliances, a few labor and social movement organizations in the United States are attempting to bring about transformative change by targeting the financial sector, which is at the core of the capitalist economic system and its most recent transformation to short-term financial orientation. The Communication Workers of America (CWA) has joined forces with Brazil's São Paulo Bank Workers' Union (SEEB/SP) to develop and implement worker organizing strategies targeting low-wage occupations in the financial industry. Partners include several community-based and alternative worker organizations such as ALIGN NY, Communities United, Make the Road New York (MRNY), and New York Communities for Change (NYCC). These groups currently constitute the Committee for Better Banks (CBB), an alliance that will likely transform over time with the expansion of the campaign.[1] Strategic support is also being provided by UNI Finance Global Union (UNI) and the broader Brazilian bank workers' organization, *Confederação Nacional dos Trabalhadores do Ramo Financiero da Central Única dos Trabalhadores* (Contraf-CUT).

A focus on the financial sector is imperative today because social and economic conditions have drastically changed since the 2008 Great Recession. Such organizing efforts come at a time when rising wealth inequality in the United States and globally is creating conditions that require an urgent and strategic response to leverage the voice of workers as a critical counterweight to other forces driving economic change. A comprehensive effort that veers from old labor organizing strategies and emphasizes grassroots organizing of workers and community members is crucial to transforming an industry that has been at the center of the global economic crisis. This effort must be locally centered with national and global coordination. Even though the work of CWA, its community and labor allies, and SEEB/SP is in its infancy in the United States, it exhibits these characteristics and provides some hope for tackling the degradation of working conditions, labor norms, and standards with the broader goal of transforming socioeconomic and political conditions.

In what follows, we first describe the significance of organizing labor in the financial sector—not just in the United States but in other countries as well. Second, we provide an analysis of the restructuring of the financial industry, its impact on labor, and its broader socioeconomic implications. The constant structural changes in the financial industry pose many challenges to the organizing efforts of CWA and its community and labor partners.

Third, we examine the Brazilian labor movement, specifically the bank workers' union, and its influence in ensuring fair labor practices for Brazilian bank workers and how their experiences can help shape strategies for U.S. financial sector workers. Fourth, we describe the future work of CWA, its community and labor partners in the United States, and the Brazilian bank worker unions in organizing U.S. bank workers. Finally, we present an outlook for the effort to organize the financial industry in the United States.

SIGNIFICANCE OF LABOR UNIONS

At peak moments of the American labor movement, unions have been able to galvanize and organize workers across industries. The drastic changes in corporate behavior toward prioritizing short-term profit may create another peak moment for the American labor movement. Unions have made major gains, such as the eight-hour workday, minimum wage, worker compensation, and improving occupational health and safety, among other worker protections.

In the 1980s, the United Auto Workers (UAW) and United Food and Commercial Workers (UFCW) were at the forefront of holding major companies such as General Motors, Chrysler, Iowa Beef Processors, and Morrell Meat Packing accountable for workplace safety violations and injuries, leading to historic multimillion-dollar settlements (Delp, Mojtahedi, and Sheikh 2014). And, as recent history has shown, labor unions have made significant strides in organizing sectors in which workers were never before organized or had lost union representation over time. The notable Justice for Janitors campaign by the Service Employees International Union (SEIU) proved that long-term investment with a multi-pronged and comprehensive strategy that extended beyond engaging workers to include the religious community, students, and community-based organizations was possible and a necessity in winning demands.

Moreover, some unions have stepped away, although reluctantly, from ineffective organizing strategies and become more inclusive. In 2006, the American Federation of Labor and Congress of Industrial Organizations (AFL-CIO) and National Day Labor Organizing Network (NDLON) formed the Worker Center Partnership to support organizing of the predominantly immigrant day laborers. According to Victor Narro, "Solidarity support and cross-fertilization between traditional labor and alternative organizing movements are creating new opportunities for collaboration" (2009:98).

Even with this progress, the reality is that union membership in the United States is in decline, with less than 7% of private sector and just over 35% of public sector workers with union representation (U.S. BLS 2014). Unions are more focused on maintaining their existing membership base and show less interest in making the long-term investments required for grassroots organizing and worker education to build a powerful and politically active base of workers across various industries.

The Occupy Wall Street (OWS) movement helped create a space for such organizing by shifting the nation's attention and public discourse toward issues of wealth inequality and the role of financial institutions in the 2008 economic downturn. Large U.S. financial institutions, through the issuance of subprime and toxic products, are the main parties responsible for the financial crisis, and workers could have played a crucial role in pointing out the systemic failures. Considering that U.S. bank workers represent one third of all bank workers globally, the importance of this struggle is clear. Therefore, it is vital that U.S. bank workers be organized so that they may have a voice in regulating the financial industry, both in the United States and globally. Weak worker representation or a complete absence of worker organization in a country that is the center of the financial industry means that there is a risk of the worst banking practices being disseminated to other countries.

Another important factor to consider is the strengthening of democracy through the organized participation of workers. Strong unions have an extremely important role in building and strengthening democracy, inasmuch as workers become educated about political participation and the class divide, and aware of their rights. The strengthening of democratic institutions such as unions in the United States would benefit workers and labor conditions in other countries.

Thus, the potential development of a campaign that comprises a grassroots, community-based, transnational strategy to organize workers in the financial sector is timely. Organizing in the financial industry is an opportunity that must be seized by the labor movement to demonstrate its ability to adapt to a new economy and build power. A long-term investment by community and labor partners—a commitment that goes beyond a few months or a couple of years and perseverance in the face of setbacks and challenges—provides hope in bringing about transformative, industry-wide, socioeconomic, and political change.

RESTRUCTURING THE FINANCIAL INDUSTRY

Since the 2008 financial crisis, many banks have returned their focus to generating large profits. However, as the banking industry restructures, it is the low- and middle-tier workers who have seen their wages, hours, and benefits dwindle and their jobs cut, while executives receive pay increases. Globally, there have also been job losses in the financial sector (UNI Global 2013). In the United States in the years 2012 and 2013, nearly 200,000 jobs were cut in the global financial services sector (Hyman 2012).[2] In the United States, about 8.35 million people were employed in the banking industry at its peak in December 2006, compared with 7.7 million at the end of 2012 (U.S. BLS via Tausche 2012). By the end of 2013, there were fewer than 6 million people employed in the financial sector in the United States (U.S. BLS 2013).

The decline in jobs is a result of multiple structural changes by the industry to cut labor costs. First, there is automation, whereby banks are phasing out consumer tellers in branches and replacing them with automated machines (Hoyt 2013). Bank of America has plans to close down 750 of its 5,700 branches over the next few years. Citigroup projects to close 84 branches, with a loss of 6,200 jobs in its consumer banking unit. And JPMorgan Chase plans to reduce staff per branch by 20% through 2015 (Fitzpatrick and Lublin 2012; Henry and Rothacker 2012; Wilchins 2013, in Hoyt 2013). Bank of America, Citigroup Inc., JPMorgan Chase, Goldman Sachs, and Morgan Stanley cut more than 3.5%, or 31,000 jobs, of their combined workforce between June 2011 and April 2013 (Hoyt 2013).

The financial industry is also near-shoring, or moving jobs to different regions and cities within the United States. Banks are relocating departments and occupations that do not require capital-intensive, highly qualified workers from expensive city centers to less costly areas. Jacksonville, Florida; Salt Lake City, Utah; and St. Louis, Missouri, have been popular destinations for banks to move their service-oriented jobs to. These jobs include accounting, trading and legal support, and human resources and compliance. In fact, St. Louis's securities-industry employment increased by 85% between January 2008 and September 2012 (Moody's Analytics via Fitzpatrick 2012 and Hoyt 2013). These relocations have had a regional impact on traditional financial regions. According to the New York Comptroller's Office, the loss of each financial services position results in the loss of two additional jobs in other industries in New York City and one loss elsewhere in the state (Office of the State Comptroller 2013). On a net income basis, there is a loss of jobs despite the growth of jobs in fields peripheral to the financial sector. A securities-industry job that on average pays $343,000 in New York City pays $102,000 in St. Louis.

Finally, certain banking sector jobs are being outsourced to countries with significantly lower labor costs and lack of labor regulations and/or labor monitoring and enforcement. For example, banks have moved call centers to countries such as India and the Philippines. Approximately 500,000 jobs over the past four years have been lost as a result of overseas outsourcing. Banks have also begun outsourcing mortgage-related work, including foreclosure reviews and loan modifications. The *Wall Street Journal* reported that in 2013, Indian outsourcing firms gained over $315 million in mortgage work, twice the amount of revenue from such work in 2009 (Schectman 2013).

Implications for Financial Sector and Its Workers in the United States

Global and domestic restructuring of the financial sector has many implications beyond reductions in the number of jobs. The types of business practices that banks engage in and working conditions are also affected.

A CBB survey of bank workers in the United States, ranging from consumer branch tellers to loan officers, found that after the financial crisis, there was an increase in sales pressure, leading to problematic and illegal practices (Hoyt 2013). The survey found that such pressure led some workers to forge signatures or open fake bank accounts to meet sales goals. The pressure to meet goals and the looming threat of losing one's job creates stress and hinders an employee's ability to provide quality services that meet consumer needs. A bank teller surveyed by the CBB described the work pressures:

> My manager was mentally abusive at Wells Fargo. At times he would not allow me to drink water. The higher ups send you over 50 emails a day pushing sales and your direct manager does most of the scowling directly. They don't care about their customers and just want them to open more products. We don't push sales for incentives at Wells Fargo. As an employee, we push sales just to be able to keep our jobs. (Hoyt 2013:11)

In an effort to increase their sales and cut labor costs, banks have enhanced the use of strategies that erode and even abandon normative labor standards. Such strategies, to name but a few, include manipulation of work hours so that employees do not qualify for benefits, expansion of unpredictable scheduling practices, and conversion of full-time jobs to part-time (Bernhardt, Boushey, Dresser, and Tilly 2008).

The CBB survey reports the following results:

- 25% of those who answered described cuts to their take-home pay.
- 24% mentioned benefit cuts (including higher insurance premiums).
- 16.6% of respondents expressed that they did not always get deserved vacation, personal, and sick days.
- 43.5% of respondents said that their life insurance and medical benefits did not cover all desired medical and life needs.

Wage cuts are an outright abandonment of norms in the labor market, especially when taking into consideration the already low wages of bank tellers. Low wages means less money is spent in local economies and more reliance on public assistance programs. In the United States, the median income for a full-time bank teller is $24,940 per year, which is $11.99 per hour (U.S. BLS 2013). At Wells Fargo, the average hourly wage for a teller is less than $11 an hour. While this is above the federal minimum wage of $7.25 per hour, it is low enough for workers to qualify for food stamp benefits (Picchi 2013). Research by the University of California, Berkeley,

Labor Center found that one third of bank tellers rely on public assistance. In New York State, almost 40% of bank tellers and their family members are enrolled in public assistance programs, costing the state and federal governments $112 million in benefits (Allegretto, Jacobs, Emiko Scott, and Graham-Squire 2014), essentially forcing taxpayers to subsidize banks that do not pay their employees a living wage.

In contrast, bankers at the top six firms have taken home more than half a trillion dollars in bonuses and compensation since the bailout (New Bottom Line 2012 in Lerner and Bhatti 2013). For instance, John Stumpf, CEO of Wells Fargo, earned $22.9 million in 2012, nearly 16% more than his pay of $19.8 million in 2011 (Allegretto, Jacobs, Emiko Scott, and Graham-Squire 2014).

There are also violations and evasion of labor laws (Bernhardt, Boushey, Dresser, and Tilly 2008) in the financial sector. For example, 32% of CBB survey respondents reported that they were not always paid for overtime work. Some workers also stated that their employers did not allow them to report overtime hours worked. There are also restrictions placed on workers through Code of Conduct rules that expressly state that an employee cannot talk about the work or the industry. Companies also evade U.S. labor laws by relocating work to other countries.

Moreover, restructuring results in further erosion of the normative workplace standard: freedom of association. Workers are dispersed and separated when work is divided geographically and occupation-wise. Lack of interaction between employees and strict monitoring of workers by supervisors inhibits people from openly discussing and organizing to improve their work conditions. Social and economic pressures external to the workplace, such as paying a home mortgage, student debt, or just the fear of losing a job during a sluggish economy, keep people from risking their jobs by attempting to organize.

Such erosion and abandonment of labor standards and evasion of laws threaten the working conditions of unionized financial sector workers globally. The constant drive by companies to down labor costs, along with a region's need for jobs, enhances political and economic conditions that are unfavorable for workers, leading to increased pressure on workers to produce for low wages and leaving them susceptible to workplace violations. This situation is even more evident in countries that do not have strong regulatory systems to monitor labor conditions and enforce existing labor laws.

Implications for Financial Sector Workers Globally

Unlike the United States, many countries have historically had labor unions in the banking sector. These include most European countries and Australia, as well as developing countries and emerging economies such as Brazil, Burkina Faso, Ghana, Grenada, Malaysia, the Philippines, and Venezuela (UNI Global 2013). CWA and its organizational partners can learn a great deal from the powerful Brazilian bank workers and from other sectoral unions that are part of the UNI Global Union. An organized workforce, not just in the financial industry but also across industries, is the most effective way to improve overall social and economic conditions. Yet it is also important to recognize that unionization does not necessarily ensure jobs in a restructuring industry and a rapidly changing economy. Unionization, however, can serve as a tool of accountability when workers are collectively and individually empowered to call out predatory and/or illegal business practices.

UNI's survey (2013) found that unions in ten countries reported the acceleration of job loss in the banking sector since the 2008 economic crisis. The remaining 18 countries either responded that job loss rates were stabilizing or leveling off, indicating that the financial sectors had already gone through their job elimination processes (UNI Global 2013). Because labor regulations vary across nations, financial institutions in various countries are not held to the same standards, which has major implications for worker protections on a global scale. For instance, when Santander, a Spanish bank, acquired Sovereign Bank, an American firm, it was not required to meet the same labor and wage standards that it provided its workers at its offices and branches around the world. According to Elk (2010), Santander immediately laid off 23% of its new subsidiary's workforce in the United States, cut pay, slashed hours, and doubled the cost of health insurance. Outside the United States, Santander branches on average are 75% unionized, in line with the fact that most other industrialized nations have unionized banking sectors. Elk (2010) also found that unionized janitors in the Boston headquarters of Sovereign Bank often make more than the firm's bank tellers and personal bankers because the janitors have collective bargaining power through union representation.

Workers' power is further threatened in other countries as Santander and other banks send their managers and executives—who are trained in performance-based models—from Wall Street and London to its branches across the world. The expansion of banking practices that are centered on meeting sales quotas and selling subprime products with hidden fees means that bank workers, even those who are unionized, face pressures that impact their working conditions. For example, some 60% of Brazilian bank workers are organized (Contraf-CUT, no date). Their strike in the fall of 2013 lasted 23 days, ending with an agreement that put the wage increase at 8.5% (the previous year's inflation rate had been about 6%). But these significant gains are under threat because of a lack of organized efforts in other countries, such as in the large and economically powerful market of the United States. Brazilian bank workers are faced with job losses and discrimination in pay. SEEB/SP recently reported that banks cut nearly 5,200 jobs throughout Brazil within a span of one year (August 2013 to August 2014). Contraf-CUT and the Inter-Union Department of Statistics and Socioeconomic Studies (DIEESE) also reported that there was a gap in salaries for female and male workers, with women earning 75.2% of the wages earned by men (*Brasil de Fato* 2014).[3]

Without a concerted effort at organizing employees who work for the same firms across national boundaries, the bargaining power of bank sector unions is threatened. Hence, the organizations of Brazilian bank workers are coordinating with CBB, CWA, and UNI to help develop an organizing campaign for better working conditions for finance workers in the United States. Brazilian financial sector workers will play an important role in assisting American bank workers build a foundation for an organized workforce.

Before delving into U.S. efforts to organize bank workers and the role the Brazilian unionists play, it is important to understand the history of the Brazilian trade union movement.

Brazil: Historical Context and Brazil's Bank Unions Today

For over a century, the Brazilian labor movement struggled to transform and build political power at national, regional, and local levels of government. These struggles demonstrate that unification of all types of movements, from social to student and labor across urban and rural areas, can lead to the transformation of power relations and socioeconomic conditions for the marginalized and disenfranchised. To better understand the contemporary Brazilian labor movement, it is important to know the historical context and the origins of the movement, which are rooted in strikes involving thousands of people; military coups; and economic, social, and political struggles.

The industrialization and expansion of factories between the years 1890 and 1914 and the large-scale immigration to Brazil from Italy, Spain, and Germany were two important factors in the growth of trade unionism. The new wave of immigrants brought with them ideologies and politics that had roots in *sindicatos* of socialist or anarchist groups. The 1930 coup by Getúlio Vargas brought a new era of regulation of unions known as the Collor Law, named after Labor Minister Lindolfo Collor (Alexander 2003). Under the decree, unions were required to register and gain recognition as legal entities, and union members were required to have professional labor cards. Under Vargas's 15 years of dictatorship, collective bargaining was abolished and replaced with a labor tribunal. Many other controls were put in place to keep labor unions from acting independently, which in turn contributed to the increased militancy of the Brazilian labor movement (Alexander 2003).

The most significant walkouts were in 1934 and 1935 at the Great Western Railroad, which eventually achieved 30% wage gains for the workers. Increased militancy of labor unions continued into the next regime and in part was due to the Communists, who were more disciplined and organized than their opponents. Under military rule, after the 1964 coup, unions were harshly repressed, especially after 1968, with the imposition of Institutional Act Number 5, which abolished all individual and political guarantees. From 1964 to 1985, the Brazilian labor movement fought against the military regime in demand of elections and democracy. During that period, multiple social, student, and labor movements joined and organized across rural and urban areas.

The most significant gains were made in the late 1970s, when a series of strikes and popular movements in favor of public health care, against the increase in the cost of living, for democracy, and for amnesty for political prisoners rocked the foundations of the dictatorship and triggered a process of political opening. Specifically, in 1978, Luiz Inácio Lula da Silva, from the northeast of Brazil, who began his working life in childhood as a shoeshine boy and later became a metalworker and union leader, organized a major strike in opposition to the military regime—something that was unthinkable at the time.

The boldness of the strike and the courage of the metalworkers inspired unionists, intellectuals, politicians, and representatives of social movements to discuss the need for a workers' movement that allowed workers to make decisions to transform the social, political, and economic conditions of the country. This movement was born of workers' desire for independence from the existing political parties and led to emergence of the *Partido dos Trabalhadores* (PT; Workers' Party) in 1980. Establishing a political party meant that labor could now work to ensure that workers were in the ranks of the national congress, a body that did not have any labor representation and did not reflect Brazilian society. Thus began the Brazilian labor movement's struggle to elect workers to all spheres of power. Lula was elected as a federal official, and Brazilians, through a coordinated effort, continued to elect workers to advocate the agendas of labor, the poor, and the working class.

But to achieve a massive social transformation, the Brazilian labor and social movements recognized that they needed more. The idea of creating unity among labor through establishment of a major central body came to fruition in 1983 with the creation of *Central Única dos Trabalhadores* (CUT) (Fontes, Macedo, and Sanches 2013). This body was founded on the principles of trade union freedom, autonomy, and independence from governments, the state, and political parties or groups. CUT embraces all social struggles—women, blacks, youth, and others who have been marginalized. Today, CUT represents more than 7.8 million workers in all production sectors. It is also the largest trade union center in Latin America and the fifth largest in the world.

Brazil's bank workers are a fundamental part of a "new unionism"[4] that is unified, politically sophisticated, and powerful and that helped bring about a renewal in the Brazilian labor movement. In the face of the impossibility of taking control of their original confederation, *Confederação Nacional dos Trabalhadores em Empresas de Crédito* (CONTEC), which did not implement more combative practices to challenge the banks, Brazil's bank workers, led by the São Paulo Bank Workers' Union, created a new confederation, the National Bank Workers' Confederation (CNB-CUT) in 1990. The São Paulo union, founded in 1923, accounts for one third of all bank workers who are members of locals and federations affiliated to this confederation.

In 2006, the union was renamed Contraf-CUT and represented all workers in the financial sector, especially those not included in the *Convenção Coletiva Nacional dos Bancários* (National Collective Agreement). Contraf-CUT also represents workers in entities that are part of all financial industry processes, including workers who are contracted by holding companies controlled by banks. Currently, Contraf-CUT represents eight federations and 101 unions, representing more than 85% of bank workers in Brazil (Cordeiro 2013).

Contraf-CUT is a pluralistic organization. When organizing bank workers' national campaigns that encompass collective bargaining efforts, a *Comando Nacional* is formed. This body comprises representatives of major local unions and state federations coordinated by the presidents of Contraf-CUT and SEEB/SP.

Bank workers in Brazil benefit greatly from the National Collective Agreement, which ensures that bank workers across the country are paid the same wages. Prior to this agreement, which was first signed in 1992, wages and benefits varied greatly depending on the region and employer. For instance, workers in northeastern Brazil were paid less than workers in the southeast (CUT, no date). The 1992 agreement was won after a three-day strike. Since 2004, bank workers have been gaining real wage increases every year, higher salary floors (38.7% gain above inflation this period), and improvements in profit-sharing plans (UNI Global 2014). By contrast, in the United States, workers in certain occupations in the banking sector earn wages low enough to qualify them for public assistance.

BRAZILIAN FINANCIAL SECTOR UNIONS AND AMERICAN WORKERS

In 2010, SEIU initiated an effort to explore organizing bank workers in the United States, with the support and encouragement of Contraf-CUT and UNI. SEIU was joined in the campaign by CWA, with SEIU focusing on retail banking workers in Boston and a number of other cities. CWA focused their organizing on call centers in Massachusetts and Rhode Island. The campaign initially homed in on the Spanish bank, Santander, which had recently purchased Sovereign Bank in the United States. Santander is unionized in much of the world, including its home country of Spain, and in Brazil, which has become a major employer and one of the most profitable units in the world.

The initial strategy was to focus on winning a card-check neutrality agreement[5] from Santander for its 7,000 U.S. employees by using relationships and pressure in Spain and Brazil, where the company is unionized. The aim was to convince the company to adopt policies toward unionization in the United States, similar to its position of recognizing and negotiating with unions in other countries. Despite some initial success in building worker committees in Boston, the campaign was put on hold when the 2008 financial crisis spread to and gripped the Spanish economy. The unions in Spain, buffeted by austerity and cutbacks, felt it was not the right time to have a battle with Spanish banks about organizing rights for U.S. workers.

Over time, SEIU decided that it did not want to focus on organizing a new industry (banks) and questioned whether there was sufficient interest among bank workers to engage and activate them at the level needed to maintain the campaign. As a result, SEIU did not continue the campaign. CWA continued its organizing of call centers, with ties to its core industries in the telephone and airline industries, but lacking involvement by SEIU, CWA did not continue the part of its campaign that focused on banks and finance.

Despite the decision of the U.S. and Spanish unions not to continue with the campaign, Brazilian bank workers, the SEEB/SP, and Contraf continued to advocate for the importance of organizing finance and bank workers in the United States. They argued that finance and banking were global and that the gains its workers were making in Brazil and other countries could not be maintained if the United States, center of the financial industry, remained unorganized.

With the birth of Occupy Wall Street in the United States and the growing understanding of the importance of finance to the U.S. and global economies, Brazilian bank workers again began advocating for the importance of organizing finance workers in the United States.

After a series of meetings in Brazil, CWA, in partnership with community groups that had long been working on the housing foreclosure crisis and other Wall Street–related issues, began laying a grassroots foundation for a long-term campaign to organize and reform the financial industry in the United States by building onto and supporting the ongoing and robust campaigns for Wall Street accountability. The campaign is a joint community and labor effort with strong support and guidance from SEEB/SP and UNI. This collaboration is in the early stages of experimenting with how U.S. unions can shift from campaigns that traditionally focus on only worksite organizing to a broader and more comprehensive strategy that includes social, economic, and racial justice movements and cross-border alliances to target an industry that is central to the U.S. and global economic systems.

THE CAMPAIGN: FROM PRINCIPLES TO FIELD STRATEGY AND IMPLEMENTATION

Five strategic principles guide the campaign to organize U.S. bank and finance workers. These principles are central to strategy development and on-the-ground implementation of the campaign.

The first principle requires *global solidarity in order to challenge global capital*. Finance is global, with bank workers in many countries being represented by unions. To protect already unionized workers and to build the strength necessary to force banks to recognize the rights of U.S. workers to form unions, there needs to be ongoing escalating global pressure on specific banks and the financial sector as a whole.

The second principle calls for *global and national transformation and reform of finance*. This principle is important because the goal of the campaign is not just to win collective bargaining rights for U.S. workers but also to challenge and reform industry practices that are bad for workers and the national and global economies. These actions range from reducing pressure on workers to meet unrealistic sales goals by peddling predatory products to consumers to supporting a national and global financial transaction tax.

Third, *building community support and supporting communities* is critical. Worker organizing in the United States must be nested in a broader campaign to challenge the power of banks. Community groups are more likely to actively support a campaign that has goals and demands beyond just improving conditions for workers, and workers are more likely to organize if they see widespread support for their organizing.

The fourth principle is to have an *industry-wide organizing approach*. The campaign will take many years—there is no shortcut—and must focus on the whole industry while trying to win initial victories at specific banks. This approach should address labor issues in the entire financial industry rather than just pushing for changes and campaign demands one bank at a time.

Finally, it is important to recognize that *collective bargaining, regulating, and reforming finance are intertwined*. Workers will not be successful in organizing in the United States if its financial industry does not have greater regulation and reform and will not work in the long run unless unionized workers are empowered to be the front line against predatory bank practices that damage consumers and threaten the economy.

These five principles help guide and establish a field strategy that can have the most impact in organizing workers while reforming a broken industry. The campaign is moving from broad rhetoric about global solidarity to the practical day-to-day work of connecting workers and unions and looking for concrete ways to build on the different strengths and experiences in each country. UNI is playing an overall coordinating role, bringing together union members and leaders from different countries to jointly strategize and plan. The Brazilian and Argentinian bank workers' unions are helping raise money to finance the campaign and connect directly to the day-to-day organizing of specific banks and cities. Examples of early transnational work include coordinated actions, meetings, and communications efforts.

December 2013 Week of Action in New York City

In December 2013, elected leaders of SEEB/SP and other local Brazilian bank worker unions joined community groups in New York City for a week of action focused on Wall Street. The week of action included meetings between Brazilian and U.S. bank workers, a report on the negative impact of Wall Street's practices on the New York economy (Hoyt 2013; New Day New York Coalition 2013), a research project documenting that one third of bank tellers receive public assistance (Allegretto, Jacobs, Emiko Scott, and Graham-Squire 2014), and a mass demonstration in support of workers' rights. In addition, SEEB/SP was honored at the annual gala of New York Communities for Change, along with the newly elected mayor of New York City, Bill de Blasio. This week of action grew directly out of the strategic principles of building global solidarity and connecting the campaign to community-based organizations and progressive political movements.

Global Strategy Meetings

In February 2013, UNI and CWA brought together bank and call-center workers from around the world to Orlando, Florida. Workers shared experiences as finance employees and developed a common calendar of activities and strategies to pressure banks in the United States to respect workers' rights to organize. The global delegation then traveled to New York City, where there was a demonstration at Citibank and issuance of the CBB report (Hoyt 2013) that documented how unionized bank workers from around the world had many benefits and rights that U.S. bank workers did not.

Reforming Banking: The Campaign on "Sales and Advice"

UNI's financial sector has been running a campaign on "sales and advice," which advocates that workers should not have unrealistic sales goals and should be able to advise consumers on quality bank products rather than pitch predatory products.[6] As part of the campaign in the United States, workers have adopted a similar theme. Thousands of Wells Fargo workers signed an online petition demanding the company eliminate unfair sales quotas. The petition was delivered to Wells Fargo at its annual shareholders meeting in conjunction with joint demonstrations by homeowners protesting Wells Fargo foreclosure practices at demonstrations around the country.

Community Issues

The bank workers' organizing campaign has joined forces with a number of community organizations that focus on the multiple levels of predatory lending by banks in the United States. By working with groups that are challenging banking practices, the campaign hopes to form a larger coalition calling for reform and regulation of the financial sector, in addition to encouraging these groups to support bank workers in their efforts to organize. The three primary issues of focus for the bank workers' campaign and community groups are housing, student debt, and predatory public debt.

Millions of people lost their homes to foreclosure during the economic collapse. Communities of color were affected disproportionately, with a loss of 60% of their wealth. Ten million homeowners are still underwater, which means their homes are worth less than they paid for them. Bank workers were often also victims of the housing collapse. In cities across the United States, the bank workers' campaign and community groups are using innovative tactics such as eminent domain to seize underwater mortgages so that they can be rewritten at current market value, dramatically reducing mortgage payments.

Students and their families have been dealing for years with increasingly exorbitant student loans and interest rates. But this issue has become even more relevant today, given the high numbers of unemployed and underemployed college graduates.[7] Forty million people have $1.2 trillion in student debt. Banks are profiting in multiple ways off of student debt and the privatization of higher education. By working with student debt groups and exposing how banks are profiting off of growing student debt the campaign connects to a huge growing movement in the United States that helps lead the charge to regulate and reform banks.

The same banks that caused the housing debacle and are profiting from the student debt crisis are also driving urban areas like Detroit into bankruptcy with predatory public loans such as interest rate swaps. In 2013, states, cities, counties, and other public entities had $3.8 trillion in outstanding bond debt, and they pay billions of dollars in interest each year (Lerner and Bhatti 2013; SIFMA 2014). Banks have increased their profits by trapping cities in toxic debt deals, even after receiving money at zero or near zero interest rates from the Federal Reserve (Lerner and Bhatti 2013). Nearly every city worker in Scranton, Pennsylvania, had to take a pay cut down to the minimum wage when the city almost ran out of funds (Lerner and Bhatti 2013). In 2014, the *Chicago Tribune* broke the story on how Chicago Public Schools had been exploited by banks for over 10 years. Two years prior, the Chicago Teachers Union and a coalition of community and labor organizations shed light on toxic swaps that had cost the school district tens of millions of dollars and, through the lifetime of the deals, could cost hundreds of millions more (Potter 2014). Today, the Chicago's elected officials are under public scrutiny and pressure to make major reforms in how the city does business with banks. Exposing the skimming of public dollars has further isolated banks by demonstrating the damage their practices have.

The three issues of housing, student debt, and predatory banking practices go to the heart of how banks take advantage of ordinary people in the United States and connect the bank workers' organizing campaign to a much broader movement calling for reform and regulation of Wall Street and big banks in the United States.

Organizing Bank Workers Industry-Wide

The early bank worker organizing has been taking place online, at work-sites, at particular banks, and in various locations. The goal is to build a national, industry-wide organizing committee, regional and local committees, and committees within certain banks.

The use of social media has led to the most active participation by bank workers. Social media platforms provide a means for workers to share and discuss how they are treated and compare conditions between banks and between countries. This effort has spawned the circulation of petitions addressing specific issues, which thousands of bank workers and supporters have signed. Bank worker organizing efforts are also taking place at worksites and key banking centers around the country. The work began in New York and New Jersey and is spreading to the middle of the country and the West Coast.

Banco do Brasil, which is partially publicly owned by the Brazilian government, has been a particular focus of attention for the campaign, which has a goal of winning a neutrality agreement for the United States. Workers from Banco do Brazil have traveled to the United States, and Banco do Brazil workers in the United States have attended union meetings in Brazil to build support for the rights of U.S. bank workers.

Banco do Brasil signed a global framework agreement (GFA) with UNI Americas on May 30, 2011, which, in addition to addressing social dialogue, corporate social responsibility, occupational safety and health, and other measures, holds the firm responsible for recognizing freedom of association. The agreement states in part:

> The Parties recognise the mutual right, without any distinction or previous authorisation, and in accordance with each country's legislation, to be represented by organisations/associations of their own choice, as well as the right of their employees and represented personnel to become members of these organisations, as long as they follow their statutes. (UNI Global 2011:5)

The GFA enables workers of Banco do Brasil to organize, whether they are in the United States or in Brazil. Because this right must conform to each country's labor laws, Banco do Brasil workers based in the United States must wage an intensive organizing campaign. U.S. labor regulations are weak in protecting the right of workers to organize without retaliation from the employer. However, the support of nearly 120,000 unionized Banco do Brasil workers in Brazil provides solidarity, opportunities to exchange knowledge and strategy, and a way to exert pressure on the bank from workers on two continents.

The U.S. business community is placing extraordinary pressure on multinational companies that are unionized in their home country to adopt an anti-union posture when they operate in the United States. SEIU's multi-year campaign to organize Group 4 Securicor (McCallum 2013), CWA's experience with German-owned T-Mobile (Early 2012), and UAW's recent experience with auto plants that are unionized everywhere in the world except the United States are examples of the difficulties of enforcing global practices and agreements in the United States.[8]

Despite the challenges faced by such campaigns, they offer the greatest opportunities for initial victories in the financial world. There are tens of thousands of workers employed in the United States by foreign-owned banks that have a history of good labor relations in their home countries. The bank workers' campaign believes that Banco do Brasil and other global banks not based in the United States could be the best places to establish a U.S. beachhead of organized bank workers. No matter what progress the bank workers' campaign makes with global banks, it will not be able to win collective bargaining for the vast majority of bank workers unless the power of big banks in the United States is severely restricted.

CONCLUSION

Since the start of global economic restructuring in the 1970s, the U.S. economy has transformed into a system that allows for greater concentration of wealth and power in the hands of bank executives. In parallel, workers in the financial industry have seen a continual decline in their labor conditions. As the mainstream discourse has shifted to wealth inequality in the United States and globally, thanks to Occupy Wall Street, the labor movement has the opportunity to organize a sector that is critical to ensuring that we have an economic system that is held accountable. The bank workers' organizing campaign in the United States has immense potential to achieve systemic transformation if attention and resources are adequately provided.

Moreover, a coordinated effort between community-based organizations, alternative worker organizations, and trade unions is required to be able to push for industry-wide reforms in terms of business practices and labor standards. This campaign has to remain grounded in the five principles (discussed previously in this chapter) with a long-term outlook geared not just to an increase in union membership but to an actual transformation. But to reach this long-term goal, the campaign must in the short term cultivate community and worker leadership. As evident in the experience of the Brazilian labor movement, without a grassroots base that is politically educated, engaged, and willing to fight for their demands despite challenges posed by the current anti-union environment, there can be no change.

In closing, we recommend the following actions be taken at the municipal, state, and federal levels to rein in a rogue financial sector.

Municipal-Level Rule-Making

- **Responsible Banking:** Many cities have responsible banking ordinances that require banks to engage in fair lending and other similar practices if they are to be eligible to win city business. These ordinances should be expanded to include language calling for fair wages and treatment for bank workers as a condition to get city business, which is a major profit center for banks.

- **Scheduling:** Pass legislation on a city-by-city basis that requires banks and other retail employers to provide regular hours to workers, instead of split and partial shifts. In December 2014, San Francisco's Board of Supervisors unanimously adopted the Retail Workers Bill of Rights, which requires employers to schedule their workers' hours at least two weeks in advance, to pay workers for hours they spend on call only to have their shifts canceled, and to offer their part-time workers more hours before they seek to hire new workers (Meyerson 2014). The ordinance applies to stores, restaurants, hotels, and banks with 11 or more outlets nationwide and aims to help people attain stable employment (Wong 2014).

- **Higher Wages by Sector:** A number of cities are passing laws that allow for legislating wages by sector. Such legislation that includes strong wage enforcement mechanisms is crucial. Higher wages are beneficial only when workers know that legislation will be enforced and there are systems in place for workers' grievances and to hold employers accountable. Passing such legislation in multiple cities and then running campaigns with bank workers to set higher bank worker minimum wage could be an important part of campaigns in targeted cities.

Monitor and Enforce Agreements

New York City and many other cities give tax breaks and similar subsidies to banks to maintain and create good-paying local jobs. However, rarely do banks deliver on what they promised on either front. Getting cities to audit, enforce and, if necessary, claw back the subsidies would improve job opportunities and demonstrate to workers that collective action works (New Day New York Coalition 2013).

Discontinue Government Financial Support for Banks

Because some of these subsidies and tax break agreements are already in place, we recommend that in the future, such government support not be provided to banks. Tax credits and subsidy-driven economic policies encourage competition among regions and do not create jobs but redistribute them. Although the City of New York provides government financial support to banks—and even after receiving a $700 billion bailout—banks there are still moving jobs to other cities, states, and countries. Thus, municipalities and states must veer from economic development policies that provide corporations with tax breaks, incentives, and subsidies paid for by taxpayers.

Monitor and Enforce Labor Laws Through Litigation

Banks regularly violate wage and hour, fair hiring, and other laws designed to protect workers. Aggressively pursuing claims against these deeds through legal channels, ideally on a class-action basis, exposes how banks take unfair advantage of workers and will lead to tangible economic gains for workers.

Expand Whistleblower Protection and Expose Bank Maleficence

The Dodd–Frank Wall Street Reform and Consumer Protection Act significantly improved protections for financial whistleblowers. Banks, however, through daily pressure on employees and by other means, still restrict and threaten employees who use social media and other venues to discuss their bank's predatory practices, which has a chilling effect on workers organizing. Ramping up protections and support for whistleblowers and encouraging workers at all levels to report bank maleficence should be supported and encouraged. Specifically, on the basis of the Government Accountability Project's work,[9] we recommend the following:

- Clarify that whistleblowers are in fact eligible for protection when they make disclosures from within their respective corporations. Further, clarify that any actions made by the wrongdoer to block the flow of whistleblowing evidence are illegal. Finally, make clear that disclosing evidence of crime or other violations of Securities and Exchange Commission (SEC) rules is a legally protected activity, despite any assertions by wrongdoers that employees have stolen their "property." These suggested solutions warrant a public hearing and careful consideration by the SEC.

- Launch a series of field hearings around the country to discuss the problem of workplace retaliation and explore new ways to increase reporting, both internally and externally.

- Create an Advisory Committee on Whistleblower Reporting and Protection to leverage worker reports from field hearings and the expertise of a diverse group of participants that meets regularly. This committee will serve as a vehicle for the SEC to collect advice, best practices, and recommendations related to whistleblower reporting and protection.

Create Municipal and State Banks

Wall Street banks made significant profits managing and investing pension fund and other public monies, usually charging hefty fees. In 2013, the City of Los Angeles paid Wall Street $204 million in fees—$41 million more than it spent on its Bureau of Street Services (Fix LA Coalition 2013). Insourcing some of these financial services to the public sector and creating municipal and state banks would demonstrate the inefficiencies of Wall Street practices and be the foundation on which a unionized public bank workforce could be built.

In addition to grassroots organizing and global coalitions, a series of local and national political, regulatory, and legislative actions could significantly add to a campaign that must achieve short-term victories while continuing an active, multi-year campaign to organize the entire industry.

ENDNOTES

[1] Additional groups working across the United States in the effort to organize financial sector workers include Cleveland Jobs With Justice (JWJ), Central Florida JWJ, St. Louis JWJ, Minnesotans for a Fair Economy (MFFE), and Missourians Organizing for Reform and Empowerment (MORE).

[2] This figure does not include administrative and human resources positions, consumer banking, and other banking services areas of employment.

[3] The average monthly wage at time of hire for men is R$3,678.54 (US$1,5962.52), while for women it is R$2,765.15 (US$1,200.10) (*Brasil de Fato* 2014).

[4] At the end of the 1970s, new unionism emerged in Brazil as an alternative to the authoritarian model of the dictatorial governments of the 1964 military regime. The discourses that attempted to define this new type of movement highlighted its democratic, demanding, and sometimes revolutionary aspect, which was grassroots oriented. The definition and affirmation of this new model arose in contrast with the unionism of the 1960s and 1970s, which was characterized as assistance oriented and bureaucratic, and was known as *atrelado* (literally, "harnessed"—a figurative term for *subservient*). This new unionism proposed that unions must be class based and undertake class struggles.

[5] A card-check neutrality agreement restricts the company from campaigning against the union and requires the company to agree to negotiate a contract with its workers when a majority of workers voluntarily sign a card authorizing the union to represent them.

[6] According to UNI Global, "In 2010, UNI Finance [Steering Group] adopted the Model Charter on Responsible Sales of Financial Products which key companies are encouraged to adopt. The charter aims to ensure the best possible framework for providing advice and responsible sales of products to customers" (UNI Global, no date).

[7] For young college graduates, the unemployment rate was 10.4% in 2010 and 9.4% in 2011, and the underemployment rate was 19.8% in 2010 and 19.1% in 2011 (Shierholz, Wething, and Sabadish 2012). In April 2014, the U.S. Department of Labor reported that the unemployment rate for 2013 college graduates was 10.9%. That rate was down from 13.3% in 2012, but unemployment for recent graduates was still higher than 9.6% for all Americans ages 20 to 29 as of October 2014. The Labor Department reported that 260,000 college graduates were working at or below the federal minimum wage of $7.35 an hour in 2013—more than twice as many as in 2007 (127,000), the year the recession began (Associated Press 2014).

[8] In February 2014, Volkswagen workers in the United States voted against joining UAW (DePillis 2014).

[9] Information was provided in an e-mail communication on August 14, 2014, with Tom Devine, legal director at the Government Accountability Project.

REFERENCES

Alexander, Robert J. 2003. *A history of organized labor in Brazil.* Westport: Praeger.

Allegretto, Sylvia, Ken Jacobs, Megan Emiko Scott, and Dave Graham-Squire. 2014 (Oct.). *The Public Cost of Low-Wage Jobs in the Banking Industry.* Berkeley: University of California–Berkeley Labor Center.

Associated Press. 2014 (Apr. 22). "Job Market for College Graduates Improves Slightly." *New York Times* (http://nyti.ms/1A6Tkzw).

Bernhardt, Annette, Heather Boushey, Laura Dresser, and Chris Tilly, Eds. 2008. *The Gloves-off Economy: Workplace Standards at the Bottom of America's Labor Market.* Cornell University ILR School. Ithaca, NY: ILR Press (http://bit.ly/1SYUbyf).

Brasil de Fato. 2014 (Mar. 26). "Pesquisa da Contraf aponta que bancos cortaram 1.864 empregos em 2014."

Central Única dos Trabalhadores (CUT). No date. "Histórico" (http://bit.ly/1DNp7Nh).

Confederação Nacional dos Trabalhadores do Ramo Financiero da Central Única dos Trabalhadores (Contraf-CUT). No date. "Contraf-CUT representa trabalhadores do ramo financeiro" (http://bit.ly/1A6Uyec).

Cordeiro, Carlos. 2013 (Apr. 2). "Convenção Coletiva Nacional, conquista histórica dos bancários." Central Única dos Trabalhadores (CUT) (http://bit.ly/1EpK5RE).

Delp, Linda, Zahra Mojtahedi, and Hina Sheikh. 2014. "A Legacy of Struggle: The OSHA Ergonomics Standard and Beyond, Part 1." *New Solutions: A Journal of Environmental and Occupational Health Policy,* Vol. 24, no. 3, pp. 365–389.

DePillis, Lydia B. 2014 (Feb. 14). "Volkswagen Workers Reject UAW in Tenn.; Union Looks for Plan B to Enter South." *Washington Post* (http://wapo.st/1EpKFij).

Early, Steve. 2012 (Jan. 17). "Going Global at T-Mobile: German Union Members Seek Better Treatment for U.S. Wireless Workers." Talking Union (http://bit.ly/1A6UX04).

Elk, Mike. 2010 (July 29). "Too Big Not to Organize." *In These Times* (http://bit.ly/1A6UZVL).

Fitzpatrick, Dan. 2012 (Dec. 13). "Meet Them in St. Louis: Bankers Move." *Wall Street Journal* (http://on.wsj.com/1EpLg3s).

Fitzpatrick, Dan, and Joann S. Lublin. 2012 (Jan. 13). "Bank of America Ponders Retreat." *Wall Street Journal* (http://on.wsj.com/1A6VcIF).

Fix LA Coalition. 2013. *No Small Fees: LA Spends More on Wall Street Than Our Streets* (http://bit.ly/1EpLyYh).

Fontes, Paulo, Francisco Macedo, and Ana Tércia Sanches (coordinators). 2013. "90 Anos Fortalecendo a Democracia—Bancários de São Paulo CUT (1923–2013)." São Paulo: Sindicato dos Bancários e Financiários de São Paulo Osasco e Região (http://bit.ly/1DNpEyz).

Henry, David, and Rick Rothacker. 2012 (Dec. 5). "Citigroup Cutting 11,000 Jobs, Taking $1 Billion in Charge." Reuters (http://reut.rs/1EpLLui).

Hoyt, Jordana. 2013. *The Committee for Better Banks Report: The State of the Bank Employee on Wall Street* (http://bit.ly/1A6VqzC).

Hyman, Simeon. 2012 (Jan. 30). "Financial-Sector Job Cuts Announced: 200,000." Bloomberg Business (http://bloom.bg/1EpM3l2).

Lerner, Stephen, and Saqib Bhatti. 2013. "Forcing Banks to the Bargaining Table: Renegotiating Wall Street's Relationship with Our Communities." In Chester Hartman and Gregory Squires, eds., *From Foreclosure to Fair Lending: Advocacy, Organizing, Occupy and the Pursuit of Equitable Credit*. New York: New Village Press.

McCallum, Jamie K. 2013. *Global Unions, Local Power: The New Spirit of Transnational Labor Organizing*. New York: Cornell Press.

Meyerson, Harold. 2014 (Dec. 10). "Employees Shouldn't Be Treated Like Products." *The Washington Post* (http://wapo.st/1sjAcAk).

Narro, Victor. 2009. "¡Sí Se Puede! Immigrant Workers and the Transformation of the Los Angeles Labor and Worker Center Movements." *Los Angeles Public Interest Law Journal*, Vol. 1 pp. 66–106.

New Day New York Coalition. 2013. *One New York for All of Us: Leveraging New York's Financial Power to Combat Inequality* (http://bit.ly/1A6VQG1).

Office of the State Comptroller, New York State. 2013. *The Securities Industry in New York City* (http://bit.ly/1A6VSxH).

Picchi, Aimee. 2013 (Dec. 5). "One-Third of Bank Tellers Rely on Public Assistance." CBS Money Watch (http://cbsn.ws/1EpMNql).

Potter, Jackson. 2014 (Nov. 11). "CPS Must Recover Losses from Toxic Financial Deals." *Chicago Public Tribune* (http://trib.in/1OwrczC).

Schectman, Joel. 2013 (May 27). "Mortgage Jobs Sent to India by U.S. Banks." *Wall Street Journal* (http://on.wsj.com/1EpMT0Y).

Securities Industry and Financial Markets Association (SIFMA). 2014. *Outstanding U.S. Bond Market Debt*. Washington, DC: Securities Industry and Financial Markets Association (http://bit.ly/1A6W2VQ).

Shierholz, Heidi, Hilary Wething, and Natalie Sabadish. 2012 (May 3). *The Class of 2012: Labor Market for Young Graduates Remains Grim*. Economic Policy Institute (http://bit.ly/1A6W9Rh).

Tausche, Kayla. 2012 (Oct. 5). "Jobs Growth? Not on Wall Street." CNBC U.S. News.

UNI Global Union. No date. "Campaigns" (http://bit.ly/1Qu2rlV).

UNI Global Union. 2011. *Global Framework Agreement for the Americas Union Network International (UNI) and Banco do Brasil* (http://bit.ly/1A6WkMu).

UNI Global Union. 2013. *Banking the Human Crisis: Job Losses and the Restructuring Process in the Financial Sector* (http://bit.ly/1EpNLCZ).

UNI Global Union. 2014. *U.S. Bank Workers Report: Better Banks for People, People for Better Banks* (http://bit.ly/1EpNQ9z).

U.S. Bureau of Labor Statistics (U.S. BLS). 2013. "Industries at a Glance: Finance and Insurance" (http://1.usa.gov/1EpNXC7).

U.S. Bureau of Labor Statistics (U.S. BLS). 2014. "Union Members Summary." Economic News Release (http://1.usa.gov/1kXdAMp).

Wong, Julia. 2014 (Aug. 5). "A 'Bill of Rights' for San Francisco's Retail Workers." *In These Times* (http://bit.ly/1A6WL9r).

Chapter 6

Labor in the 21st Century: The Top 0.1% and the Disappearing Middle Class

WILLIAM LAZONICK

University of Massachusetts Lowell

and

The Academic–Industry Research Network

WHERE HAVE ALL THE GOOD JOBS GONE?

Over the past four decades, real gross domestic product (GDP) per capita has about doubled in the United States. Yet most Americans are not all that better off. The ongoing explosion of the incomes of the richest households and the erosion of middle-class employment opportunities for most of the rest raise serious questions about whether the U.S. economy is beset by deep structural problems. My research on the evolution of the U.S. economy over the past half century shows that a structural explanation is indeed warranted.[1]

Since the beginning of the 1980s, employment relations in U.S. industrial corporations have undergone three major structural changes— which I summarize as "rationalization," "marketization," and "globalization"—that have permanently eliminated middle-class jobs in the United States. From the early 1980s, rationalization, characterized by plant closings, terminated the jobs of high-school-educated blue-collar workers, most of them well-paid union members. From the early 1990s, marketization, characterized by the end of a career with one company as an employment norm, placed the job security of middle-aged white-collar workers, many of them college educated, in jeopardy. From the early 2000s, globalization, characterized by the movement of employment offshore to lower-wage areas of the world, left all members of the U.S. labor force, even those with advanced educational credentials and substantial work experience, vulnerable to displacement.

Initially, each of these structural changes in employment could be justified as a business response to major changes in industrial conditions related to technologies, markets, and competition. During the onset of the rationalization phase in the early 1980s, the plant closings were a reaction to the superior productive capabilities of Japanese competitors in consumer-durable and related capital-goods industries that employed significant numbers of unionized blue-collar workers.[2] During the onset of the marketization phase in the early 1990s, the erosion of the one-company-career norm among white-collar workers was a response to the dramatic technological shift from proprietary systems to open systems, integral to the microelectronics revolution. This shift favored younger workers with the latest computer skills, acquired in higher education and transferable across companies, over older workers with many years of company-specific experience with systems integration.[3] During the onset of the globalization phase in the early 2000s, the sharp acceleration in the offshoring of jobs was a response to the emergence of large supplies of highly capable, and lower-wage, labor in developing nations such as China and India, which, linked to the United States through inexpensive communications systems, could take over U.S. employment activities that had become routine.[4]

Once U.S. corporations transformed their employment relations, however, they often pursued rationalization, marketization, and globalization to cut current costs rather than to reposition themselves to produce competitive products. That is, they closed manufacturing plants, terminated experienced workers, and offshored production to low-wage areas of the world simply to increase profits, often at the expense of the companies' long-term competitive capabilities and without regard for displaced employees' long years of service. As this new approach to corporate resource allocation became embedded in the new structure of U.S. employment, business corporations failed to invest in new, higher-value-added capabilities on a scale sufficient to create middle-class employment opportunities that could provide a new foundation for equitable and stable growth in the U.S. economy.

On the contrary, from the mid-1980s, with superior corporate performance defined as meeting Wall Street's expectations for ever-higher quarterly earnings per share, corporations turned to massive stock repurchases to "manage" their own stock prices. Trillions of dollars that could have been spent on innovation and job creation in the U.S. economy over the past three decades have instead been used to buy back stock for the purpose of manipulating stock prices. Legitimizing this financialized mode of corporate resource allocation has been the ideology, itself a product of the 1980s and 1990s, that a business corporation should be run to "maximize shareholder value."[5] Through their stock-based compensation in the forms of stock options and stock awards, corporate executives who make these decisions are themselves prime beneficiaries of this focus on rising stock prices as the sole measure of corporate performance.

As a result of these three major transformations in employment relations, the paucity of well-paid and stable employment opportunities in the U.S.

economy is largely structural. But the structural problem is not, as some economists have argued, a labor-market mismatch between the skills that prospective employers want and the skills that potential workers have.[6] If major employers need and want a match, they can train, and then through pay incentives retain, employees. That, in fact, was the primary reason why U.S. business corporations adopted the norm of a career with one company under the Old Economy model and why, from the 1940s through most of the 1970s, the real incomes of corporate employees, both blue collar and white collar, kept pace with productivity growth. For innovative companies, the match between what employers demand and what employees can supply is made in the workplace, not on the labor market.

Nor is the problem automation, a common refrain of economists who view "skill-biased technical change" (SBTC) as the most plausible explanation for the disappearance of good jobs for members of the U.S. labor force who have only a high-school education.[7] As I shall elaborate in the conclusion to this chapter, SBTC focuses on labor-market supply and demand to determine employment outcomes. But, especially where the adoption of new technologies is involved, employment outcomes in terms of pay and promotion are determined within the employing organizations, not in labor markets. In the United States, the roots of the employment problem are systemic changes in employment relations related to rationalization, marketization, and globalization. The concomitant "financialization" of the resource-allocation decisions of U.S. business corporations has deepened the job-destroying impacts of rationalization, marketization, and globalization.

Given the dramatic changes in technology, markets, and competition that have occurred in the world economy since the 1970s, it would be foolish to think that the types of employment relations that most members of the U.S. labor force (especially white males) experienced in the three decades or so after World War II could have been sustained without substantial changes in conditions of work and pay. Nevertheless, as previously existing middle-class jobs disappeared, U.S. business corporations could have used their substantial profits to invest in new rounds of innovation to create the new high-value-added jobs that a prosperous economy requires. As even the proponents of SBTC recognize, technological change can create high-skill jobs even as it may be eliminating low-skill jobs.[8]

The fundamental problem is the obsessive focus of the top executives of U.S. corporations on their companies' stock prices. While the old structures of stable and remunerative employment were being undermined by rationalization, marketization, and globalization, U.S. business corporations became afflicted with a socioeconomic disease known as financialization. The prime manifestations of financialization have been, and remain, the distribution of corporate cash to shareholders through stock repurchases, often in addition to generous cash dividends, and, incentivizing these distributions, the stock-based explosion of the remuneration of top corporate executives.

In the following section, "The Disappearance of Middle-Class Jobs," I review evidence on the fundamental structural changes related to rationalization, marketization, and globalization that, since the early 1980s, have eroded U.S. middle-class employment opportunities. In the section titled "Financialization of the U.S. Business Corporation," I analyze the emergence of stock buybacks as a massive and systemic way in which corporate executives seek to boost their companies' stock prices. In that section, I identify how, in many different ways and in many different industries, this financialized mode of corporate resource allocation has undermined the prosperity of the U.S. economy. Then, in "Maximizing Executive Compensation," I show how this financialized behavior, justified by the ideology that companies should be run to "maximize shareholder value," boosts the remuneration of top corporate executives, providing a major explanation for the increasing concentration of income among the top 0.1% of U.S. households.

Finally, in "Exploding Executive Pay, Eroding American Prosperity," which is based on the evidence and arguments presented in this chapter, I focus on the ill-conceived SBTC approach to understanding the creation and destruction of employment opportunities in the U.S. economy. I also argue that Thomas Piketty, who has done a great service in documenting the concentration of income at the top, misnamed his recent best-selling book, *Capital in the Twenty-First Century*.[9] By Piketty's own analysis of the sources of the incomes of the top 0.1% in the United States over the past three decades, his book should have been called *Labor in the Twenty-First Century*. The analysis of the relation between the concentration of income at the top and the disappearance of middle-class jobs that I present here should make clear why I have chosen to give that title to this chapter.

THE DISAPPEARANCE OF MIDDLE-CLASS JOBS
Rationalization

During the post–World War II decades, for both blue-collar and white-collar workers, the norm in large, established U.S. business corporations was career employment with one company.[10] When layoffs occurred, they tended to be temporary and, in unionized workplaces, on a last-hired, first-fired basis. Supported by a highly progressive income tax system, countercyclical government fiscal policy sought to reduce the severity of business fluctuations while employment generated by ongoing government spending, particularly on higher education, health care, advanced technology, and physical infrastructure (for example, the interstate highway system), complemented the employment opportunities provided by the business sector. The result from the late 1940s to the beginning of the 1970s was relatively equitable and stable economic growth, especially for households headed by white males.

From the late 1970s, however, in industries that had been central to U.S. innovation, employment, and growth, U.S. corporations faced formidable Japanese competition.[11] The Japanese challenge came in industries such as automobiles, consumer electronics, machine tools, steel, and microelectronics in which the United States was a world leader. The critical source of Japan's competitive advantage over the United States was "organizational integration": through the hierarchical integration of shop-floor workers and the functional integration of technical specialists into processes of organizational learning, the Japanese perfected, and outcompeted, the U.S. "Old Economy" business model.[12]

As I have shown in my book *Sustainable Prosperity in the New Economy?*, the Old Economy business model had provided a large measure of stable and equitable growth to both blue-collar and white-collar male workers in the United States in the post–World War II decades. Yet, even though unionized blue-collar workers had a high degree of job security in this era, they had historically been excluded from the processes of organizational learning within the corporation, reflecting a uniquely American hierarchical segmentation between "management" and "labor."[13] In the face of Japanese competition, this exclusion of shop-floor workers from the processes of organizational learning proved to be the Achilles heel of U.S. manufacturing.

An institutional pillar of Japan's economic development in the last half of the 20th century was permanent salaried employment for male workers at both the blue-collar and white-collar levels.[14] The prime source of Japanese competitive advantage was the extension of organizational learning—which is the essence of innovative enterprise—from the managerial structure populated by college-educated professional, technical, and administrative employees to shop-floor production workers, almost all with high-school educations, so that both groups working together could contribute to productivity improvements. Complementing this hierarchical integration of the learning of white-collar and blue-collar workers was the collaboration of Japanese technical specialists in solving productivity problems in manufacturing. The functional integration of their skills and efforts contrasted with the relatively high degree of functional segmentation of technical specialists in the United States.[15] In sum, it was a more hierarchically and functionally integrated system of organizational learning that from the 1970s enabled Japanese manufacturers to outcompete U.S. manufacturers in a range of industries in which U.S. companies had previously been world leaders.

The particular impact of Japanese competition varied markedly across U.S. industries. It virtually wiped out the U.S.-based consumer electronics industry. For example, in 1981, RCA, with 119,000 employees, was one of the leading consumer electronics companies in the world and the 44th largest U.S. industrial company by revenues.[16] By 1986, General Electric had taken over RCA and had sold it off in pieces. During the 1980s, U.S. automobile manufacturers attempted to learn from the Japanese, but three decades later, the U.S. companies were still producing lower-quality, higher-cost cars and, not surprisingly, had lost significant market share.[17] In the machine-tool industry, the overwhelming success of the Japanese against the major U.S. companies was followed in the 1990s by the emergence of export-oriented, small- and medium-size enterprises producing for specialized niche markets.[18] In the steel industry, the innovative response of the United States was the emergence of mini-mills, using electric arc furnaces and scrap metal, as distinct from the traditional vertically integrated mills that converted iron ore into crude steel before making finished products. In the 1980s, the mini-mills had the technological capability to manufacture only long products such as bars and rails, but the introduction of compact strip-production technology, led by Nucor in 1989, enabled the mini-mills to compete with integrated mills in flat products such as plates and sheets as well.[19]

The most perilous, but ultimately successful, U.S. response to Japanese competition was in the semiconductor industry. By the middle of the 1980s, the Japanese had used their integrated skill bases to lower defects and raise yields in the production of memory integrated circuits, transforming one of the most revolutionary technologies in history into mass-produced goods known as "commodity chips." This development forced major U.S. semiconductor companies to retreat from the memory segment of the market, with Intel, a key U.S. chip company, facing the possibility of bankruptcy in the process.[20] Since 1981, however, Intel had been producing microprocessors for the IBM PC and its clones, and on this basis emerged by the beginning of the 1990s as the world's leading chip manufacturer. More generally, during the 1980s, as the Japanese (and then the South Koreans) were taking over the memory chip market, U.S. companies became world leaders in the production of logic integrated circuits, where value was added through chip design rather than manufacturing yield, the area in which the Japanese now excelled. Indeed, relying on the Intel microprocessor and the Microsoft operating system, the rapid emergence of the IBM PC as the industry "open systems"—or "Wintel"—standard in the years after its launch in 1981 was the basis for the rise of a "New Economy business model" with rationalization, marketization, and globalization of employment relations in its DNA.[21]

The adverse impact on U.S. employment of Japanese competition in consumer electronics, automobiles, steel, and machine tools became particularly harsh in the double-dip recession of 1980 through 1982 when large numbers of blue-collar jobs permanently disappeared from U.S. industry.[22] Previously, in a more stable competitive environment, U.S. manufacturing companies would lay off workers with the least seniority in a downturn and re-employ them when economic conditions improved. In the 1980s, however, it became commonplace for companies to shutter whole plants.[23] From 1980 through 1985, employment in the U.S. economy increased from 104.5 million to 107.2 million workers, or by 2.6%. But employment of operators, fabricators, and laborers fell from 20 million to 16.8 million, a decline of 15.9%.[24]

As Daniel Hamermesh observed, "each year during the eighties, plant closings in the U.S. displaced roughly one-half million workers with three-plus years on the job."[25] Over the course of the 1980s, the stock market came to react favorably to permanent downsizings of the blue-collar labor force.[26] As secure middle-class jobs for high-school-educated blue-collar workers permanently disappeared, there was no commitment on the part of those who managed U.S. industrial corporations, or the Republican administrations that ruled in the 1980s, to invest in the new capabilities and opportunities required to upgrade the quality, and expand the quantity, of well-paid employment opportunities in the United States on a scale sufficient to reestablish conditions of prosperity for these displaced members of the labor force.

Among blue-collar workers, blacks were extremely hard hit by the rationalization of employment in the 1980s. They were overrepresented in the declining mass-production sectors of the Old Economy, such as steel, autos, and consumer electronics, and underrepresented in the rising sectors of the New Economy related to the microelectronics revolution. Besides losing jobs when plants were closed, many blacks had recently moved into unionized jobs so that when some workers in an establishment were laid off, blacks, who were more likely to have been the last hired, were the first fired.[27] The disappearance of these middle-class jobs had devastating impacts on the abilities and incentives of blacks to accumulate the education and experience required to position themselves for the types of well-paid and stable employment opportunities that remained.[28]

In retrospect, we now know that the recoveries that followed the recessions of 1990–1991, 2001, and 2007–2009 were "jobless": macroeconomic growth was not accompanied by job growth. Technically, the recovery from the recessionary conditions of 1980–1982 was not "jobless" because employment opportunities created by the microelectronics boom in the first half of the 1980s offset the joblessness that remained in the traditional manufacturing sector as the U.S. economy began to grow. For example, from 1980 through 1985, employment of mathematical and computer engineers increased from 330,000 to 571,000, or by 73%, and employment of computer programmers increased from 318,000 to 534,000, or by 67.9%.[29] In the expansion of 1983–1985, however, workers in traditional manufacturing industries, who typically held only high-school diplomas, experienced the first of four jobless recoveries of the past three decades.

Marketization

As for the New Economy, the recovery from the recession of 1980–1982 saw the emergence of the Wintel architecture around the IBM PC.[30] In 1982, IBM's PC sales were $500 million. Just two years later, sales had soared to 11 times that amount—more than triple the 1984 revenues of Apple, its nearest competitor, and about equal to the revenues of IBM's top eight rivals. Subsequently, the very success of the IBM PC, combined with open access to the Microsoft operating system and the Intel microprocessor, meant that, in the last half of the 1980s and beyond, IBM lost market share to lower-priced PC clones produced by New Economy companies such as Compaq, Gateway, and Dell.[31] Competition based on open systems had become the norm.[32]

With the microelectronics revolution of the 1980s, New Economy companies in the information and communication technology (ICT) industries found themselves in competition for professional, technical, and administrative labor with Old Economy ICT companies such as Hewlett-Packard, IBM, Motorola, Texas Instruments, and Xerox that in the 1980s still offered employees the realistic prospect of a career with one company.[33] As young firms facing a highly uncertain future, New Economy companies could not attract labor away from Old Economy companies by promises of career employment. Instead, the New Economy start-ups used the inducement of employee stock options to attract and retain employees—very high proportions of whom were college educated. As the successful New Economy companies grew large, most, if not all, employees were partially compensated in stock options. For example, Cisco Systems had 250 employees in 1990, the year in which it became publicly traded. After it had come to dominate the Internet router market a decade later, it had over 34,000 employees, virtually all of whom received stock options as part of their compensation.[34]

So that stock options would perform a retention function as well as an attraction function, the practice evolved in New Economy firms of making option grants annually, with 25% of an annual block of option grants vesting at the end of each of the first four years after the grant date. Once the options are vested, they can typically be exercised for a period of ten years from the grant date, so long as the employee remains with the company.

Without creating the Old Economy expectation among employees of life-long careers with the company, the perpetual pipeline of unvested options functions as a tangible retention mechanism. Indeed, for most employees, the amount of options that an individual can expect to receive is tied to his or her position in the firm's hierarchical and functional division of labor so that the retention function of stock options is integrally related to the employee's career progress within the particular company.[35]

Nevertheless, it is important to recognize that the original labor-market function of broad-based employee stock-option programs from the early 1980s was to induce high-tech personnel to leave secure employment in established Old Economy corporations for insecure employment in New Economy start-ups. When New Economy companies such as Dell, Microsoft, and Cisco grew to be large, the Old Economy norm of a career with one company did not reappear. Rather, during the 1990s, the norm of a career with one company disappeared at Old Economy corporations as well.[36]

Old Economy companies such as IBM, Hewlett-Packard, and Motorola had valued career employees because of their organizational experience in developing and utilizing the company's proprietary technologies. At many of the leading companies, the corporate research lab was the main source of this intellectual property. Investment in new products and processes was often done under military contracts, with the adaptation of the technologies to commercial production occurring as process technologies improved and unit costs fell through achieving economies of scale. Old Economy companies passed on some of their productivity gains to their employees in the forms of higher wages and employment security, thus underpinning higher standards of living in the economy as a whole. In short, the Old Economy norm of a career with one company provided the foundation for relatively stable and equitable economic growth in the post–World War II decades.[37]

The recession and recovery of the early 1990s witnessed the marketization of the employment relation and marked the beginning of the end of the career-with-one-company norm, as, in effect, long-established companies made the transition from the Old Economy business model to the New Economy business model. Although in absolute terms, blue-collar workers suffered more unemployment than white-collar workers did during the recession of the early 1990s, the extent to which professional, technical, and administrative employees were terminated was unprecedented in the post–World War II decades. Hence, the downturn of 1990–1991 became known as the white-collar recession.[38] Increasingly over the course of the 1990s, including during the Internet boom in the second half of the decade, the career-long employment security that people in their 40s and 50s had come to expect under the Old Economy business model vanished as employers replaced more-expensive older workers with less-expensive younger workers.[39]

Given its size, reputation, and central position in ICT industries, the dramatic changes at IBM in the early 1990s marked a fundamental juncture in the transition from employment security to employment insecurity in the U.S. corporate economy. Through the 1980s, IBM touted its practice of "lifelong employment" as a source of its competitive success.[40] From 1990 through 1994, however, IBM cut employment from 373,816 to 219,839; this net reduction of 154,000 jobs dropped its labor force to only 59% of its year-end 1990 level.[41] During this period, much of IBM's downsizing was accomplished by making it attractive for its employees to accept voluntary severance packages, including early retirement at age 55. But in 1993 and 1994, after the recruitment from RJR Nabisco of Louis V. Gerstner, Jr. as IBM's CEO, many thousands of IBM employees were fired outright. In 1995, IBM rescinded the early-retirement offer that had helped downsize its labor force. The offer had accomplished its purpose, and, in any case, IBM no longer wanted to encourage all employees to remain with the company even until the age of 55.

Of IBM's losses of $15.9 billion from 1991 through 1993 (including an $8.1 billion deficit in 1993, the largest annual loss in U.S. corporate history to that time), 86% came from workforce-related restructuring charges, including the cost of employee separations and relocations. This loss was, in effect, the cost to the company of ridding itself of its once-hallowed tradition of lifelong employment. Ignoring restructuring charges, IBM recorded positive net incomes before taxes of $939 million in 1991, $2.619 billion in 1992, and $148 million in 1993. Although IBM continued to downsize at a torrid pace in 1994, most of the layoffs were done outside the United States and without voluntary severance provisions. During 1994, the company booked no restructuring charges and had after-tax profits of $3.021 billion. By that time, lifelong employment at IBM was a thing of the past.

In line with the IBM transition, John Abowd and his co-authors found a general shift in U.S. employment from older experienced workers to younger skilled workers from 1992 through 1997 as companies adopted computer technologies.[42] Using Current Population Survey data, Charles Schultze discovered that "middle-aged and older men, for whatever reason, are not staying as long with their employers as they once did."[43] He went on to show, moreover, that the job displacement rate for white-collar workers relative to blue-collar workers had risen substantially in the 1980s and 1990s, starting at 33% in 1981–1982 and increasing to about 80% in the 1990s. As Lori Kletzer wrote in a 1998 survey article on "job displacement":

Job loss rates fell steadily from the 1981–83 rate, which encompassed the recession of 1981–82, through the expansion period of 1983–89. Job loss rates then rose again in 1989–91 as the economy weakened. The latest job loss figures are surprising. In the midst of a sustained (if uneven) expansion, 1993–95 job loss rates are the highest of the 14-year period: about 15 percent of U.S. workers were displaced from a job at some time during this three-year period. These high rates of job loss are consistent with public perceptions of rising job insecurity.[44]

In a survey of changes in job security from 1973 through 2008, Henry Farber stated that "there is ample evidence that long-term employment [with one company] is on the decline in the United States."[45] Using Current Population Survey data, Farber found that

mean tenure for males employed in the private sector has declined substantially, particularly for older workers. For example, mean tenure for private sector males at age fifty declined from 13.5 years in the 1973 to 1983 period to 11.3 years in the 1996 to 2008 period. The pattern in the public sector is the opposite. For example, mean tenure for public sector males at age fifty increased from 13.6 years in the 1973 to 1983 period to 15.8 years in the 1996 to 2008 period.[46]

Moreover, it appears that education as a guarantor of employment security weakened significantly from the early 1980s through the late 2000s. Using Displaced Worker Survey data to analyze rates of job loss, Farber found that

in 1981 to 1983, the private-sector three-year job loss rate was 16 percent for high school graduates and 9.4 percent for college graduates. By 2001 to 2003 (also a period of weak labor markets), the gap had fallen to virtually zero, with a private-sector three-year job loss rate of 10.7 percent for high school graduates and 11 percent for college graduates. Interestingly, the education gap in job loss rates increased in the 2005 to 2007 period with 8.3 and 10.0 percent job loss rates for high school and college graduates, respectively.[47]

Globalization

In the 2000s, globalization joined rationalization and marketization as a source of structural change in U.S. employment relations. In the ICT industries that were central to the growth of the U.S. economy in the 1980s and 1990s, the globalization of employment dated back to the 1960s, when U.S. semiconductor manufacturers had set up assembly and testing facilities in East Asia, making use of low-paid but literate female labor.[48] Over time, a combination of work experience with multinational and indigenous companies, as well as the return of nationals who had acquired graduate education and work experience abroad, enhanced the capability of the Asian labor force to engage in higher-value-added activities.

By the beginning of the 2000s, Indians had become world leaders in the offshore provision of IT services, while the Chinese had become adept in a wide range of manufacturing industries, especially in ICT. China and India inserted themselves into the global value chains that became an organizational characteristic of the New Economy business model. In the 2000s, the availability of capable, college-educated labor supplies in developing economies, along with high-quality, low-cost communications networks, enabled a vast acceleration of the movement of jobs by U.S. companies to China and India.[49] In both countries, indigenous and foreign-owned high-tech companies were by the 2000s well positioned to move rapidly up the global value chains.

Offshoring depressed U.S. employment in the recession of 2001 and in the subsequent jobless recovery that stretched into 2003. As U.S.-based companies hired workers abroad, well-educated high-tech workers in the United States found themselves vulnerable to displacement.[50] Given huge increases in the issuance of nonimmigrant (H-1B and L-1) work visas in the United States in the late 1990s and early 2000s, there were hundreds of thousands of high-tech workers, especially Indians, who had accumulated U.S. work experience that they could now take back home.[51] In February 2003, after more than a year of jobless recovery, *BusinessWeek* gained considerable attention when its cover blared the rhetorical question: "Is Your Job Next?"[52] The subtitle read: "A new round of globalization is sending upscale jobs offshore. They include chip design, engineering, basic research—even financial analysis. Can America lose these jobs and still prosper?"

For three decades now, the U.S. economy has been losing unionized blue-collar jobs. As it turns out, Democratic administrations have been no better than Republican administrations in stanching the decline.[53] In 2014, the U.S. rate of business sector unionization was 6.6%, having declined steadily from over 15% in 1983.[54] Since the early 1990s, non-unionized white-collar workers, including professional, technical, and administrative employees who are deemed to be members of management, have found that they can no longer expect that they will have a career with one company. The shift to open-systems technologies and the globalization of high-tech jobs have rendered highly educated and highly experienced members of the U.S. labor force vulnerable to loss of career employment. Meanwhile, since 1960, through a tax policy that exempts U.S. companies from paying corporate taxes on their foreign profits until those profits are repatriated to the United States, the U.S. government has given U.S. companies an incentive to make profits abroad and keep them there. The Obama administration has promised to get rid of this tax loophole, but, even before the Republicans took control of the House of Representatives in November 2010, the president caved in the presence of vociferous opposition from high-tech executives.[55]

It should be emphasized once again that the displacement of workers from middle-class jobs has often had a productive rationale: manufacturing plants may become uncompetitive; recently educated workers may possess more relevant skills than experienced (older) workers; and the productive capabilities of workers in low-wage areas of the world may be on a par with, if not superior to, those of workers in the United States. Nevertheless, once changes in the structure of employment have become widespread for productive reasons, corporations have been known to terminate employees in order to increase short-term profits for the sake of inciting speculative increases in their companies' stock prices. As documented in the following section, under a regime of financialized corporate resource allocation, the tendency has been to allocate those extra profits to stock buybacks for the purpose of giving a company's stock price a manipulative boost.

Unlike the recessions of 1980–1982, 1990–1991, and 2001, the Great Recession of 2008–2009 was a purely financial downturn caused by speculation in, and manipulation of, securities markets by the financial sector of the economy. This speculation and manipulation exploited the fragility of home ownership in an economy that, since the 1980s, had been eliminating the stable and remunerative middle-class jobs that had made home ownership affordable. The jobless recovery that followed the Great Recession was far more prolonged than earlier ones. While Wall Street has become, and remains, a gambling casino, the more fundamental fragility of the U.S. economy emanates from the industrial sector to which the vast majority of households look for employment that can sustain middle-class living standards. In the following sections of this chapter, I shall show that, as a general rule, the executives who run U.S. industrial corporations have become focused on creating profits for the sake of higher stock prices rather than creating the high-value-added jobs that are the essence of a prosperous economy.

FINANCIALIZATION OF THE U.S. BUSINESS CORPORATION
Income Inequality
In the generally prosperous U.S. economy of the post–World War II decades, there was a movement toward more equality in the distribution

of income, as illustrated by the time series for the Gini coefficient in Figure 1. In the late 1970s, there was a reversal of this trend, followed by accelerating inequality from the early 1980s. As measured by the Gini co-efficient, income inequality increased in almost all of the countries in the Organisation for Economic Co-operation and Development (OECD) from the mid-1980s through the late 2000s. The United States, however, has had the most unequal distribution in the OECD except for Turkey and Mexico.[56]

For the post–World War II decades, the guiding principles of corporate resource allocation can be summed up as "retain-and-reinvest."[57] Business corporations retained earnings and reinvested them in productive capabilities, including the capabilities of employees who, in helping to make the enterprise more productive and competitive, benefited in the forms of higher incomes and more employment security. Retain-and-reinvest is a resource-allocation regime that supports *value creation* at the business level and implements a process of *value extraction* through which the firm shares the productivity gains with a broad base of employees.[58]

Figure 2a shows that from the late 1940s through the late 1970s, changes in real wages tracked changes in productivity in the U.S. economy. In my view, the retain-and-reinvest employment policies of major U.S. corporations largely accounted for this result.[59] The sharing of the gains of productivity growth with white-male career employees, including both union blue-collar workers with high-school educations and non-union white-collar workers with college educations, underpinned the resultant trend toward greater income equality in the United States from the late 1940s well into the 1970s, as charted by the Gini coefficient in Figure 1.

As shown in Figure 2b, however, since the late 1970s there has been a widening gap between the growth in productivity and the growth in real wages. This gap, I would argue, is largely the result of a shift of corporate resource allocation to a downsize-and-distribute regime in which corporate executives look for opportunities to downsize the labor force and distribute earnings to financial interests. Had corporate executives made different allocation decisions, a portion of the earnings that were paid out to share-holders could have been invested in, among other things, the productive capabilities of the people thrown out of work. Downsize-and-distribute is a resource-allocation regime that supports *value extraction* at the business level that may enrich financial interests at the expense of employees who contributed to the process of *value creation* that generated those earnings in the first place. As a result, a downsize-and-distribute allocation regime contributes to employment instability and income inequity.[60]

Downsizing of the existing U.S. labor force is inherent in rationalization, marketization, and globalization. As stated earlier, initially it was possible

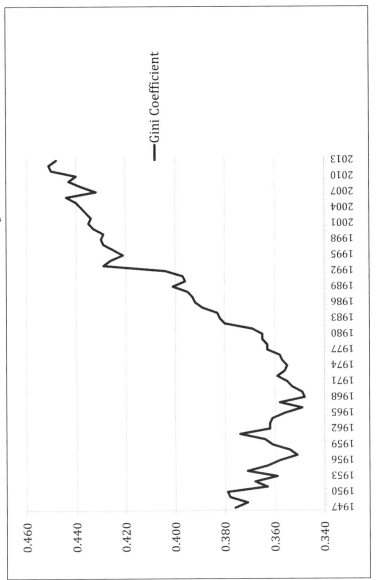

FIGURE 1

Gini Coefficient as an Indicator of Income Distribution Among All U.S. Families, 1947–2013

Source: U.S. Census Bureau, Historical Income Tables Families, Table F-4 (http://1.usa.gov/1CZ6eVN).

Note: The Gini coefficient is a widely used measure of income inequality. A Gini coefficient of 0 would mean perfect equality in the distribution of income among all families in the economy, while a coefficient of 1 would mean that one family has all the income and all of the remaining families in the economy have none. The higher the Gini coefficient, therefore, the greater the income inequality among families in the economy concerned.

FIGURE 2a
Cumulative Annual Percent Changes in Productivity
and Real Wages in the United States, 1948–1983

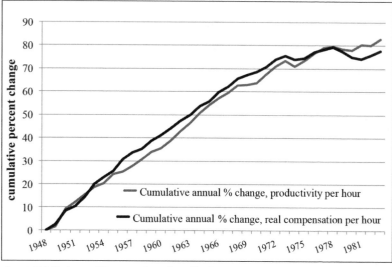

Source: U.S. Budget and Economic Data (http://bit.ly/1DaOiVI).

FIGURE 2b
Cumulative Annual Percent Changes in Productivity
and Real Wages in the United States, 1963–2012

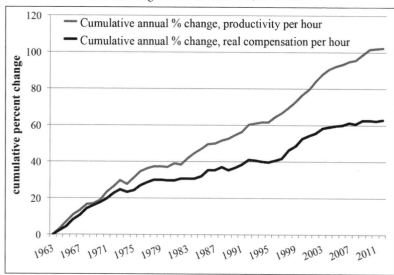

Source: U.S. Budget and Economic Data (http://bit.ly/1DaOiVI).

to justify these changes in employment relations as responses to changes in technological, market, and competitive conditions that even powerful business enterprises could not ignore. The critical issue is how the business enterprise reallocates its productive resources in the face of these changing industrial conditions. Is the corporation downsizing its labor force for the sake of reallocating the company's resources to investment in new productive capabilities, or is it engaging in downsizing just to boost its short-term profitability? And if the purpose of downsizing is the latter, what does the corporation do with the increased profits that downsizing makes possible? Do executives who make corporate decisions concerning the allocation of labor and capital use the cash flow generated by downsizing to increase payouts to shareholders? And if so, why?

Stock Buybacks

In answering these questions, it must be recognized that for a business enterprise that has made the transition from a new venture to a going concern, earnings retained out of profits provide the financial foundation for investing in the productive capabilities that it needs to generate competitive goods and services in the future. Corporate retentions can be used to invest in plant and equipment, research and development, and retraining and retaining the labor force (some but not all of which are included in R&D expenses). The higher incomes that retained workers receive can serve as both incentives for these employees to continue to supply their skills and efforts to the company and rewards for their past contributions to the company's current profitability. In addition, the taxes that corporations pay out of their profits help fund government investments in physical infrastructure and human knowledge that business enterprises are unable (or unwilling) to finance themselves.[61]

Downsize-and-distribute occurs, therefore, when the business enterprise not only downsizes its labor force but distributes the resultant cash flow to shareholders in the name of maximizing shareholder value (MSV). During the 1980s, the retain-and-reinvest mode of resource allocation that characterized the post–World War II decades came under attack from Reaganite deregulation, hostile takeovers, and corporate restructuring, all of which gained legitimacy from MSV ideology.[62] Embracing this new agenda, by the last half of the 1980s, U.S. corporate executives became focused on distributing corporate cash to shareholders through open-market stock repurchases, which had previously been infrequent and of relatively modest amounts. These large-scale stock buybacks have since been on top of cash dividends, the traditional way of paying out corporate cash to shareholders.

MSV portrays downsize-and-distribute as a mode of resource allocation that disgorges cash from inefficient companies for the sake of reinvestment in efficient ones. In fact, the disgorged cash has supported the rise of the financial sector of the economy, with the augmented value that financial interests have been able to extract increasing the amount of "capital" chasing high yields on financial markets instead of investing in the productive capabilities that can create new sources of value. Since the 1980s, stock buybacks have become integral to downsize-and-distribute, and hence a prime reason for both the erosion of stable, remunerative employment opportunities and the extreme concentration of income among the very richest households.

Dividends provide shareholders with a yield for, as the name says, holding stock. In contrast, buybacks provide shareholders with a yield for selling stock—that is, for ceasing to be shareholders. While increasing buybacks, U.S. companies have not been stingy with their dividend payouts. The ratio of dividends to net income for all U.S. corporations rose from 37% in both the 1960s and 1970s, to 46% in the 1980s, to 58% in the 1990s, and to 63% in the 2000s.[63] Meanwhile, especially for the largest and most profitable corporations on which economic prosperity relies, stock buybacks became an even larger source of cash distributions to public shareholders.

Figure 3 shows net equity issues of U.S. corporations from 1946 through 2014. Net equity issues are new corporate stock issues minus outstanding stock retired through stock repurchases and mergers and acquisitions activity. Since the mid-1980s, corporations have in aggregate funded the stock market rather than vice versa (as is conventionally assumed).[64] Over the decade 2004 through 2014, net equity issues of nonfinancial corporations averaged −$399 billion per year.[65]

That buybacks are largely responsible for negative net equity issues is clear from the chart on the evolution of gross repurchases shown in Figure 4. For the 248 companies in the S&P 500 Index in March 2014 that were publicly listed back to 1981, the buyback payout ratio—that is, repurchases as a proportion of net income—was less than 5% in 1981–1983 but 42% in 2011–2013, with a three-year peak of 68% in 2006–2008. From 1981 to 1985, 1994 to 1999, and 2003 to 2008, the proportion of net income devoted to buybacks by these 248 companies moved up sharply. In 2007, on the eve of the financial crisis, profits of these 248 companies totaled $478 billion, with 72% (or $345 billion) used for buybacks. In that year, those companies also distributed $187 billion as dividends, making the total payout ratio 110%.

In his 1999 letter to Berkshire Hathaway shareholders, Warren Buffett argued that buybacks could be beneficial to the "continuing shareholder" when done at below "intrinsic value" and when all shareholders "have been supplied all the information they need for estimating that value."[66] These types of repurchases are done as *tender offers* in which the company

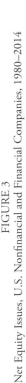
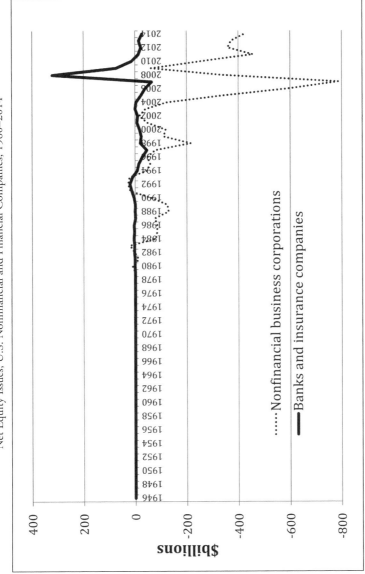

FIGURE 3

Net Equity Issues, U.S. Nonfinancial and Financial Companies, 1980–2014

Source: Board of Governors of the Federal Reserve System, Federal Reserve Statistical Release Z.1, "Financial Accounts of the United States: Flow of Funds, Balance Sheets, and Integrated Macroeconomic Accounts," Table F-213: Corporate Equities, March 12, 2015.

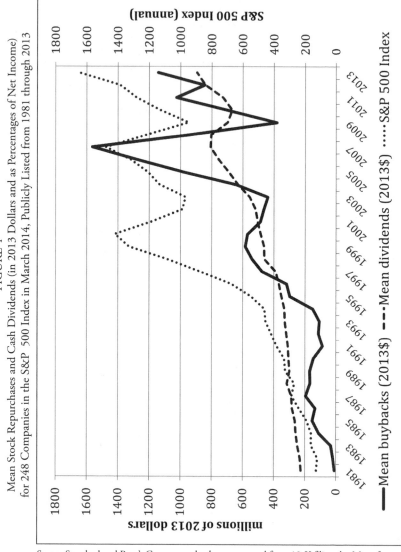

FIGURE 4
Mean Stock Repurchases and Cash Dividends (in 2013 Dollars and as Percentages of Net Income)
for 248 Companies in the S&P 500 Index in March 2014, Publicly Listed from 1981 through 2013

Source: Standard and Poor's Compustat database, corrected from 10-K filings by Mustafa Erdem Sakinç of The Academic–Industry Research Network.

announces its intention to repurchase shares at a stipulated price. The vast majority of buybacks done since the mid-1980s, however, have been open-market repurchases that are virtually unregulated: a corporation is required to inform neither public shareholders nor the Securities and Exchange Commission (SEC—the federal government agency that is supposed to regulate the stock market) of the actual days on which its top corporate executives have decided to repurchase the company's stock. Only the top executives of the repurchasing company know the timing of the buybacks, creating the possibility that they might trade for their own benefit on this valuable inside information.

SEC Sanctions Stock-Market Manipulation

On November 17, 1982, the SEC promulgated Rule 10b-18, which gives a company a safe harbor against manipulation charges in doing open-market repurchases.[67] The safe-harbor provision states that a company will not be charged with manipulation if, among other things, its buybacks on any single day amount to no more than 25% of the previous four weeks' average daily trading volume (ADTV). Under Rule 10b-18, moreover, there is no presumption of manipulation should the corporation's repurchases exceed the 25% ADTV limit.[68]

Rule 10b-18 is intended to cover only open-market repurchases, which nonetheless have been estimated to comprise as much as 90% of all buybacks, because it is in the open market that undetected stock-price manipulation can most easily occur. Private, off-market transactions such as tender offers are not regulated under the rule. In 1982, the SEC also excluded block trades (which it defined as trades at or above $200,000 in value or numbering at least 5,000 shares with a minimum value of $50,000) from the 25% ADTV calculation, apparently because in the early 1980s block trades, although done on the open market, were viewed as exceptional. In a revision of Rule 10b-18 in 2003, however, the SEC included most block trades in the 25% ADTV calculation.[69]

It has become customary for a company that wants to do open-market repurchases under the Rule 10b-18 safe harbor to announce a stock repurchase *program* that has been approved by its board of directors. But Rule 10b-18 does not require disclosure of the particular days on which top corporate executives instruct the company's broker to execute *actual buybacks*. In its lack of disclosure, its 25% safe-harbor limit, and the absence of a presumption of manipulation even when the 25% limit is exceeded, Rule 10b-18 is highly permissive of, and even encourages, stock buybacks.

In a 1984 article, "Issuer Repurchases," Lloyd H. Feller, a former associate director of the SEC's Division of Market Regulation, and Mary Chamberlin, the then-current deputy chief counsel of that division, called

Rule 10b-18 a "regulatory about-face" from previous SEC views on the detection and prevention of manipulation through open-market repurchases.[70] Since the SEC's inception as a result of the Securities Exchange Act of 1934, the regulatory agency had sought to prevent stock-price manipulation by insiders and to require companies to disclose all material information to all stock-market investors. In 1955, the SEC adopted Rule 10b-6 to try to prevent an issuing company from manipulating its stock price during a *distribution* of its stock, such as during a public stock offering or an mergers and acquisitions deal, or when it had convertible bonds or warrants outstanding. In the 1960s, the "go-go years" of conglomeration and takeovers,[71] the SEC sought to extend this anti-manipulative regulation to open-market repurchases more generally, and not just when a company had a distribution in process.

The result was Rule 13e-2, which emerged out of the Williams Act of 1968 (amending the Securities Exchange Act to require disclosure of information in cash tender offers), and made its first appearance in 1969. Rule 13e-2 was proposed in 1970, 1973, and 1980 but never passed. It emphasized disclosure of full information to investors to maintain the integrity of the stock market. In sharp contrast to Rule 10b-18, which in the "regulatory about-face" was adopted in 1982, Rule 13e-2 would have put a 15% ADTV limit on open-market repurchases, required disclosure of the days on which buybacks were actually done, and presumed that a company was manipulating the market if it exceeded the 15% ADTV limit. Whereas Rule 13e-2 proposed regulation of stock-price manipulation, without by any means banning open-market repurchases, Rule 10b-18 in effect gave corporations license to use open-market repurchases to manipulate the market.[72]

This regulatory reversal resulted from the 1980 election of Ronald Reagan as U.S. president on a platform of government deregulation and his appointment in 1981 of John Shad, vice chairman of the stock brokerage firm E.F. Hutton, to head the SEC. Shad had been the first Wall Street executive to back Reagan for president and had served as head of fundraising in New York State for the Reagan campaign.[73] Not since Joseph Kennedy had been the inaugural chair of the SEC in 1934–1935 had a Wall Street executive led the agency.

A *Wall Street Journal* article on the adoption of Rule 10b-18 noted that "the new, deregulation-minded commission, with its 3–2 majority of Reagan appointees, has been revamping many SEC policies." It went on to say that Shad hoped that buybacks would help to fuel increases in stock prices and thus be beneficial to shareholders. The longest-serving SEC commissioner, John Evans, appointed by President Nixon in 1973, expressed concern that Rule 10b-18 represented deregulation of buybacks that could result in market manipulation.[74] In the end, however, Evans agreed to make the adoption of Rule 10b-18 unanimous.

The 2003 amendment to Rule 10b-18 included block trades within the 25% safe harbor because, as the SEC stated in its release, "during the late 1990s, it was reported that many companies were spending more than half their net income on massive buyback programs that were intended to boost share prices—often supporting their share price at levels far above where they would otherwise trade." The SEC went on to warn that the unregulated use of block trades in doing buybacks could exacerbate "the potential for manipulative abuse," and "mislead investors about the integrity of the securities trading market as an independent pricing mechanism."[75]

In seeking to rectify these problems, the 2003 amendment to Rule 10b-18 initiated quarterly reports on stock buybacks. But the SEC still did not require disclosure of the actual days on which buybacks were done so that it would be able to determine, without a special investigation, whether a company had in fact exceeded the 25% ADTV safe-harbor limit. And, given the escalation of buybacks after 2003, it is clear that the 2003 amendment did nothing to bring "the potential for manipulative abuse" under control. For the 248 major U.S. corporations included in Figure 4, the repurchase payout ratio for 2004 through 2007 was 56%, far higher than the 45% it had been in 1997 through 2000, a period in which the SEC had viewed buybacks as possibly contributing to market manipulation. Compared with 1997–2000, the absolute value of buybacks in inflation-adjusted dollars was 2.1 times higher in 2004–2007 and 1.4 times higher in 2010–2013.

The daily buybacks that are permissible within the 25% ADTV limit are sufficiently large to enable a company to manipulate its own stock price. Table 1 shows the top ten stock repurchasers for 2004–2013, and the proportions of net income that each company spent on buybacks and dividends over the decade. In most cases, total distributions to shareholders exceeded net income. Assuming that block trades are included in the ADTV calculations, under Rule 10b-18, Exxon Mobil, by far the biggest stock repurchaser with $217 billion in the decade 2004–2013, could have bought back up to $210 million worth of shares on (as an illustration) July 29, 2014, without fear of facing manipulation charges. That same day's safe-harbor limits for the next nine top repurchasers for 2004–2013 ranged from $76 million in buybacks for Hewlett-Packard to $369 million for Microsoft. Apple Inc., which did $22.9 billion in buybacks in fiscal year 2013 and another $45 billion in 2014 (after having largely refrained from the practice during the reign of Steve Jobs) could have done up to $1.2 billion on July 29, 2014, while still availing itself of the safe harbor.[76] Within the limits of the total value of buybacks set by a

TABLE 1
Repurchases (RP) and Dividends (DV) as Percentages of Net
Income (NI), Ten Largest Repurchasers for the Decade 2004–2013

Buyback rank	Company name	NI ($b)	RP ($b)	DV ($b)	RP/NI (%)	DV/NI (%)	(RP+DV)/ NI (%)
1	Exxon Mobil	360	217	84	60	23	84
2	IBM	126	116	26	92	21	113
3	Microsoft	160	113	77	71	48	119
4	Cisco Systems	70	72	5	103	8	110
5	Procter & Gamble	100	71	47	71	47	118
6	Hewlett-Packard	44	65	9	148	20	168
7	Walmart Stores	142	64	40	45	28	73
8	Pfizer	93	62	65	67	70	137
9	Intel	83	58	31	70	37	107
10	General Electric	162	57	87	35	54	89

Source: Standard and Poor's Compustat database, corrected from company 10-K filings by Mustafa Erdem Sakinç, The Academic–Industry Research Network.

board-authorized repurchase program, Rule 10b-18 permits open-market repurchases of these manipulative magnitudes to be repeated trading day after trading day.

Over the decade 2004–2013, the 454 companies in the S&P 500 Index in March 2014 that were publicly listed back to 2004 expended 51% of net income, or $3.4 trillion, on stock buybacks and another 35% of net income on dividends. That left scant profits available for funding new investment in productive capabilities or passing on profits to a company's employees as increased remuneration. And with much of the retained profits held abroad (avoiding, as we have seen, U.S. corporate taxes), many companies have borrowed to do buybacks.[77] Substantial research carried out under my direction by The Academic–Industry Research Network and the University of Massachusetts Lowell Center for Industrial Competitiveness has revealed the economic damage at the industry and company levels caused by these distributions to shareholders.

The Economic Damage That Buybacks Can Do

When, as shown in Table 1 for the ten largest repurchasers in 2004–2013, those who exercise strategic control over resource allocation in the nation's major corporations distribute most, all, or even more of their companies' earnings to shareholders, we have to question what innovative investment opportunities they are failing to fund. Given the importance of these companies in the industries in which they operate, this type of financial behavior has enormous costs for economic performance at both the industry and the company levels. Considering the activities of some of the ten largest repurchasers listed in Table 1, here are three industry examples and three company examples of how stock buybacks harm the economy.

Industries

Alternative Energy. Exxon Mobil spends about $21 billion a year on buybacks while receiving U.S. government tax breaks of $600 million annually for oil exploration.[78] It spends virtually no money on alternative-energy research. Meanwhile, other companies that want alternative energy expect the U.S. government to fill the gap. The American Energy Innovation Council (AEIC), an association of six corporate executives and a venture capitalist, has lobbied the U.S. government to triple its investment in alternative-energy research and subsidies to $16 billion per year.[79] Yet just two of the AEIC companies, Microsoft and General Electric, have spent about that amount annually on buybacks over the past decade. AEIC corporate executives want the U.S. taxpayer to fund investment in the development of alternative energy while the companies that they head waste billions of dollars of corporate profits manipulating their stock prices.

Nanotechnology. Intel executives have long lobbied the U.S. government to increase spending on nanotechnology research, arguing as its then-CEO Craig R. Barrett did in 2005 that "it will take a massive, coordinated U.S. research effort involving academia, industry, and state and federal governments to ensure that America continues to be the world leader in information technology."[80] Yet from 2001, when the U.S. government launched the National Nanotechnology Initiative (NNI), through 2013, Intel's expenditures on buybacks were almost four times the total NNI budget. Given how much a company such as Intel has benefited from decades of government investment in microelectronics and related fields, one might expect that Intel would use its cash flow to play a major role in the "massive, coordinated effort" of which Barrett spoke rather than squander billions of dollars manipulating its stock price.

Pharmaceutical Drugs. In response to complaints voiced in Congress and elsewhere that the prices of drugs in the United States are at least twice those in any other country, Pfizer and other U.S. pharmaceutical companies have made the argument that the profits from these high prices permit more R&D to be done in the United States than in other nations.[81] Yet in 2004–2013, the equivalent of 60% of Pfizer's profits went to buybacks, along with 63% distributed as dividends. In reality, Americans pay high drug prices so that major pharmaceutical companies can boost their stock prices. Congress should be aware of these facts and regulate pharmaceutical drug prices of companies that throw away their profits doing buybacks.

Companies

International Business Machines (IBM). In the post–World War II decades through the 1980s, IBM had a "lifelong employment" policy that exemplified the employment norm of a career-with-one-company characteristic of most established Old Economy companies.[82] Yet, as mentioned previously, from 1990 to 1994 IBM's worldwide employment dropped from 374,000 to 220,000. By 1994, IBM's top executives had deliberately obliterated the system of lifelong employment. From the mid-1990s, focusing on software and services and shedding most of its manufacturing capacity, IBM led the U.S. offshoring movement. By 2008, the company employed 398,000 people, but only 30% of them were in the United States, down from 52% in 1996. In 2011, with its operating earnings per share (EPS) at $13.44, IBM announced its "2015 EPS Road Map," the objective of which is to reach at least $20 EPS by the end of 2015.[83] Along with revenue growth and operating leverage, IBM cited stock repurchases as a driver in achieving its EPS objective. One way in which IBM has been increasing "operating leverage," and hence raising EPS, has been through layoffs of U.S. employees. Another way is through stock buybacks.[84] From 2010 to 2014, IBM did $70 billion in buybacks, equal to 92% of net income, including $13.7 billion (114% of net income) in 2014, as it reduced its worldwide employment by 51,620, or 12% of its labor force at the end of 2013. Apparently, the company had not been downsizing and distributing hard enough. In October 2014 IBM announced that it was abandoning the 2015 EPS Road Map.[85]

Hewlett-Packard (HP). As described by founder David Packard in his 1995 book, *The HP Way*, HP, like IBM, provided stable careers and equitable pay to its employees as a foundation for continuous innovation.[86] But in 1999, it spun off its engineering division as Agilent and then did away with employment security, becoming known as a "hire-and-fire" company that engaged in "employee churn."[87] From 2004 to 2011, HP did $61.4 billion in buybacks, equal to 120% of its net income, along with distributing $6.8 billion in dividends. Unlike IBM, however, HP largely failed in its attempt to shift from selling hardware to selling high-margin software and services.[88] In both 2013 and 2014, HP had declining revenues as its services business floundered, but the company restored its profitability by cutting its labor force from 349,600 on October 31, 2011, to 302,000 on October 31, 2014. With another 14,000 layoffs envisioned for fiscal 2015, HP announced its intention to split in two, with one company producing printers and other computer hardware, and the other company providing computer-related services.[89] Meanwhile, even with this restructuring in process, this "downsize-and-distribute" company could not kick the buyback habit. As it incurred huge losses in 2012, HP distributed $1.6 billion in buybacks and $1 billion in dividends. In 2013–2014, HP disgorged 65% of net earnings to shareholders, of which $4.3 billion were buybacks and $2.3 billion dividends.

Cisco Systems. In the 1990s, Cisco Systems, founded in Silicon Valley, was the fastest-growing company in the world as it captured more than 70% of the global Internet router market. Using its stock as an acquisition currency, from 1993 through 2000, Cisco did 71 acquisitions for over $35 billion, of which 98% was paid in its shares. In March 2000, Cisco had the highest market capitalization in the world, but by September 2001, despite increased revenues, Cisco's stock price had fallen to just 14% of its peak value.[90] At that point, Cisco started buying back its stock and, from 2002 through 2014, expended $89.3 billion on buybacks, equal to 108% of its net income. In the process, Cisco has eschewed investment in sophisticated communication technologies, despite the fact that it was well positioned to make such investments at the beginning of the 2000s. Many of Cisco's new products have quickly become commodities, and, in recent years, the company has engaged in rounds of large-scale layoffs to sustain its buyback habit. Among its global competitors, the company that has made the high-end investments in communication technology that Cisco has ignored is Huawei Technologies, an employee-owned Chinese company founded in 1988 that is now challenging Sweden's Ericsson—another company that does not do buybacks—for top spot in the global communication-equipment industry.[91]

MAXIMIZING EXECUTIVE COMPENSATION
Stock-Based Pay
In its release on the amendment to Rule 10b-18 in 2003, the SEC articulated clearly why it needs to get rid of Rule 10b-18. "In summary," wrote the SEC, "Rule 10b-18 is intended to protect issuer repurchases from manipulation charges when the issuer has no special incentive to interfere with the ordinary forces of supply and demand affecting its stock price. Therefore, it is not appropriate for the safe harbor to be available when the issuer has a heightened incentive to manipulate its share price."[92]

Yet the stock-based pay of the executives who decide to do repurchases on any given day provides the issuer with "a heightened incentive to manipulate its share price." As shown in Table 2, from 2006 through 2013, the 500 highest-paid corporate executives named on proxy statements received from 66% to 84% of their total remuneration in stock-based pay—mainly in the form of gains from exercising stock options before the financial crisis but since then increasingly in the form of stock awards that require that the company hit stock-performance targets such as quarterly EPS. In 2012 and 2013, the average total compensation of the 500 highest-

TABLE 2

Mean Total Direct Compensation of the 500 Highest-Paid
Executives Named in U.S. Corporate Proxy Statements, and
the Components of Total Direct Compensation, 2006–2013

Year	Mean total direct comp. (million $)	Percentage shares of components of total direct compensation						
		Salary	Bonus	Non-equity incentive plan	All other comp.	Deferred earnings	Realized stock option gains	Realized stock award gains
2006	27.4	3.3	7.0	7.6	5.9	0.5	58.9	16.8
2007	30.0	3.0	4.1	6.9	7.6	0.1	58.8	19.6
2008	22.9	4.1	4.2	8.7	4.1	0.1	43.9	34.9
2009	14.4	7.0	4.8	14.9	7.4	0.1	39.9	25.9
2010	18.5	5.5	4.8	15.0	6.2	0.1	40.3	28.1
2011	19.4	5.5	3.8	12.3	4.3	0.2	40.9	33.0
2012	30.3	3.6	2.7	8.2	3.2	0.1	41.5	40.7
2013	32.2	3.3	1.9	7.6	3.5	0.1	55.4	28.2

Source: Standard and Poor's ExecuComp database, with calculations by Matt Hopkins, The Academic–Industry Research Network.

paid executives was in real terms about three times the level of executive pay that had prevailed in the early 1990s, when executive compensation was already viewed as excessive.[93]

Given the fact that in the United States companies are not required to announce the dates on which they actually do open-market repurchases, there is an opportunity for top executives to do buybacks to benefit themselves. Buybacks can enable companies to hit quarterly EPS targets, with the manipulation invisible to the public. The manipulation of EPS can make executives look good to Wall Street, in some cases offsetting EPS declines that reflect "bad news."[94] And it can also directly pad their pay, as is often the case with stock awards that are contingent on EPS performance.[95]

Moreover, top executives who are privy to the company's repurchasing activity can use this inside information (finding ways to evade or abuse SEC Rule 10b5–1 enacted in 2000 to control such insider trading) to time their option exercises and stock sales to increase their pay. Indeed, in 1991 the SEC made it easier for top executives to do just that. Until 1991, Section 16(b) of the 1934 Securities Exchange Act prevented top executives from reaping short-swing profits when they exercised their stock options by requiring that they wait at least six months before selling the acquired shares. In 1991, by arguing that a stock option is a derivative, the SEC determined that henceforth the six-month waiting period would begin at the grant date, not the exercise date. Since the option grant date is always at least one year before the option exercise date, this reinterpretation of Section 16(b) means that top executives, as company insiders, can sell the shares acquired from stock options immediately upon exercise and keep the short-swing gains.

With this reinterpretation pending in 1989, a Towers Perrin consultant told the *New York Times* that the change was "great news for executives because they give insiders much more flexibility in buying and selling stock." The same article noted that the proposed change to Section 16(b) "would provide a dual benefit. Since corporate insiders could immediately sell the stock, they could qualify for loans from brokers that would enable them to exercise stock options without laying out their own cash. They would also no longer face the risk that the shares might decline in value during the holding period."[96] After the Section 16(b) reinterpretation went into effect in May 1991, a compensation consultant was quoted as saying that senior executives "now have an opportunity of making a decision of when to get in and out at the most propitious time."[97]

Do top executives actually trade on this inside information? We do not know because the SEC does not require that, even after the fact, companies disclose the days on which they have done open-market repurchases. What we do know is that stock-based pay creates a strong incentive for corporate executives to orient themselves toward downsize-and-distribute rather than retain-and-reinvest. And, since the 1980s, downsize-and-distribute has been the clear-cut winner in the corporate resource-allocation game.

Corporate Executives in the Top 0.1%

We also know that stock-based pay has enabled corporate executives to become the most populous members of the top 0.1% in the U.S. income distribution. Figure 5 displays data for 1916 to 2011 on the income shares of the top 0.1% of U.S. households, collected from tax returns. As can be seen, the biggest component of executive pay over the past quarter century has been salaries, supplemented by spikes in capital gains at the peaks of stock-market booms such as in 2000 and 2007. Note, however, that the salary data include substantial stock-based pay, which is not reported as such in tax returns.[98] Indeed, as we have seen from the ExecuComp data in Table 2, as components of total executive compensation, gains from stock options and stock awards dwarf not only salaries but also bonuses.

We can use the ExecuComp database to get an initial idea of the representation of high-paid corporate executives among the top 0.1% of households in the income distribution. In 2012, the threshold income (excluding capital gains) for inclusion in the top 0.1% of the income distribution was $1,549,616.[99] From the ExecuComp proxy statement data on "named" top executives, in 2012, 4,627 executives had total compensation

FIGURE 5

Share of Total U.S. Incomes of the Top 0.1% of Households in
the U.S. Income Distribution and Its Components, 1916–2011

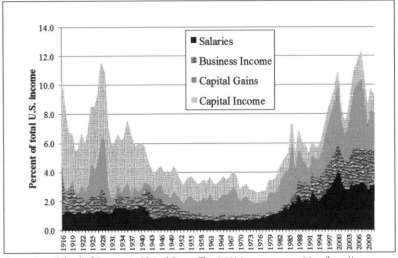

Source: Paris School of Economics United States, Top 0.1% income composition (http://
bit.ly/1K6RINX).

Note: Salaries include compensation from the realized gains on exercising stock options
and the vesting of stock awards.

greater than this threshold amount, with a mean income of $6,824,000,
of which 31% was gains from exercising stock options and 37% gains
from vesting of stock awards.

The number of corporate executives who in 2012 were members of
the top 0.1% club was, however, far higher than 4,627, for two reasons.
First, total corporate compensation of the named executives does not
include other noncompensation income (from securities, property, fees
for sitting on the boards of other corporations, etc.) that would be included
in their federal tax returns. If we assume that named executives whose
corporate compensation was below the $1.55 million threshold were able
to augment that income by 25% (to pick a plausible number) from other
sources, then the number of named executives in the top 0.1% in 2012
would have been 5,398.

Second, included in the top 0.1% of the U.S. income distribution were
a potentially large, but unknown, number of U.S. corporate executives
whose pay was above the $1.55 million threshold for the top 0.1% but
who were not named in proxy statements because they were neither the
CEO nor one of the four other highest paid in their particular companies.

For example, of the highest-paid IBM executives in 2012 named in the company's proxy statement, the lowest paid had a total compensation of $9,052,761. There were presumably large numbers of other IBM executives whose total compensation was between this amount and the $1.55 million threshold for inclusion in the top 0.1%. These "unnamed" executives would have been among the top 0.1% in the income distribution.

There is another, more direct, method for gauging the representation of corporate executives among the top 0.1%. Federal tax returns include information on a filer's occupation and, through an employer identification number, the type of business sector that provides the taxpayer with his or her primary employment income. Jon Bakija, Adam Cole, and Bradley Heim accessed federal tax return data for selected years from 1979 to 2005 to analyze the occupations of federal taxpayers at the top of the U.S. income distribution. They found that "executives, managers, supervisors, and financial professionals account for about 60 percent of the top 0.1 percent of income earners in recent years and can account for 70 percent of the increase in the share of national income going to the top 0.1 percent of the income distribution between 1979 and 2005."[100]

For 2005, they found that of taxpayers whose incomes including capital gains placed them in the top 0.1%, executives, managers, and supervisors in nonfinance businesses made up 41.3% of the total, while financial professionals (including management) were another 17.7%. Of the 41.3% who were nonfinance executives, managers, or supervisors, 19.8% were salaried and the rest were in closely held businesses.[101] Besides the 6.2% of the top 0.1% who were "not working or deceased," the next largest occupational groups were lawyers with 5.8%, real estate with 5.1%, and medical with 4.1%.

The bottom line is that top executives of U.S. business corporations—industrial as well as financial—are very well represented among the top 0.1% of the U.S. income distribution, with much, and often most, of their compensation coming from the realized gains from exercising stock options and the vesting of stock awards. Especially since the 1980s, when Wall Street has judged the performance of corporations by their quarterly stock-price performance, stock-based pay gives top executives a powerful personal incentive to boost their companies' stock prices from quarter to quarter. In stock buybacks, these executives have found a potent, and SEC-approved, instrument for stock-market manipulation from which they can personally benefit, even if the stock-price boosts are only temporary. Top executives of U.S. corporations have been given both the incentives and the tools for deciding, as the previously quoted compensation consultant put it, "when to get in and out at the most propitious time."

The Self-Serving Ideology of Maximizing Shareholder Value

Legitimizing both stock buybacks and stock-based pay is the economic ideology that business corporations should be run to "maximize shareholder value" (MSV). In the 1970s and 1980s, agency theorists trained in the conservative economics tradition of the University of Chicago propounded the theory that a corporation will maximize the efficiency of the economy if it maximizes the value of the company's shares.[102] The problem, as they saw it, was that the managers of large corporations, in control of the allocation of significant resources, had a tendency, if left to their own devices, to build empires and invest in wasteful projects.

The MSV perspective viewed hostile takeovers, or what more generally became known as the market for corporate control, as one way in which shareholders could force managers to stop wasting corporate resources and distribute cash to shareholders. Agency theorists had a stock-market carrot to go along with this stock-market stick. They argued that by making stock-based pay a major proportion of executive compensation, the incentives of corporate managers in the allocation of resources could be aligned with those of public shareholders.[103] Only by disgorging the corporation's "free cash flow" to shareholders, the MSV proponents contended, would the economy's resources be allocated to their most efficient uses. The money from the corporate coffers could be distributed to shareholders in the forms of cash dividends and stock repurchases. In short, by maximizing shareholder value, corporate resource allocation would result in the best possible performance of the economy as a whole.

The theory that underpins the MSV argument is that, of all participants in the business corporation, shareholders are the only economic actors who make productive contributions *without a guaranteed return*. All other participants, such as creditors, workers, suppliers, and distributors, allegedly receive a market-determined price for the goods or services that they render to the corporation, and hence take no risk of the company making or losing money. On this assumption, only shareholders have an economically justifiable claim to the "residual"—the profits left over after the company has paid all other stakeholders their guaranteed contractual claims for their productive contributions to the firm.

By the MSV argument, shareholders are the only stakeholders who need to be incentivized to bear the risk of investing in productive resources that may result in superior economic performance. As the only "residual claimants," moreover, shareholders are the only stakeholders who have an interest in monitoring managers to ensure that they allocate resources efficiently. Furthermore, by buying and selling corporate shares on the stock market, public shareholders, it is argued, can directly reallocate resources to more efficient uses.

The fundamental problem with MSV lies in the assumption that shareholders are the only corporate participants who bear risk. Taxpayers through government agencies and workers through the firms that employ them make risky investments in productive capabilities on a regular basis. From this perspective, both the state and labor have residual-claimant status—that is, an economic claim on the distribution of profits.

Through government investments and subsidies, *taxpayers* regularly provide productive resources to companies without a guaranteed return. As an important example, but only one of many, the annual budget of the National Institutes of Health (NIH) in 2014 was $30.1 billion, with a total NIH investment from 1938 through 2014 of $927 billion in 2014 dollars.[104] As risk bearers, taxpayers have a claim on corporate profits if and when they are generated. But these profits, and hence the tax revenues on them, are not guaranteed. Through the tax system, governments, representing taxpayers in general, seek to extract this return from corporations and individuals that reap the rewards of government spending. Through the political process, however, tax rates and tax revenues are subject to change, thus creating further uncertainty about the returns to taxpayers that will actually accrue when tax dollars are used to invest in the economy.

Workers regularly make productive contributions to the companies for which they work through the exercise of skill and effort beyond those levels required to lay claim to their current pay—but without guaranteed returns.[105] Any employer who is seeking to generate higher-quality, lower-cost products knows the profound productivity difference between employees who just punch the clock to get their daily pay and those who engage in learning to make productive contributions through which they can build their careers and thereby reap future returns in work and in retirement. Yet these careers and the returns that they can generate are not guaranteed.

As risk bearers, therefore, taxpayers whose money supports business enterprises and workers whose efforts generate productivity improvements have economic claims on corporate profits if and when they occur. MSV ignores the risk–reward relation for these two types of economic actors in the operation and performance of business corporations. Instead it erroneously assumes that only shareholders are residual claimants.[106]

The irony of MSV is that the public shareholders whom it holds up as the only risk bearers typically never invest in the value-creating capabilities of the company at all. Rather, they invest in outstanding shares in the hope that they will rise in price on the market. And, following the directives of MSV, a prime way in which corporate executives fuel this hope is by disgorging the so-called free cash flow in the form of dividends but, even more important, with buybacks.

EXPLODING EXECUTIVE PAY, ERODING AMERICAN PROSPERITY

I have argued that the increasing concentration of income at the top of the distribution is both cause and effect of the disappearance of middle-class jobs over the past three decades. It is a cause of the loss of middle-class jobs because of the incentives that stock-based pay gives to top corporate executives to downsize-and-distribute rather than retain-and-reinvest. It is an effect of the disappearance of middle-class jobs because trillions of dollars of "free" corporate cash flow, through distributions to shareholders, into the compensation packages of top executives in particular, and, more generally, into the coffers of financial interests that then seek to extract yet higher returns from financial markets. Investments in productive resources that can generate competitive industrial products require "patient," not "impatient," finance.[107] And when finance is patient, the returns from generating competitive products tend to go to employees in the forms of pay increases and promotions—not to shareholders in the forms of higher dividends and massive stock buybacks.[108]

The analysis that I have provided calls into question the main explanation propounded by labor economists for growing income inequality, namely skill-biased technical change (SBTC).[109] The SBTC argument is that the machine technologies made possible by the computer revolution have automated away the relatively lower-level skills that high-school-educated workers provided to the production process coming into the 1980s while creating new demand for the higher-level skills of college-educated workers. SBTC, so the argument goes, decreases the demand for high-school-educated members of the labor force and increases the demand for college-educated members, thus increasing the wage premium for higher education levels. In the presence of SBTC, a polarization of the U.S. labor market occurs.[110]

SBTC was first put forward at the end of the 1980s in an attempt to explain the loss of blue-collar manufacturing jobs and the widening premium to a college education during that decade. It is clear that in the 1980s the microelectronics revolution greatly increased the demand for college-educated workers with computer-related skills. But the notion that it was SBTC that threw blue-collar employees out of work in the 1980s has little empirical basis. Rather, from the beginning of the decade, it was Japanese competition that precipitated the plant closings that became endemic in the United States, resulting in the transformation of shop-floor employment relations that I have summarized as rationalization. Instead of confronting the new competition by upgrading the knowledge and capabilities of blue-collar workers through a strategy of retain-and-reinvest, increasing numbers of senior executives of established U.S. corporations imbibed the new ideology that corporations should be run to maximize shareholder value—an ideology that legitimized downsize-and-distribute.

As for "skill-biased" technologies, in the 1980s and beyond it was Japan, with its focus on retain-and-reinvest, not the United States, with its new creed of downsize-and-distribute, that emerged as the world leader in factory automation. Japan was in the forefront in introducing flexible manufacturing systems and robotics. Both the development and adoption of factory automation depended on the existence of a blue-collar labor force with a high degree of employment security as well as a high level of integration into their companies' organizational learning processes—two key characteristics of Japanese employment relations. Japanese production workers, virtually all of them with only high-school educations, were much more willing and much more able than their American counterparts to cooperate with engineers in their companies in the development and utilization of flexible manufacturing systems and robotics.[111]

As a result, Japan, not the United States, became the world leader in factory automation, a position that it still holds by a wide margin.[112] In the new digital age, U.S.-style rationalization reflected a weakness, not a strength, of U.S. manufacturing, especially when the elimination of previously well-paid blue-collar jobs transformed from a reaction to for-midable Japanese competition to a finance-driven quest for higher profits in the name of MSV. Invoking this destructive ideology to legitimize their actions, U.S. corporate executives terminated millions of previously well-paid and stable blue-collar jobs without bearing any responsibility for reinvesting corporate profits to help create new middle-class employment opportunities for an upgraded blue-collar labor force. Rather, invoking MSV ideology, these corporations turned to using billions, and in aggregate trillions, of dollars to manipulate their companies' stock prices.

If the proponents of SBTC misunderstand the rationalization movement of the 1980s, they completely ignore the marketization of U.S. employ-ment relations that occurred from the early 1990s. The shift from proprietary technology systems to open technology systems associated with the rise of the New Economy business model represented a pronounced "skill bias" that favored younger employees over older employees among the college educated. As we have seen, IBM, which among the Old Economy companies led the move to open systems, abruptly and dramatically ended its decades-long system of lifelong employment in the early 1990s. After that, other Old Economy companies followed suit, and, by the end of the 1990s, the previous norm of a career with one company had all but disappeared.[113]

In the jobless recovery subsequent to the "white-collar" recession of 1990–1991, earnings of college-educated workers stagnated. At the begin-ning of 1996, AT&T announced that, as part of its planned spinoff of

Lucent Technologies and NCR, it would lay off 40,000 employees, most of them middle managers.[114] For the following months, the media ruminated on "the downsizing of America," including a seven-part series of front-page articles in the *New York Times* that was subsequently published as a book.[115]

Over the course of 1996, however, talk of downsizing disappeared as the initial surge of what would become the Internet (or New Economy) boom became evident. In December 1996, Federal Reserve chairman Alan Greenspan shifted the focus of concern from labor to capital, asking whether "irrational exuberance" in the booming financial markets might be setting the stage for "unexpected and prolonged contractions," as had indeed happened in Japan.[116] As it turned out, there was a lot of "irrational exuberance" left in the U.S. economy, as the New Economy stock-market boom swept the nation for the next three-plus years.[117]

During the boom of 1997–2000, wages rose rapidly, especially for college-educated members of the U.S. labor force. For substantial numbers of high-tech employees, this run-up in wages reflected the rise of the New Economy business model, with its broad-based stock-option plans that, as we have seen, had functioned since the 1970s to lure professional, technical, and administrative personnel from secure career employment in Old Economy companies to insecure employment in New Economy start-ups.

The substantial impacts of broad-based employee stock options on increases in earnings are visible in Figure 6, which shows real wages (in 2000 dollars) from 1994 to 2012 for U.S. employees at companies engaged in semiconductors, software publishing, computer programming, and computer system design. Together, in 2000, these four ICT fields employed 1,554,000 people in the United States—more than double the number in 1994, and a total that would rise by 6.5% to 1,656,000 in 2012.[118]

Note the spikes in earnings in 2000, especially in software publishing in which annual employee earnings went from $64,700 in 1994 to $75,600 in 1997 and then exploded to $132,100 in 2000 before falling to $91,400 in 2002. Starting from a lower 1994 base, movement in semiconductor earnings was similar to that in software publishing. Figures 7 and 8, which disaggregate the U.S.-level data into selected high-tech occupations, show that the most dramatic income spikes were in software publishing in Washington State, where earnings went from $112,600 in 1996 (almost double 1994 earnings) to $380,000 in 2000 and in semiconductors in Silicon Valley, where the increase was from $79,600 in 1996 to $156,300 in 2000.

The County Business Patterns (CBP) data, on which Figures 6, 7, and 8 are based, do not actually tell us that these spikes are the result of broad-based stock-option plans, since all the data are reported simply as

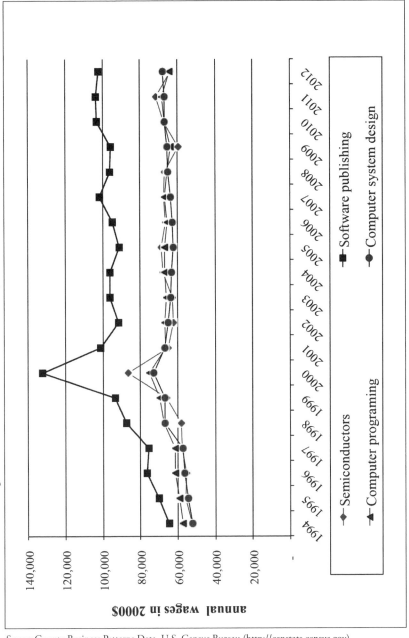

FIGURE 6

Annual Earnings (in 2000 Dollars) of Full-Time U.S. Employees in Four High-Tech Fields, 1994–2012

FIGURE 7

Annual Earnings (2000 Dollars) of Full-Time U.S. Employees in Software Publishing, 1994–2012

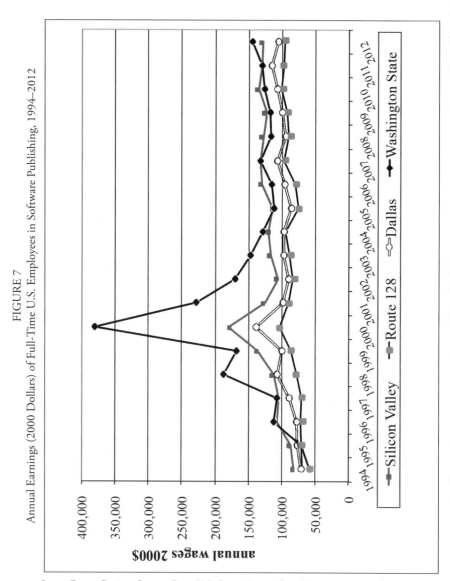

Source: County Business Patterns Data, U.S. Census Bureau (http://censtats.census.gov).

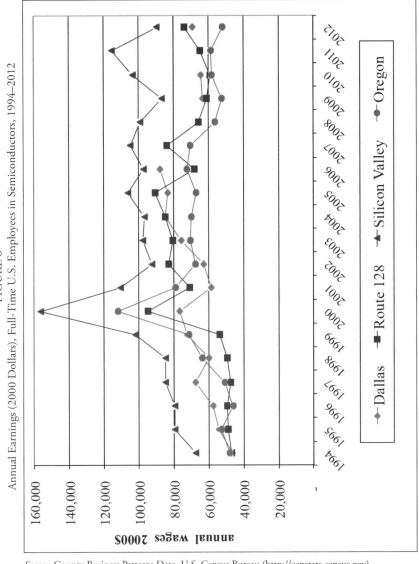

FIGURE 8

Annual Earnings (2000 Dollars), Full-Time U.S. Employees in Semiconductors, 1994–2012

earnings. But since 1994 in the notes to their financial statements in 10-K annual filings to the SEC, companies have provided data on their employee stock-option plans, including the total options exercised in the year and the average weighted exercise price.[119] From this information, we can estimate the average gains per employee from exercising stock options at the company in a given year. (Except for the five executives named in proxy statements for whom individual data on stock-option gains are available, we do not know the distribution of these gains across a company's employees.) The most extreme case, and one that corroborates the stock-based interpretation of the remarkable spike in the CBP data for Washington State in Figure 7, was for Seattle-based Microsoft where (excluding the five named executives) the average gains from exercising stock options were $79,000 across 19,200 employees in 1996 before soaring to a peak of $449,100 across 35,200 employees in 2000 and then falling back to $80,300 across 52,800 employees in 2003.

These dramatic changes in "wages" cannot be attributed to SBTC. Rather they reflect the fact that in using stock options to lure professional, technical, and administrative personnel from secure employment in established companies to insecure employment in start-ups, the New Economy companies in effect "outsourced" a substantial portion of the pay of these employees to the wildly volatile stock market. In 2003 Microsoft decided to do away with its stock-option program, in part because of a new ruling from the Financial Accounting Standards Board that requires companies to expense stock-option awards, thus lowering reported earnings with a potentially negative impact on a company's stock price. But the massive gains from stock options going well down into the business organization in the Internet boom and even beyond had already wreaked a different type of havoc on Microsoft, namely the loss of many key employees who had suddenly become extremely rich and left the company to "retire," do a start-up, become an angel investor, or take up employment with another company that might offer them even more stock options. This mobility of highly remunerated labor disrupted Microsoft's organizational learning processes, undermining the ability of the company to engage in innovation in new lines of business.[120]

The marketization of employment relations in the New Economy business model, reflected in the use of broad-based stock-option plans, created problems for technological development in the United States more generally, even as it facilitated the transfer of U.S. technology abroad as part of the globalization process. In the United States, the disruption to organizational learning caused by the movement of high-tech personnel from Old Economy to New Economy companies bears a substantial part of the responsibility for the precipitous decline, beginning in the late 1980s, of the corporate research labs that over the course of the 20th century had helped to make the United States the world's most technologically advanced economy.[121] Proponents of MSV within the top executive ranks and on Wall Street were then better positioned to ask why the company was wasting its money on basic and applied research that might not result in commercial products. Meanwhile "open system" companies that, in large part through mobile high-tech labor, could tap into the ostensibly proprietary technologies of the Old Economy companies could focus on product development to generate, in relatively short order, product revenues.

At a 1993 conference at Harvard Business School that sought to understand the decline of the corporate research lab, Gordon Moore, the co-founder of Intel and its long-time chairman of the board, clearly articulated this relation between basic and applied research done in Old Economy companies and product development done in New Economy companies:

> Running with the ideas that big companies can only lope along with has come to be the acknowledged role of the spin-off, or start-up. Note, however, that it is important to distinguish here between exploitation and creation. It is often said that start-ups are better at creating new things. They are not; they are better at *exploiting* them. Successful start-ups almost always begin with an idea that has ripened in the research organization of a large company. Lose the large companies, or research organizations of large companies, and start-ups disappear.[122]

The focus on product development was characteristic of the region where Intel was founded in 1968 and that, by the beginning of the 1970s, had become known as Silicon Valley. In the last half of the 1960s, when this new industrial district spawned dozens of semiconductor start-ups, intense competition, not only from within the United States but also from Japanese chip producers, led virtually every semiconductor company in the United States to seek to cut costs by offshoring assembly and testing operations to lower-wage areas of the world.[123] The high value and low weight of semiconductor chips meant that, as an alternative to sourcing production in the expanding *maquiladora* of northern Mexico, transportation costs posed no barrier to offshoring to far-off places such as Hong Kong, Singapore, South Korea, and Taiwan. These Asian nations had much lower wages and far more literate female labor forces than Mexico could offer. From the early 1970s, Malaysia also became a location of choice for the offshored activities of U.S. companies engaged in microelectronics. Meanwhile U.S. tariff policy facilitated the offshoring movement: Sections 806.30 and 807 of the Tariff Schedule of the United

States permitted goods that had been exported from the United States for foreign assembly to be imported with duty charged only on the value added abroad.[124]

As the offshored Asian factories expanded their employment of female operatives, with at most a high-school education, they also increased the employment of college-educated managers and engineers. They needed the college-educated personnel to run the facilities, upgrade process technologies, and move into the fabrication of various electronics components—that is, in the presence of digitization of production processes, the Asian microelectronics industries experienced a complementarity between the employment of high-school-educated and college-educated labor to generate higher-quality, lower-cost products.[125]

Meanwhile, companies such as Motorola, Texas Instruments, Hewlett-Packard, and Intel, which were offshoring their more routine work to Asian factories, were increasing their employment of college-educated labor at home. Indeed, a New Economy company such as Cisco Systems, which grew to dominate the Internet equipment market in the 1990s while outsourcing all of its manufacturing (be it in the United States or abroad), increased its U.S. employment from 244 in 1990 (the year of its initial public offering) to 27,000 in 2001, while its rest-of-world employment grew from 10 to 11,000.[126]

In the period 1990–2001, when Cisco did a relatively small amount of buybacks (21% of net income in 1995–1997) and paid no dividends, the company added 15,800 more U.S. employees than rest-of-world employees. But from 2002 to 2014, when Cisco expended 107% of its net income on buybacks and another 11% on dividends, it added 16,600 more rest-of-world employees than U.S. employees. In 2013 and 2014, for the first times, rest-of-world employees surpassed U.S. employees at Cisco, and the trajectory for the future seems clear.

While U.S. companies have been offshoring jobs to Asia, Asians have been coming to the United States for jobs. Since the 1990s, vast numbers of college-educated Asians, first and foremost from India, have found employment in the United States under H-1B and L-1 temporary immigrant visa programs.[127] U.S. companies value these foreign employees not only for their educational backgrounds (the majority have computer-related college degrees, and many of them have acquired further higher education in high-tech fields in the United States before being employed on an H-1B or L-1 visa) but also for their lack of labor mobility within the United States. These employees are beholden to the particular companies that provide them with their visas in industrial sectors where labor mobility can give workers who are citizens or permanent residents considerable bargaining power.

Many employees on H-1B and L-1 visas transition to permanent immigration visas in the United States, but most have gone back to their countries of origin with enhanced education and experience that are extremely valuable for developing innovative capabilities there.[128] Indeed, Indian IT companies such as TCS, Infosys, and Wipro have been among the largest users of H-1B and L-1 visas, employing Indians in the United States to acquire more sophisticated capabilities that can be "near-shored" back to India to support the movement of their companies up the global value chains.[129]

As with the rationalization and marketization of employment relations, SBTC has little to offer as an explanation of how, why, and in which industries globalization has been eroding middle-class employment opportunities in the United States.[130] Like all well-trained neoclassical economists, the proponents of SBTC look for the determination of wages in labor markets. People compete for entry-level jobs through labor markets. But the earnings that result in higher standards of living are determined in business organizations, with wages serving as both inducements for contributing to a company's productivity and rewards for prior contributions to a company's profitability.[131] Rationalization, marketization, and globalization represent fundamental structural changes in employment relations that disrupted the Old Economy relation between productivity and pay as portrayed, toward the beginning of this chapter, in Figure 2a. But the financialization of the U.S. corporation, characterized by the shift from retain-and-reinvest to downsize-and-distribute, has prevented a reconstruction of employment relations that can provide the foundations for stable and equitable economic growth. Instead, since the 1980s, the United States has experienced the growing income inequality inherent in the widening gap between productivity and wages displayed in Figure 2b.

If SBTC has little to say about the reasons for the disappearance of middle-class jobs in the United States, it has even less to say about the concentration of income at the top.[132] In *Capital in the Twenty-First Century*, Thomas Piketty criticizes SBTC for "its inability to adequately explain the explosion of very high incomes from labor observed in the United States since 1980." Indeed, notwithstanding the title of his book, Piketty's own explanation for the "explosion of very high incomes" in the United States is not a story of "returns to capital" but rather of "returns to labor." As he says, "Let me turn now to the US case, which stands out precisely because it was there that a subclass of 'supermanagers' first emerged over the past several decades."[133] Apparently referring to the work of Bakija, Cole, and Heim that I cited earlier, Piketty states: "Recent research, based on matching declared income on tax returns with corporate compensation records, allows me to state that the vast majority (60 to 70 percent, depending on what definitions one chooses) of the top 0.1 percent of the income hierarchy in 2000–2010 consists of top managers."[134]

What then, in Piketty's view, has driven the explosion of executive pay? "Simply put," Piketty tells the reader, "wage inequalities increased rapidly in the United States and Britain because US and British corporations became much more tolerant of extremely generous pay packages after 1970."[135] He sees this growing tolerance for exploding executive pay as the result of changes in "social norms," but he provides no analysis of what these norms are or when, how, and why they changed. For example, he makes only an oblique reference in his book to "shareholder value" ideology, a social norm that arose in the 1980s and that, as I have shown, has legitimized the stock-based incomes of the people who control the allocation of resources in U.S. business corporations.[136]

Nor does Piketty raise the possibility that the mode of compensation of top corporate executives may bear some responsibility for the decline in middle-class employment opportunities. As I have argued in this chapter, the compensation of U.S. corporate executives gives them incentives to make corporate resource-allocation decisions that are destructive of employment opportunities for the vast majority of Americans. The exploding incomes of the top 0.1% and the erosion of the American middle class are integrally related. The attainment of stable and equitable growth in the U.S. economy in the 21st century will require an organizational revolution far more profound than the managerial revolution that occurred in the opening decades of the 20th century. And it is the employees at the top of the major corporations, the legatees of that managerial revolution, who now must be brought under control. If not, inequity and instability in the U.S. economy will only get worse.

ACKNOWLEDGMENTS

This paper builds on research and ideas in a number of my published papers including "The Financialization of the U.S. Corporation," *Seattle University Law Review*, 36, 2013:857–909; "Innovative Enterprise and Shareholder Value," *Law and Financial Markets Review*, 8, 1, 2014:52–64; "Taking Stock: Why Executive Pay Results in an Unstable and Inequitable Economy," Roosevelt Institute White Paper, June 5, 2014; and "Profits Without Prosperity: Stock Buybacks Manipulate the Market and Leave Most Americans Worse Off," *Harvard Business Review*, September 2014:46–55; as well as on my book *Sustainable Prosperity in the New Economy? Business Organization and High-Tech Employment in the United States*, Upjohn Institute for Employment Research, 2009.

The research has been funded by the Ford Foundation project on Financial Institutions for Innovation and Development; two Institute for New Economic Thinking (INET) projects, The Stock Market and Innovative Enterprise followed by Impatient Capital in High-Tech Industries; and the European Commission Project on Finance, Innovation, and Growth.

Mustafa Erdem Sakinç has coordinated the development and maintenance of the stock-buyback database, and Dongxu Li, Qiaoling Ma, Xiahui Xia, and Yue Zhang have provided research assistance. I am grateful to Tom Ferguson, Matt Hopkins, Ken Jacobson, Phil Moss, Lynn Parramore, Hal Salzman, and Öner Tulum for discussions on the issues treated in this chapter, as well as to Justin Fox and Steve Prokesch of the *Harvard Business Review* for probing questions in the process of writing the *HBR* article, "Profits Without Prosperity." I also thank Ken Jacobson for proofreading and editorial comments.

ENDNOTES

[1] William Lazonick, *Sustainable Prosperity in the New Economy? Business Organization and High-Tech Employment in the United States*, Upjohn Institute for Employment Research, 2009; William Lazonick, "The Financialization of the U.S. Corporation: What Has Been Lost, and How It Can Be Regained," *Seattle University Law Review*, 36, 2013:857–909.

[2] William Lazonick, "Innovative Business Models and Varieties of Capitalism: Financialization of the U.S. Corporation," *Business History Review*, 84, 4, 2010:675–702.

[3] Lazonick, *Sustainable Prosperity*, chs. 2–4.

[4] Ibid., ch. 5.

[5] William Lazonick and Mary O'Sullivan, "Maximizing Shareholder Value: A New Ideology for Corporate Governance," *Economy and Society*, 29, 1, 2000:13–35; William Lazonick, "Innovative Enterprise and Shareholder Value," *Law and Financial Markets Review*, 8, 1, 2014:52–64.

[6] See, for example, Narayana Kocherlakota, "Back Inside the FOMC," president's speeches, Federal Reserve Bank of Minnesota, 2010; Marcello Estevão and Evridiki Tsounta, "Has the Great Recession Raised U.S. Structural Unemployment?" IMF Working Paper No. 11/105, 2011 (http://bit.ly/1Br569c).

[7] Daron Acemoglu, "Technical Change, Inequality, and the Labor Market," *Journal of Economic Literature*, 40, 1, 2002:7–72; David H. Autor, Lawrence F. Katz, and Melissa S. Kearney, "The Polarization of the U.S. Labor Market," *American Economic Review*, 96, 2, 2006:189–194; Claudia Goldin and Lawrence Katz, *The Race between Education and Technology*, Harvard University Press, 2010; Erik Brynjolfsson and Andrew McAfee, *The Second Machine Age: Work, Progress, and Prosperity in a Time of Brilliant Technologies*, W.W. Norton, 2014.

[8] Frank Levy and Richard Murnane, *The New Division of Labor: How Computers Are Creating the Next Job Market*, Princeton University Press, 2004.

[9] Thomas Piketty, *Capital in the Twenty-First Century*, Harvard University Press, 2014.

[10] Lazonick, *Sustainable Prosperity*, chs. 1–4.

[11] Lazonick, "Innovative Business Models."

[12] William Lazonick, "Organizational Learning and International Competition," in Jonathan Michie and John Grieve Smith, eds., *Globalization, Growth, and Governance*, Oxford University Press, 1998:204–238.

[13] See William Lazonick, *Competitive Advantage on the Shop Floor*, Harvard University Press, 1990.

[14] William Lazonick, "The Institutional Triad and Japanese Development" [translated into Japanese] in Glenn Hook and Akira Kudo, eds., *The Contemporary Japanese Enterprise*, Yukikaku Publishing, 2005, 1:55–82.

[15] Kim B. Clark and Takahiro Fujimoto, *Product Development Performance: Strategy, Organization, and Management in the World Auto Industry*, Harvard Business School Press, 1991; Lazonick, "Organizational Learning"; Lazonick, "Innovative Business Models."

[16] Alfred D. Chandler, Jr., *Inventing the Electronic Century: The Epic Story of the Consumer Electronics and Computer Industries*, Free Press, pp. 13–49.

[17] Michaela D. Platzer and Glennon J. Harrison, "The U.S. Automotive Industry: National and State Trends in Manufacturing Employment," Congressional Research Service, R40746, 2009 (http://bit.ly/1K77yb6).

[18] Ronald V. Kalafsky and Alan D. MacPherson, "The Competitive Characteristics of U.S. Manufacturers in the Machine Tool Industry," *Small Business Economics*, 19, 4, 2002:354–369.

[19] Frank Giarratani, Gene Gruver, and Randall Jackson, "Clusters, Agglomeration, and Economic Development Potential: Empirical Evidence Based on the Advent of Slab Casting by U.S. Steel Minimills," *Economic Development Quarterly*, 21, 2, 2007:148–164.

[20] Robert A. Burgelman, "Fading Memories: A Process Theory of Strategic Business Exit in Dynamic Environments," *Administrative Science Quarterly*, 39, 1, 1994:24–56; Daniel I. Okimoto and Yoshio Nishi, "R&D Organization in Japanese and American Semiconductor Firms," in Masahiko Aoki and Ronald Dore, eds., *The Japanese Firm: The Sources of Competitive Strength*, Oxford University Press, 1994:178–208.

[21] Lazonick, *Sustainable Prosperity*.

[22] Robert W. Bednarzik, "Layoffs and Permanent Job Losses: Workers' Traits and Cyclical Patterns," *Monthly Labor Review*, September 1983:3–12.

[23] Daniel S. Hamermesh, "What Do We Know About Worker Displacement in the U.S.?" *Industrial Relations*, 28, 1, 1989:51–59; Candee S. Harris, "The Magnitude of Job Loss from Plant Closings and the Generation of Replacement Jobs: Some Recent Evidence," *Annals of the American Academy of Political and Social Science*, 475, 1984:15–27.

[24] U.S. Department of Commerce, Bureau of the Census, *Statistical Abstract of the United States 1984*, 104th edition, U.S. Government Printing Office, 1983, p. 416; U.S. Department of Commerce, Bureau of the Census, *Statistical Abstract of the United States 1987*, 107th edition, U.S. Government Printing Office, 1986, p. 386.

[25] Hamermesh, "What Do We Know?" p. 53.

[26] John M. Abowd, George T. Milkovich, and John M. Hannon, "The Effects of Human Resource Management Decisions on Shareholder Value," *Industrial and Labor Relations Review*, 43, Special Issue: 1990:203S–233S; Oded Palmon, Huey-Lian Sun, and Alex P. Tang, "Layoff Announcements: Stock Market Impact and Financial Performance," *Financial Management*, 26, 3, 1997:54–68.

[27] Lori Kletzer, "Job Displacement," *Journal of Economic Perspectives*, 12, 1, 1998:115–136; Ronald Fairlie and Lori Kletzer, "Jobs Lost, Jobs Regained: An Analysis of Black/White Differences in Job Displacement in the 1980s," *Industrial Relations*, 37, 4, 1998:460–477; Rochelle Sharpe, "Unequal Opportunity: Losing Ground on the Employment Front," *Wall Street Journal*, September 14, 1993.

[28] William Julius Wilson, "When Work Disappears," *Political Science Quarterly*, 111, 4, 1996–1997:567–595.

[29] U.S. Department of Commerce, *Statistical Abstract 1984*, p. 416; *Statistical Abstract 1987*, p. 386.

[30] Michael Borrus and John Zysman, "Wintelism and the Changing Terms of Global Competition: Prototype of the Future?" BRIE Working Paper No. 96B, University of California, Berkeley, 1997.

[31] Chandler, *Inventing the Electronic Century*, pp. 118–119, 142–143.

[32] Henry Chesbrough, *Open Innovation: The New Imperative for Creating and Profiting from Technology*, Harvard Business School Press, 2006.

[33] Lazonick, *Sustainable Prosperity*, pp. 81–113.

[34] Ibid., pp. 39–79.

[35] Ibid., pp. 39–79, 115–147.

[36] Ibid., ch. 3.

[37] Ibid., pp. 81–113; William Lazonick, "Alfred Chandler's Managerial Revolution: Developing and Utilizing Productive Resources," in William Lazonick and David J. Teece, eds., *Management Innovation: Essays in the Spirit of Alfred D. Chandler, Jr.*, Oxford University Press, 2012:3–29.

[38] Randall W. Eberts and Erica L. Groshen, "Is This Really a 'White-Collar Recession'?" *Economic Commentary*, Federal Reserve Bank of Cleveland, 1991; Jennifer M. Gardner, "The 1990–91 Recession: How Bad Was the Labor Market?" *Monthly Labor Review*, June 1994:3–11.

[39] Lazonick, *Sustainable Prosperity*, pp. 81–113, 249–279.

[40] Joel Kotkin, "Is IBM Good for America?" *Washington Post*, October 6, 1985; Thomas J. Watson, Jr., and Peter Petrie, *Father, Son, and Company: My Life at IBM and Beyond*, Bantam, 1990, pp. 288–289.

[41] The following account is based on Lazonick, *Sustainable Prosperity*, pp. 85–89.

[42] John Abowd, John Haltiwanger, Julia Lane, Kevin L. McKinney, and Kristin Sandusky, "Technology and the Demand for Skill: An Analysis of Within and Between Firm Differences," NBER Working Paper No. 13043, National Bureau of Economic Research, 2007.

[43] Charles L. Schultze, "Downsized & Out: Job Security and American Workers," *Brookings Review*, 17, 4, 1999:9–17.

[44] Kletzer, "Job Displacement."

[45] Henry Farber, "Job Loss and the Decline of Job Security in the United States," in Katharine G. Abraham, James R. Spletzer, and Michael Harper, eds., *Labor in the New Economy*, University of Chicago Press, 2010:223–262.

[46] Ibid., p. 230.

[47] Ibid., p. 253.

[48] Lazonick, *Sustainable Prosperity*, ch. 5.

[49] Kate Bronfenbrenner and Stephanie Luce, "The Changing Nature of Corporate Global Restructuring: The Impact of Production Shifts on Jobs in the US, China, and Around the Globe," submitted to the US–China Economic and Security Review Commission, October 14, 2004 (http://bit.ly/1Br5BjB); Robert W. Bednarzik, "Restructuring Information Technology: Is Offshoring a Concern?" *Monthly Labor Review*, August 2005:11–20; Alan S. Blinder, "How Many U.S. Jobs Might Be Offshorable?" CEPS Working Paper No. 142, Princeton University, March 2007; Rona Hira and Anil Hira, *Outsourcing America: The True Cost of Shipping Jobs Overseas and What Can Be Done About*

It?, revised edition, AMACOM, 2008; Susan N. Houseman, "Measuring Offshore Outsourcing and Offshoring: Problems for Economic Statistics," *Employment Research*, 16, 1, 2009:1–3; Susan N. Houseman, "The Role of Manufacturing in a Jobs Recovery," Center on Budget and Policy Priorities, April 2, 2014 (http://bit.ly/1Br5EvN).

[50] C. Alan Garner, "Offshoring in the Service Sector: Economic Impact and Policy Issues," *Economic Review*, Federal Reserve Bank of Kansas City, Third Quarter, 2004:5–37; J. Bradford Jensen and Lori B. Kletzer, "Tradable Services: Understanding the Scope and Impact of Services Outsourcing," Institute for International Economics Working Paper 05-9, September 2005.

[51] Ron Hira, "Bridge to Immigration or Cheap Temporary Labor? The H-1B & L-1 Visa Programs Are a Source of Both," Economic Policy Institute Briefing Paper #257, February 17, 2010.

[52] Pete Engardio, Aaron Bernstein, and Manjeet Kripalani, "The Great Global Job Shift," *BusinessWeek*, February 3, 2003.

[53] Louis Uchitelle, *The Disposable American: Layoffs and Their Consequences*, Vintage, 2007.

[54] Bureau of Labor Statistics, "Union Members—2013," January 24, 2014 (http://1.usa.gov/1kXdAMp).

[55] William Lazonick, "The Global Tax Dodgers: How Big Business Keeps Money Overseas Instead of Creating Jobs at Home," *AlterNet*, August 31, 2011; Lazonick, "The Financialization of the U.S. Corporation," pp. 900–903. For the amount of cash that U.S. corporations are holding abroad, see International Strategy and Investment (ISI), "Accounting and Tax Research: Cash & Earnings Parked Overseas," ISI Report, March 17, 2014.

[56] OECD, "Growing Income Inequality in OECD Countries: What Drives It and How Can Policy Tackle It?" OECD Forum on Tackling Income Inequality, Paris, May 2, 2011.

[57] Lazonick and O'Sullivan, "Maximizing Shareholder Value."

[58] Lazonick, *Sustainable Prosperity*. See also Lazonick, *Competitive Advantage on the Shop Floor*.

[59] Lazonick, *Sustainable Prosperity*, ch. 3.

[60] William Lazonick, "Creating and Extracting Value: Corporate Investment Behavior and American Economic Performance," in Michael Bernstein and David Adler, eds., *Understanding American Economic Decline*, Cambridge University Press, 1994:79–113; William Lazonick, "Corporate Restructuring," in Stephen Ackroyd, Rose Batt, Paul Thompson, and Pamela Tolbert, eds., *The Oxford Handbook of Work and Organization*, Oxford University Press, 2004:577–601; William Lazonick and Mariana Mazzucato, "The Risk–Reward Nexus in the Innovation–Inequality Relationship," *Industrial and Corporate Change*, 22, 4, 2013:1093–1128.

[61] William Lazonick, "The Innovative Enterprise and the Developmental State: Organizational Foundations for Economic Prosperity," AIR Working Paper, revised version forthcoming.

[62] Lazonick and O'Sullivan, "Maximizing Shareholder Value."

[63] Federal Reserve Bank of St. Louis, *Federal Reserve Economic Data*, "Corporate Profits After Tax with IVA and CCAdj: Net Dividends" (http://bit.ly/1Br5Wmp).

[64] The spike in equity issues for financial corporations in 2009 occurred when they sold stock to the U.S. government in the bailout. The banks that were bailed out had been

major repurchasers of their stock in the years before the financial meltdown. See William Lazonick, "Everyone Is Paying the Price for Share Buy-Backs," *Financial Times*, September 26, 2008, p. 25; William Lazonick, "The Buyback Boondoggle," *BusinessWeek*, August 24 and 31, 2009, p. 96.

[65] For 12 months ending March 31, 2014, net equity issues of nonfinancial corporations were –$451 billion. Board of Governors of the Federal Reserve System, Federal Reserve Statistical Release Z.1, "Financial Accounts of the United States: Flow of Funds, Balance Sheets, and Integrated Macroeconomic Accounts," Table F-213, "Corporate Equities," June 5, 2014.

[66] Warren Buffett, "Letter to the Shareholders of Berkshire Hathaway, Inc." (http://bit.ly/1Br61GS).

[67] Securities and Exchange Commission, "Purchases of Certain Equity Securities by the Issuer and Others; Adoption of Safe Harbor," November 17, 1982, *Federal Register*, Rules and Regulations, 47, 228, November 26, 1982:53333–53341.

[68] For the safe harbor to be in effect, Rule 10b-18 also requires that the company refrain from doing buybacks at the beginning and end of the trading day and that it do all the buybacks through one broker only (http://1.usa.gov/1K78zAc).

[69] Securities and Exchange Commission, "Purchases of Certain Equity Securities by the Issuer and Others" (November 10, 2003), *Federal Register*, Rules and Regulations, 68, 221, November 17, 2003:64,952–64,976. In response to comments on the proposed amendments to Rule 10b-18 that expressed concern that the elimination of the block exception would have an adverse impact on issuers with moderate or low ADTV that relied mainly on block purchases to implement their repurchase programs, the SEC amendment permitted a company to do one block trade per week that would remain an exception to the 25% ADTV calculation so long as no other repurchases were made on that day.

[70] Lloyd H. Feller and Mary Chamberlin, "Issuer Repurchases," *Review of Securities Regulation*, 17, 1, 1984:993–998.

[71] John Brooks, *The Go-Go Years*, Weybright and Talley, 1973.

[72] See Douglas O. Cook, Laurie Krigman, and J. Chris Leach, "An Analysis of SEC Guidelines for Executing Open Market Repurchases," *Journal of Business*, 76, 2, 2003: 289–315.

[73] See Jeff Gerth, "Shad of S.E.C. Favors Bright Corporate Image," *New York Times*, August 3, 1981, p. D1.

[74] Richard L. Hudson, "SEC Eases Way for Repurchase of Firms' Stock," *Wall Street Journal*, November 10, 1982, p. 2.

[75] Securities and Exchange Commission, "Purchases of Certain Equity Securities," Nov. 17, 2003, pp. 64, 959.

[76] See William Lazonick, Mariana Mazzucato, and Öner Tulum, "Apple's Changing Business Model: What Should the World's Richest Company Do With All Those Profits?" *Accounting Forum*, 37, 4, 2013:249–267.

[77] Lazonick, "The Financialization of the U.S. Corporation," pp. 895–896; Steven C. Johnson and Jennifer Ablan, "Rise of Shareholder Activism Gives Bondholders Headaches," *Reuters News*, December 13, 2013.

[78] Daniel J. Weiss and Seth Hanlon, "Romney Tax Plan: Many Happy Returns for Big Oil," Center for American Progress, July 2012 (http://bit.ly/1Br6cBU).

[79] AEIC website (http://bit.ly/1Br6fO5); John M. Broder, "A Call to Triple U.S. Spending on Energy Research," *New York Times*, June 9, 2010, p. B3; Lazonick, "The Financialization of the U.S. Corporation," pp. 890–891.

[80] "U.S. Could Lose Race for Nanotech Leadership, SIA Panel Says," *EDN Network*, March 16, 2005 (http://ubm.io/1Br6k4j).

[81] William Lazonick and Öner Tulum, "US Biopharmaceutical Finance and the Sustainability of the Biotech Business Model," *Research Policy*, 40, 9, 2011:1170–1187.

[82] Lazonick, *Sustainable Prosperity*; Lazonick, "The New Economy Business Model."

[83] "Generating Higher Value at IBM" (http://ibm.co/1K78VGO).

[84] Heidi Moore, "IBM Fires Small-Town Workers for Wall Street Numbers," *The Guardian*, March 2, 2014. See also Nick Summers, "The Trouble with IBM," *Bloomberg BusinessWeek*, May 22, 2014; Steve Denning, "Why IBM Is in Decline," *Forbes*, May 30, 2014. In an interview conducted by Justin Fox of *Harvard Business Review*, former IBM CEO Sam Palmisano in essence states that his major role as the company's top executive was to keep shareholders happy by distributing cash to them: "Managing Investors," *Harvard Business Review*, June 2014:80–85.

[85] Alex Barinka, "IBM Plummets as CEO Abandons 2015 Earnings Forecast," *Bloomberg*, October 20, 2014 (http://bloom.bg/1BwVPuU).

[86] David Packard, *The HP Way: How Bill Hewlett and I Built Our Company*, Harper-Business, 1995.

[87] Lazonick, *Sustainable Prosperity*, ch. 3.

[88] Rachelle Dragani, "HP Rearranges Chairs in Hopes of Propelling Turnaround," *E-Commerce Times*, August 23, 2013.

[89] Jack Hough, "Meg Whitman's Turnaround at HP," *Barron's*, April 7, 2014, p. 19; Spencer E. Ante, "Hewlett-Packard Layoffs Reflect Effort to Keep Pace with Revenue Slide," *Wall Street Journal*, May 29, 2014; Quentin Hardy and David Gelles, "Hewlett-Packard Announces Breakup Plan as Technology Landscape Shifts," *New York Times*, October 6, 2014 (http://nyti.ms/1J5QDGc).

[90] Marie Carpenter, William Lazonick, and Mary O'Sullivan, "The Stock Market and Innovative Capability in the New Economy: The Optical Networking Industry," *Industrial and Corporate Change*, 12, 5, 2003:963–1034.

[91] Bob Bell, Marie Carpenter, Henrik Glimstedt, and William Lazonick, "Cisco's Evolving Business Model: Do Massive Stock Buybacks Affect Corporate Performance?" Paper presented at the Edith Penrose Centenary Conference, SOAS, University of London, November 15, 2014; Kaidong Feng, William Lazonick, and Yin Li, "Huawei Technologies: A Learning Organization," AIR Working Paper, The Academic–Industry Research Network, forthcoming; see also Henrik Glimstedt, William Lazonick, and Hao Xie, "Evolution and Allocation of Stock Options: Adapting US-Style Compensation to the Swedish Business Model," *European Management Review*, 3, 3, 2006:1–21.

[92] SEC, "Purchases of Certain Equity Securities," Nov. 17, 2003, pp. 64, 965.

[93] See Graef S. Crystal, *In Search of Excess: The Overcompensation of the American Executive*, Norton, 1991; William Lazonick, "Taking Stock: How Executive Pay Results in an Inequitable and Unstable Economy," Franklin and Eleanor Roosevelt Institute White Paper, June 5, 2014, in which I show how stock-based pay permits the ratcheting up of total compensation.

[94] See Lazonick, "The Financialization of the U.S. Corporation," p. 897, for Amgen's use of buybacks to offset bad news in 2007.

[95] See, for example, Paul Hribar, Nicole Thorne Jenkins, and W. Bruce Johnson, "Repurchases as an Earnings Management Device," *Journal of Accounting and Economics*, 41, 1–2, 2006:3–27; Steven Young and Jing Yang, "Stock Repurchases and Executive Compensation Contract Design: The Role of Earnings per Share Performance Conditions," *The Accounting Review*, 86, 2, 2011:703–733.

[96] Carole Gould, "Shaking Up Executive Compensation," *New York Times*, April 9, 1989, p. F13.

[97] Jan M. Rosen, "New Regulations on Stock Options," *New York Times*, April 27, 1991, p. 38.

[98] Almost all gains from exercising employee stock options and the vesting of employee stock awards are taxed at the ordinary personal income tax rate, not at the capital gains tax rate, with taxes withheld by the employer at the time that options exercise or awards vest. Hence, these stock-based gains are reported as part of salary income.

[99] United States, P99.9 income threshold (http://bit.ly/1Br6HvW).

[100] Jon Bakija, Adam Cole, and Bradley T. Heim, "Jobs and Income Growth of Top Earners and the Causes of Changing Income Inequality: Evidence from U.S. Tax Return Data," Working Paper, April, 2012 (http://bit.ly/1Br6M2L). The quotation is from the paper's abstract. I am grateful to Thomas Piketty for bringing this study to my attention.

[101] Bakija, Cole, and Heim, "Jobs and Income Growth," p. 38.

[102] See Michael C. Jensen, "Agency Costs of Free Cash Flow, Corporate Finance, and Takeovers," *American Economic Review*, 76, 2, 1986:323–329.

[103] Michal C. Jensen and Kevin J. Murphy, "Performance Pay and Top Management Incentives," *Journal of Political Economy*, 98, 2, 1990:225–264.

[104] William Lazonick and Öner Tulum, "US Biopharmaceutical Finance and the Sustainability of the Biotech Business Model," *Research Policy*, 40, 9, 2011:1170–1187; National Institutes of Health (http://1.usa.gov/1K79rEO).

[105] Lazonick, *Competitive Advantage on the Shop Floor*; Lazonick, "Innovative Business Models."

[106] Lazonick, "Innovative Enterprise and Shareholder Value."

[107] William Lazonick, "Patient Capital Is a Virtue," *FT Alphaville*, July 24, 2014 (http://on.ft.com/1K79tg3).

[108] Lazonick, *Sustainable Prosperity*; Lazonick, "Innovative Business Models"; William Lazonick, "The Chandlerian Corporation and the Theory of Innovative Enterprise," *Industrial and Corporate Change*, 19, 2, 2010:317–349.

[109] For an elaboration of this critique of SBTC, see William Lazonick, Philip Moss, Hal Salzman, and Öner Tulum, "Skill Development and Sustainable Prosperity: Cumulative and Collective Careers versus Skill-Biased Technical Change," Institute for New Economic Thinking Working Group on the Political Economy of Distribution Working Paper No. 7, December 2014 (http://bit.ly/1NqV0u4).

[110] David H. Autor, Lawrence F. Katz, and Melissa S. Kearney, "The Polarization of the U.S. Labor Market," *American Economic Review*, 96, 2, 2006:189–194.

[111] Lazonick, "Organizational Learning."

[112] See the website of the International Federation of Robotics (http://bit.ly/1K79yjH).

[113] See, for example, William Lazonick and Edward March, "The Rise and Demise of Lucent Technologies," *Journal of Strategic Management Education*, 7, 4, 2011.

[114] Abby Goodnough, "A Crack in the Bedrock," *New York Times*, January 14, 1996; see also Tim Jones, "Amid Uproar About Layoffs, AT&T Retreats," *Chicago Tribune*, March 16, 1996.

[115] New York Times, *The Downsizing of America*, Three Rivers Press, 1996.

[116] "Allan Greenspan, Chairman of the Federal Reserve Board, Delivers Remarks at the American Enterprise Institute Dinner," NBC Professional Transcripts, December 5, 1996.

[117] It was in March 2000, at the peak of the Internet boom, that Robert Shiller published his book *Irrational Exuberance* (Princeton University Press, 2000).

[118] These data are from County Business Patterns Data (SIC & NAICS), U.S. Census Bureau (http://censtats.census.gov). I am grateful to Yue Zhang for continually updating these time series as well as for calculating the average gains per employee from exercising stock options at the company level, to which I refer below.

[119] See Lazonick, *Sustainable Prosperity*, pp. 16–28.

[120] The arguments in this paragraph are based on work in progress at The Academic–Industry Research Network. See also William Lazonick, "The New Economy Business Model and the Crisis of US Capitalism," *Capitalism and Society*, 4, 2, 2009, article 4.

[121] For an elaboration of this argument, see Matt Hopkins and William Lazonick, "Who Invests in the High-Tech Knowledge Base?" Institute for New Economic Thinking Working Group on the Political Economy of Distribution Working Paper No. 6, September 2014 (revised December 2014) (http://bit.ly/1D6HTNJ).

[122] Gordon E. Moore, "Some Personal Perspectives on Research in the Semiconductor Industry," in Richard Rosenbloom and William Spencer, eds., 1996, *Engines of Innovation: U.S. Industrial Research at the End of an Era*, Harvard Business School Press, 1996, p. 171.

[123] Y. S. Chang, "The Transfer of Technology: Economics of Offshore Assembly, The Case of the Semiconductor Industry," UNITAR Research Report No. 11. Geneva: United Nations Institute for Training and Research, 1971; Warren E. Davis and Daryl G. Hatano, "The American Semiconductor Industry and the Ascendancy of East Asia," *California Management Review*, 27, 4, 1985:128–143; Lazonick, *Sustainable Prosperity*, ch. 5.

[124] Kenneth Flamm, "Internationalization in the Semiconductor Industry," in Joseph Grunwald and Kenneth Flamm, eds., *The Global Factory: Foreign Assembly in International Trade*, Brookings Institution, 1985:38–136.

[125] Lazonick, *Sustainable Prosperity*, ch. 5.

[126] Cisco Systems annual 10-K filings to the SEC, 1990–2013. The proportion of Cisco labor force in engineering increased from 21% in 1990 to 28% in 1996 and to 34% in 2001 and since then has ranged from 29% in 2009 to 36% in 2002 and 2005. In 2012, Cisco changed the "engineering" classification to "R&D." We do not know the distribution of these engineering employees between the United States and the rest of the world.

[127] Lazonick, *Sustainable Prosperity*, ch. 5; see "Professor Norm Matloff's H-1B Web Page" (http://bit.ly/1Br7gFX).

[128] Hira, "Bridge to Immigration or Cheap Temporary Labor?"

[129] For the top H-1B visa holders in 2014, see http://bit.ly/1Br7g8T; for L-1 visas, see Deepak Chitnis, "USCIS to Increase Scrutiny of Indian IT Firms, L-1 Visa Holders Will Be Under the Scanner," *The American Bazaar*, January 28, 2014 (http://bit.ly/1Br7m0m).

[130] For recognition by SBTC proponents of the impact of Chinese manufacturing on U.S. employment in the 2000s, see David H. Autor, David Dorn, and Gordon H. Hanson, "The China Syndrome: Local Labor Market Effects of Import Competition in the United States," *American Economic Review*, 103, 6, 2013:2121–2168. But this paper offers no analysis of the roles of key organizations—the developmental state and the innovative enterprise—in driving China's remarkable development. For an analytical framework, see William Lazonick and Yin Li, "China's Path to Indigenous Innovation," AIR Working Paper, August 2014 (revision forthcoming).

[131] The relation between productivity and earnings was recognized in the "efficiency wage" arguments put forward by a number of economists in the early 1980s; see Janet L. Yellen, "Efficiency Wage Models of Unemployment," *American Economic Review*, 74, 2, 1094:200–205; George A. Akerlof and Janet L. Yellen, eds., *Efficiency Wage Models of the Labor Market*, Cambridge University Press, 1986. This body of research invoked "wage stickiness" as a possible explanation of the stagflation of the 1970s. When stagflation disappeared in the 1980s, the interest in efficiency wages waned.

[132] In *The Second Machine Age*, pp. 151–152, Brynjolfsson and McAfee make the dubious SBTC argument that the high pay of top executives results from the availability of digital technologies that gives them the ability to increase their direct oversight of factories throughout the world.

[133] Piketty, *Capital in the Twenty-First Century*, p. 291.

[134] Ibid., p. 302.

[135] Ibid., p. 332.

[136] The closest Piketty comes to acknowledging the existence of shareholder-value ideology as a central social norm of American capitalism in the 21st century is in his discussion of the difference between the German stakeholder model and the Anglo-Saxon shareholder model on pp. 145–146 of his book. He states: "The point here is not to idealize this [stakeholder] model of shared social ownership, which has its limits, but simply to note that it can be at least as efficient economically as Anglo-Saxon market capitalism or 'the shareholder model' (in which all power lies in theory with shareholders, although in practice things are always more complex), and especially to observe that the stakeholder model inevitably implies a lower market valuation but not necessarily a lower social valuation."

Chapter 7

Investors as Managers: How Private Equity Firms Manage Labor and Employment Relations

Rosemary Batt
Cornell University

Eileen Appelbaum
Center for Economic Policy and Research

INTRODUCTION

Labor relations scholars have long paid attention to the role of labor market institutions—labor and employment laws, unions, and educational institutions—in shaping the managerial behavior of firms. They also have incorporated an analysis of changing product market structures into their theories—from early studies of how the expansion of the U.S. national market led to the need for national industrial unions to recent research on how deregulation and globalization of product markets has led to intra-industry, head-to-head competition among firms cross-nationally, and in turn put downward pressure on workers' jobs and wages. Now the field needs to incorporate a theoretical understanding of how capital markets and new financial actors affect firm behavior and labor–management relations.

Private equity (PE) firms are an important group of new financial actors to examine because, more than others, they take an active role in managing the companies they buy. Private equity firms are financial "intermediaries" in that they raise large pools of capital from wealthy individuals and institutions for investment funds, which they use to buy out companies. They attract investors by promising higher than average returns, and to deliver those returns, they use high levels of debt—referred to as leverage—that is loaded onto the companies they buy. The private equity firm wagers that it will sell the company at a profit in a five-year window. If the wager pays off, the high level of debt magnifies private equity's returns. But high debt also magnifies the likelihood of financial distress or bankruptcy. And the costs of bankruptcy do not fall on private equity but on the portfolio company and other stakeholders—employees, retirees, suppliers, creditors, and others.

Of particular interest for management, labor, and employment relations scholars and practitioners is that the law treats private equity firms as *investors* even though they behave as *managers* of the companies they buy and *employers* of workers in those companies. As a result, they are often not held accountable for their actions in the way that most companies are.

Private equity is not just a minor side show in the American economy. Between 2000 and 2012, private equity firms invested over $3.4 trillion in about 18,300 leveraged buyouts of U.S. companies employing roughly 7.5 million people (PEGCC 2013). That is slightly more workers than are currently members of U.S. unions. In 2014, about 3,300 private equity firms and 11,120 PE-backed companies were headquartered in the United States (PEGCC 2014). And private equity's influence goes beyond the direct employment of people in the companies it owns because its strategies affect vendors and their workers along the supply chain.

In addition, many public companies have emulated private equity's "innovative" financial strategies, particularly in the greater use of debt financing. And private equity affects the lives of working people in other ways. Retirement savings—"workers' capital"—accounts for roughly 35% of all investments in private equity funds, and, while pension funds may gain from those investments, private equity firms take a disproportionate share of the returns. Moreover, investors often don't receive the high returns that private equity firms promise. Furthermore, after the financial crisis, private equity firms began buying up foreclosed homes on the cheap and renting the homes back at inflated rates to working people who cannot afford home ownership.

In sum, the imprint of private equity ownership and control of Main Street companies extends broadly into the U.S. economy—affecting a large cross section of Americans as workers, consumers, and retirees.

Private equity firms and the investment funds they sponsor are not simply financial firms that passively invest in businesses but rather are employers who actively manage the companies they acquire. Laws such as the Employee Retirement Income Security Act (ERISA), the Worker Adjustment and Retraining Notification (WARN) Act, and Internal Revenue Service (IRS) rules governing the tax treatment of private equity profits need to be updated to address the problems that arise when investors act as employers without being held legally accountable for their actions.

THE PRIVATE EQUITY BUSINESS MODEL

The private equity business model represents an extreme version of the shareholder value model of the firm, which posits that the only purpose of the corporation is to return profits to its shareholders. That view—popularized by Milton Friedman in a 1972 *New York Times* essay and developed as "agency theory" by economist Michael Jensen, among others—argues that shareholders are the principals who own and control the corporation and managers are the agents. As such, shareholders are entitled to discipline and direct the actions of corporate managers to act in the shareholders' best interests. Agency theory turned on its head the assumptions of the then-dominant managerial business model, which views the corporation and its board of directors as the principals—and shareholders as one group of many stakeholders with whom the corporation contracts (Stout 2012).

The managerial model assumes that professional managers with deep industry expertise and organizational experience are in the best position to make decisions about how to run a company—what strategies to use, where and when to invest, and how to manage the workforce. It assumes that the effective management of labor and the production process are critical to creating and extracting wealth. And because these managers' careers depend on long-term growth and sustainability, they tend to prioritize the investment of retained earnings in innovation and long-term operational improvements and to share productivity gains with workers to ensure their commitment to the firm (Lazonick 1992). These priorities are at odds with the shareholder value model, which posits that equity investors are entitled to larger returns and should determine how retained earnings are used.

Agency theory legitimized the leveraged buyout (LBO) movement of the 1980s, when corporate raiders took over large public companies using high levels of debt and high-risk (junk) bonds to finance the deals. While LBOs were discredited by the financial scandals of the late 1980s, they reappeared in the form of private equity in the late 1990s and 2000s. Private equity firms have been at the forefront of perfecting an extreme form of the shareholder value concept—a financial business model in which companies are viewed as assets to be bought and sold for the purpose of maximizing profit—rather than as organizations to produce goods and services.

In general, shareholders can realize returns from their investments through two primary mechanisms. On the one hand, returns may come from capital's contribution to *productive activities*—the economic pie gets bigger and capital's share grows larger too. On the other hand, shareholders can gain from economic *rents*—by using financial strategies to increase their slice of the economic pie at the expense of others. Under the managerial business model, most returns to capital occur through productive activities that lead to real economic growth in the economy as a whole. Under financial models, spearheaded by intermediaries such as private equity, a larger share of returns to capital accrues through financial engineering or rent-seeking strategies than was true in the past. Because operational improvements are not as central to capital accumulation, the shared interest in productivity gains that traditionally linked owners and workers is weaker, and owners don't have to worry as much about negotiating with employees to ensure their cooperation in generating economic value.

The relative growth of returns from financial engineering compared with that from productive investments has occurred in many large American corporations, but the private equity model represents a more extreme version of this pattern. Here, financial engineering or rent-seeking activities take place through a much wider variety of mechanisms inside and outside of companies; these activities affect people not only in their role as workers but also as customers, taxpayers, homeowners, and community members.

Publicly held companies are also under pressure to maximize short-term shareholder value, and they use a range of financial and productive strategies to do so. But the incentives and constraints that public companies face limit their risk-taking behavior. The Securities and Exchange Commission (SEC) regulates public corporations and requires them to submit detailed, publicly available, qualitative and quantitative financial reports to ensure transparency and accountability to shareholders. Reporting requirements for private equity firms, only recently adopted under the 2010 Dodd–Frank Wall Street Reform and Consumer Protection Act, include only a general narrative about the firm's activities. In addition, because private equity typically buys companies and takes them private, the companies in their portfolio face no reporting requirements at all.

More important, the structure of private equity firms and their agreements with their investors (the limited partners) encourage excessive risk taking. These agreements require the limited partners to commit their investments to a private equity fund for ten years in exchange for PE's promise to deliver returns that greatly exceed the stock market. During those ten years, the PE general partners make all of the decisions about how to use the money—which companies to buy, how much debt to use, how to manage the companies, when to sell them, and for how much.

Typically, private equity general partners invest less than 2% of the capital committed to a private equity fund, while pension funds and other limited partners provide 98% of the fund's capital. Yet the general partners receive 20% of the returns once the fund achieves a "hurdle"—usually about 8%. This asymmetry between how much PE partners invest and how much they stand to gain encourages them to take high risks using other people's money—in particular, the excessive use of debt to finance deals. Private equity funds typically acquire companies using about 30% equity, while loading the companies with 70% debt. Thus, the general partners have less at risk than 1% (2% of 30%) of the purchase price of the acquired company.

If the deal goes well, debt magnifies the returns to the PE fund, but it also increases the company's likelihood of financial distress or bankruptcy. While the high debt burden subjects the operating company to increased risk of failure, it is a low-risk, high-reward model for the private equity fund's general partners. This is a classic case of what economists call "moral hazard." The general partners, who make the decision to load the company with debt (that the company not the PE firm or its funds is obligated to repay) gain disproportionately if things go well but bear few of the costs if things go badly.

This leveraged buyout model is replicated any number of times by a private equity firm. An investment fund that it sponsors can buy out several companies, in part because the fund's equity goes much further with the extensive use of debt—and the PE firm may have more than one investment fund going at any time. Thus, the private equity firm, which is typically structured as a limited liability partnership, may own many companies across different industries. In that sense, it resembles the discredited diversified corporate conglomerate model but with centralized control over legally separate portfolio companies.

This structure, shown in Figure 1, allows the PE firm to reduce its legal liability for the companies in its funds' portfolios while taking advantage of market power and economies of scale to maximize shareholder value at the level of the PE firm. Thus, if any one or a few companies do poorly, the returns to private equity are barely affected. The PE firm and the general partners also can collect advisory fees and management fees that can run into millions of dollars annually.

In sum, private equity firms differ from public corporations in substantial ways that push the envelope on the shareholder value model. The light regulation and low transparency and accountability that PE firms face—coupled with the incentive structure embedded in their business model—lead them to engage in more risky behavior than their publicly traded counterparts. Private equity reverses the equity/debt ratio of public companies, which typically use 70% equity and 30% debt. Private equity–owned companies are usually financed with 30% equity and 70% debt.

Private equity firms also make substantial use of junk bonds, sales of real estate and other assets of the companies they own for their own profit, and "dividend recapitalizations," in which the PE firm takes out additional debt (usually high-risk, junk bond status) and loads it on the company to pay itself and its investors dividends. Private equity firms also charge large fees not available to public corporations, are taxed at a 20% capital gains rate rather than the corporate income tax rate (up to 35%)

FIGURE 1

The Structure of Private Equity Firms, Funds, and Portfolio Companies

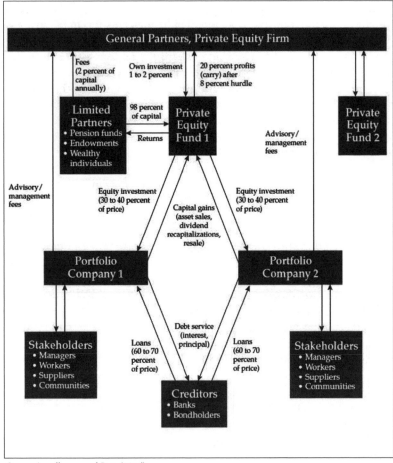

Source: Appelbaum and Batt (2014).

on their share of funds' earnings, and face little legal oversight—leading to low transparency and accountability. They can engage in a broader range of risky financial strategies than public corporations because the latter worry about reputational consequences and the opposition of shareholders, who can sell their stock at any time. Private equity limited partners, by contrast, commit their funds for a ten-year period. And if a PE portfolio company suffers distress or bankruptcy, the negative attribution typically falls on the company—not the PE firm behind the scenes. These critical differences are summarized in Table 1.

TABLE 1
Differences Between Private Equity–Owned and Public Corporations

	Private equity	Public corporations
Capital structure	70% debt/30% equity	30% debt/70% equity
Regulatory oversight	Low	High
Transparency	Low	Higher
Accountability	Low	Higher
Risk taking	High	Low
"Moral hazard"	High	Lower
Use of junk bonds	Considerable	Low
Asset sales	Proceeds go to PE owners	Proceeds go to company
Dividend recaps	Frequent	Rare
Fees	Key part of PE firm earnings	No advisory fees
Taxes	Capital gains rate	Corporate income rate
Reputational effects	Low	High

INVESTORS AS MANAGERS: CAPITAL STRUCTURE DRIVES BUSINESS STRATEGY

The private equity business model is an extreme enactment of agency theory concepts. It tightly links ownership to organizational control because the PE general partners take control of the company they buy and act as the employer of its workers. The general partners set the strategic direction for portfolio companies, appoint members to the company's board of directors, and serve as board members themselves. Private equity–owned companies tend to have smaller boards of directors, and they meet more often so that they are able to more closely monitor and control their portfolio companies (Acharya, Hahn, and Kehoe 2009).

The decision about which company to buy is based on a long process of due diligence in which the private equity partners and their staff carefully examine all of the company's financial records and growth over time as well as its position in the industry and prospects for sale within a three- to five-year window. Given that the PE partners promise outsized returns to investors, they target companies that have strong fundamentals, are performing well, and have high cash flow but are undervalued. Post-buyout, the strategic goal is to manage for cash flow, not necessarily for high profits.

In contrast to what industry spokespeople often say, PE firms rarely target distressed companies because speedy debt retirement requires high cash flow. Distressed investing accounts for only 2% of private equity investments and is undertaken by a small number of specialist firms (Strömberg 2008). Indeed, the best econometric studies show that private equity firms tend to buy healthy, better-performing companies with higher employment growth and wage levels compared with similar public companies (Davis, Haltiwanger, Handley et al. 2013). Obviously, healthier companies are more likely to deliver higher returns in PE's preferred three- to five-year window.

Like the leveraged buyouts of the 1980s, private equity firms today create a management plan for each portfolio company that is driven by its capital structure. The partners and top management draft a "100-day plan" that serves as a guide for restructuring the company's operations—one designed to allow the company to service its heightened debt load and meet the PE fund's targets. In some instances, the general partners put in place their own management team to implement the new business strategy.

Note that in contrast to the assumptions of strategic management theory—that *business strategy drives structure* (Chandler 1977)—in the private equity model, *capital structure drives strategy*; that is, the structure of debt determines private equity's strategy for each portfolio company, which varies depending on the kind and level of assets available to serve as collateral for debt. The way that the debt structure drives strategy is illustrated in the case of Freescale Semiconductor, which in 2006 was bought out by Blackstone, Carlyle Group, TPG, and Permira Advisers. The then largest tech buyout in history at $17.6 billion, the deal was financed with almost $10 billion in debt. The company fit the profile that private equity firms seek: profitable, good fundamentals with a rich customer and technology base, little debt of its own, and a generous cash flow to service the debt from the buyout, which had increased the company's debt load tenfold.

The PE partners in that buyout, however, did not factor in the normal volatility of the high-tech industry, which was accentuated by the effects of the recession. In 2007, Freescale's cash flow fell to $1.5 billion, leaving it barely able to service the $750 million interest on its debt that year. The company's bonds were soon rated junk level and trading for pennies on the dollar. Subsequently, the debt load drove a series of financial engineering strategies to stave off bankruptcy. Between 2008 and 2013, the private equity owners refinanced the company's debt four times and issued two initial public offerings (IPOs) to raise money to pay down the debt. Ongoing high interest payments undermined its ability to invest in R&D, the lifeblood of technology companies. And it restructured several times to reduce costs, eliminating about one third of its workforce between 2006 and 2014—from 24,000 to just 16,800. As of March 2014, the company was still burdened with $6.4 billion in debt (Deener 2010; Manners 2014; PitchBook 2014a).

Industry differences are also notable. In industries where companies own their own property—as in retail stores, restaurant chains, and nursing homes—private equity firms may rely on the sale of assets—often referred to as asset stripping—to pay themselves back or service the debt. They typically split the company into an operating company (OpCo) and a property company (PropCo), sell off the latter to quickly repay themselves for their initial investment, and require the operating company to lease back the property it once owned, sometimes at inflated rates. Especially in cyclical industries, this puts the operating company at financial risk because property ownership is a buffer against downturns in the market.

The sell-off of property was a central factor that drove the Mervyns department store chain into bankruptcy. A consortium of private equity firms, led by Sun Capital, purchased the chain in 2004 in a leveraged buyout worth $1.2 billion. They immediately split Mervyn's into a property company that owned Mervyn's real estate and an operating company that ran the stores. Within a year, they sold off the property, retired the debt backed by those assets, and paid themselves back the $400 million in equity they had invested. They also paid themselves and their investors dividends by taking out an additional loan and loading the debt on the portfolio company—known as a dividend recapitalization. When Mervyns filed for bankruptcy in 2008, it had a $64 million loss that year—less than the $80 million increase in rent payments following the private equity buyout. Thirty-thousand people lost their jobs (Appelbaum and Batt 2014).

Small and mid-size companies, by contrast, offer less collateral for leveraging debt. In deals with enterprise values of under $200 or $300 million, private equity firms are constrained in their use of leverage—to perhaps 40% to 50% of the purchase price. Here, the debt structure and interest payments are not as central in driving business and labor strategy, and financial engineering often plays a lesser role. Instead, private equity firms can take advantage of opportunities for operational improvements—so-called low-hanging fruit—that smaller companies have not had the resources or capacity to undertake. Private equity firms have the resources and expertise to manage upgrades to technology, operations, accounting and HR systems, marketing, and so on.

A case in point is Awarix, a very small company that developed software systems for large-screen displays for hospitals to improve patient visibility and monitoring. The systems allow health care providers to coordinate clinical and location information—to know about each patient's needs and move the patients more seamlessly through the treatment process, improving cost efficiencies as well as the quality of care. New Capital Partners, a PE firm specializing in health care, acquired Awarix for $3 million two years after it was founded. At that time in 2005, Awarix had implemented its technology in only two Alabama hospitals. Within 18 months, New Capital expanded that number to 19, and by mid-2007, New Capital sold the company to a strategic buyer, McKesson Corporation, for four times what it had paid. McKesson, one of the largest suppliers of health care delivery solutions, had more than 400 sales reps available to market the Awarix software. In this case, private equity was able to capitalize on an opportunity for small company growth that proved beneficial to the original entrepreneur and the strategic buyer (Appelbaum and Batt 2014).

The majority of private equity capital in buyouts, however, has not gone to small companies but rather to large corporate buyouts. In such cases, easy productive or operational improvements are few because large companies have taken care of low-hanging fruit—they already have sophisticated systems for functions such as finance and accounting, HR, and marketing. But financial engineering opportunities are great, given sizable corporate assets. Here the use of dividend recapitalizations, asset sales, plant closures, layoffs, and wage reductions is extensive.

INVESTORS AS EMPLOYERS: HR AND LABOR STRATEGIES

Private equity partners also play a central role in managing people in the businesses they buy. When they first negotiate a buyout, they enter into agreements with top managers about their compensation, which typically includes a substantial equity stake in the company. If top managers successfully execute private equity's strategic plan, they will become exceedingly rich once the company is sold. If they don't execute it effectively, however, they are likely to be fired. Empirical research shows that private equity owners replace top management teams more rapidly than do comparable public companies: in one study, new private equity owners replaced 39% of CEOs in the first 100 days after the LBO and 69% at some point during the deal (Acharya, Hahn, and Kehoe 2009).

In the Mervyn's case, the private equity partners immediately replaced the top management team, including the president, CEO, CFO, finance VP, CIO, and supply chain manager. The partners also called a meeting of the top finance directors a month after they took over and told them to make 10% to 15% headcount reductions across the board, regardless of whether their area was making a profit or not. Notes one former manager, "With employees, we were more or less told how to rate employees. We always had standards at Mervyn's and were expected to have so many employees in each category. But we never had this type of oversight before" (Mervyn's Department Store 2011). In four years, four CEOS entered and exited the retail chain.

As in the case of Mervyn's, private equity partners establish the plan for staffing levels and headcount reductions in business units, as well as which units should be sold, downsized, or closed. The best quantitative evidence of these patterns comes from a series of rigorous econometric studies covering PE activities from 1980 to 2005, based on industry data on private equity transactions (from the Capital IQ database) linked to the U.S. Census Bureau's longitudinal business database, which covers the entire nonfarm private sector. The researchers found that private equity–owned companies are much more likely than comparable public corporations to close lower-performing establishments, move operations to higher-performing ones, and acquire new plants or facilities (Davis, Haltiwanger, Jarmin et al. 2008, 2009, 2011; Davis, Haltiwanger, Handley et al. 2013). Thus, private equity firms play a central role in determining which employees will be laid off and which will be hired.

Clearly, the consequences of decisions made by private equity–owned companies are substantial. The studies by Davis and colleagues found that, post-buyout, private equity–owned companies had significantly lower levels of employment and wages than comparable publicly traded companies. It is notable that in the year of the private equity buyouts, the target companies had *higher* levels of wages and employment growth than comparable public companies, but post-buyout, both wages and employment levels were *lower* in the PE-owned companies. Estimates of the difference in employment levels range from 3% to 6.7% lower in PE-owned establishments compared with other similar establishments in the first two years after the buyout and 6% lower after five years, depending on the precise data and estimation techniques used (Davis, Haltiwanger, Jarmin et al. 2008, 2011).

Net employment effects depend on the relative size of job destruction and job creation. Private equity–owned companies created more "green-field" establishments but closed more existing ones, and the net effect was negative: they destroyed more jobs than they created, compared with their publicly traded counterparts (Davis, Haltiwanger, Jarmin et al. 2008, 2011). About half of the greater risk of job loss was due to a higher likelihood that a worksite would be shut down post-PE buyout (Davis, Haltiwanger, Jarmin et al. 2011). In manufacturing sectors, this pattern of closing lower-productivity plants and shifting operations to better-performing plants allowed private equity–owned companies to have higher productivity; that is, the majority of higher productivity, about 75% in these studies, was due to the reallocation of labor across sites in private equity–owned companies—or organizational restructuring—rather than investments in continuing or existing plants.

Chief Manufacturing provides an example in which private equity owners helped the company expand and reach a national market, but employment growth was not commensurate. Chief was a niche manufacturer of stands for slide projectors in 2003, which was bought out by private equity firm Friedman Fleischer & Lowe Capital (FFL) for an undisclosed amount in a leveraged buyout. The company had a strong reputation for high-quality products serving the professional market but did not have the capacity to move into retail where demand for technology mounts for flat screen TVs was accelerating. FFL set out a strategic plan for growth into retail markets and hired new top managers for sales and operations, one of whom later became president and CEO. FFL then identified and acquired a retail-oriented company, SANUS, as a strategic add-on to complement Chief's manufacturing strengths. Within a few years, the new company, named Milestone AV Technologies, succeeded in getting major retailers—including Best Buy, Target, Costco, and Walmart—to carry its products. While the company prospered and expanded, employment grew only modestly because FFL sent 60% of manufacturing offshore, compared with 1% that Chief offshored prior to the buyout. The PE firm, in effect, taught a small manufacturing company how to offshore production (Appelbaum and Batt 2014).

In the buyout of Delphi Corporation, the critical parts supplier to General Motors, a private equity and hedge fund consortium was also instrumental in offshoring 25,000 jobs. Following the bankruptcy of Delphi in 2005, GM began working with the U.S. Treasury and United Auto Workers to develop a joint venture with Platinum Equity, a buyout firm owned by Tom Gores, a Michigan native. His firm had worked with Delphi for years, understood the auto parts business, and was loyal to Delphi and GM. The plan would have returned key Delphi operations to GM, closed 14 plants, and kept the remaining union plants open (Beaudette 2009; Palast 2012). The new Delphi would have assumed the majority ($2.1 billion) of pension liabilities.

Delphi's PE and hedge fund creditors, however, who had been buying up a majority of Delphi's bonds at a fraction of their value—rejected the deal and demanded twice as much as the deal could pay for the bonds they held. They persuaded the bankruptcy judge to hold an auction for all of Delphi's stock and were able to easily outbid Platinum Equity (Beaudette 2009). In 2009, the court approved the sale of Delphi's steering business and four plants to GM, with the remaining businesses going to the PE and hedge fund creditors, who sent the work and 25,000 union jobs to China. Two years later, they took Delphi public. Shorn of its health care and pension liabilities and with its debt burden substantially reduced, Delphi commanded a price of $22 per share at its IPO, earning a profit of more than 3,000% for the PE firms and hedge funds that owned it. The company is now incorporated overseas (Palast 2012; PitchBook 2012a).

While these organizational restructuring strategies often improve the productivity and profitability of private equity–owned companies, the wages and benefits of surviving employees are often negatively affected. In the analyses conducted by Davis and colleagues (2009), overall, earnings per worker at PE-owned companies in the acquisition year were 1.1% higher than comparable publicly traded companies, but they fell considerably in the two years post-buyout. In manufacturing, where productivity data are available, they found that productivity in PE-owned companies, post-buyout, had increased, but wages were stagnant. The authors concluded that "private equity firms are increasing the gap between productivity and earnings per worker" (Davis, Haltiwanger, Handley et al. 2013; Davis, Haltiwanger, Jarmin et al. 2009)—that is, shifting the distribution of performance gains from workers to themselves.

The findings by Davis and colleagues also show that private equity restructuring strategies increase wage inequality by depressing wages in already lower-wage industries and raising them in already higher-wage industries (Davis, Haltiwanger, Jarmin et al. 2009). In addition, workers employed in private equity buyouts are more likely to lose their jobs— accentuating wage inequality because when unemployed workers find new jobs, they typically earn lower wages and benefits and have lower-wage earnings profiles over their lifetimes (Von Wachter 2013).

Negotiating Union Contracts

The control over business decisions and employment relations exerted by private equity partners is also evident in the prominent role they play in collective bargaining negotiations with unions. When unions represent workers in the companies that private equity partners intend to buy, the partners often become deeply involved in relations with the unions pre- and post-buyout. Even when they appear to stay out of direct negotiations, their strategic plan for the company is an important factor in driving contract outcomes.

Some private equity firms promote their ability to work constructively with unions as one of their competitive advantages. Blue Wolf Capital Partners, for example, has expertise in working with unions to overcome legacy problems and views labor unions as a potential source of added value (Blue Wolf Capital Partners 2013). KPS Partners also highlights its positive work with unions, noting that it "has resulted in the creation of enterprises that are profitable and positioned for success over the long term" (KPS Partners 2013). In a 2013 acquisition of Wausau Paper, for example, it negotiated a collective bargaining agreement with the unions as a condition for acquiring the company and agreed to assume liability for defined benefit pension and other post-retirement benefit obligations (Business Wirevia 2013; Primack 2013).

In the cases we examine here, the outcomes of private equity negotiations with unions are varied; but, more often than not, PE firms have negotiated concessions in job levels, wages, and benefit levels—regardless of whether the company was in financial distress or not. That is because union workers typically have above-market wage and benefit packages, which private equity views as inefficient. The level of concessions depends on a number of industry and firm-level factors and the relative power of the union.

An early example of successful negotiations between private equity and unions occurred in the steel industry in 2001. The industry was on the verge of collapse in 2000 because of industry overcapacity and the dumping of cheap imports on the U.S. market after the Asian financial crisis and China's entry into the World Trade Organization in 2001. Between 1998 and 2003, 45 steel companies declared bankruptcy, 18 mills were shut down, and 55,000 steelworkers lost their jobs. Sixteen pension plans covering over 250,000 employees, with $10 billion in underfunded benefits, were terminated and turned over to the Pension Benefit Guaranty Corporation (PBGC, the federal agency that provides insurance to cover benefits when a defined benefit plan is unable to do so). And more than 210,000 retirees and their dependents lost their retiree health care benefits (USWA 2004).

In this context, Wilbur Ross, owner of the WL Ross & Co. investment firm, formed the International Steel Group (ISG) in 2002 to serve as a platform to buy four facilities owned by LTV Steel, a U.S. Steel plate mill, and Bethlehem Steel Corporation's liquidated plants, which gave him a 20% stake in the industry (Stein 2003). In 2004, he added Georgetown Steel, Weirton Steel, and facilities in Trinidad and Tobago owned by HBI to his empire.

Ross approached the steelworkers in 2001 and began negotiating with them prior to the purchase of LTV. The union leaders clearly understood how to restructure the integrated steel mills to make them competitive with the mini-mills, which had introduced Japanese-style innovations to improve quality and efficiency. But the legacy of conflict precluded a joint labor–management approach with the former owners. Ross, by contrast, was pragmatic: "He took the USW work plan and implemented it. He had the capital, could talk to labor, and avoided the drama," according to Tom Conway, international vice president for administration for United Steelworkers (USWA 2012).

The agreement with Ross was a handshake, and the steelworkers worked without a full contract until December 2002. Ross hired a new management team from Nucor Steel and reopened the LTV operations with about 3,000 workers (Stein 2003). While the union accepted a 20% workforce reduction, Ross fired 40% of the plant managers, in consultation with the union (USWA 2012). The December 2002 contract became the model for a 2003 integrated steel agreement covering all workers in the former LTV, Acme, and Bethlehem operations. It set base wages at $15 to $20.50

per hour; guaranteed full-time work hours, overtime pay, and seniority; provided for health care coverage; and established a "layoff minimization plan," a neutrality clause, and limits on pay for top managers. It expanded the union's role in work redesign, extensive training, and health and safety committees and added a union nominee to the ISG board of directors. Active union members were folded into the Steelworkers Pension Trust, a multi-employer defined benefit pension plan (USWA 2002, 2003).

Large productivity improvements ensued, with ISG reducing man-hours of labor per ton and the cost of production by more than 50%, compared with the past (Brynes 2003; Stein 2003). Timing and political support also mattered. A month after Ross purchased LTV, then–President George W. Bush imposed a 30% temporary tariff on 14 categories of steel. This gave Ross a critical window to take advantage of rising steel prices, heightened demand from China, and a 0% financing scheme for car buyers from the U.S. auto industry (Gross 2005; USWA 2004).

At the same time, Ross's strategy for making a profit depended on buying the mills out of bankruptcy at a discount and then ridding the companies of legacy health care and pension liabilities. He bought the Cleveland steel mills and other LTV assets out of bankruptcy at the low price of $325 million, using $90 million of his own and investors' cash and assuming 74% debt. Their cash payment equaled 3.6% of the $2.5 billion value of the assets on the books (Brynes 2003).

Hardest hit in the restructuring were older workers targeted for layoffs, who received up to $50,000 in severance and one year of health care coverage; and retirees, who under the bankruptcy rulings lost their health care coverage and saw their pensions diminished under the PBGC insurance plan. To cover retiree health care costs beyond the initial year, the union negotiated a Voluntary Employees' Beneficiary Association (VEBA), with contributions contingent on corporate profitability (USWA 2002, 2003).

Ross's negotiations with the steelworkers union saved the industry—in 2014, the ISG mills continued to operate competitively. But Ross's profits of $4.5 billion almost exactly equaled the losses sustained in the pension and health care programs for retirees. When Ross sold ISG to Mittal Steel in April 2005, only three years after his initial purchase, he made an estimated 14 times his investment. In 2006, Mittal merged with Arcelor Steel, based in Belgium, to become the world's largest steel producer (Gross 2005).

While Wilbur Ross exited the steel industry almost a decade ago, other cases illustrate the ongoing role of private equity firms in negotiating with unions and other stakeholders in the companies they own.

Energy Future Holdings (EFH), formerly known as Texas Utilities, is a particularly important case. In 2007, KKR & Co., the Texas Pacific

Group, and the PE arm of Goldman Sachs acquired the utility company in the largest buyout in history, valued at $48.1 billion. Texas Utilities was the fifth largest utility in the United States, with 7,262 workers serving over 2 million customers. The PE consortium invested $8.3 billion in equity and borrowed $39.8 billion for the remaining 82% of the purchase price (Anderson and Creswell 2010; PitchBook 2014b).

The deal's size and impact made it controversial because union workers, consumers, environmental groups, and key state political actors had a stake in the outcome. Many of them welcomed the private equity buyers because then-CEO of the company, C. John Wilder, was planning to build 11 new coal-fueled power plants and create a new company to outsource workers' jobs, but he alienated consumers and politicians by refusing to lower electricity prices that rose after hurricanes.

The private equity consortium built a political constituency to support the takeover—including the union, environmentalists, community groups, local and state legislators, and businesses. They proposed to build three rather than 11 coal-powered plants, which won the support of the Natural Resources Defense Council and the Environmental Defense Fund. They hired James Baker III as an advisor and lobbyist and spent some $17 million on lobbying to minimize legislative opposition and regulatory oversight of the project.

The new owners negotiated a very favorable union contract with the International Brotherhood of Electrical Workers (IBEW). They used the Gephardt consulting group (led by Richard Gephardt, former U.S. Congressman) to facilitate the union relationship. The 2007 union contract called for no staff reductions, a neutrality clause, and a commitment to terminate outsourcing and bargain in good faith with newly organized IBEW members. The PE owners agreed to quarterly meetings with the IBEW. They also set up a Sustainable Energy Advisory Board, which includes representatives from the union, environmental groups, and the community (Beeferman 2009; IBEW 2012; Kosman 2009).

The PE consortium restructured EFH into a holding company and three operating companies: TXU (the unregulated customer service and sales company), Luminant (the unregulated power generation company), and Oncor (the regulated transmission company). After the buyout, the union worked closely with the PE consortium and reported that the company was well run. The PE owners maintained their no-layoff pledge and hired some 1,600 workers (mainly retiree replacements) between 2007 and 2012 (IBEW 2012). By 2014, employment had grown by almost 25%, to 9,000 (PitchBook 2014b).

Despite these constructive dealings with EFH management, union, and other stakeholders, the private equity owners failed in their business plan. Their strategy to pay off the 82% in debt financing assumed that the price of natural gas would continue to rise; instead, it fell to less than half of its 2007 value and never recovered. To prevent bankruptcy, the PE owners refinanced the debt several times by offering to exchange debt for pennies on the dollar, so-called distressed exchanges. Moody's downgraded the company's rating to a "Caa3 Probability of Default," calling the company's capital structure untenable and its business model unsustainable (Global Credit Research 2012). In April 2014, the company filed for Chapter 11. Creditors lost millions, and the limited partners had written off their investments years earlier.

Ironically, the stodgy regulated part of EFH—Oncor, the cash cow—was doing well in 2014. It was not part of the bankruptcy because it remained state regulated and "ring-fenced" from the holding company. Electricity continued to flow to its 10 million customers. While EFH as a whole had $36.5 billion in assets and $49.7 billion in debt in 2014, Oncor had about $7 billion in assets and $7 billion in debt because state regulations limit the size of debt. Fortunately, most of the union members work for Oncor. But their fate depends on how the bankruptcy is structured and whether the company retains pension liabilities rather than shifting them to the PBGC, in which case workers might lose a hefty share of their retirement savings (Creswell 2013; Spector, Glazer, and Smith 2014).

A third case also demonstrates private equity's important role in negotiating with unions prior to and after leveraged buyouts. Onex Partners, a Canadian private equity firm, purchased Boeing's Wichita Aircraft Division in 2005, using 31% equity and 69% debt for the $1.5 billion buyout (PitchBook 2013). Onex viewed the role of the unions as critical because they represented a highly skilled workforce needed to run the plant. Before the buyout, it tried unsuccessfully to gain assurances from the International Machinists Union (IAM) that it would agree to negotiate job cuts and wage and work rule concessions. Post-buyout, the new company (Spirit AeroSystems) negotiated a five-year contract that included job cuts of roughly 15%, wage reductions of 10%, and minor work rule changes. In exchange, union members, who were "first day" hires (but not new hires), would receive stock and cash payouts when the company went public. The contract maintained a defined benefit pension plan (IAM 2012a).

The technical, professional, and engineering employees, represented by the Society of Professional Engineering Employees in Aerospace, negotiated a contract that maintained their wage rates, but they accepted workforce reductions of 6% and concessions in the medical retiree program. They also introduced an innovative job security plan that replaced the conventional layoff system with a "short week" system in the event of economic difficulties (SPEEA 2012, 2013).

The cost-cutting measures, coupled with a dramatic increase in demand for aircraft, led to a major turnaround for Spirit that far exceeded expectations. Spirit's revenues climbed from $3.2 billion in 2006 to $4.1 billion in 2007. The company went public in November 2006 and raised $1.4 billion in the IPO (more than enough to repay Onex's initial investment); machinist members received $61,000 each in cash and stock—double what they had expected.

Between 2007 and 2014, Spirit negotiated two additional rounds of union contracts, with generally positive results according to the unions. The leadership of both unions characterized their relationship with Onex as positive. While negotiations have been tough and disagreements are not uncommon, both unions say they have had a more productive relationship with management than under the previous ownership of Boeing. In April 2012, the IAM organized 126 workers at a newly opened facility in Kingston, North Carolina, which Spirit built to design and manufacture major parts for Airbus aircraft (IAM 2012b).

We have highlighted the more positive cases in which private equity has negotiated constructively with unions. Even here, however, concession bargaining has been the rule. In many other cases, private equity owners have undermined or marginalized unions, refused to bargain in good faith, or driven companies into bankruptcy, leading to loss of jobs and retirement savings (Appelbaum and Batt 2014).

In sum, the case study and econometric evidence show that when private equity partners take control of a company, major changes ensue in the structure of the organization; human resource management; staffing, wage, and benefit levels; and union contracts. Regardless of the outcomes, private equity partners are managers and employers of the portfolio companies they own.

Getting Rid of Pension Obligations

Private equity partners also shape the retirement income of employees—even those who worked for the company before the PE owners took control. Imagine an employee who worked for a company from 1975 to 2005. After 30 years, he or she retires with a defined benefit pension plan. In 2006, the company is bought out by a private equity firm. In 2008, it goes bankrupt, and the private equity firm walks away—shifting the pension liability to the PBGC and substantially reducing the employee's retirement income. A corporate buyout that occurs after his or her retirement destroys a large part of the employee's 30-year investment.

Private equity–owned businesses are twice as likely to go bankrupt as comparable publicly traded companies (Strömberg 2008), largely because of their much greater use of leverage in capital financing. The problem of bankruptcy exploded during and after the 2008 financial collapse, with a much higher proportion of private equity–owned companies entering bankruptcy in that period. U.S. bankruptcy laws are designed to protect a struggling company from the demands of its creditors while it reorganizes its operations and finances so that it can emerge from bankruptcy as a viable business with a sustainable level of debt. The bankruptcy court oversees the establishment of a plan of reorganization that provides for the successful reorganization of the company and the equitable satisfaction of creditors' claims. Secured creditors—for example, those whose loans are guaranteed against a company's assets—take precedence over unsecured creditors, including employees, retirees, and others.

If employees are covered by a defined benefit plan when a bankruptcy occurs, then the PBGC guarantees that the employees will receive basic benefits, although not necessarily at the level they would have received had the pension remained solvent. This occurred, for example, in the steel industry case, previously discussed, as well as in the Delphi case. There, the private equity and hedge fund consortium that took over Delphi refused to pay any U.S. worker pensions, forcing the PBGC to take over the Delphi pension system. By its own rules, the PBGC had no choice and had to cut the pension benefits of higher-paid, mainly salaried, workers; 20,000 workers were forced to accept substantially reduced pensions (Eisenstein 2012; Palast 2012).

Given the higher rates of bankruptcy in private equity–owned companies, the PBGC has disproportionately absorbed the liabilities for the pensions of workers in those companies. Following the recession, that number accelerated—often a result of the financial engineering activities of PE owners that put their companies at risk. Harry & David, the food and gift mail-order business, is a case in point. It was bought out in 2004 by Wasserstein & Co. and Highfields Capital Management for $253 million, with a one-third equity investment ($82.6 million). A year later, the PE owners took out three dividends totaling $101.6 million, thereby giving themselves a 23% return no matter what happened to the company. In March 2011, the company—sinking under a debt load of $200 million—declared bankruptcy (PitchBook 2012b). The PBGC assumed responsibility for the retirement benefits of 2,513 Harry and David's employees and retirees (PBGC website, no date).

Private equity firms have also figured out a number of ways to take advantage of the bankruptcy code and more easily shift pension liabilities to the PBGC. One strategy is to use a special provision in the bankruptcy code (Section 363) that allows for the streamlined sale of company assets, including the sale of an entire company, without first putting in place a plan for reorganization or distribution of proceeds. Although the secured creditors get paid, there is no requirement to renegotiate union contracts or pension obligations—typically the largest unsecured creditor in a bankruptcy case. As a result, the pension liabilities typically get shifted to the PBGC, and employees receive only the minimally guaranteed level of pension payouts. Under a normal bankruptcy proceeding, the PBGC can present evidence on behalf of the bankrupt company's workers and retirees regarding whether the company can afford its pension plan and whether freezing the plan is a better alternative than terminating it.

Section 363 sales were intended to be used only in cases when delays might pose a serious threat to the value of the company's assets. While they were extremely rare in the 1990s (only 4% of large publicly traded companies), they represent 21% of bankruptcies since 2000. And between 2003 through 2012, employees and retirees lost more than $650 million in Section 363 sales of bankrupt companies owned or controlled by private equity firms, according to the PBGC (Gotbaum 2013). Exploiting the 363 loophole has severely strained the financial stability of the PBGC in recent years.

Some private equity firms have developed even more sophisticated ways to use the 363 loophole to rid themselves of pension liabilities while retaining ownership of the company once it comes out of bankruptcy. Under normal bankruptcy procedures, that is difficult to do, but 363 sales make it easier. Sun Capital, for example, bought Friendly's ice cream chain in 2007 for $337 million. The leveraged buyout left Friendly's with $297 million in debt, most of it taken out in 2008. After the buyout, Sun Capital sold Friendly's corporate headquarters property and the buildings housing 160 of its restaurants in a sale–leaseback arrangement in which the restaurants paid above-market rents to stay in the same buildings that the chain used to own. Under those circumstances, Friendly's could not make the investments and operational changes needed to make the turnaround that Sun Capital had promised (for more details, see Appelbaum and Batt 2014).

Friendly's filed for Chapter 11 bankruptcy in November 2011, after closing 65 stores and laying off 1,260 workers. Sun Capital then sold Friendly's in a 363 sale to another Sun Capital private equity fund, but with its pension obligations offloaded onto the PBGC. This strategy allowed the Sun Capital PE firm to retain ownership of Friendly's, but neither the PE firm nor any of its funds had any responsibility for pension obligations to Friendly's 6,000 employees and retirees. Friendly's is far from the only example. Oxford Automotive and Relizon, among other companies that went bankrupt while in private equity hands, were also sold from one affiliate of a PE firm to another affiliate (Gotbaum 2013).

Sun Capital was also the focal point in a lawsuit over its obligations to a multi-employer pension fund when the company it owned, Scott Brass, went bankrupt. Scott Brass was a high-end brass- and copper-producing company that Sun Capital purchased in 2006. Its workers were covered by a multi-employer pension plan—the New England Teamsters and Trucking Industry Pension Fund. In October 2008, Scott Brass withdrew from the Teamsters' pension fund and a month later declared bankruptcy. The Teamsters argued that Sun Capital was responsible for paying a "withdrawal liability" of $4.5 million to the Teamsters' multi-employer fund. According to ERISA, an employer that withdraws from a multi-employer pension plan must pay the pension plan a withdrawal liability—that is, "a sum sufficient to cover the employer's fair share of the pension's unfunded liabilities" (U.S. District Court for the District of Massachusetts 2012).

The case turns on whether Sun Capital is in fact an employer for purposes of ERISA. The law defines an employer as any parent or subsidiary that is a "trade or business" and has at least an 80% ownership stake in a company that contributes to a multi-employer pension plan. Sun Capital argued that it is not a trade or business and, furthermore, it did not meet the 80% threshold. Rather, it had purchased Scott Brass using two different private equity funds: Sun Fund IV acquired 70% of Scott Brass and Sun Fund III acquired the remaining 30%. The Teamsters argued that together, the two Sun Capital funds owned 100% of Scott Brass and were its parent company for purposes of ERISA.

In October 2012, the District Court of Massachusetts found that the Sun Funds did not qualify as a trade or business because the Sun Funds do not have employees, own any office space, or make or sell goods (U.S. District Court for the District of Massachusetts 2012). Even though Sun Capital admitted that one purpose of the 70/30 ownership split was to limit the potential that it would face withdrawal liability, the district court found that this was not the major goal of the 70/30 structure. In July 2013, however, the First U.S. Circuit Court of Appeals in Boston reversed part of the district court ruling. It found that the PE fund was not just a passive investor in Scott Brass but was actively engaged in managing the company. The appeals court did not rule on whether the 70/30 ownership split between two Sun Funds counts as an 80% ownership stake in Scott Brass and sent that question back to the lower court for a decision on the issue and on whether Sun Capital is liable for Scott Brass's pension liabilities (U.S. District Court for the District of Massachusetts 2012).

The appeals court's decision that the PE fund is engaged in a trade or business is significant because it collapses a legal structure intended to keep separate the activities of the general partner and the limited partners in a fund (Fleischer 2013) and establishes that private equity funds are not necessarily passive investors and may actively control the companies they buy. The PBGC, which has argued since 2007 that PE funds are trades or businesses for ERISA purposes, welcomed the ruling, but the industry's lobbying association, the Private Equity Growth Capital Council (PEGCC), raised alarms that the decision would lead to major shifts in the liabilities of private equity funds (Bradford 2013).

Pensions are deferred compensation for workers—income that will be received by workers in the future instead of higher wages today—for work performed today. ERISA was designed to ensure that private sector workers would receive the pensions due them when they retired. The intent of Congress was to protect the pensions of working people so that employers cannot escape their responsibilities by adopting organizational structures that obscure ownership and control. While the Boston appellate court decision is a step toward ensuring that private equity funds are held liable for pension liabilities, it is not clear that it is sufficient to protect the retirement benefits in defined benefit pension plans for workers in companies acquired by private equity funds.

Private equity funds' strategies to avoid pension liabilities are particularly noteworthy given that over one third of the investors in private equity are union, corporate, and public pension funds. These large pension funds are in the contradictory position of hoping to benefit from activities that at times undermine their own *raison d'etre*—the retirement security of beneficiaries in funds like their own. And this raises serious questions about whether pension funds that invest in private equity are behaving in ways that are consistent with the interests and values of their own members.

PUBLIC POLICIES TO HOLD PRIVATE EQUITY FUNDS ACCOUNTABLE AS EMPLOYERS

The examples in this chapter illustrate the wide variety of ways in which private equity partners act as managers and employers of the companies they take over, even though they are viewed as investors in the public eye and under the law. With the exception of a handful of large private equity firms that are now publicly traded (including Blackstone, Apollo, and Carlyle), they are not required to file the kind of detailed financial and operational information that public corporations must file with the SEC. For the portfolio companies that PE funds acquire and take private, there is silence—no reporting requirements at all. Moreover, even the limited partners who invest in private equity funds have only modest information about how private equity partners manage the companies that the PE funds have bought and how financial performance and returns to investors are measured.

One solution is for Congress to pass legislation that requires greater transparency for private equity firms, in keeping with what is currently required of publicly traded companies. While the Dodd–Frank Act improved reporting requirements (virtually nonexistent before that), private equity funds still are not required to disclose which companies they own, the incomes earned by senior managers and partners in the private equity firm that sponsors the fund, or the financial statements of portfolio companies. Current evaluation methodologies used by private equity firms do not compare their returns to those of comparable investments in the stock market. Yet creditors, vendors, suppliers, managers, workers, and unions need this information to make informed decisions about their interactions with PE-owned companies. Workers and their unions are often unaware that the company that employs them is owned by a private equity fund—especially when private equity investors acquire the company through holding companies located off shore. Simple requirements for more detailed financial accounting would provide employees, investors, and other stakeholders with information needed to accurately assess how private equity ownership affects their livelihoods.

Beyond corrections for lack of transparency, private equity partners are not held accountable for their actions in managing the companies they own in the way that public corporations are. If employees are dismissed or laid off, it is not the private equity partners but the company they own that is the likely target of a lawsuit over unjust dismissal or severance pay. If a company goes bankrupt, private equity partners can walk away from liabilities owed to pension funds, vendors, suppliers, and creditors. If a company owned by private equity provides bad service or faulty products, or enters bankruptcy, the reputational effects fall on the company itself, not on the PE partners behind the scenes.

Part of the problem is the light regulation and privileged position that private equity firms enjoy under the law. In addition to the modest reporting requirements for private equity firms under the Dodd–Frank law, they also receive greater or additional tax breaks not available to public corporations. Because they make much greater use of debt in their capital structure, companies owned by private equity are able to take greater advantage of the tax deductions allowed for interest on debt under the tax code. In addition, the share of fund earnings paid to private equity partners, so-called carried interest, is taxed as capital gains—at a rate of 20%—rather than as income at a rate of up to 35%.

The incentives built into the business model of private equity firms, and their deals with their investors, take advantage of this lack of transparency, accountability, and light regulation. As we explain in the first part of this chapter, because private equity partners invest only 1% or 2% of their own money in the purchase price of a company but reap 20% of the returns, they have little at stake—creating a low-risk, high-reward model for the PE firm—and the moral hazard that comes with it. The excessive fees charged to limited partners and portfolio companies—for services that add questionable value to investors or companies—came under particular scrutiny by the SEC in 2014 (Bowden 2014).

Several regulatory changes would curb the negative effects of private equity on companies and working people, while preserving the benefits of private pools of capital to stimulate growth and development in small and mid-size companies.

The first would reduce incentives for the excessive use of debt. Three approaches have been used: placing a cap on the amount of debt that can be used, limiting or eliminating the tax deductibility of interest, and establishing rules designed to limit risky behavior. A cap limits the use of debt over a specific amount—for example, 40% or 50% of purchase price. During the 1930s, the SEC established Regulation T, which limits the amount of debt an individual can run up in a brokerage account when buying shares of stock. Regulation T currently allows an individual to borrow up to 50% of the initial purchase price of a qualified security.

The second approach, eliminating or reducing the tax deductibility on debt, reduces incentives for using leverage. There is no economic argument for a government subsidy to business to encourage the use of debt rather than equity—and no economic reason that taxpayers should subsidize borrowing by corporations. Limiting the tax deductibility of interest payments on debt would not prevent the use of debt in financial transactions, but it would remove a major incentive to do so.

The third approach—requiring private equity to explicitly take risk into account in deciding how much debt to use—was adopted by the European Union following the financial crisis under the Alternative Investment Fund Manager Directive (AIFMD 2011). This directive requires private equity funds to report on their use of debt relative to a number of factors, including their portfolio companies' assets and ability to amortize debt. While this approach puts PE funds under pressure to manage risk more appropriately, it is more difficult to monitor and enforce.

A second regulatory change—eliminating the capital gains tax loophole on private equity profits—would complement regulations that limit tax deductions on debt. Both go hand in hand. Private equity partners' use of excessive debt magnifies their returns to investment. Then, with higher returns, the partners also enjoy lower taxes via the capital gains rate as opposed to the more appropriate income tax rate. The idea that private equity profits are the equivalent of capital gains has been repeatedly questioned by legal scholars on a number of counts.

One of the most convincing arguments compares private equity partners to real estate developers, who in their day-to-day business, typically take years to buy, develop, and resell real estate at a profit. During that time, the tax code is clear that the real estate held by a developer is not a capital asset; rather, it is viewed as being held for sale to customers. Similarly, corporations held by PE funds should not be treated as a capital asset by the IRS. In the ordinary course of doing business, private equity funds buy, develop, and resell corporations to customers at a profit—and this profit constitutes remuneration for their work to improve them. In sum, the profits of a PE fund from the sale of a portfolio company arise from the everyday operation of the fund and are the type of profits that Congress sought to exclude from preferential capital gains treatment (Rosenthal 2013).

A third set of regulations would hold private equity accountable for its role in plant closures and company bankruptcies. One set of issues concerns whether and how private equity should be required to pay severance pay to workers who suffer layoffs as a result of private equity owners' business strategies. When private equity's use of excessive leverage, asset stripping, financial engineering, and cost cutting leads to layoffs, then it should be held accountable and should pay workers severance commensurate with their seniority. In addition, private equity employers should be liable for plant closures under the federal WARN Act, which requires an employer with 100 employees or more (or a plant shutdown of 50 employees or more) to provide 60 days' advance notice in the event of a plant closing or mass layoff. Thus far, courts have ruled in a small number of cases that the private equity partners who own the company are liable under the WARN Act, but other cases are pending.

Whether private equity owners are covered under bankruptcy and ERISA laws is less clear. As our cases have shown, in the event of bankruptcy of their portfolio companies, private equity partners have often been able to shift liability for the company's defined benefit plan contributions or payouts to the PBGC. Their liability for payments to multi-employer plans in bankruptcy cases is in question in light of the Scott Brass case. The appeals court, for the first time, found that the private equity funds that owned Scott Brass were engaged in a trade or business and thus are potentially liable for the payments. However, the technical question of whether the funds met the 80% ownership rule was still pending at the time of this writing in 2015. In the meantime, the private equity industry and its legal consultants are promoting a strategy of "co-investment" in which no one private equity fund has 80% or more ownership in a particular company. That approach is designed to ensure that private equity owners are not held accountable for pension liabilities in the case of financial distress or bankruptcy.

CONCLUSION

Our brief overview provides case study and quantitative evidence that private equity owners are managers and employers of the companies they buy. They set the agenda for corporate restructuring, downsizing, or layoffs; assume responsibility for human resource practices such as hiring and compensation; and negotiate contracts with unions where they are present. They are also more likely to drive a company into financial distress and even bankruptcy than are comparable publicly traded companies. They should, therefore, be held accountable for their actions.

A set of legal and regulatory changes is needed to ensure that private equity firms are transparent and accountable for their actions, that they pay their fair share of taxes, and that they assume liability for any negative effects of their actions on the jobs, income levels, and pensions of the workers in the companies they own.

ACKNOWLEDGMENTS

This chapter draws heavily on the extensive research and case evidence found in Appelbaum and Batt (2014).

REFERENCES

Acharya, Viral, Moritz Hahn, and Conor Kehoe. 2009. *Corporate Governance and Value Creation: Evidence from Private Equity* (http://bit.ly/1xsTZdo).

Alternative Investment Fund Manager Directive (AIFMD). 2011. "Directive 2011/61/EU of the European Parliament and of the Council of 8 June 2011 on Alternative Investment Fund Managers and Amending Directives 2003/41/EC and 2009/65/EC and Regulations (EC) No. 1060/2009 and (EU) No. 1095/2010."

Anderson, Jenny, and Julie Creswell. 2010 (Feb. 28). "For Buyout Kingpins, the TXU Utility Deal Gets Tricky." *Wall Street Journal.*

Appelbaum, Eileen, and Rosemary Batt. 2014. *Private Equity at Work: How Wall Street Manages Main Street.* New York: Russell Sage Foundation.

Beaudette, Marie. 2009 (Jun. 10). "Delphi and the 'Guys in Suits.'" *Wall Street Journal* (http://on.wsj.com/1CegIPF).

Beeferman, Larry. 2009. "Private Equity and American Labor: Multiple, Pragmatic Responses Mirroring Labor's Strengths and Weaknesses." *Journal of Industrial Relations*, Vol. 5, no. 4, pp. 543–556.

Blue Wolf Capital Partners. 2013. "What We Do Well" (http://www.bluewolf.com).

Bowden, Andrew J. 2014 (May 6). "Spreading Sunshine in Private Equity. Private Equity International (PEI), Private Fund Compliance Forum." Presentation by Andrew Bowden, Director, Office of Compliance Inspections and Examinations, New York, NY.

Bradford, Hazel. 2013 (Aug. 15). "Private Equity Group Backs Sun Capital Partners Over Pension Liability." *Pensions & Investments* (http://bit.ly/1xsVjwK).

Business Wirevia. 2013 (May 20). "Wausau Paper Announces Definitive Agreement to Divest Specialty Paper Business" (http://aol.it/1xsVqII).

Byrnes, Nanette. 2003 (Dec. 22). "Is Wilbur Ross Crazy?" *Businessweek* (http://buswk.co/1Ceh9t9).

Chandler, A.D., Jr. 1977. *The Visible Hand: The Managerial Revolution in American Business.* Cambridge, MA: The Belknap Press.

Creswell, Julie. 2013 (Apr. 8). "Battle Heats Up Over Fate of Troubled Energy Buyout." Dealbook. *New York Times* (http://nyti.ms/1xsVV5y).

Davis, Steven, John Haltiwanger, Kyle Handley, Ron Jarmin, Josh Lerner, and Javier Miranda. 2013. *Private Equity, Jobs, and Productivity*. NBER Working Paper No. 19458. Cambridge, MA: National Bureau of Economic Research (http://bit.ly/1DZdJwG).

Davis, Steven, John Haltiwanger, Ron Jarmin, Josh Lerner, and Javier Miranda. 2008. "Private Equity and Employment." In A. Gurung, and J. Lerner, eds., *Globalization of Alternative Investments Working Papers Volume 1: The Global Economic Impact of Private Equity Report 2008*. New York: World Economic Forum (http://bit.ly/1AIJGTC).

Davis, Steven, John Haltiwanger, Ron Jarmin, Josh Lerner, and Javier Miranda. 2009. "Private Equity, Jobs, and Productivity." In A. Gurung and J. Lerner, eds., *Globalization of Alternative Investments Working Papers Volume 2: Global Economic Impact of Private Equity Report 2009*. New York: World Economic Forum (http://bit.ly/1AIKl7j).

Davis, Steven, John Haltiwanger, Ron Jarmin, Josh Lerner, and Javier Miranda. 2011. *Private Equity and Employment*. NBER Working Paper 17399. Cambridge. MA: National Bureau of Economic Research (http://bit.ly/1AIKBn0).

Deener, Will. 2010 (Aug. 22). "Chip Maker Freescale Semiconductor's Taken Drastic Steps to Make a Dent in Its Debt." *Dallas Morning News* (http://bit.ly/1DZeTYO).

Eisenstein, Paul A. 2012 (Oct. 31). "Romney Accused of Personally Profiting as 1000s of Delphi Retirees Lost Pensions." *The Detroit Bureau* (http://bit.ly/1AIL34L).

Fleischer, Victor. 2013 (Aug. 1). "Sun Capital Court Ruling Threatens Structure of Private Equity." *New York Times* (http://nyti.ms/1AILhsC).

Global Credit Research. 2012 (Jan. 30). "Moody's Changes Energy Future Holdings Corp's Rating Outlook to Negative from Stable" (http://bit.ly/1AILyM4).

Gotbaum, Josh. 2013. Statement before the ABI Commission to Study Reform of Chapter 11. Washington, DC, March 14 (http://commission.abi.org).

Gross, Daniel. 2005 (May 21). "The Bottom-Feeder King: Never Mind Hedge Funds. Wilbur Ross Gets Rich the Unfashionable Way—In Steel Plants, Textile Mills, and Other Stuff Nobody Wants." *New York Magazine* (http://nym.ag/1AIMhNd).

International Brotherhood of Electrical Workers (IBEW). 2012. Interview, IBEW representative, November 27.

International Machinists Union (IAM). 2012a. Interview, IAM staff, December 19.

International Machinists Union (IAM). 2012b (Apr. 5). "Big Victory at Spirit AeroSystems in North Carolina." *Machinists News Network* (http://bit.ly/1AIMHTP).

Kosman, Josh. 2009. *The Buyout of America: How Private Equity Will Cause the Next Great Credit Crisis*. New York: Penguin Group.

KPS Partners. 2013. "Who We Are." KPS Capital Partners (http://bit.ly/1AIMSyo).

Lazonick, William. 1992. "Controlling the Market for Corporate Control: The Historical Significance of Managerial Capitalism." *Industrial and Corporate Change*, Vol. 1, no. 3, pp. 445–488.

Manners, David. 2014 (Mar. 10). "Private Equity, NXP, and Freescale. *Electronics Weekly* (http://bit.ly/1DZguOu).

Mervyn's Department Store. 2011. Interview with former manager. June 30.

Palast, Greg. 2012 (Oct. 17). "Mitt Romney's Bailout Bonanza." *The Nation* (http://bit.ly/1DZgLRw).

Pension Benefit Guaranty Corporation (PBGC). No date. PBGC website (http://www.pbgc.gov).

PitchBook. 2012a. Delphi Corporation Company Profile.

PitchBook. 2012b. Harry & David Company Profile.

PitchBook. 2013. Spirit AeroSystems Company Profile.

PitchBook. 2014a. Freescale Semiconductor Company Profile.

PitchBook. 2014b. Energy Future Holdings Company Profile.

Primack, Dan. 2013 (May 21). "The Big Deal." *Term Sheet*. Fortune.com.

Private Equity Growth Capital Council (PEGCC). 2013. PEGCC website (http://www.pegcc.org).

Private Equity Growth Capital Council (PEGCC). 2014. PEGCC website (http://www.pegcc.org).

Rosenthal, Steven M. 2013 (Jan. 21). "Taxing Private Equity Funds as Corporate 'Developers.'" *Tax Notes: Commentary/Policy Perspectives*. Washington, DC: Tax Policy Center of the Urban Institute and Brookings Institution (http://tpc.io/1AUTNuP).

Society of Professional Engineering Employees in Aerospace (SPEEA). 2012. Interview, SPEEA staff, December 17.

Society of Professional Engineering Employees in Aerospace (SPEEA). 2013. Interview, SPEEA Staff, January 6.

Spector, Mike, Emily Glazer, and Rebecca Smith. 2014 (Apr. 29). "Energy Future Holdings Files for Bankruptcy Chapter 11: Filing by Texas Power Firm, Formerly TXU, Is Among the Biggest Ever" (http://on.wsj.com/1AUTTm1).

Stein, Nicholas. 2003 (May 26). "Wilbur Ross Is A Man Of Steel … and Textiles and Optical Networking and Anything Else in Deep, Deep Trouble." *Fortune* (http://for.tn/1DZiJkE).

Stout, Lynn. 2012. *The Shareholder Value Myth: How Putting Shareholders First Harms Investors, Corporations, and the Public*. San Francisco: Berrett-Koehler.

Strömberg, Per. 2008. "The New Demography of Private Equity." In A. Gurung and J. Lerner, eds., *Globalization of Alternative Investments Working Papers Volume 1: The Global Economic Impact of Private Equity Report 2008*. New York: World Economic Forum (http://bit.ly/1AIJGTC).

United Steelworkers of America (USWA). 2002 (Dec. 12). "Summary: Proposed Agreement Between International Steel Group, Inc., and the United Steelworkers of America."

United Steelworkers of America (USWA). 2003 (Dec. 12). "Summary: Proposed Agreement Between International Steel Group, Inc., and the United Steelworkers of America on Behalf of Former Bethlehem Steel Employees."

United Steelworkers of America (USWA). 2004. "Steel Industry Restructuring: Steel Crisis, Bankruptcies, Pension Plan Terminations, and Consolidation." USWA–IG Metall seminar, Sprockhovel, Germany, October 11–15.

United Steelworkers of America (USWA). 2012. Interview, Tom Conway, International Vice President for Administration, June 1.

U.S. District Court for the District of Massachusetts. 2012. *Sun Capital Partners III, LP et al. v. New England Teamsters and Trucking Industry Pension Fund*. Civil Action No. 10-10921-DPW, October 18.

Von Wachter, Till. 2013. "Survey of the Literature of Job Displacement." *Journal of Economic Literature*, Fall.

CHAPTER 8

Employee Stock Ownership and Profit Sharing in the New Era of Financialization and Inequality in the Distribution of Capital Income

JOSEPH R. BLASI
Rutgers University

RICHARD B. FREEMAN
Harvard University

DOUGLAS L. KRUSE
Rutgers University

INTRODUCTION

Concentration of capital ownership in the hands of a few contributes massively to income and wealth inequality in the United States and in the rest of the world. As capital's share of national output has risen, inequality in capital ownership has become an even greater driver of inequality than in the past. In this paper, we build on analysis in *The Citizen's Share: Reducing Inequality in the 21st Century* (Blasi, Freeman, and Kruse 2015) to make the case that firm-based policies that broaden capital ownership and access to capital income are the best way to reduce the concentration of capital ownership and capital income and that federal and state and local governments should adopt tax and other incentives to encourage such behavior.

We ground our argument in the position of capital ownership in U.S. history, the extent of worker share ownership and profit sharing at the present, and the role of unequal capital ownership in the distribution of income. We argue that policies favoring greater employee sharing of equity and profits are likely to improve the economic performance of firms and the income distribution. We recognize the potential for policies beyond those considered in this chapter to improve workers' well-being and the need for extensive simulations of changes in policy against alternative hypothetical future economic worlds to provide better guidance to policy makers.

CAPITAL OWNERSHIP IN AMERICAN HISTORY

When the Revolutionary War for independence from Great Britain ended in 1783, the cod fishery, one of the mainstays of the colonial economy, was in dire straits. Cod was the fourth most valuable export of the colonies. The fish were caught off the coast of New England and to the north. The cod were dried and exported to Europe—particularly to Spain, Portugal, southern Europe around the Mediterranean, Great Britain, and France—and to slave colonies in the West Indies. During the war, the British had destroyed many American ships, closed many European markets to American fish, and made life difficult for the fishermen who manned the cod ships.

Soon after taking office as first president of the United States, George Washington asked Secretary of State Thomas Jefferson to find a way to help citizens resurrect the cod fishery and make it prosper. Neither Washington nor Jefferson favored direct state ownership or state subsidies and state control. They wanted a policy that best fit the new American republic. To devise the policy Jefferson conducted the first research on inclusive capitalism in American history, working with Tench Coxe, who was the assistant secretary of the treasury under Treasury Secretary Alexander Hamilton. Coxe, a well-known colonial political economist, asked Philadelphia shipper Joseph Anthony about work practices on the cod ships and was told in a 1790 letter from Anthony that "they (the crew) were generally found the most attentive, when their Dependence was on a Share of what they Caught" rather than fixed wages not tied to productivity.

In fact, broad-based profit sharing had been the norm in the cod and the whale fisheries for over a century in the colonies. The problem that most concerned cod fishermen and ship owners in rebuilding the industry was high tariffs on imports of equipment that they needed to operate the fishery. The high tariffs put a burden on the fishermen and owners of the ships, but they were important to support the Treasury. What was needed was a policy to encourage the cod fishery sector that included the broad group of fishermen in sharing the fruits of this industry without bankrupting the Treasury. Jefferson gave his analysis of the industry in a *Report on the American Fisheries*, which he delivered to the Speaker of the House of Representatives on February 1, 1791.

On February 16, 1792, Congress passed and President Washington signed a new law that essentially gave tax credits to cod ships that went out during fishing season based on the weight of the vessels. The tax credits were divided five eighths to the crew and three eights to the owners of the ships, recognizing the tax burden that fell on both parties. This was probably the first time in American history that a tax credit was divided between the owners of capital and the workers in the industry in question. Moreover, as a condition for receiving the tax credit, President George Washington's law required a signed agreement between the captain and the crew, before the ship went to sea, in which the captain and owners of the ship agreed to additionally continue to practice broad-based profit sharing on the entire catch. This was the first time in American history that capital shares, in this case in the form of profit sharing, was a condition of a federal tax credit. The law stayed in force for decades.[1]

The founders of the United States favored Jefferson's solution because, despite some fundamental differences over how the economy should be structured, they believed that a republic required a strong middle class and equitable distribution of wealth in order to survive and be sustainable.[2] To maintain the middle class, they supported policies to make capital ownership and capital income broadly available to the citizens.

In a June 19, 1788, letter, Washington explicitly recognized the value of broad-based land ownership: "It is also believed that it will not be less advantageous to the happiness of the lowest class of people because of the equal distribution of property." The chartering of the first joint stock corporation in the new Commonwealth of Pennsylvania in April 1786 generated heated debate over whether corporations would facilitate the concentration of wealth that was the antithesis of a democratic polity (Blasi, Freeman, and Kruse 2014).

John Adams, the second president, repeatedly articulated his fear that concentrated property ownership could undermine the republic and worked hard to distribute public lands to citizens in Massachusetts to prevent such concentration. Alexander Hamilton and Benjamin Franklin expressed support and understanding of the role of broad-based property ownership.

Jefferson, the third president, argued that a higher proportion of property owners reduced political corruption and recommended that the Virginia Constitution contain clauses to require the state to make public land available to every citizen. In a letter to James Madison on October 28, 1785, Jefferson declared that "legislators cannot invent too many devices for subdividing property, only taking care to let their subdivisions go hand in hand with the natural affections of the human mind." Jefferson drafted Washington's first policy on distributing public lands to landless citizens and set up land distribution offices during his presidency.

James Madison, the fourth president and in many ways the deepest thinker about the conflict between inequality and democracy, wrote in his speech on the right of suffrage in 1821 that "the United States have a precious advantage, also, in the actual distribution of property, and in the universal hope of acquiring property." He warned that citizens would call for redistribution of property if they did not have the opportunity to be property owners themselves. Looking a hundred years into the future, Madison projected in 1829 that the acreage of fertile land would not keep up with the population, making the dream of the yeoman farmer impossible to sustain. He sought new policies to maintain wide distribution of property ownership, meeting with others concerned about inequality of ownership, including Robert Owen, the proponent of various worker cooperative ideas. In his essay in the *National Gazette* on January 23, 1792, Madison called for specific new policies to solve this problem, which he viewed as the most serious one facing the republic (Blasi, Freeman, and Kruse 2014).

The ownership policies that resulted from the concerns of the founders were comprehensive, radical, and far reaching. In 1787, before the signing of the Constitution of the United States, founders all agreed on the Northwest Ordinance that offered cheap land in what would become Ohio, Indiana, Michigan, Illinois, Wisconsin, and part of Minnesota, and they abolished servitude in those territories. To expand the yeoman farmer idea and what Jefferson called the "empire of liberty," the United States made the Louisiana Purchase of almost a million square miles (later forming parts of 15 of the current U.S. states) in 1802 to have cheap land available to citizens. Until the Civil War, the idea of a far-reaching "homestead act," first articulated by Democratic Senator Thomas Hart Benton in 1809 and supported in Republican and Democratic Party platforms, was the most popular public policy in the entire nation, except for postal service.

In 1862, President Abraham Lincoln asked Speaker of the House of Representatives, Republican Galusha Grow, an anti-slavery representative from Lancaster, Pennsylvania, to steer a Homestead Act through Congress. The act allowed citizens over age 21 to claim a homestead at little or no cost, by making available 20% of public land and 10% of the entire U.S. land mass for that purpose. For the first time, women could be homesteaders, and they made up a significant proportion of homestead grants. The act led to homestead acts in many states such as Texas. Echoing Madison's concern about the limits of land, Grow pointed out that the future of the broad-based property idea lay in ways of spreading shares of corporations to citizens, recognizing that corporate assets, unlike land, were limitless (Blasi, Freeman, and Kruse 2014).

The Spread of Profit Sharing and Equity Sharing, 1865–1889

The idea that broad-based capital shares in corporations was the next step in the property ownership/yeoman farmer ideal of the United States developed further as business capital increased in importance. In the mid-1880s, John Bates Clark, one of the country's leading economists, argued in *The Philosophy of Wealth: Economic Principles Newly Formulated* (1886) that capital shares and financial inclusion was the only private market economy solution to the deep conflict of interests between labor and capital in a democratic society. He advised several doctoral students on their theses about equity and profit sharing at Johns Hopkins University that covered several regional geographic sectors of the United States and made sure that articles on their findings appeared in the first issues of the newly created American Economic Association (AEA) economics journal (Clark was the third president of the AEA, while the author of one of the theses on capital shares, Richard T. Ely, was the AEA's sixth president).

In his 1915 presidential address to the AEA, John H. Gray, the 16th president of the AEA, laid out clearly the relation between ownership and the well-being of labor, echoing the broad-based property ideal:

> When the American Economic Association was formed about a quarter of a century ago, the prevailing system of economics taught that the state or organized society as such had nothing to do with economics. The sole function of the state was to preserve law and order, and to prevent physical violence to persons and injury to property. The philosophy did not provide for a condition of affairs in which the mass of workmen were unskilled, working for wages, and the instruments of industry were owned by another class of society for the most part devoid of technical knowledge.

> But it was not until the days of capitalistic industry and the enormous surplus resulting therefrom, with the consequent class cleavage and the creation of the great wage-earning non-propertied classes, that we began to discover that the majority of personally free adult males, because of economic conditions, were quite [as] unfree economically as many of those whose personal freedom was limited by law. Should the decline of real wages continue for many years, the tension is likely to become very great, for inequality, with the consequent lack of bargaining ability, tends to increase at an every accelerating rate. Our free land has heretofore obscured the real tendencies of our economic development.

> On the other hand, it offered opportunities to vast numbers of people to make individual fortunes and rise to the capitalistic classes … Whatever the final outcome may be it must accomplish two important results: give the workman a conscious share in the direction of industry; and it will also … give him a share in the speculative gains and profits of the industry.

> With concentrated wealth and large production, in the absence of a wise and conscious social policy, increased population and consequent rise in rents will tend to shut out an ever increasing

part of the population from dominion over or ownership in
the natural resources and implements and tools of production.
(Gray 1915:5–18)

From 1865 through 1889, social entrepreneurs, both from management
and the labor movement, experimented with and invented approaches to
make profit shares and equity shares (employee stock ownership and
worker cooperatives) available to regular workers and managers. At the
end of his life, Andrew Carnegie explicitly tied industrial profit shares
and ownership shares to the yeoman farmer idea, mentioning profit sharing
in the cod industry, and suggesting that capital shares be encouraged
through the tax system. Skilled workers organized cooperatives. Trade
unions of different kinds, including the Knights of Labor, made share
ownership a key part of their ideology, but put only limited organizational effort behind it and were unable to develop worker-owned cooperatives
as a sustainable system. Unions abandoned this strategy in favor of collective
bargaining by the time the American Federation of Labor was founded.

Economists from the AEA's first president, Francis Amasa Walker (later
president of MIT), through John Commons (19th AEA president) argued
that the problem lay in difficulties of worker-owned firms in hiring
managerial talent and in paying the market price for such talent. Believing
that worker ownership and profit sharing would excel in economic performance as long it had top talent and room for "the entrepreneur" to take a
leadership role, Walker helped set up a national association to promote
employee ownership and profit sharing. Walker explicitly wrote that pure
worker cooperatives could be successful if his conditions were met.

Ownership and profit-sharing systems initiated by business had greater
success than workers' cooperatives at the time with larger businesses.
Charles S. Pillsbury showed that broad-based profit sharing could work
efficiently in the world's largest grain flour mill. Pillsbury also helped
demonstrate that worker cooperatives could succeed with strong management talent and advice; Pillsbury himself contributed his personal support
and expertise to the Minneapolis worker co-ops. William Cooper Procter
at Procter & Gamble funded worker purchases of company stock with
cash profit sharing rather than wage investments and later used sales of
stocks at a discount and dividends on those stocks to fund worker share
ownership.

Elements of Procter's installment payments for purchasing worker stock,
such as short-term company loans, discounts, matching company contributions, and funding worker ownership with cash profit sharing and
dividends are key aspects of the popular employee share-purchase plan
today (which has discounts), the widespread employee stock ownership
plan, or ESOP (which uses installments, worker access to company loans

from banks or other lenders in order to buy the shares, and dividend payments), and worker acquisition of shares through 401(k) plans (where companies often match worker contributions in company shares) today. George Eastman probably created the first broad-based stock option in a high-technology firm, which Kodak was in its day.

There were also mistaken business efforts to introduce greater employee profit sharing and ownership. Andrew Carnegie's general idea to tie the income of steelworkers to the world price of steel probably played a role in the Homestead Massacre. The effort of John D. Rockefeller, Jr.'s Special Conference Committee (a group of 10 to 20 corporations that tried to reform capitalism using worker capital shares) to fund worker ownership mainly with worker savings collapsed with the 1929 stock market crash. Unions were correctly suspicious of the risk facing workers who were buying equity shares with their own cash and wages. As a solution to this and other problems that could limit the applicability of worker ownership, in 1973 the U.S. Congress enacted the Employee Retirement Income Security Act (ERISA), which contained provisions for a new institutional form for funding worker ownership, known as employee stock ownership plans (ESOPs). Based on ideas of political economist Louis O. Kelso and championed by Senator Russell Long, chairman of the Senate Finance Committee, ESOPs allowed firms to borrow funds to buy stock for the trust without the workers putting up collateral or paying for the shares themselves. The loan would be paid back by the company, and the workers would receive grants of stock as the loan was paid back. ERISA also included a number of fairness tests and standards to be sure that the tax benefits were used to benefit a broad-based group of workers in each firm.

Kelso's concept was that corporations and the rich often funded their purchases of capital with loans paid for by the future income on the capital itself, so why not apply this financial engineering to workers? While ESOPs are no guarantee that a business will succeed, the evidence presented later in this chapter (Policies to Encourage Profit Sharing and Worker Equity) shows that they have for the most part worked well. Buyouts of failing firms in which workers purchase company stock with wage and benefit and work rule concessions, which all too often just postpone company closure, were never part of Kelso's concept of the ESOP and never envisioned in ERISA. The other worker ownership idea that has generally failed is the over-concentration of worker investments in company stock in their 401(k) plans (Blasi, Freeman, and Kruse 2014).

The lesson from American experience is that *grants* of equity and profit shares to workers above a fair fixed wage are the only low-risk form of broad-based profit sharing and worker ownership that make long-term sense in an enterprise-based model of ownership. Substituting profit sharing or equity shares for low wages or benefits may play a role in entrepreneurial cultures for 20- to 30-year-olds in tech start-ups and some small businesses, but it is too risky for most workers (Blasi, Freeman, and Kruse 2014; Kruse, Freeman, Blasi 2010). Any publicly supported efforts to extend worker ownership of capital or capital income should focus on lower-risk grants of equity through an ESOP (where workers do not purchase the stock or make concessions) through grants of restricted stock or stock options, grants of profit sharing or equity sharing, or combinations of all of these plans. Workers sacrificing to buy worker ownership or turning 401(k) retirement plans into their major retirement plan is, in retrospect, too risky (Blasi, Freeman, and Kruse 2014).

The Extent of Profit Sharing and Equity Sharing Today

To find out the extent of workplace-based profit sharing and equity ownership, we commissioned a special supplement to the General Social Survey (GSS) of the National Opinion Research Center at the University of Chicago for 2002, 2006, 2010, and 2014. The GSS is based on a national representative sample of all adult workers in the nation. The data are based on the 2006 and 2010 General Social Surveys and will be updated when the 2014 survey data are available in July 2015.

Figure 1 shows that 47% of adult workers in the United States have some form of profit or equity sharing or broad-based stock options, or a combination. About a third of all workers with shares have all three. The 2010 GSS shows that 17.4% of adult workers had stock in their companies and 8.7% held stock options. More union workers proportionally than non-union workers have stock options and almost as many have employee stock ownership. The 2006 GSS established that about a third had profit sharing and a fourth had gain sharing.

Figure 2 shows the median and mean value of equity and profit shares. For profit shares and gain sharing, the median share granted in the last year for which data were available was $2,000, which compares with $6,935 for the mean. For worker ownership shares, the $10,000 median and $32,692 mean are the total value of all equity shares currently held at the time of the survey from all past years in which they were bought or granted. Other data suggest that workers with stock options would have a median profit net of exercise of those stock options of $75,000 (mean of $249,900). Figure 2 illustrates that shares of profits and equity reach modest levels at the median.

Figure 3 contrasts workers at different income levels in the national representative sample. The black bars show typical or median employee ownership only for workers who reported to the GSS that they were paid at or above the market for their fixed wage, so those amounts net out possible substitution of wages for ownership. The white bars represent workers in the top quarter of incomes. Workers making less than $50,000

FIGURE 1
Citizens' Shares in the United States

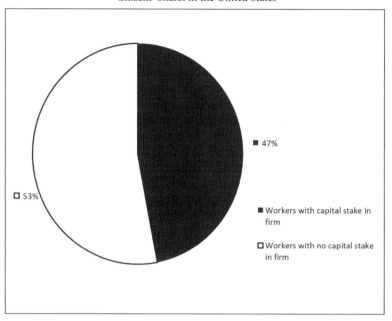

FIGURE 2
How Much Is the Typical Citizen's Share?

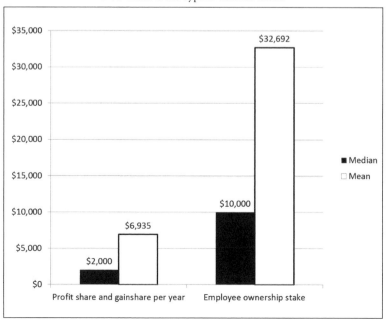

FIGURE 3
Employee Ownership and Income Levels

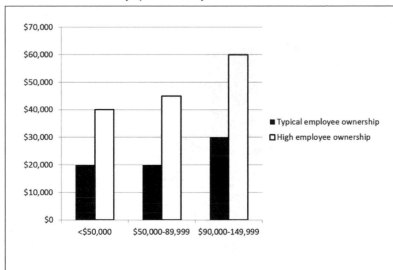

have about $20,000 in worker ownership shares, but those with shares in the 25% most generous plans accumulated about $40,000.

Figure 4 illustrates the incidence of worker owners in the United States by company size, industry, and occupation. It shows that just over 40% of all workers in companies of more than 10,000 employees own stock in the company where they work. Larger companies have more employee stock ownership. Worker shares are frequent in most industries except for the wholesale sector and are quite common in communications/utilities and nondurable manufacturing, representing more than 25% of all the workers in the industry (Blasi, Freeman, and Kruse 2014).

The figures on company size categories show that over 15% of all workers in firms with 100 to 499 employees have equity shares, while over 30% of workers in all firms with 500 to 999 workers have equity shares. These data largely reflect the importance of the ESOP sector in ownership in the United States. ESOPs are common, especially among closely held firms in these company size categories. Because of specific reporting requirements for ESOPs in federal administrative datasets, we are able to look more closely at this form of employee ownership. On the basis of U.S. Department of Labor data from Form 5500, which each ERISA benefit plan, including ESOPs, must fill out annually, the National Center for Employee Ownership estimates there were 8,926 ESOPs and ESOP-like plans with 14.7 million employee participants and almost $1 trillion

FIGURE 4
Employee Ownership in Different Parts of the Economy

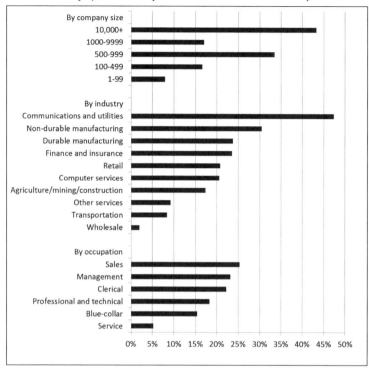

in market value in 2014. For comparative purposes, the value of the NYSE and NASDAQ were valued at approximately $25 trillion dollars at the end of October 2014.[3]

Table 1 delves deeper into the data on ESOPs. Almost half of ESOPs are in S corporations. C corporations pay corporate taxes directly, but S corporations pass on their federal tax liability to individual employee shareholders, who pay the taxes. It is estimated that, as of 2015, about 30% to 40% of ESOPs are 100% worker owned—which is substantially above the estimated 15% to 20% of ESOPs that were all worker owned in 1988 and 1990. This trend reflects the fact that many ESOPs today form when successful small and medium-size business owners sell the business to the workers upon the retirement of the founding entrepreneurs. Business founders often make a schedule to sell the equity to the workers in stages until they are totally cashed out. About 3% of ESOPs are currently in publicly traded companies.

Looking at other datasets, some form of equity sharing is found in about 10% of the Fortune 100 and 20% of the Fortune 500, while equity

TABLE 1
Basic Characteristics of ESOPs, 2015

Percentage of ESOPs that are in S corporations	40%–45%
Percentage of ESOPs that are 100% ESOP owned	30%–40%
Percentage of private companies with more than minimum equired voting rights	17%
Mean allocation to accounts, as a percentage of payroll (private companies)	5%–8%
Mean allocation to accounts, as a percentage of payroll (public companies)	3%–4%
Median number of employees, private companies	125
Mean number of employees, private companies	1,500
Median number of employees, public companies	2,100
Mean number of participants, public companies	14,000
Percentage of ESOPs that are in public companies	3%

Source: National Center for Employee Ownership (http://www.nceo.org).
Note: Data for this table were compiled from Ohio and Michigan studies, NCEO databases, and Form 5500s.

or profit sharing is in about half of the list of winners in *Fortune* magazine's annual 100 Best Companies to Work For in America competition. Profit or equity sharing in worker cooperatives is relatively rare (223 worker co-ops with about 7,500 workers according to the census of the University of Wisconsin Center for Cooperatives, although there may be as many as double this number) but is now on the rise as cooperative development and management has become more informed. These data and the survey of different industrial sectors and types of firms in the economy establish a fact useful in policy development: that broad-based employee ownership and profit sharing have sufficient institutional presence as share mechanisms in the United States to be part of a national policy on shares (Blasi, Freeman, and Kruse 2014).

CAPITAL OWNERSHIP AND CAPITAL INCOME IN INCOME AND WEALTH INEQUALITY

Employee equity and profit sharing, while spread more widely in the United States than in other advanced economies, does not yet have the breadth or magnitude nationally to greatly impact inequality in the ownership of capital or in labor incomes, where U.S. statistics treat incomes to employees based on capital, including stock options, profit-related bonuses, and stock options as labor income rather than as part of capital income. Ownership of capital is highly concentrated in the United States. The richest 5% of households have over half of all wealth, while the richest 10% have over three quarters. Eighty percent of financial assets are owned by the richest 20%. Half of all households own no stock or equity of any kind.

Over time, the share of income on capital going to the top 1% of households increased from one third of such income in 1979 to about three fifths in 2005. From 1993 to 2010, income in general from the bottom 99%, including capital gains, grew about 6% adjusted for inflation, while the overall income for the top 1% grew by 58%, according to the Economic Policy Institute (Blasi, Freeman, and Kruse 2014). In the Clinton administration, the wealthiest 1% of families received 57% of total income growth. In the Bush administration that followed, the number was 45%. Adding to the trend in inequality, the proportion of income accruing to capital has gone up in the United States, as in most countries.

Figure 5 illustrates data from the Urban Institute and the Brookings Institution Tax Policy Center showing that 86% of all capital gains and all capital income in 2011 were concentrated in the richest 20% of the population.

These data indicate that while the top 1% had 56.8% of capital gains and capital income, the extension of the top group to the top 20% pushes

FIGURE 5
Distribution of Capital Income by Percentile

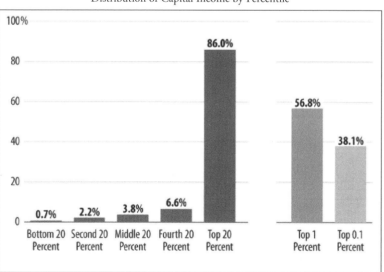

Source: Urban Institute–Brookings Institution Tax Policy Center.

Note: Figures are for calendar year 2011, current law. Capital income includes taxable and nontaxable interest income, income from dividends, realized capital gains or losses, and imputed corporate tax liability. The cash income percentile classes used are based on the income distribution of the entire population and contain an equal number of people, not tax units.

the levels of concentration to 86%. This approximates the concentration of property under English feudalism before the American Revolution, against which the American Experiment was in part a reaction. The founders' notion that broad-based property ownership was necessary for democracy (albeit one with slavery in some states and a class- and gender-based electorate) was intrinsically tied to fears that democracy was incompatible with such levels of inequality in ownership.

In an article that he wrote for the *National Gazette* on January 23, 1792, James Madison sketched out several criteria for developing policies to combat the political divisions in society that he expected to result from wide divergences in economic interests:

> In every political society, parties are unavoidable. A difference of interests, real or supposed is the most natural and fruitful source of them. The great objects should be to combat the evil: 1. By establishing political equality among all. 2. By withholding unnecessary opportunities from a few, to increase the inequality of property, by an immoderate, and especially unmerited, accumulation of riches. 3. By the silent operation of laws, which, without violating the rights of property, reduce extreme wealth towards a state of mediocrity, and raise extreme indigence towards a state of comfort. 4. By abstaining from measures which operate differently on different interests, and particularly such as favor one interest, at the expense of another. 5. By making one party a check on the other, so far as the existence of parties cannot be prevented, nor their views accommodated—If this is not the language of reason, it is that of republicanism.[4]

Our recommended policies closely follow James Madison's criteria and his concern about the connection between political corruption, the commandeering of the tax system by the powerful, and the lack of broad-based property ownership.

It is possible that the United States can prosper without addressing the inequality of ownership. Perhaps a resurgence of trade unions and collective bargaining could lift the earnings of American workers and shift income from capital to labor and reduce inequality of labor incomes as well. Perhaps a huge tax on capital income and a more progressive income tax could reduce the concentration of wealth and after-tax inequality of income. We do not see either of these possibilities as highly likely in the United States currently. Our proposed solution is for government policies to support the classical republican idea of broad-based property ownership to address the problem of inequality and to improve the functioning of the economy (Blasi, Freeman, and Kruse 2014).

POLICIES TO ENCOURAGE PROFIT SHARING AND WORKER EQUITY

This section seeks to convince readers that federal, state, and local tax incentives and/or related policies for firms to broaden low-risk forms of profit sharing and equity sharing at the workplace will improve economic performance and begin the process of reversing the trend toward greater inequality.

The starting point for our claim is a large and growing literature that shows that the key indicators of economic performance, productivity, and many other measures related to firm performance are on average higher for firms that operate with profit sharing and employee stock ownership than otherwise comparable firms that do not follow those practices. The statistics also show that workers in firms with shares and participatory work relations have higher compensation, stay on the job longer, and offer more suggestions for improvement than workers in other firms. Most striking, workers in these businesses try to correct the behavior of workers who are not producing up to par more than do workers without a property stake in their firm.

While most of the analyses are cross sectional in design, studies that compare firms before and after they adopt profit sharing or employee stock ownership relative to firms that did not change policies also show that shares and participatory work practices improve performance. Beneath the averages, several studies find that success with broad-based and related work practices depends as much or more on the company building a supportive corporate culture than on pecuniary rewards.[5] And in the few cases in which firms have experimented with different forms of shares or structures of work, or in which researchers have varied modes of pay and work in social science laboratories, the data show that workers also do better when they earn "what are usually two distinct revenues, belonging to two distinct persons, the profits of stock, and the wages of labour," as Adam Smith wrote in *The Wealth of Nations*.

Several researchers, including ourselves in *The Citizen's Share*, have reviewed this literature.[6] In 1995, Christopher Doucouliagos did a meta-statistical analysis of the evidence, combining results from many disparate studies to assess the magnitude and significance of coefficients. A meta-statistical summary combines different findings from different datasets into a single estimate covering all studies. This is done by combining estimates from different datasets and studies along with samples of different sizes from different studies—which are, understandably, subject to different biases or data imperfections—into a single estimate covering all studies. Thus, the meta-statistical summary presumptively averages imperfections across studies that are random to obtain a more accurate assessment of reality than that given in any individual study. The reviews cover many published studies and some unpublished ones—which together with newer studies not covered that we have identified—provide over 100 study/data points.

The finding from these reviews is that firms with share arrangements average better outcomes than otherwise comparable firms without share arrangements, with an order of magnitude in the range of 2% to 5%. Meaningful profit sharing generally has larger effects on output than does employee stock ownership. The weaker effect of ownership than of profit sharing may reflect the fact that meaningful profit sharing is a more immediate reward than employee stock ownership, which is a more long-term reward. Employee stock ownership tends to have positive performance effects but generally usually when combined with a supportive corporate culture. Combinations of programs—employee stock ownership and profit sharing or a stock purchase plan and profit sharing—have larger effects on output than do individual programs by themselves. In fact, such combinations of equity and profit sharing are common.

To gain greater insight into the reasons for these general results, we undertook two additional studies. The first, the National Bureau of Economic Research (NBER) Shared Capitalism Study, surveyed over 40,000 employees in 14 corporations. The companies included large multinationals traded on major U.S. stock markets, important high-technology innovators large and small, medium-size corporations and smaller factories with ESOPs and financial service firms, and other service-oriented companies spread across over 300 workplaces around the country and in their foreign divisions. This study gave us data on lots of workers but a small, almost case study–size sample of firms. Business school researchers call studies like this "insider econometrics" (Bartel, Ichniowski, and Shaw 2004), by which they mean a study that gathers sufficient quantitative data on performance to test hypotheses in a small number of companies (sometimes just one) but combines the quantitative analysis with discussions with the firm to help interpret the data. We report the results in *Shared Capitalism at Work* (Kruse, Freeman, and Blasi 2010).

For our analysis, we created an index of worker financial participation in the firm's performance for each worker based on how much ownership he or she had in the company and how much he or she shared in profits and stock options. The scores varied substantially among workers. Some had a large ownership stake. Some had little. Some were in establishments with a strong gain-sharing or profit-sharing programs. Others were not. We then compared workers who had different shared capitalism scores but were similar in occupation, fixed wages, supervisory responsibilities, tenure with the company, gender, age, disability, and so forth. We and our co-workers analyzed how economic outcomes varied among workers within the same company and how economic outcomes varied among workplaces.

The NBER study found that workers with higher shared capitalism scores were more committed to their employer in several ways than workers with lower scores and that these workers were better off in important aspects of their work lives as well. Workers with greater property in corporations in firms are more likely to stay with the company, are more loyal, are more willing to work harder, make more suggestions, and have better fixed pay and working conditions. These characteristics resemble those that many of the founders ascribed to the independent proprietor of land in early American history. Our analysis of the NBER data also found that workers with employee stock ownership or profit sharing or gain sharing are more likely than workers without shares to take action to get a shirking fellow employee to work harder or better. This suggests the fears that free riding undermines the incentives of ownership or profit sharing are exaggerated. We further found that the effects of shared capitalism were most pronounced with workers who reported a supportive corporate culture consisting of employee involvement in solving company problems, high training relative to other workers, employment security, fixed wages at or above the market, and a higher-trust type of supervision.

Finally, to deal with the limited number of firms in the NBER survey, we used the General Social Survey sample of workers described earlier to test the effects based on variation among workers in different firms. Because the GSS selects workers at random from the country as a whole, each observation is likely to represent a single firm. The weakness of the GSS is the opposite of that of the NBER study: many firms but essentially only one worker per firm rather than many workers but few firms. Despite the difference in sampling design, most findings of the NBER study were replicated with the analysis of the GSS dataset.

Our second study used data from the Great Place to Work Institute, which reviews the applications of major corporations that were named one of the 100 Best Companies to Work For in America that *Fortune* magazine presents annually with great fanfare. Because being named one of the hundred best is an honor that can attract additional and better job applicants and help retain and spur current employees as well as positive publicity, about 400 corporations apply for consideration every year. The shares of half of the corporations that apply are traded on the NYSE and the NASDAQ, where they represent 20% of the market value of the public stock market and 10% of employment and sales of all stock market companies, representing a substantial segment of the American economy.

To determine the 100 Best Companies to Work For, the Great Place to Work Institute queries the top management of each firm about their corporate culture and practices and obtains data on turnover and other aspects of work practices and corporate culture. The institute then surveys a random group of each company's workers and asks them how they are paid—with cash profit sharing, employee stock ownership, or broad-based stock options—and queries them about their attitudes toward the company and behaviors at work. Between 2006 and 2008, over 1,300 corporations applied for the competition. Over 300,000 of their workers filled out the Great Place to Work Institute survey that ultimately determines whether a corporation makes the 100 Best list and where it places on the list. The institute uses the survey responses to develop an indicator of corporate culture that it calls the Trust Index based on workers' view of the credibility, respect, fairness, pride, and camaraderie of their company. The Great Place to Work Institute gave us access to its data under strict confidentiality procedures to examine the relation between employee stock ownership and profit sharing and work practices and the performance of applicant firms.

Our first finding from analyzing these data was that a larger proportion of the applicants for the 100 Best Companies to Work For competition were more likely than the general population of firms to have some form of employee stock ownership or profit sharing for their workers. Eighteen percent had ESOPs. Eighteen percent had cash profit- or gain-sharing plans. Twenty-two percent had deferred profit-sharing plans. The average ESOP in the sample owned about 17% of company stock. One tenth of the companies were majority worker owned. One in six companies granted stock options to a majority of their workers. Another 17% of the companies granted stock options to between a quarter and half of all the corporation's workers. The average profit-sharing or gain-sharing plan provided workers a 7% bonus on top of their pay.

Our second finding was that corporations with more extensive employee ownership and profit sharing had higher scores on the Trust Index. The workers in these corporations rated their company as more credible, more respectful of workers' interests, fairer, and as providing greater participation in decisions than workers at other firms. ESOPs and profit-sharing plans where profits added a lot to annual salary topped the list in the Trust Index. Workers with stock options did not differ much on the Trust Index from workers without those options.

Our third finding was that corporations with more extensive broad-based capitalism also had reduced voluntary turnover, increased employees' intentions to stay with the firm, and higher return on equity for the firm. Corporations that combined shares with participative work practices and a supportive corporate culture had the biggest payoff in reduced turnover and higher return on equity. Finding these effects in the nonrepresentative 100 Best Companies to Work For sample strengthens the likelihood that the policies have a causal impact on employee well-being and firm performance (Blasi, Freeman, and Kruse 2014).

What Policies Could Encourage Economy-Wide Capital Shares for Workers?

A reasonable policy objective for a country that seeks to improve its economy and its future distribution of income is to give every firm—no matter what its size or industry, public or private—a strong incentive to share prosperity with workers. Blasi, Freeman, and Kruse (2014) give a fairly comprehensive list of possible policies to accomplish this objective. Here we focus on a few large policies.

The first step to increasing the citizen's share is for the United States to make increasing the property ownership and capital income of citizens a national goal. Given the "bully pulpit" of the White House, a president who declared that increasing the citizen's share was a priority for his or her administration would put broad-based capitalism front and center in the national economic discourse. To make such a commitment real, the president could also establish a White House Office of Inclusive Prosperity to coordinate federal policies dealing with broad-based capitalism and to work with the private sector to publicize and encourage best practices (lack of coordination of policies has led to a number of policy errors and disasters, which we review in Blasi, Freeman, and Kruse 2014).

The second step would be to reform the Section 162(m) deduction in the tax code. What is 162(m) and why should reforming it be part of the commitment to broad-based ownership? In 1993, seeking to rein in executive pay in a weak economy, the Clinton administration proposed to allow firms to deduct as a cost of business the fixed salary for the top five executives in stock market corporations only up to a million dollars. Corporations could pay higher amounts of fixed pay, but they could not claim that against the corporate profits tax. As this initial proposal wound its way through bipartisan passage in the Congress, Congress enacted the limitation of one million dollars of salary as deductible from corporate profits but added in Section 162(m), a provision that allowed firms to deduct unlimited "performance-based pay" as a cost of business. This performance-related pay included various employee stock ownership and profit-sharing plans only for the top five executives of all public corporations—namely, stock options, grants of stock, or bonuses paid for nonequity incentive plans—without requiring any evidence that the performance pay had any actual effect on performance.

The result was an unintended tax system that subsidized "unshared capitalism" in which firms achieve tax savings by paying the top five executives with ownership stakes and profit shares in the firm. We estimate that the exemption may have cost taxpayers $5 to $10 billion per year since 1993. In addition to this tax subsidy for unshared capitalism, many publicly traded corporations offer various narrow employee stock ownership or profit-sharing plans to the top 5% of their employees that cost taxpayers from 2001 to 2007 many more billions per year. Our proposal is simple: if a corporation traded on a stock market offers any type of profit-sharing, gain-sharing, employee stock ownership, restricted stock, stock option, or equity plan to its top five executives, the business can deduct this equity and profit sharing beyond the $1 million dollar limit only if it offers the same plan to all workers.[7]

Our third suggestion is to link federal tax subsidies to businesses that offer some form of broad-based ownership. The U.S. corporate tax contains numerous provisions that enable firms to decrease their tax liability and improve their bottom line. By a recent estimate, businesses were to receive about a trillion dollars in tax relief from 2008 through 2014 from the three largest federal tax subsidy programs: accelerated depreciation, deductions for U.S. production and manufacturing activities, and research and development tax credits.[8] Without assessing the virtue or vice of particular provisions that reduce firms' tax liabilities, our proposal is that these tax deductions go only to businesses that offer a broad-based cash or deferred profit-sharing plan or a broad-based employee stock ownership plan not financed by worker savings.[9]

Employee stock ownership will never be a meaningful part of the economy if it is not adopted by a large number of the 5,000 public corporations traded on the NYSE and NASDAQ. Grants of stock to workers (i.e., that workers do not purchase either directly or indirectly through lower wages) are the low-risk way to do this. We propose a plan to encourage stock market companies to make grants of stock to all of their employees in a way that will be easy, favorable to the employees, favorable to the company, and free of bureaucratic red tape. Our idea is to facilitate small increments in employee stock ownership year after year to move most publicly traded corporations to the point where they have employee ownership in the 5% to 25% range, as is done in a number of corporations that integrate employee ownership into their business model. Legislation has been introduced to the House of Representatives that seeks to accomplish this goal.

A publicly traded company would make grants of stock to all of its employees within some simple "safe harbor," straightforward limit of fairness that Congress would determine. For example, it could be equal grants. The company would receive an immediate deduction based on the market value of the stock in the year it was granted. To give corporations the ability to promote these grants to their employees widely, the grants would be excluded from ordinary income taxes and other employment taxes and subject to capital gains taxes and dividend taxes depending on the amount of time the stock has been held. Because the goal is to create a positive environment for company-wide grants of stock to workers, any such proposal should include a provision to make the accounting for such grants favorable to the corporations and transparent to workers, shareholders, and the public.[10]

If, by the logic of the evidence or happenstance, some or all of these policies or others seeking the same goal were adopted, we do not claim they would solve the many current and potential future economic problems facing the country. What they would do is make capital ownership and capital income part of the solution to problems rather than one of the problems. That, we believe, fits with U.S. history and the surprisingly relevant views on ownership that accompanied the founding of our democracy.

ENDNOTES

[1] Many lower-court labor disputes just after the American Revolution involved conflicts between sailors and shipowners about the fairness of paying the profit sharing. See Blasi, Freeman, and Kruse (2014:1–9) for a discussion of the cod fishery case in more detail.

[2] The biggest disagreement was over slavery. Moreover, the founders paid little attention to exclusion of women and minorities from early American society.

[3] See "A Statistical Profile of Employee Ownership," National Center for Employee Ownership (http://bit.ly/18pvKHC) and "Monthly Reports: Labor Statistics," World Federation of Exchanges (http://bit.ly/1PaGlab).

[4] See "Parties" in *The Papers of James Madison* (digital edition, 2010). J.C.A. Stagg, ed. Charlottesville: Rotunda, University of Virginia Press (original source: Congressional Series, Vol. 14 [6 April 1791–16 March 1793], *The National Gazette*, circa January 23, 1792).

[5] See the following:

Doucouliagos, Christopher. 1995. "Worker Participation and Productivity in Labor-Managed and Participatory Capitalist Firms: A Meta-Analysis," *Industrial and Labor Relations Review*, Vol. 40, no. 1, pp. 58–77, especially pp. 67–72.

Kruse Douglas, and Joseph Blasi. 1995. *Employee Ownership, Employee Attitudes and Firm Performance*. National Bureau for Economic Research Working Paper 5277. Cambridge, MA: National Bureau for Economic Research, pp. 1–52, especially 24 and 26 summarizing 26 studies of employee attitudes and 29 studies of firm performance and examining over 128 studies.

Kaarsemaker, Eric. 2006. "Employee Ownership and Human Resource Management." Doctoral dissertation, Radboud University, Nijmegen, The Netherlands, pp. 29–37 (Table 2.2) and pp. 37–44 (Table 2.3).

[6] See the following:

Weitzman, Martin L., and Douglas L. Kruse. 1990. "Profit Sharing and Productivity." In Alan S. Blinder, ed., *Paying for Productivity*. Washington, DC: Brookings Institution, pp. 95–141.

Blasi, Joseph, and Douglas Kruse. 1995.

Bryson, Alex, and Richard Freeman. 2007. *Doing the Right Thing? Does Fair Share Capitalism Improve Workplace Performance?* London: UK Department of Trade and Industry, Employment Relations Research Series, Number 81.

In addition, the following studies reviewed research for the United Kingdom:

Oxera Economic Consultancy. 2007 (Aug.). *Tax Advantaged Employee Share Schemes: Analysis of Productivity Effects, Report 1, Productivity Measured Using Turnover.* Report 33. Prepared for Her Majesty's Revenue and Customs, London.

Oxera Economic Consultancy. 2007 (Aug.). *Tax Advantaged Employee Share Schemes: Analysis of Productivity Effects, Report 2, Productivity Measured Using Gross Value Added.* Report 33. Prepared for Her Majesty's Revenue and Customs, London.

Oxera Economic Consultancy. 2007 (Aug.). *Tax Advantaged Employee Share Schemes: Analysis of Productivity Effects, Overview.* Report 33. Prepared for Her Majesty's Revenue and Customs, London.

Oxera Economic Consultancy. 2007 (Aug.). *Tax Advantaged Employee Share Schemes: Analysis of Productivity Effects, Appendices to Report 1.* Report 33. Prepared for Her Majesty's Revenue and Customs, London.

[7] For the detailed policy proposal, see Freeman, Richard, Joseph Blasi, and Douglas Kruse. 2011. *Inclusive Capitalism for the American Workforce.* Washington, DC: Center for American Progress.

[8] Accelerated depreciation allows corporations to deduct the value of capital equipment to deliver products and services to customers in fewer years, thus reducing taxes; the R&D tax credit allows firms to take a tax credit for incurring R&D expenses in the United States.

[9] By "not financed by worker savings," we mean broad-based plans that grant workers equity or profit sharing and not plans that require workers to buy company stock.

[10] The legislation was most recently introduced in the 112th Congress, First Session, on February 17, 2011, by Congressman Dana Rohrabacher of California with Congressman Walter Jones of North Carolina, Thaddeus McCotter of Michigan, and David McKinley of West Virginia.

REFERENCES

Bartel, Ann, Casey Ichniowski, and Kathryn Shaw. 2004. "Using 'Insider Econometrics' to Study Productivity." *The American Economic Review,* Vol. 94, no. 2, May, pp. 217–223. (Papers and Proceedings of the 116th Annual Meeting of the American Economic Association, San Diego, California, January 3–5, 2004.)

Blasi, Joseph R., Richard B. Freeman, and Douglas L. Kruse. 2014. *The Citizen's Share: Reducing Inequality in the 21st Century.* New Haven and London: Yale University Press.

Clark, John Bates. 1886. *The Philosophy of Wealth.* Boston: Ginn and Company.

Gray, John H. 1915. "Economics and the Law, Annual Address of the President." *The American Economic Review,* Vol. 4, no. 1 (suppl.), March. (Papers and Proceedings of the 27th Annual Meeting of the American Economic Association, Princeton, NJ, December 1914.)

Kruse, Douglas, Joseph Blasi, and Richard Freeman. 2011. *Does Shared Capitalism Help the Best Firms Do Even Better?* NBER Working Paper 7745. Cambridge, MA: National Bureau for Economic Research.

Kruse, Douglas L., Richard B. Freeman, and Joseph R. Blasi. 2010. *Shared Capitalism at Work.* Chicago and London: University of Chicago Press and National Bureau of Economic Research.

CHAPTER 9

Household Wealth Inequality, Retirement Income Security, and Financial Market Swings 1983 Through 2010

EDWARD N. WOLFF
New York University

INTRODUCTION

This chapter summarizes evidence on household wealth inequality trends in the United States from 1983 through 2010. The chapter highlights rising wealth inequality, particularly during the 1980s and throughout the Great Recession from 2007 through 2010, and the increasing reliance on defined contribution plans and financial market returns for the current and future economic security of households. It then analyzes the consequences of these changes for retirement income security, particularly with regard to the aftershocks of the Great Recession.

Three main factors came into play over these years. First, there was a radical transformation of the pension system, with the share of middle-aged householders (ages 47–64) with a traditional defined benefit (DB) pension plan plummeting from 69% in 1983 to 30% in 2010 and the share with a defined contribution (DC) plan such as a 401(k) rising from 12% to 60%. Whereas DC wealth increased by a factor of 14 over these years, DB wealth fell by 27%.

Second, the middle class (defined here as the middle three wealth quintiles) got heavily into debt, with their ratio of total debt to net worth almost doubling from 37% in 1983 to 72% in 2010. Third, this high indebtedness coupled with a heavy concentration of their asserts in housing (two thirds of gross assets) made the middle class "over-leveraged" when the housing market tanked from 2007 through 2010 and resulted in a catastrophic decline in their net worth. Indeed, while housing prices fell by 24% in real terms, median net worth collapsed by 47% in real terms. The same process also led to a decline in retirement security over the Great Recession.

Differential leverage between the rich and the middle class also caused a sharp rise in overall wealth inequality. Though stock prices declined by 26% in real terms over the Great Recession, the very wealthy were much less leveraged than the middle class and, as a result, their wealth fell by much less (in percentage terms).

How did the asset price meltdown and resultant collapse in household wealth affect retirement preparedness of those households approaching retirement? I find somewhat surprisingly that despite the financial meltdown and steep drop in household wealth, average projected retirement income fell by only 6% from 2007 through 2010. However, median expected retirement income was down by a more sizeable 16.4%, a consequence of the steep drop in median net worth. The share of households meeting a 75% replacement rate standard remained unchanged, though this was partly a consequence of declining incomes. However, the projected poverty rate among these households increased by 1.9 percentage points to 12.1%.

The rest of this chapter is organized as follows: The next section is a brief literature review on retirement adequacy, followed by a section providing some background on the Great Recession. After that, sections discuss the measurement of household wealth and describe the data sources used for this study. The chapter continues by presenting time trends in median and average wealth holdings, changes in wealth concentration, and the composition of wealth, followed by an analysis of the effects of leverage on wealth movements over time. A subsequent section investigates changes in wealth holdings by race and ethnicity. Additional sections contain discussions about the concept and measurement of retirement income security, estimates of expected retirement income, the projected poverty rate at retirement, and replacement rates.

BACKGROUND LITERATURE

Several studies have documented changes in pension coverage in the United States, particularly the decline in DB pension coverage among workers over the past few decades. Bloom and Freeman (1992), using the Current Population Survey (CPS) for 1979 and 1988, were among the first to call attention to the drop in DB pension coverage. They reported that the percentage of all workers in age group 25 through 64 covered by these plans fell from 63% to 57% over this period. Gustman and Steinmeier (1992) were among the first to document the changeover from DB to DC plans. On the basis of IRS 5500 filings between 1977 and 1985, they estimated that only about half of the switch was due a decline in DB coverage conditional on industry, size, and union status and that the other half was due to a shift in employment mix toward firms with industry, size, and union status historically associated with low DB coverage rates. Even and Macpherson (1994) also found a pronounced drop in DB pension coverage among male workers, particularly those with low levels of education.

A U.S. Department of Labor (2000) report found that a large proportion of workers, especially low-wage, part-time, and minority workers, were not covered by private pensions. The coverage rate of all private sector wage and salary workers was 44% in 1997. Coverage of part-time, temporary, and low-wage workers was especially low. This appeared to be ascribable to the proliferation of 401(k) plans and the frequent requirement of employee contributions to such plans. Pension participation was found to be highly correlated with wages. While only 6% of workers earning less than $200 per week had a pension plan, 76% of workers earning at least $1,000 per week participated.

Using data from the CPS, Munnell and Perun (2006) reported a sharp drop-off in pension coverage between 1979 and 2004. In 1979, 51% of nonagricultural wage and salary workers in the private sector in age group 25 through 64 participated in a pension plan. By 2004, that figure was down to 46%. The authors also found that the decline in pension coverage occurred for all five earnings quintiles, though it was particularly pronounced for the middle quintile.

In general, these studies report an overall increase in pension coverage during the 1980s and 1990s despite the collapse of DB plans because of an offsetting rise in DC plans. However, they also indicate a drop-off in pension coverage during the 2000s.

There is also extensive literature on retirement adequacy that addresses the question of whether working individuals have saved enough (or will save enough) to meet their needs during retirement. Pension accumulations, Social Security wealth, and savings in nonretirement assets all play a role in determining whether accumulated wealth at retirement will be sufficient to meet retirement needs.

Measuring retirement adequacy is usually done by comparing predicted income at time of retirement with previous income (the so-called replacement rate). It should be noted that estimates of the replacement rate are quite sensitive to the choice of denominator. Some studies use family income at the time of the survey, others use a measure of permanent income, and still others use actual (or predicted) income as of the age just before retirement. Usually, 75% or 80% of pre-retirement income is considered adequate because the income needs of retirees are likely to be lower than those of the same individuals when working. In particular, households no longer need to save for retirement, taxes are lower, work-related expenses disappear, the family size of retirees is often smaller than when working, and households eventually pay off their debts.

The studies on retirement income adequacy have produced differing results. Gustman and Steinmeier (1998) found, using the Health and Retirement Survey (HRS), that the average household could replace only 60% of pre-retirement income in real terms. Engen, Gale, and Uccello (1999), using the Survey of Income and Program Participation (SIPP) and the Survey of Consumer Finances (SCF), estimated that about half of households fell short of what they needed for adequate retirement income but the other half could be expected to meet the target retirement savings. Nevertheless, they calculated an average replacement ratio for the median income household of 72%, a result that led the authors to conclude that households were close to being adequately prepared for retirement. In a later study, Engen, Gale, and Uccello (2005) found that the upswing in stock prices from 1995 through 1998 did not substantially alter their earlier findings on retirement income. This finding suggests that much of the increase in retirement wealth was concentrated among households that were already adequately prepared for retirement. These three studies appeared to indicate that households in the main had saved enough for retirement.

In contrast, several studies concluded that households were inadequately prepared. Moore and Mitchell (2000) found, using the 1992 HRS, that the median-wealth households would have to save an additional 7% of earnings annually if they were to retire at age 65 to finance an adequate real replacement ratio. Moore and Mitchell's estimate of a savings rate of 7.3% for households wishing to retire at age 65 was three times as much as what households actually saved. Similarly, Bernheim (1997) calculated that, on average, baby boomer households were saving only at 34% of what their target savings rate should be.

As wealth is unequally distributed, there may be a large share of households for which the shortfalls are larger. Engen, Gale, and Uccello (1999) calculated that households in the 75th percentile had 121% to 172% of what they needed for retirement. For the median household, the same ratios ranged from 47% to 124%. Gustman and Steinmeier (1998) found that households in the bottom quartile had real replacement rates of 33%, compared with 81% for the top quartile.

Shortfalls in retirement savings vary with household demographics. Moore and Mitchell (2000) and Engen, Gale, and Uccello (1999) found that black and Hispanic married households experienced a larger shortfall in retirement income adequacy than whites and that less educated households had lower retirement income adequacy than more educated ones.

A number of studies also looked at the changes of retirement income adequacy over time. Smith (2003) found, using data from the Panel Study of Income Dynamics (PSID) and the CPS, that median after-tax income replacement ratios in retirement showed an increasing trend since the early 1990s. Sorokina, Webb, and Muldoon (2008), using data from the HRS for age group 51 through 56, calculated that replacement rates fell between 1992 and 2004.

With regard to the financial crisis of 2007 through 2009, Gustman, Steinmeier, and Tabatabai (2009) offered a rather sanguine view of the effects of the stock market crash on retirement preparedness. Their findings indicated that the average person approaching retirement was not likely to suffer a life-changing financial loss from the stock market downturn. Using HRS data, they found that pension coverage was much more extensive than was usually recognized. Over three quarters of households aged 51 through 56 in 2004 were either currently covered by a pension or had pension coverage in the past. Pension wealth accounted for 23% of their total wealth (including Social Security wealth), but DC plans remained small. As a result, 63% of their pension wealth was in the form of a DB plan. The authors argued that the fact that such a high share of their pension wealth was in the form of DB plans should cushion the drop in overall pension wealth resulting from the stock market crash.

In sum, these studies document the changeover from a retirement system dominated by DB pension plans to one dominated by DC plans. Despite the transformation of the pension system, studies generally report an overall increase in pension coverage during the 1980s and 1990s and also during the 2000s. The literature does differ on both the level of and trends in retirement adequacy. However, there is a general belief that the financial crisis of the late 2000s did not notably impair retirement adequacy.

HISTORICAL BACKGROUND

The past three decades witnessed some remarkable asset price movements. While the median house price in real terms was virtually the same in 1989 and 2001,[1] house prices suddenly took off thereafter, rising 19% in real terms from 2001 through 2007. Then the Great Recession hit and home prices plummeted by 24%. This was followed by a partial recovery. Median house prices rose 7.8% through September 2013, still way below their 2007 value.

The stock market trended differently during this same period. In contrast to the housing market, the stock market boomed in the 1990s, surging 59% in real terms between 1989 and 2001.[2] However, from 2001 through 2007, the S&P 500 was up only 6%. During the Great Recession, it nosedived 26%. In this case, there was a strong recovery after 2010, with stock prices up 41% through September 2013.

It will be shown in this chapter that the Great Recession abruptly reversed a trend of robust growth in middle-class wealth since the early 1980s and also brought about the first growth in wealth inequality since the early 1980s. Median wealth plummeted 47% over the years 2007 through 2010, and the inequality of net worth, after almost two decades of little movement, rose sharply. Relative indebtedness of the middle class also continued to expand, even though the middle class had stopped taking on new debt.

What drove these changes? This chapter will show that the recent sharp fall in median net worth and the recent rise in the inequality of net worth are traceable to the high leverage of middle-class families and the high share of homes in their portfolios.[3] Median net worth fell because middle-class homeowners were not able to shed mortgage debt. At the same time, their home values declined.

Wealth inequality increased because home values composed 67% of middle-class wealth but only 9% of the portfolios of the wealthiest 1%. It follows that the wealthiest were better protected against the sharp decline in housing prices during the Great Recession.

DATA SOURCES

The primary data source used in this study is the Survey of Consumer Finances (SCF) conducted by the Federal Reserve Board. Each survey consists of a core representative sample combined with a high-income supplement. The high-income supplement is selected as a list sample derived from tax data from the IRS Statistics of Income.

The wealth concept used here is marketable wealth (or net worth), which is defined as the current value of all marketable assets less current debt. Total assets are defined as the sum of (1) homes; (2) other real estate; (3) liquid assets such as bank deposits and money market accounts; (4) bonds and other financial securities; (5) pension plans, including IRAs, Keoghs, and 401(k)s; (8) corporate stock and mutual funds; (9) unincorporated businesses; and (10) trust funds. Total liabilities are the sum of (1) mortgage debt and (2) other debt.[4]

THE GREAT REVERSAL IN WEALTH

It is useful to begin by examining trends in mean and median household wealth. These trends evince what may be called the "great reversal" in which the relatively high rates of growth in recent decades came to a sudden end with the Great Recession.

Table 1 and Figure 1 show this robust growth in wealth from 1983 through 2007. Median wealth grew at 1.1% per year from 1983 through 1989, 1.2% per year between 1989 and 2001, and then at 2.9% per year from 2001 through 2007. Then, between 2007 and 2010, median wealth plunged by a staggering 47%! The primary reasons, as we shall see, were the collapse in the housing market and the high leverage of middle-class families.

Mean net worth, which is of course more sensitive to the long "right tail" of the distribution, also grew vigorously throughout the beginning of our time series. It grew at 2.3% per year from 1983 through 1989, at 3% per year from 1989 through 2001, and at 3.1% per year from 2001 through 2007. A point of note is that mean wealth grew more than twice as fast as the median between 1983 and 2007, indicating widening inequality of wealth over those years.

The Great Recession also saw an absolute decline in mean household wealth. However, whereas the median plunged by 47%, mean wealth fell

TABLE 1
Mean and Median Wealth and Income, 1983–2010 (average annual growth rates, %)

	1983–1989	1989–2001	2001–2007	2007–2010	1983–2010
Net worth					
Median	1.13	1.22	2.91	−21.23	−0.92
Mean	2.27	3.02	3.10	−6.50	1.81
Income (CPS)					
Median	1.76	0.19	0.27	−2.21	−1.69
Mean	2.40	0.91	−0.13	−1.72	2.07

Source: Author's computations from the 1983, 1989, 2001, 2007, and 2010 SCF.

FIGURE 1
Mean and Median Net Worth, 1983–2010

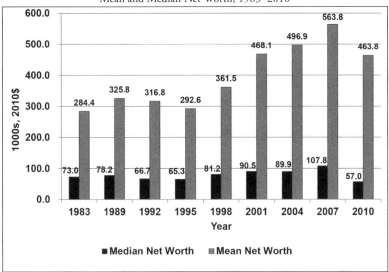

by (only) 18%. Here, too, the relatively faster growth in mean wealth than median wealth (that is, the latter's more moderate decline) from 2007 through 2010 was coincident with rising wealth inequality.

Changes in income distribution were rather different. When the CPS is used to track median income in real terms, it gained 11% between 1983 and 1989, grew by only 2.3% (in total) from 1989 through 2001, and then grew by another 1.6% (in total) from 2001 through 2007 (Figure 2). From 2007 through 2010, it fell off by 6.4%. This reduction was not nearly as great as that in median wealth.

Mean income surged by 2.4% per year from 1983 through 1989, advanced by 0.9% per year from 1989 through 2001, and then dipped by

FIGURE 2
Mean and Median Household Income, 1983–2010

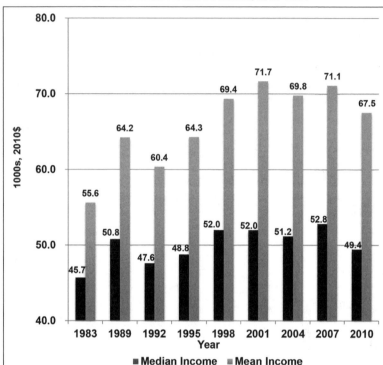

−0.1% per year from 2001 through 2007. Mean income also dropped in real terms from 2007 through 2010, by 5% overall, slightly less than that of median income.

The upshot is that the Great Recession was indeed a "great reversal" of what had been a long period of expansion in wealth. By contrast, the effects of the Great Recession on income were less profound, although here again it interrupted what had been a long period of increase (except that mean income was roughly stable from 2001 through 2007).

TRENDS IN INEQUALITY

What about trends in inequality? Figure 3 shows that the Gini coefficient (an inequality index that ranges from zero, meaning no inequality, to one, meaning total inequality) for wealth, after rising steeply between 1983 and 1989 from 0.8 to 0.83, remained virtually unchanged from 1989 through 2007, at 0.83. In contrast, the years of the Great Recession saw a very sharp elevation in wealth inequality, with the Gini coefficient rising to 0.87.

FIGURE 3
Wealth and Income Inequality, 1983–2010 (Gini coefficients)

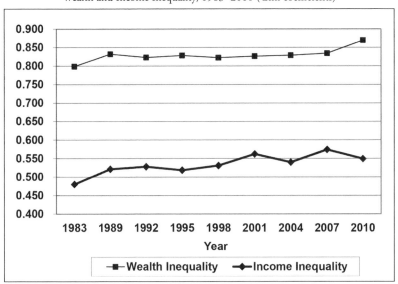

The time trend for income inequality contrasts with that for wealth inequality. Income inequality showed a sharp rise from 1982 through 1988, with the Gini coefficient expanding from 0.48 to 0.52, and again from 1988 through 2006, with the Gini index advancing to 0.57. Perhaps somewhat surprisingly, the Great Recession witnessed a rather sharp contraction in income inequality. According to the SCF data, the Gini coefficient fell from 0.574 in 2006 to 0.549 in 2009. One of the puzzles we have to contend with is that wealth inequality rose sharply over the Great Recession while income inequality contracted.

It is of course well known that wealth is more unequally distributed than income (see Wolff 2009, for example). This result is quite dramatically revealed in Figure 3. Because the Great Recession increased wealth inequality but reduced income inequality, this disparity has become even more pronounced in recent years.

PORTFOLIOS AND DEBT

It is also important to monitor portfolio composition because some types of assets, particularly housing assets, were especially vulnerable during the Great Recession. In 2010, homes accounted for 31% of total assets among all households (Figure 4). However, net home equity—home value minus mortgage debt—amounted to only 18%. Liquid assets made up 6% and pension accounts 15%. "Investment assets" (nonhome real estate,

FIGURE 4

Composition of Household Wealth by Wealth Class, 2010 (percentage of gross assets)

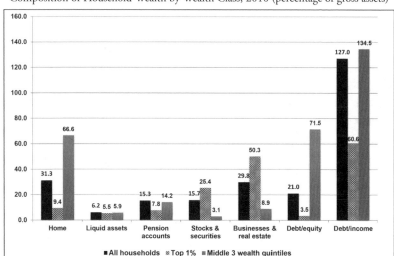

business equity, financial securities, corporate stock, mutual funds, and trust funds) collectively amounted to 45%. The debt–equity ratio (the ratio of debt to net worth) was 0.21 and the debt–income ratio was 1.27.

There are marked differences in portfolio composition by wealth class. As shown in Figure 4, the wealthiest 1% invested over three quarters of their savings in investment assets. Housing accounted for only 9%, liquid assets 5%, and pension accounts 8%. Their debt–equity ratio was only 0.03, their debt–income ratio was 0.61, and their ratio of mortgage debt to house value was 0.19. In contrast, 67% of the assets of the middle three wealth quintiles were invested in their home, a crucial difference relative to the portfolios of the wealthier. Home equity amounted to only 32% of total assets, a reflection of their large mortgage debt. Another 20% went into monetary savings and pension accounts. Together housing, liquid, and pension assets accounted for 87%, with the remainder in investment assets. Their debt–equity ratio was 0.72 and their debt–income ratio was 1.35, both much higher than those of the top 1%. Finally, their mortgage debt amounted to a little more than half the value of their home.

The rather staggering debt level of the middle class in 2010 raises the question of whether this was a recent phenomenon. It indeed was. There was a sharp rise in the debt–equity ratio of the middle class from 0.37 in 1983 to 0.61 in 2007, mainly a reflection of a steep rise in mortgage debt. The debt–income ratio more than doubled from 1983 through 2007, from 0.67 to 1.57. The rise in the debt–equity ratio and the debt–income ratio was much steeper than for all households. In 1983, the debt–income ratio was about the same for the middle class as for all households, but by 2007 the ratio was much larger for the middle class.

Then the Great Recession hit. The debt–equity ratio continued to rise, reaching 0.72 in 2010, but there was actually a retrenchment in the *debt–income* ratio, which fell to 1.35. The reason is that, from 2007 through 2010, the mean debt of the middle class actually contracted by 25% in constant dollars. Mortgage debt fell by 23% as families paid down their outstanding balances, and other debt dropped by 32% as families paid off credit card balances and other consumer debt. The steep rise in the debt–equity ratio was due to the sharp drop in net worth, while the decline in the debt to income ratio was exclusively due to the sharp contraction of overall debt.

THE ROLE OF LEVERAGE

Two major puzzles emerge. The first is the steep plunge in median net worth in real terms of 47% between 2007 and 2010 despite an only moderate drop in median income of 6.4% and less steep declines in housing and stock prices of 24% and 26%, respectively. The second is the steep increase of wealth inequality of 0.035 Gini points despite a decline in income inequality of 0.025 Gini points.

Changes in median wealth and wealth inequality from 2007 through 2010 can be explained by leverage, the ratio of debt to net worth. The steep fall in median wealth was due in large measure to the high leverage of middle-class households. The spike in wealth inequality was largely due to *differential leverage* between the rich and the middle class.

Table 2 shows average annual *real* rates of return for both gross assets and net worth over the period 1983 through 2010.[5] Results are based on the average portfolio composition over the period. It is of interest to examine the results for all households. The overall annual return on gross assets rose from 2.2% in the period 1983 through 1989 to 3.25% in the period 1989 through 2001 and then to 3.34% in the period 2001 through 2007 before plummeting to –6.95% in the period 2007 through 2010.

The average annual rate of return on net worth among all households also increased from 3.17% in the first period to 4.25% in the second and to 4.31% in the third but then fell off sharply to –7.98% in the last period. It is notable that the returns on net worth are uniformly higher—by about one percentage point—than those on gross assets over the first three periods, when asset prices were rising. However, in the period 2007 through 2010, the opposite was the case, with the annual return on net worth 1.03 percentage points lower than that on gross assets. These results illustrate the effect of leverage—raising the return when asset prices rise and lowering the return when asset prices fall.

TABLE 2
Average Annual Real Rates of Return by Period and Wealth Class, 1983–2010 (%)

	1983–1989	1989–2001	2001–2007	2007–2010	1983–2010
Gross Assets					
All households	2.20	3.25	3.34	−6.95	1.90
Top 1%	3.00	3.88	3.86	−6.94	2.48
Next 19%	2.17	3.33	3.19	−6.70	1.93
Middle 3 quintiles	1.21	2.23	2.95	−7.52	1.08
Net Worth					
All households	3.17	4.25	4.31	−7.98	2.67
Top 1%	3.38	4.15	4.03	−7.10	2.70
Next 19%	2.82	3.97	3.80	−7.35	2.42
Middle 3 quintiles	3.15	4.55	5.95	−11.37	2.78

Source: Author's computations from the 1983, 1989, 2001, 2007, and 2010 SCF.

Note: Calculations are based on household portfolios averaged over the period.

There are striking differences in returns by wealth class. In the first three periods, the return on net worth was higher for the middle quintiles (except for the period 1983 through 1989 when its return was slightly lower than that of the top 1%), but in the period 2007 through 2010, the middle three quintiles registered a lower (that is, more negative) return. Differences in returns between the top 1% and the middle quintiles were quite substantial in some years. In the period 2001 through 2007, the annual return was 1.92 percentage points higher for the middle quintiles, while in the period 2007 through 2010, it was 4.27 percentage points lower. The spread in returns between the top 1% and the middle quintiles reflects the much higher leverage of the middle class.

The huge negative rate of return on net worth of the middle quintiles was largely responsible for the precipitous drop in median net worth between 2007 and 2010. This factor, in turn, was attributable to the steep drop in housing prices and the very high leverage of the middle class. The substantial differential in returns on net worth between the middle quintiles and the top percentile (over a point and a half lower) helps explain why wealth inequality rose sharply between 2007 and 2010 despite the decline in income inequality.

THE RACIAL DIVIDE WIDENS

Striking differences are found in the wealth holdings of specific racial and ethnic groups. In 2007, while the ratio of mean incomes between black and white households was an already low 0.48, the ratio of mean wealth holdings was even lower, at 0.19 (Figure 5). This was the same ratio as in 1983. The ratio of mean income between Hispanics and whites in 2007 was 0.5, almost the same as that between black and white households. The ratio of mean net worth was 0.26 compared with a ratio of 0.19 between blacks and whites. This was up from 0.16 in 1983.

The picture changed radically by 2010. The ratio of mean net worth between black and white households dropped from 0.19 to 0.14 between 2007 and 2010. The proximate causes were the higher leverage of black households and their higher share of housing in gross assets. In 2007, the debt–equity ratio among blacks was an astounding 0.55, compared with 0.15 among whites, while housing as a share of gross assets was 0.54 for the former as against 0.31 for the latter. The sharp drop in home prices from 2007 through 2010 thus led to a relatively steeper loss in home equity for blacks (25%) than for whites (21%), and this factor, in turn, led to a much steeper fall in mean net worth for black households than white households.

From 2007 through 2010, the mean net worth in 2010 dollars of Hispanics fell almost *by half* so that the mean wealth ratio relative to whites plummeted from 0.26 to 0.15. The same factors were responsible as in the case of black households. In 2007, the debt–equity ratio for Hispanics was 0.51, compared with 0.15 among whites, while housing as a share of gross assets was 0.53 for the former as against 0.31 for the latter. As a result, net home equity dropped by 48% among Hispanic homeowners, compared with 21% among white homeowners, and this factor, in turn, was largely responsible for the huge decline in Hispanic net worth both in absolute and relative terms. Next, we will see how this reversal in both

FIGURE 5

Ratio of Mean Net Worth by Race and Ethnicity, 1983–2010

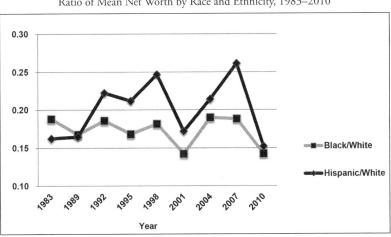

the absolute and relative wealth of minorities played out in terms of retirement security.

RETIREMENT INCOME SECURITY

As discussed previously, retirement income security refers to the ability of households to provide an adequate stream of income during the period of their retirement from the labor force. The empirical analysis involves three steps. The first is a calculation of how much wealth, including marketable wealth, pension wealth, and Social Security wealth, households held in 2010 and how that amount changed compared with 1983, 1989, and 2001. The second step is a calculation of the stream of retirement income that today's older workers can expect from their accumulated wealth at the time of their retirement. For this purpose, I convert the stock of wealth into an annuity flow on the basis of the historical rate of return on household assets and on the basis of life expectancy by age, race, and gender.

The third step is a comparison of the expected income stream to two standards of adequate retirement income: the poverty level and the share of final income replaced by retirement income. These measures allow us to assess whether households have saved enough for retirement and how this has changed over time. This chapter also analyzes changes in retirement income security for households with different demographic characteristics, as defined by age, race or ethnicity, marital status, education, and income class.

MEASURING RETIREMENT INCOME ADEQUACY
Retirement Income Projections

Retirement income is based here on four components: (1) standard nonpension wealth holdings (NWX), (2) DC pension holdings, (3) DB pension entitlements, and (4) Social Security benefits. I then convert NWX into an annuity equivalent (ANN) based on the following formula:

$$ANN_i = r_i \cdot Asset_i / [1 - (1 + r_i)^{-max(LERH, LERW)}]$$

where r_i is the rate of return on asset i, LERH is the life expectancy of the husband at year of retirement, and LERW is the life expectancy of the wife at year of retirement. An annuity is calculated for each asset (and debt) based on the historical rate of return on that asset.

The rationale for converting household wealth into an annuity to gauge retirement adequacy is that the annuity value indicates the sustainable level of withdrawals from each asset that will last the (estimated) remainder of the person's life (or, in the case of a couple, the life of the longest-living spouse) and that will totally exhaust the asset value at time of death. In a sense, this is the wealth equivalent to the concept of permanent income. The rates of return include both capital gains and asset income such as dividends and interest so that the annuity value replaces any projected property income. Though a family need not actually withdraw the annuity value of their wealth each year, the annuity value does indicate the level of *potential* consumption that can be maintained over time from their wealth holdings.

With regard to the second component, DC wealth, I also add DCEMP (the present value of future projected employer contributions to the worker's DC plan) and DCEMPW (the present value of future employee contributions into the DC plan). These two components are estimated with data provided in the SCF, which indicates what fraction of the employee's salary is currently contributed into the employee's DC account by both employer and employee. It is assumed that the worker continues to work for the same employer until retirement and that the employer's and worker's contribution rate remains unchanged over time. I then define total DC wealth (DCTOT) as the sum of DC, DCEMP, and DCEMPW. I then treat the second component, DCTOT, in exactly the same way as NWX and convert it into an annuity.

The third component is the actual or expected DB plan benefit, as indicated by the respondent. The fourth component is the Social Security benefit currently being received or the future expected Social Security benefit. The latter is based on a computation of the primary insurance amount (PIA), which, in turn, is based on the estimated work history for both husband and wife (see Wolff 2011 for more details).

I then add to NW the sum of current NWX and DC plan holdings, the estimated amount of additional wealth accumulations up to the time of retirement. My method uses a straightforward projection of net worth based on historical changes in the net worth of age group 47 through 64 over the period 1989 through 2010. Moreover, these computations are made for seven income classes (results are very similar using wealth classes as well).[6]

Retirement Adequacy

Retirement adequacy is measured in three ways. The first is the annual projected retirement income. The second is the percentage of households whose projected retirement income is greater than the poverty threshold.[7] The third is the income replacement rate, which is based on projected household income at time of retirement (typically age 64). I use a 1.7% annual growth rate of real income, an estimate based on the growth of real income for age group 47 through 64 over the period 1989 through 2010. It should be noted that this is a stringent measure of the replacement rate compared with that found in most of the literature on the subject because it compares (projected) retirement income against (projected) pre-retirement income at the eve of retirement (see the Background Literature section of this chapter for a review of the pertinent literature). Other studies have used a measure akin to average income over the lifetime or a measure of permanent income as the basis of comparison.

EXPECTED RETIREMENT INCOME

The mean retirement income for all households in age group 47 through 64 is projected to be $117,100 in 2010 dollars in 2007 (Table 3). There is little difference in projected retirement income for age groups 47 through 55 and 56 through 64. However, there is a big difference between minorities and whites—a ratio of 2.3.

There are also wide gaps by family type. The projected mean retirement income of married couples is 1.9 times that of single males and 3.5 times that of single females. Wide variation is also seen in educational attainment.

TABLE 3
Projected Mean Retirement Income, Ages 47–64 (in thousands, 2010 dollars)

| | 1989 | 2001 | 2007 | 2010 | Percentage change | | |
					1989–2001	2001–2007	2007–2010
All, ages 47–64	77.0	108.2	117.1	110.0	40.4	8.2	−6.0
Ages 47–55	88.3	110.2	118.4	108.0	24.9	7.4	−8.8
Ages 56–64	64.3	105.1	115.3	112.4	63.6	9.7	−2.4
Non-Hispanic white	87.9	123.9	132.0	129.0	41.0	6.5	−2.3
African American or Hispanic	32.8	43.7	56.6	43.8	33.3	29.5	−22.7
Married couples	99.0	143.8	155.1	149.2	45.3	7.9	−3.8
Single males	60.4	78.1	81.5	56.3	29.4	4.3	−30.9
Single females	34.5	42.5	43.7	41.8	23.2	2.9	−4.4
Less than 12 years of schooling	38.1	33.0	27.7	26.4	−13.5	−16.0	−4.8
12 years of schooling	80.5	56.5	58.9	58.0	−29.9	4.3	−1.4
13–15 years of schooling	91.0	73.9	80.3	66.3	−18.8	8.7	−17.4
16 or more years of schooling	183.0	213.2	216.7	212.4	16.5	1.7	−2.0
Income quintile 1	12.9	23.9	25.5	31.8	84.5	6.6	25.0
Income quintile 2	35.5	39.9	41.9	39.2	12.3	5.0	−6.5
Income quintile 3	55.3	63.7	70.3	57.8	15.2	10.4	−17.8
Income quintile 4	74.7	98.7	104.2	94.2	32.2	5.6	−9.6
Income quintile 5	211.2	326.5	353.3	338.6	54.6	8.2	−4.2
Memo: Median, ages 47–64	45.1	50.9	55.1	46.1	12.9	8.3	−16.4

Source: Author's computations from the 1989, 2001, 2007, and 2010 SCF.

The projected mean retirement income of college graduates in 2007 is 2.7 times that of those with some college, 3.7 times that of high school graduates, and 7.8 times that of those with the least schooling. There is also great variation by income quintile. The projected mean retirement income of the top quintile in 2007 is (a huge) $335,800, 3.4 times that of the fourth quintile, 5 times that of the middle quintile, 8.4 times that of the second quintile, and 13.9 that of the bottom quintile.

Projected mean retirement income advanced very strongly between 1989 and 2001, 40% overall. However, changes in retirement income were generally much lower from 2001 through 2007—only 8% overall. For households with less than 12 years of schooling, a 16% drop is found in their mean retirement income. Median retirement income rose less than the mean—only 13% from 1989 through 2001 and by another 8% from 2001 through 2007.

Some gaps in retirement income between groups widened over time, whereas others narrowed. Retirement income for households nearer retirement (age group 56 through 64) grew faster—79% between 1989 and 2007—than for age group 47 through 55, only 34%. Minorities saw greater gains in retirement income than whites, 73% versus 50%. While mean retirement income of whites grew somewhat faster than minorities over the 1990s, the reverse was true for the 2000s. Indeed, minorities were the only group with sizeable gains (30%) in retirement income over the period 2001 through 2007. As a result, the ratio of retirement income between minorities and whites, after falling from 0.37 in 1989 to 0.35 in 2001, advanced to 0.43 in 2007.

Married couples experienced greater gains over the period 1989 through 2007 (57%) than single males (35%) and single females (27%), and the retirement income gaps widened among these groups. In 2007, the mean expected retirement income of single females was only 28% that of married couples, down from 35% in 1989.

The only educational group with positive growth in retirement income from 1989 through 2007 was college graduates, which saw a modest 18% gain. The other groups experienced negative growth, ranging from –27% for the least educated group and for high school graduates to –12% for those with some college.[8] As a result, the gap in retirement income between college graduates and the other groups widened over those years. In contrast, the bottom income quintile recorded the fastest growth in retirement income at 97%, with the top income quintile second at 67%, whereas the middle three quintiles had the lowest gains over the period.

Over the Great Recession, from 2007 through 2010, mean projected retirement income dropped by a rather small amount—6% overall. However, the median fell by 16.4%, reflecting the steep decline in median wealth. The decline in mean retirement income was greater for ages 47 through 55 than ages 56 through 64 (8.8% versus 2.4%), much greater for minorities than whites (23% versus 2.3%), much greater for single males than married couples or single females (31% versus 3.8% and 4.4%), greatest for those with some college only (17%), and greatest for the third income quintiles (18%). Once again, the lowest income quintile showed a sizeable gain (35%).

Further details are provided in the next two tables. Table 4 shows the percentage composition of projected retirement income in 2007. In 2007, 52% of total retirement income of all households in age group 47 through 64 is projected to come from NWX, with another 18% from DCTOT, 17% from Social Security benefits, and only 13% from DB benefits. There

TABLE 4
Composition of Projected Mean Retirement Income, Ages 47–64, 2007 (%)

	Nonpension wealth (NWX)	DC plans (DCTOT)	DB pensions	Social Security	Total
All, ages 47–64	51.8	18.3	12.7	17.2	100.0
Ages 47–55	50.9	19.3	12.5	17.3	100.0
Ages 56–64	53.1	16.8	13.0	17.0	100.0
Non-Hispanic white	53.0	18.6	12.3	16.1	100.0
African American or Hispanic	40.2	15.1	17.8	26.9	100.0
Married couples	52.9	18.3	12.1	16.7	100.0
Single males	52.2	19.8	12.8	15.1	100.0
Single females	42.8	17.1	17.4	22.7	100.0
Less than 12 years of schooling	34.7	9.2	7.0	49.1	100.0
12 years of schooling	41.8	15.2	14.2	28.7	100.0
13–15 years of schooling	44.4	18.2	15.9	21.5	100.0
16 or more years of schooling	56.6	19.4	11.8	12.2	100.0
Income quintile 1	44.3	4.4	9.0	42.3	100.0
Income quintile 2	37.2	11.5	15.3	36.0	100.0
Income quintile 3	32.7	19.7	19.4	28.2	100.0
Income quintile 4	32.4	23.8	19.5	24.3	100.0
Income quintile 5	64.0	18.2	9.3	8.5	100.0
Memo					
1989	55.4	8.1	19.0	17.5	100.0
2001	50.9	17.0	13.8	18.4	100.0
2010	44.9	24.7	11.6	18.8	100.0

Source: Author's computations from the 1989, 2001, 2007, and 2010 SCF.

is a big variation in the composition by demographic group. Expected Social Security benefits will make up 27% of the expected retirement income of minorities in 2007, compared with 16% for whites, whereas the expected annuity from NWX for minorities will constitute 40%, compared with 53% for whites. Likewise, Social Security will comprise 23% for single females, compared with 17% for married couples, whereas NWX will make up 43% for single females, compared with 53% for married couples. Social Security benefits decline from 49% for the least educated group to 12% for college graduates, while the share from NWX rises from 14% to 44%. The share from Social Security falls from 42% to 9% across the five income quintiles, while the share from NWX rises from 24% to 52%.

Over time, DC income is projected to become an increasingly important source of retirement income, rising from an 8% share in 1989 to 25% in 2010. This change reflects the sharp rise in the share of DC wealth in the overall household portfolio. Correspondingly, DB income will become less important, declining from 19% in 1989 to 12% in 2010. Together, the contribution of total pension wealth will rise from 27% in 1989 to 36% in 2010. Correspondingly, the proportion of projected retirement income from NWX will decline over time, from 55% in 1989 to 52% in 2007 and then to 45% in 2010, while that from Social Security will rise slightly from 17.5% to 18.8%.

Overall, the mean projected retirement income climbed by 40% between 1989 and 2001 but advanced by only 8% from 2001 through 2007, for an overall gain of 52% (Table 5). In contrast from 2007 through 2010, it was down by 6%. The expected annuity from NWX grew strongly during the 1990s, by 33%, but by only 3% from 2001 through 2007. From 2007 through 2010, it fell by 19%, reflecting the steep decline in household wealth. The expected annuity from DCTOT showed a huge gain in the first period, almost tripling in value, and a much smaller increase in the second period, 17%. It continued to advance by 27% from 2007 through 2010. Expected DB benefits remained largely unchanged from 1989 through 2007 but then plummeted by 14% from 2007 through 2010. Expected Social Security benefits rose sharply in the first period, by 48%, and then remained largely unchanged in the second and third periods.

The ratio of projected retirement income between minorities and whites jumped from 0.37 in 1989 to 0.43 in 2007. The convergence was due largely to the growth in Social Security benefits among minorities, which outstripped that among whites (90% versus 42%), and the growth in DCTOT (1,017% versus 225%). In 2010, the ratio was down to 0.34, as annuities from NWX fell much more for minorities than whites (43% versus 14%), reflecting the steep absolute and relative drop in wealth

TABLE 5
Change in Projected Mean Retirement Income by Component, Ages 47–64 (%)

	Nonpension wealth (NWX)	DC plans (DCTOT)	DB pensions	Social Security	Total
1989–2007	42.1	243.5	1.6	49.6	52.0
Ages 47–55	22.7	133.1	–0.7	42.1	34.2
Ages 56–64	72.9	801.8	4.5	59.3	79.4
Non-Hispanic white	40.8	225.4	2.0	44.2	50.2
African American or Hispanic	66.3	1,017.1	–2.4	89.9	72.6
Married couples	49.2	258.4	0.1	50.2	56.8
Single males	6.1	412.1	16.1	52.4	35.0
Single females	12.7	102.4	2.9	46.3	26.8
Less than 12 years of schooling	–42.3	–4.9	–80.0	49.4	–27.3
12 years of schooling	–46.4	141.3	–35.5	–5.6	–26.9
13–15 years of schooling	–24.1	57.0	–28.8	2.5	–11.8
16 or more years of schooling	5.3	131.7	–14.0	41.3	18.4
Income quintile 1	113.7	41,473.1	64.2	71.9	96.7
Income quintile 2	3.4	317.9	–12.9	26.6	18.0
Income quintile 3	–3.3	373.5	–6.2	41.7	27.2
Income quintile 4	14.3	222.6	–4.3	56.6	39.6
Income quintile 5	57.2	220.4	13.8	62.7	67.3
Memo					
1989–2001	28.9	194.6	1.6	47.8	40.4
2001–2007	10.2	16.6	0.0	1.2	8.2

Table 5 continues, next page

among minorities, as did income from DCTOT (13% decline versus a 34% gain).

In contrast, the expected retirement income of single females grew much more slowly than that of married couples from 1989 through 2007, 27% versus 57%. As a result, the ratio in expected retirement income between the two groups fell from 0.35 in 1989 to 0.28 in 2007. The relative decline was due mainly to slower growth in DCTOT (102% versus 258%). From 2007 through 2010, expected retirement income declined about the same extent for the two groups.

Absolute declines in expected retirement income were recorded for each of the three lowest educational groups between 1989 and 2007, whereas college graduates expected to see an 18% increase. Here, too, there were

TABLE 5 (continued)
Change in Projected Mean Retirement Income by Component, Ages 47–64 (%)

	Nonpension wealth (NWX)	DC plans (DCTOT)	DB pensions	Social Security	Total
2007–2010	−18.6	27.1	−14.1	2.5	−6.0
Ages 47–55	−23.8	28.0	−20.0	2.3	−8.8
Ages 56–64	−12.4	26.9	−7.0	3.1	−2.4
Non-Hispanic white	−14.3	34.0	−12.4	3.3	−2.3
African American or Hispanic	−43.1	−12.7	−20.3	0.6	−22.7
Married couples	−16.7	33.8	−13.1	2.8	−3.8
Single males	−45.7	−25.8	−11.2	−3.4	−30.9
Single females	−10.6	19.5	−24.6	4.5	−4.4
Less than 12 years of schooling	−32.1	12.5	41.3	4.7	−4.8
12 years of schooling	−7.4	17.2	−2.2	−2.4	−1.4
13–15 years of schooling	−33.6	−3.7	−17.9	5.0	−17.4
16 or more years of schooling	−14.8	39.8	−16.0	5.0	−2.0
Income quintile 1	39.9	98.7	−33.7	14.3	25.0
Income quintile 2	−24.2	19.9	−10.1	5.1	−6.5
Income quintile 3	−26.4	−22.6	−17.8	−4.5	−17.8
Income quintile 4	−19.3	0.4	−12.4	−4.4	−9.6
Income quintile 5	−19.6	49.5	−13.4	7.4	−4.2

Source: Author's computations from the 1989, 2001, 2007, and 2010 SCF.

steep declines in the expected annuity from NWX both absolutely and relative to college graduates from 1989 through 2007 (the ratio between high school and college graduates plummeted from 0.35 to 0.14!) and in expected DB benefits relative to college graduates. Less educated households became more dependent on Social Security, whose share in total expected retirement income more than doubled from 24% in 1989 to 49% in 2007 among the least educated and increased from 22% to 29% among high school graduates. From 2007 through 2010, there was relatively little change in relative retirement income among the four schooling groups (except for those with some college).

In summary, Social Security was a more important source of projected retirement income among the lower-income groups—minorities, single females, the less educated, and the lower-income quintiles—than among higher-income groups—whites, married couples, college graduates, and the top income quintile. It has thus served as an important equalizing factor in retirement adequacy. Moreover, the importance of Social Security benefits in expected retirement income grew over time between 1989 and 2010 for the low-income groups previously described.

THE EXPECTED POVERTY RATE AT RETIREMENT

Trends in projected poverty rates at retirement tend to follow trends in mean retirement income (Table 6). In 2007, 10.2% of households in age group 47 through 64 were projected to have retirement income less than the poverty line. The percentage was smaller for the older age group (8.2% for ages 56 through 64) than for age group 47 through 55 (11.6%). Only 4.8% of white households are projected to fall below the poverty standard, compared with 13.9% of minorities (a 9.1 percentage point difference). Differences are also marked by marital status, with only 5.7% of married couples compared with 12.8% of single males and 19.7% of single females falling below the poverty line. Poverty rates are smaller for the better educated, varying between 28.1% for the least educated and 6.4% for college graduates.

All of the poverty reduction took place between 1989 and 2001—by 4.6 percentage points overall. From 2001 through 2007, there was no change and from 2007 through 2010, it increased by 1.9 percentage points. By and large, groups with the highest projected poverty rate in 1989 experienced the largest reduction from 1989 through 2007. Percentage

TABLE 6
Households with Expected Retirement Income Less Than Poverty Line, Ages 47–64 (%)

					Percentage point change		
	1989	2001	2007	2010	1989–2001	2001–2007	2007–2010
All, ages 47–64	14.8	10.2	10.2	12.1	–4.6	0.0	1.9
Ages 47–55	13.2	10.7	11.6	11.6	–2.5	0.8	0.1
Ages 56–64	16.7	9.4	8.2	12.6	–7.3	–1.2	4.4
Non-Hispanic white	3.2	4.0	4.8	5.6	0.8	0.8	0.7
African American or Hispanic	48.1	21.6	13.9	16.1	–26.5	–7.6	2.1
Married couples	7.3	3.9	5.7	6.0	–3.4	1.8	0.3
Single males	11.4	11.9	12.8	16.7	0.4	1.0	3.9
Single females	33.2	24.4	19.7	24.9	–8.8	–4.7	5.2
Less than 12 years of schooling	26.7	23.8	28.1	26.9	–2.8	4.3	–1.1
12 years of schooling	1.6	10.6	9.0	12.2	9.1	–1.7	3.2
13–15 years of schooling	0.4	6.8	9.0	10.3	6.4	2.1	1.3
16 or more years of schooling	5.4	5.7	6.4	8.2	0.3	0.7	1.8

Source: Author's computations from the 1989, 2001, 2007, and 2010 SCF.

point declines were much greater for age group 56 through 64 than age group 47 through 55. In contrast, from 2007 through 2011, it increased much more among the older age group.

Minority households experienced a precipitous decline in their projected poverty rate, 34.1 percentage points from 1989 through 2007, while white households experienced a slight increase. However, the gap widened a bit from 2007 through 2010. Single females also saw a large decline from 1989 through 2007—13.4 percentage points. However, from 2007 through 2010, the gap with married couples widened substantially (by 4.9 percentage points).

Table 7 shows the expected poverty rate by component. I have added these components sequentially. Of course, the results depend on the order in which the components are included, so these results give particular influence to Social Security, the last component.

On the basis of NWX alone, the projected poverty rate at retirement is 45% overall.[9] Adding in DCTOT lowers it to about a third, and adding

TABLE 7
Households with Expected Retirement Income Less
Than the Povery Line by Component, Ages 47–64, 2007

	Nonpension wealth (NWX)	NWX + DCTOT	NWX + DCTOT + DB	Total: NWX + PW + SS
All, ages 47–64	45.2	33.2	27.9	10.2
Ages 47–55	45.5	31.7	28.6	11.6
Ages 56–64	44.9	35.3	27.0	8.2
Non-Hispanic white	38.9	25.9	20.5	4.8
African American or Hispanic	60.2	49.7	43.9	13.9
Married couples	37.1	24.9	20.6	5.7
Single males	50.3	44.0	36.8	12.8
Single females	62.4	48.0	41.0	19.7
Less than 12 years of schooling	80.1	74.6	68.7	28.1
12 years of schooling	54.3	39.9	32.8	9.0
13–15 years of schooling	50.4	32.5	27.4	9.0
16 or more years of schooling	23.9	15.5	11.7	6.4
Memo				
1989	45.1	40.7	27.5	14.8
2001	50.2	38.9	30.2	10.2
2010	56.7	41.4	34.3	12.1

Source: Author's computations from the 1989, 2001, 2007, and 2010 SCF.

in DB benefits lowers it to 28%. Finally, adding in the Social Security benefits lowers the expected poverty rate by 18 percentage points, to 10%.

There is considerable variation across groups in the importance of these various components in reducing expected poverty. The poverty rate on the basis of NWX is much lower for whites, 39%, than for non-whites, 60%, reflecting the latter's much lower wealth. Adding in all expected pension benefits lowers the rate for whites by 18 percentage points, to 21%, and that for minorities by 16 percentage points, to 44%. Adding in Social Security causes a huge reduction for non-whites, by 30 percentage points, to 14%, compared with a 16 percentage point drop for whites, to 5%.

A similar pattern holds for the comparison between married couples and single females. The expected poverty rate for the former is 37% on the basis of NWX alone. Adding in pensions reduces it to 21%, and including Social Security further reduces it to 6%. For single females, the predicted poverty rate is 62% from NWX alone. It falls to 41% when private pensions are included and then through 20% when Social Security is included.

The expected poverty rate for college graduates on the basis of NWX is quite low, 24%. Adding pensions lowers it to 12%, and then including Social Security reduces it further, to 6%. In contrast, the poverty rate on the basis of NWX alone varies from a high of 80% for the least educated to 50% for those with some college. Adding in private pensions reduces the expected poverty rate by 11 to 23 percentage points, and then including Social Security lowers it by another 18 to 41 (for the least educated group) percentage points. Indeed, for the least educated group, Social Security reduces the projected poverty rate from 69% to 27%.

Over time, the importance of Social Security grows as a weapon to reduce poverty among the low-income elderly. On the basis of NWX alone, the expected poverty rate actually increases from 45% in 1989 to 57% in 2010. With the inclusion of private pensions, the expected poverty rate is slightly higher in 2010, at 41.4%, than in 1989, at 40.7%. The main effect comes from Social Security. When that income is included, the expected poverty rate declines from 14.8% in 1989 to 12.1% in 2010.

REPLACEMENT RATES

There was relatively little change over time in the share of households with expected retirement income greater than or equal to three quarters of projected income at retirement, the "three-quarters replacement rate" (Table 8). The reason is that a replacement rate is a relative standard, and changes in the replacement rate reflect changes in both expected retirement income and pre-retirement income.

In 2007, only 49% of all households in age group 47 through 64 were expected to meet the three-quarters replacement rate. The share meeting

TABLE 8
Households Meeting the Three-Quarters Replacement Rate Standard, Ages 47–64 (%)

	1989	2001	2007	2010	Percentage point change 1989–2001	Percentage point change 2001–2007	Percentage point change 2007–2010
All, ages 47–64	45.4	46.5	49.3	49.4	1.2	2.8	0.1
Ages 47–55	38.8	40.7	43.7	44.0	1.9	2.9	0.3
Ages 56–64	53.0	55.3	57.1	56.0	2.3	1.8	−1.1
Non-Hispanic white	49.7	50.5	53.6	55.0	0.8	3.1	1.4
African American or Hispanic	35.2	37.4	41.5	40.4	2.3	4.1	−1.2
Married couples	47.3	49.7	49.7	52.6	2.4	0.0	2.9
Single males	54.0	47.1	57.2	49.3	−6.9	10.1	−7.9
Single females	37.6	38.2	44.0	41.0	0.5	5.9	−3.1
Less than 12 years of schooling	42.1	44.3	34.6	38.6	2.2	−9.7	4.0
12 years of schooling	47.8	44.8	42.6	47.5	−3.0	−2.2	4.9
13–15 years of schooling	44.8	43.1	45.9	45.2	−1.7	2.8	−0.7
16 or more years of schooling	52.7	51.5	61.4	57.4	−1.2	9.9	−4.1
Income quintile 1	51.8	62.2	57.3	59.9	10.4	−5.0	2.6
Income quintile 2	45.8	45.1	47.0	49.9	−0.7	1.9	3.0
Income quintile 3	56.4	38.4	47.8	39.5	−18.0	9.4	−8.2
Income quintile 4	33.6	41.3	47.1	45.3	7.7	5.8	−1.8
Income quintile 5	39.2	45.1	47.3	52.0	5.9	2.2	4.7

Source: Author's computations from the 1989, 2001, 2007, and 2010 SCF.

this standard increased moderately from 1989 through 2007 (by 3 percentage points) but then showed no change from 2007 through 2010. The lack of change may appear surprising, but it reflects the decline in mean (and median) income from 2007 through 2010.

Surprisingly, the percentage of households meeting this replacement rate standard is generally higher for the higher-income groups, despite their higher pre-retirement income. The share projected to meet the three-quarters replacement rate in 2007 is greater for ages 56 through 64 than ages 47 through 55 (57% versus 44%), for whites than blacks (54% versus 42%), for married couples than single females (50% versus 44%), and for college graduates than other schooling levels (61% versus 43% for high school graduates, for example).

However, younger households achieved greater gains in replacement rates from 1989 through 2007 relative to older households, as did minorities relative to whites and single females relative to married couples. In contrast, the share meeting the replacement rate standard climbed much more for college graduates than for the other educational groups (indeed, changes were negative for the two lowest educated groups). From 2007 through 2010, the reverse was generally the case, with higher-income groups achieving greater gains in replacement rates (or smaller losses) than poorer groups, with the notable exception of college graduates.

As already noted, in 2007, the percentage of all households in age group 47 through 64 with a three-quarters replacement rate is projected to be 49%. However, the share is only 10% on the basis of NWX (Table 9). The share rises to 17% when DCTOT is also included, to 29% with the addition of DB benefits, and then to 49% with the addition of Social Security.

TABLE 9
Households Meeting the Three-Quarters
Replacement Rate Standard by Component, Ages 47–64 (%)

	Nonpension wealth (NWX)	NWX + DCTOT	NWX + DCTOT + DB	Total: NWX + PW + SS
All, ages 47–64	10.0	16.8	28.5	49.3
Ages 47–55	8.1	14.7	26.1	43.7
Ages 56–64	12.5	19.6	31.8	57.1
Non-Hispanic white	11.0	18.9	31.2	53.6
African American or Hispanic	7.8	11.4	23.2	41.5
Married couples	8.7	16.5	28.4	49.7
Single males	14.9	20.8	35.8	57.2
Single females	10.5	15.4	25.1	44.0
Less than 12 years of schooling	3.1	4.4	7.5	34.6
12 years of schooling	7.6	11.7	19.9	42.6
13–15 years of schooling	10.2	15.2	27.5	45.9
16 or more years of schooling	13.9	25.7	42.7	61.4
Income quintile 1	16.8	19.4	25.6	57.3
Income quintile 2	9.3	14.8	25.1	47.0
Income quintile 3	7.6	16.0	29.2	47.8
Income quintile 4	3.2	12.4	29.2	47.1
Income quintile 5	12.9	21.5	33.8	47.3
Memo, Ages 47–64				
1989	10.8	13.0	27.8	45.4
2001	10.5	16.1	26.8	46.5
2010	8.0	17.4	27.7	49.4

Source: Author's computations from the 1989, 2001, 2007, and 2010 SCF.

The share of households meeting this replacement standard rose overall from 45% to 49% between 1989 and 2007. DCTOT made a larger marginal contribution in the later years, increasing the replacement rate by 6.8 percentage points compared with 2.2 percentage points in 1989, whereas DB benefits made a correspondingly smaller marginal contribution, 11.7 compared with 14.8 percentage points. The marginal contribution of Social Security increased between the two years—17.6 in 1989 versus 20.8 percentage points in 2007.

There is a sizeable gap in the share of households meeting the replacement rate standard between whites and minorities, 12.1 percentage points in 2007. Most of the gap comes from differences in NWX and DCTOT. Differences in the share meeting the replacement rate standard are from 7 to 27 percentage points higher for college graduates than for the other education groups in 2007. The differences are primarily due to the much higher value of DCTOT among college graduates.

CONCLUSIONS

Median wealth showed robust growth during the 1980s and 1990s and an even faster advance from 2001 through 2007. However, from 2007 through 2010, house prices fell by 24% in real terms, stock prices by 26%, and median wealth by a staggering 47%. Wealth inequality, after remaining relatively stable from 1989 through 2007, also showed a steep increase over the Great Recession, with the Gini coefficient climbing from 0.834 to 0.870.

The key to understanding the plight of the middle three wealth quintiles over the Great Recession was their high degree of leverage and the high concentration of assets in their home. The steep decline in median net worth between 2007 and 2010 was attributable to their very high degree of leverage and the precipitous fall in home prices. High leverage, moreover, helps explain why median wealth fell more than house (and stock) prices over those years and declined much more than median household income.

The large spread in rates of return on net worth between the middle three wealth quintiles and the top percentile also largely explains why wealth inequality increased steeply from 2007 through 2010 despite the decline in income inequality. Though there was also a radical transformation of the pension system over those years, with DC plans substituting for DB plans, this changeover does not seem to be accountable for the precipitous drop in median net worth nor for the spike in wealth inequality over the Great Recession.

The racial disparity in wealth holdings was almost exactly the same in 2007 as in 1983. However, the Great Recession hit black households much harder than whites. Black households suffered substantial relative (and absolute) losses from 2007 through 2010 because they had a higher share of assets invested in the home than did whites and a much higher debt–equity ratio. Hispanic households made sizeable gains on whites from 1983 through 2007. However, Hispanic households got hammered by the Great Recession. The relative (and absolute) losses suffered by Hispanic households over those three years are likewise traceable to the much larger share of assets invested in the home and a much higher debt–equity ratio.

There was also a marked slowdown in the growth of mean expected retirement income for age group 47 through 64 in the period 2001 through 2007 compared with the 1990s, even before financial meltdown. Whereas retirement income gained 40% overall from 1989 through 2001, it advanced by only 8% from 2001 through 2007. There was also a large reduction in the expected poverty rate at retirement for that age group, from 15% in 1989 to 10% in 2001. However, there was no further reduction from 2001 through 2007. In contrast, the percentage of households meeting the 75% replacement standard rose somewhat more in the later period, from 45.4% to 46.5% from 1989 through 2001 and from 46.5% to 49.3% from 2001 through 2007. From 2007 through 2010, despite the steep decline in household wealth, mean expected retirement income declined by "only" 6%. However, the median fell by a more sizeable 16.4%, reflecting the steep drop in median wealth. Moreover, the projected poverty rate increased by 1.9 percentage points. There was no change in the expected percentage of households meeting the 75% replacement standard because incomes also fell over the Great Recession.

It might seem surprising that the growth of projected retirement income slowed down between the periods 1989 through 2000 and 2001 through 2007 because the growth rate of net worth actually accelerated. However, after titanic gains in the first period, the growth of DCTOT noticeably slowed down in the second, and increases in both DB pension benefits and Social Security also diminished. The reduction in expected retirement income between 2007 and 2010 is traceable primarily to the sharp decline in net worth and secondarily to a plunge in DB pension benefits.

The ratio of expected retirement income between minorities and whites jumped from 0.37 in 1989 to 0.43 in 2007 but then fell sharply to 0.34 in 2010. The convergence from 1989 through 2007 was due largely to the growth in expected Social Security benefits among minorities, which outstripped that among whites. The reversal from 2007 through 2010 was due to sharp relative declines in both NWX and DCTOT among minorities.

Minorities also made dramatic inroads with regard to their projected poverty rate at retirement, which fell from 48% in 1989 to 14% in 2007. Still, whites had a much lower expected poverty rate in 2007 than minorities did, 5% versus 14%. However, from 2007 through 2010, the projected poverty rate was up somewhat more for minorities than whites. Minorities also saw a slightly greater increase in the share meeting the 75% replacement rate from 1989 through 2007. However, minorities still had a lower proportion who met this replacement standard in 2007—42% versus 54%. Moreover, from 2007 through 2010, the share increased somewhat among whites but fell a bit among minorities.

The projected retirement income of single females grew much more slowly than that of married couples from 1989 through 2007, 27% versus 57%. As a result, the ratio between the two groups fell from 0.35 in 1989 to 0.28 in 2007. The relative decline was due mainly to a steep drop in the relative holdings of NWX and DCTOT. From 2007 through 2010, there was little relative change.

Less educated households did not fare well at all. The three lowest groups all saw absolute declines in their expected retirement income from 1989 through 2007 (27% for those with a high school degree or less). The only group showing positive gains was college graduates. From 2007 through 2010, expected retirement income was down for all four schooling groups, though most notably for those with some college. The less educated groups were much more dependent than college graduates on Social Security (29% of expected retirement income for high school graduates in 2007 versus 12% for college graduates), but the reverse was true for NWX—42% for high school graduates versus 57% for college graduates.

The expected poverty rate at retirement was much higher for the least educated group, 28% in 2007, compared with 6% to 9% for the more educated ones. However, those with 12 years of schooling and those with some college saw the biggest increase in expected poverty, 7 and 9 percentage points, respectively, from 1989 through 2007. From 2007 through 2010, projected poverty rates were up for all educational groups except the least educated one.

The share of households meeting a 75% replacement rate at retirement was much higher for college graduates in 2007, 61%, than the other schooling groups, between 35% and 46%. The percentage meeting this standard increased for college graduates between 1989 and 2007 but declined for the least educated group and high school graduates and essentially remained the same for those with some college. In contrast, from 2007 through 2010, the share increased for the lowest two educational groups, fell slightly for those with some college, and declined steeply for college graduates.

Expected retirement income also varies directly with income quintile, and the gaps were quite large. The ratio of expected retirement income between the top and bottom quintile was 13.9 in 2007. Advances in projected retirement income from 1989 through 2007 had a U-shaped pattern, with the strongest gains for the bottom quintile and the second strongest for the top quintile. From 2007 through 2010, projected retirement income fell for the top four quintiles but increased strongly, by 25%, for the bottom quintile.

Social Security was much more important as a source of expected retirement income among the lower-income groups—minorities, single females, the less educated, and the lower-income quintiles—than among higher-income groups—whites, married couples, college graduates, and the top income quintile. Social Security thus serves as an important equalizing factor in retirement adequacy. The share of Social Security in expected retirement income descended with income quintile, from 42% for the bottom to 9% for the top in 2007.

Moreover, the importance of Social Security benefits in expected retirement income grew between 1989 and 2007 for the low-income groups indicated previously. The faster growth of expected Social Security benefits among minorities largely explains the decline in the gap in expected retirement income between them and whites from 1989 through 2007. Likewise, the faster growth of Social Security benefits for the bottom income quintile was the principal factor explaining the faster growth in their expected retirement income relative to that of the top quintile. Social Security also prevented median retirement income from falling even more than 16.4% over the Great Recession, given the 47% drop in median net worth.

In 2007, Social Security caused a huge reduction in the expected poverty rate for low-income groups—non-whites (30 percentage points), single females (21 percentage points), households with less than 12 years of school (41 percentage points), and high school graduates (24 percentage points). Between 1989 and 2007, the drop in the expected poverty rate from adding in expected Social Security benefits increased from 15 to 30 percentage points for minorities, from 15 to 21 percentage points for single females, from 16 to 40 percentage points for least educated, and from 15 to 24 percentage points for high school graduates.

In conclusion, it has been found, first, that Social Security fulfills its expected role of a solid, broadly shared retirement benefit. Second, private savings, including home ownership, is the second most important retirement savings vehicle. Third, private savings still leave future retirees potentially exposed to enormous financial risks. Fourth, private retirement savings plans, including both traditional defined benefit and the more recent defined contribution varieties, leave large holes, even after growing sharply from 1989 through 2010.

ENDNOTES

[1] The source for 1989 through 2007 is U.S. Bureau of the Census, 2009 Statistical Abstract, Table 935 (http://1.usa.gov/16YHIau). The source for 2007 through 2013 is National Association of Realtors, Median Sales Price of Existing Single-Family Homes (http://bit.ly/16BuWOf). The data are for metropolitan areas only.

[2] The source for these data is Table B-96 of the Economic Report of the President, 2013 (http://1.usa.gov/16YHNuU, with updates to September 2013 at http://us.spindices.com/indices/equity/sp-composite-1500).

[3] Also see Weller (2013) for a related analysis on the risk exposure of older Americans.

[4] It should be noted that I exclude vehicles and other consumer durables, as well as defined benefit pension and Social Security wealth, in the standard definition. The latter two are included in my measure of retirement adequacy.

[5] See Wolff, Zacharias, and Masterson (2009) for sources and methods, with updates through 2010 provided by the author.

[6] At first glance, the sensible procedure might seem to be to project nonpension wealth NWX to year of retirement and add that to a projection of DC wealth. However, the problem with this procedure is that there is likely to be substitution between DC contributions and savings in nonpension wealth. Employees who contribute to a DC plan are likely to save less in other forms of wealth, ceteris paribus, than workers who do not contribute. My approach avoids the difficulty of determining whether DC contributions add to net savings over time or not.

[7] I use the official U.S. poverty thresholds for this analysis and assume that the family's marital status remains unchanged over time and that at time of retirement there are no children in the household.

[8] These results might appear to be inconsistent with an overall gain of 39%. However, the paradox is explained by the fact that the share of households with a college degree also climbed sharply over the period (from 17% to 37%).

[9] It should be noted that the poverty rates reported in Table 7 are for the household, not the individual (head count).

REFERENCES

Bernheim, B. Douglas. 1997. "The Adequacy of Personal Retirement Saving: Issues and Options." In David A. Wise, ed., *Facing the Age Wave*. Stanford, CA: Hoover Institute Press, pp. 30–56.

Bloom, David E., and Richard B. Freeman. 1992. "The Fall in Private Pension Coverage in the United States." *American Economic Review Papers and Proceedings*, Vol. 82, pp. 539–558.

Engen, Eric M., William G. Gale, and C.E. Uccello. 1999. "The Adequacy of Household Saving." *Brookings Papers on Economic Activity*, Vol. 2, pp. 65–165.

Engen, Eric M., William G. Gale, and C.E. Uccello. 2005. "Effects of Stock Market Fluctuations on the Adequacy of Retirement Wealth Accumulation." *Review of Income and Wealth*, Vol. 51, no. 3, pp. 397–418.

Even, William E., and David A. Macpherson. 1994. "Why Did Male Pension Coverage Decline in the 1980s?" *Industrial and Labor Relations Review*, Vol. 47, pp. 429–453.

Gustman, Alan L., and Thomas L. Steinmeier. 1992. "The Stampede Toward Defined Contribution Pension Plans: Fact or Fiction?" *Industrial Relations*, Vol. 31, pp. 361–369.

Gustman, Alan L., and Thomas L. Steinmeier. 1998 (Aug.). *Effects of Pensions on Saving: Analysis with Data from the Health and Retirement Study*. NBER Working Paper 6681. Cambridge, MA: National Bureau of Economic Research.

Gustman, Alan L., Thomas L. Steinmeier, and Nahid Tabatabai. 2009. *How Do Pension Changes Affect Retirement Preparedness? The Trend to Defined Contribution Plans and the Vulnerability of the Retirement Age Population to the Stock Market Decline of 2008–2009*. Michigan Retirement Research Center Working Paper 206. Ann Arbor: Michigan Retirement Research Center.

Moore, James F., and Olivia S. Mitchell. 2000. "Projected Retirement Wealth and Saving Adequacy." In Olivia S. Mitchell, P. Brett Hammond, and Anna M. Rappaport, eds., *Forecasting Retirement Needs and Retirement Wealth*. Philadelphia: University of Pennsylvania Press.

Munnell, Alicia H., and Pamela Perun. 2006 (Aug.). *An Update on Private Pensions*. Issue in Brief 50. Boston: Center for Retirement Research at Boston College.

Smith, James P. 2003. "Trends and Projections in Income Replacement During Retirement." *Journal of Labor Economics*, Vol. 21, no. 4, pp. 755–781.

Sorokina, Olga, Anthony Webb, and Dan Muldoon. 2008. *Pension Wealth and Income: 1992, 1998, and 2004*. Issue in Brief 8-1. Boston: Center for Retirement Research at Boston College.

U.S. Department of Labor, Pension and Welfare Benefits Administration. 2000. *Coverage Status of Workers Under Employer Provided Pension Plans: Findings from the Contingent Work Supplement to the February 1999 Current Population Survey*. Washington, DC: U.S. Department of Labor.

Weller, Christian E. 2013 (Mar.). *Making Sure Money Is Available When We Need It: Protecting Household Assets Must Become an Integral Part of U.S. Savings Policies*. Washington, DC: Center for American Progress.

Wolff, Edward N. 2009. *Poverty and Income Distribution* (2nd ed.). Oxford, UK: Wiley-Blackwell.

Wolff, Edward N. 2011. *The Transformation of the American Pension System: Was It Beneficial for Workers?* Kalamazoo, MI: W.E. Upjohn Institute for Employment Research.

Wolff, Edward N., Ajit Zacharias, and Thomas Masterson. 2009. *Long-Term Trends in the Levy Institute Measure of Economic Well-Being (LIMEW), United States, 1959–2004*. Working Paper No. 556, Annandale-on-Hudson, NY: Levy Economics Institute of Bard College.

CHAPTER 10

Debt Lock-In: Household Debt Burdens and Voluntary Quits

SARA M. BERNARDO

University of Massachusetts Boston

INTRODUCTION

U.S. households accumulated debt at an unprecedented pace in the period from 1980 until the start of the financial crisis of 2007–2008. Total debt to disposable income—a measure that indicates households' ability to service their debt burdens out of current income—was stable throughout the 1960s and 1970s, hovering around 70%. The steady increase in debt to disposable income began in the mid-1980s—increasing to 90% by 1995 and reaching a historic peak of 135% in 2007.[1] This massive growth of household indebtedness has generated significant research interest and policy attention over the past two decades. Research regarding the causes and consequences of U.S. household indebtedness grew in urgency after the global financial crisis of 2007, given that economists generally identify the U.S. subprime mortgage market as the catalyst that set the crisis in motion.

While the financial crisis marks an unmistakable tipping point in the debate about the sustainability of debt growth among U.S. households, theoretical and political examinations regarding the main drivers of this growth have yet to reach a productive consensus of sorts. The literature about this debate is more nuanced than the dominant policy positions, partially because there is more room and institutional requirements to take seriously the plausibility of alternative hypotheses. Policy debates must overlook many of these nuances while still making use of the empirical research from the literature. It is thus easier to distill the policy arguments into two distinct drivers of the growth that are reflected in the literature: supply-side factors and demand-side factors.

The supply-side positions argue that technological innovations in credit scoring and government re-regulation of banking activities—including re-regulation of interest rate caps and mandated anti-discrimination policies such as the Community Reinvestment Act—greatly expanded the supply of credit to U.S. households. Optimizing households then used this access to credit to maximize their lifetime consumption, thus increasing indebtedness.

Demand-side positions argue that households have increasingly had to rely on their personal access to financial instruments to maintain their standard of living amid an environment of decreased access to government-funded income support programs and declining direct government funding of welfare state goods such as education, adequate health insurance programs, and Social Security retirement earnings (Crouch 2009; dos Santos 2009; Draut 2006; Lapavitsas 2009; Sullivan 2008). Job insecurity increased during this same period, resulting in both the instability of labor market income and the erosion of the real value of employer-provided benefits. Households thus had to turn to credit markets to finance their consumption (Montgomerie 2013; Pollin 1988) and to financial markets to manage their future retirement security (Blackburn 2006; Soederberg 2007, 2009).

Other demand-side theories focus on the new cultural and ideological attitudes about the credit access and debt use that have developed since the 1970s. In the decades following the Great Depression, debt use was considered to be imprudent financial management. The cultural understanding of household debt has transformed since the 1970s, and savvy debt use is now considered to be an indispensable component of achieving economic security and wealth. Households with enough financial sophistication accumulate *good debt*, such as housing and education debt, that is used as investments in future wealth or higher lifetime labor market earnings. Therefore, debt has risen as a consequence of the increased rationality and sophistication of U.S. households.

While there is certainly some merit to all of these theoretical explanations about the rise of household indebtedness, there is a lack of literature that brings these incomplete arguments together. In the next section of this chapter, I discuss the economic environment in which household debt grew at historic rates and argue that both supply- and demand-side factors are equally important. The structure of the U.S. economy has transformed radically since the mid-1970s, which is often characterized as an era of *financialization*—that is, the increased role of financial markets, products, and incentives in the U.S. economy (Epstein 2005). Financialization has increased both financial and labor market uncertainty and dependence on access to financial instruments to maintain economic security. I argue that the financialization-induced transformations within financial and labor markets have been the main drivers of growing household debt.

The second portion of this chapter offers an interpretation of the consequences of increased indebtedness for labor market mobility. I argue that high levels of debt that are coupled with high debt service burdens constrain workers' abilities to quit undesirable jobs, potentially leading to labor market inefficiencies. Debt service burdens (DSBs) measure the percentage of current disposable income that is devoted to making principal and interest payments on outstanding debts. Debt service burdens signify the extent of households' financial fragility because a higher DSB increases the economic consequences associated with income drops or disruptions. Households with high DSBs use a larger portion of current income to service past consumption. If income drops or is disrupted by a period of unemployment, it is more difficult for a household with a high DSB to continue to meet economic obligations than an otherwise similar household. Therefore, households with higher DSBs face a larger cost of job loss, which limits their ability to quit undesirable jobs. As a result, workers with high debt service burdens are exposed to similar job mobility constraints that are characteristic of "job lock"—caused by the nonportability of employer-provided health insurance.

The growth of household indebtedness in the United States may thus contribute to labor market inefficiencies as a result of suboptimal levels of voluntary turnover. Labor market efficiency depends partly on optimal employment matches at which workers are employed in a position where they are most productive.[2] Sufficient voluntary turnover increases the chances of optimal matches for the labor market as a whole and for an individual's career and wage growth trajectory.

This chapter concludes with a discussion of the theoretical and policy implications that stem from this broader view of the causes and consequences of growing household indebtedness. I argue that financialization has produced a reinforcing cycle of labor market insecurity and financial risk exposure. Labor market insecurities are managed by credit use to maintain economic security, which often results in increased indebtedness. Higher indebtedness, if coupled with a high debt service burden, increases the cost of job loss and magnifies the degree of labor market insecurity. A comprehensive policy program that addresses the larger economic insecurities faced by U.S. households in the era of financialization, rather than just regulation of the supply- or demand-side factors, is needed to effectively improve the economic security of U.S. households.

FINANCIALIZATION AND MARKET DEVELOPMENTS

Household debt growth has been a response to both supply and demand factors that developed from the new economic dynamics ushered in during the era of financialization. The major economic events of the 1970s—end of the gold standard, stagflation of the U.S. economy, the globalization of production, and the liberalization of the regulations on international capital flows—created the conditions for the emergence of financial markets and motives as fundamental elements of social and economic activity (Stockhammer 2013).

Scholars of financialization examine the influence of the financial sector in important economic institutions including development of the shareholder value maximization structure of corporate governance (Fligstein 1993; Lazonick and O'Sullivan 2000) and the resulting increase of financial investments vis-á-vis real investments by nonfinancial firms (Orhangazi 2008; Stockhammer 2008), the growth of the share of national income going to owners of financial assets (Epstein and Jayadev 2005), the resulting increase of income and wealth inequality in the United States (Onaran, Stockhammer, and Grafl 2011; Tomaskovic-Devey and Lin 2011; Van Arnum and Naples 2013), and the growing indebtedness of all sectors of the economy (Krippner 2011; Palley 2007).

These dynamics of financialization have all contributed to the increase in job insecurity and labor market risk exposure of U.S. households as well as their financial market dependence and risk exposure. Financialization has enabled households to maintain their standard consumption levels amid labor market earnings stagnation and insecurity by increasing their access to credit markets. Households have not only increased their use of credit markets as a substitute for rising incomes, however; they have also increased their use of both credit and financial markets in response to the new economic requirements of individual provision schemes of standard welfare goods (Lapavitsas 2011; Montgomerie 2013).

Financialization has thus ushered in a new era of magnified financial and labor market risk exposure among U.S. households, creating economic insecurity among the mass of U.S. households not seen since the beginning of the 20th century. The following sections highlight the major transformations within financial and labor markets that have contributed to this increase in economic insecurity.

Financial Market Transformations

U.S. and global financial systems have undergone profound changes since the 1970s. The focus of this chapter requires an examination of the major changes that expanded access to financial markets and contributed to the rise of household indebtedness in the United States—namely, the development of a new commercial banking model, the regulatory changes that increased the profitability of lending to households, and the growth of securitization.

The current business of commercial banking is nearly unrecognizable from that of the post–World War II period. During the course of the past 30 years, industrial and commercial firms have been able to turn to retained profits and direct fund-raising in open markets to finance investment (Lapavitsas 2009). This financialization of productive enterprises narrowed the scope for conventional commercial banking that had traditionally generated business-sustaining profits by lending to these industrial and commercial firms.

Households also began to shift their financial resources away from commercial banks and into more direct financial market accounts to take advantage of the higher rates of returns that these financial institutions offered. Most important, households withdrew their funds from traditional bank savings accounts—which in 1979 could legally pay no more than 6% interest on deposit accounts—and deposited their savings in the newly created money market mutual funds that offered interest rates as high as 10% more than what banks could provide (Geisst 2009).

Commercial banks, facing a profitability crisis caused by the exodus of household and business deposit accounts, pursued several regulatory and business strategies to regain their customer base. The New Deal financial regulatory structure, established in the aftermath of the 1929 stock market crash, limited the ability of commercial banks to compete with the cheaper sources of financing and higher returns offered by other growing financial institutions: the Glass–Steagall Act of 1933 prevented banks from using funds from customers' deposit accounts to invest in the stock market, and Regulation Q prevented banks from paying interest on checking deposits and limited the interest rates they could offer to savers and charge to borrowers. In addition to those regulations, the Federal Deposit Insurance Corporation (FDIC) was established to ensure the safety of U.S. households' savings. While these regulations succeeded in stabilizing the banking system to avoid another systemic financial crisis—which was on everyone's mind in the decades following the crash—they became serious obstacles to the profit rate of commercial banks as economic and financial market developments increased the competitive advantage of other financial institutions.

A series of important policies were enacted beginning in the early 1980s that enabled banks to gradually regain their competitiveness in financial markets. The Depository Institutions and Monetary Deregulation Act of 1980 removed the interest rate ceilings imposed by Regulation Q. Banks created deposit accounts with higher interest rates, which brought many depositors—who had transferred their savings to money market mutual funds—back to the banks, thus expanding the pool of funds available for lending. The 1980 act also removed interest rate ceilings imposed by many state usury laws, enabling banks to charge higher rates of interest to borrowers (Gindin and Panitch 2012).

The relaxation of interest rate regulations was accompanied by advances in credit scoring techniques that spread the use of risk-based pricing as a business strategy (Cynamon and Fazzari 2008; Langley 2008). Technological advances facilitated the development of accurate standardized statistical methods to determine borrowers' creditworthiness (Langley 2008). Prior to these advances, credit was extended more on a relational basis that had relatively high information costs. Lenders assessed the creditworthiness of borrowers through more direct interactions and relationship development, which took significant amounts of time and resources (Geisst 2009). With a standardized mechanism that enables lenders to plug in income, credit history, and other relevant data about potential borrowers, the determination of credit worthiness became much easier. Credit scoring, as the primary means of determining the likelihood of default and thus the cost of credit, was heralded as a monumental efficiency improvement in credit markets (Greenspan 2004).

The spread of standardized credit scores led to the dominance of a new pricing mechanism known as risk-based pricing (Burhouse 2003). Through risk-based pricing, lenders are willing to extend credit to higher-risk borrowers by increasing the interest rates and fees charged in accordance with their default risk, making it easier to estimate the expected profitability of lending to individuals. The combination of interest rate deregulation and credit scoring techniques expanded credit market access, and thus the supply of credit, to households that were previously excluded based on their weaker financial profiles—in particular, low-income and non-white households (Dobos 2012; Weller 2009).

Lending to individual households grew significantly since that period. The proportion of total bank lending that involved individual households, rather than both small and large businesses, rose from around 35% in the early 1970s to nearly 50% in 2007 (Lapavitsas 2009). This growth of loans to individuals underscores the shift in commercial banking practices—from lending primarily to productive business enterprises to lending primarily to households. As individual incomes became the source of banks' profits, it was rational to expand the supply of credit to households.

The supply of credit to households was also facilitated by the development of securitization in credit markets (Langley 2008; Montgomerie 2007). Securitization is the practice of bundling together many small loans into a master trust—a special-purpose vehicle that creates an asset-backed security—that investors buy shares of and receive portions of the principal and interest payments made by the underlying borrowers throughout the term of the loans (Burhouse 2003; Geisst 2009). Securitization makes it possible for originating banks to move loans off of their balance sheet, enabling a re-capitalization of their existing capital stock—that is, the ability to issue new loans from the same source of funds (Langley 2008; Montgomerie 2007).

Securitization became common practice in the mortgage market in the late 1970s and early 1980s and by the early 1990s had spread to other consumer finance markets that had predictable streams of repayment such as car loans, credit card accounts, and educational loans (Langley 2008; Montgomerie 2007). One of the underlying functions of securitization is a systemwide transfer of risk that, especially in the case of the subprime mortgage market, is often seen as a source of the relaxation of underwriting standards (Dymski 2009; Guttmann and Plihon 2010). Securitization meant that lenders no longer had to absorb the total default risk of the loans they generated. Instead, the risk is transferred to the purchasers of the asset-backed securities. This risk transfer incentivized the expansion of credit supply to U.S. households, which, as the next section will show, was met with an increased demand for credit.

Labor Market Transformations

Several labor market indicators show distinctly divergent trends between the post–World War II years to the 1970 period and the period from the early 1970s until about the present. Job insecurity rose significantly for workers who had been employed in industries and occupations that had birthed the middle class in the years after the war (Cockshott and Zachariah 2010). The steady real wage and living standard growth won by the unionized working class throughout the post-war period stopped in the early 1970s when international competition and persistent stagflation significantly reduced the profitability of U.S. firms (Brenner 2006; Glyn 2007; Krippner 2005). Firms pursued policy strategies to weaken the labor market regulations that were keeping labor costs high and instituted business strategies to develop more profitable firm organization and investment patterns. Labor market insecurity rose for the mass of U.S. workers as a result; real wages and incomes stagnated; income inequality rose; and unemployment, underemployment, and precarious work became standard (Glyn 2007; Hacker 2004).

U.S. firms cut their production costs by successfully pushing labor and financial market deregulation to the forefront of policy priorities. Combating inflation had firmly replaced a full-employment priority as the dominant policy agenda by the time Paul Volcker became chair of the Federal Reserve in 1979.[3] Volcker attributed the high inflation rates to pressures caused by a wage–price spiral induced by the growing strength of labor's bargaining power in the low-unemployment, highly unionized post-war economy (McNally 2010). Volcker immediately fought inflation with tight monetary policy by sharply increasing interest rates (Epstein and Jayadev 2005). Although Volcker's interest rate shocks succeeded in reducing inflation to 4% within three years, high interest rates caused businesses to significantly reduce investments, resulting in a severe economic contraction and an unemployment rate above 11% (McNally 2010). Real wage growth remained close to zero for roughly two decades since the period of high unemployment in 1982, successfully reducing firms' labor costs (Brenner 2006).

During this period of high inflation and tight monetary policy, U.S. firms aggressively pursued labor market deregulations as a more structural approach to reducing labor costs. Labor unions were an indispensable organizational tool and institution that U.S. workers used throughout the post-war period to achieve a growing share of productivity gains in the form of rising real wages and employment-based benefits. As the source of the working-class power that became a serious impediment to the bottom lines of firms during the profitability crisis of the 1970s, firms effectively eroded labor union power by the mid-1980s by securing the support of key policy makers who were desperate to alleviate the economic crisis that Keynesian policies seemed to both create and exacerbate (Gindin and Panitch 2012; Van Arnum and Naples 2013).

The real turning point in the mission to eliminate restrictive wage, benefit, and working conditions secured by collective bargaining came at the beginning of Reagan's presidency. Reagan ended the air traffic controllers' strike in 1981 by firing 12,000 workers and arresting many of the strike leaders (Gindin and Panitch 2012). Firms had won the support of the Reagan administration and through this historic action sent a clear message to workers: the era of union-won gains in employment and standard of living is over. The timing of Reagan's strike break—during a time of high rates of unemployment induced by monetary policy—further broke workers' confidence and resulted in significant labor concessions in major U.S. industries (Moody 1988).

This combination of inflation-focused monetary policy and labor market deregulations was a boon to nonfinancial U.S. firms throughout the 1980s. Without collective bargaining pressure from unionized workers, firms have been able to capture the majority of the labor productivity gains since that time. Real wage gains broke with productivity growth, resulting in higher profit rates than would have been the case if wages kept pace with productivity growth, as they had done throughout the post-war period (McNally 2010).

U.S. firms also greatly benefited from the financial market liberalization discussed in the previous section of this chapter. Large U.S. firms bolstered their profitability by engaging in new financial market activities that produced quicker returns on investments than they could achieve through productive investments. Scholars of financialization refer to this turn to financial investments by firms as the *financialization of nonfinancial corporations.*[4] As this profit strategy spread throughout industries during the 1980s and 1990s, the corporate governance strategy of "shareholder value maximization" dominated the structure and management of U.S. corporations (Krippner 2011; Lazonick and O'Sullivan 2000). Shareholder value maximization shifted the priority of corporate management from providing long-term growth, stability, and profitability of firms to producing large-share price gains and dividend payouts. The growth of corporate takeovers—the process of buying firms at low prices and then selling their assets for a major profit—further ingrained the trend of shareholder value maximization as managers' top priority because corporations with low stock prices were more vulnerable to takeovers (Krippner 2011).

This financialization of nonfinancial firms increased labor market instability for workers. The priority of raising share prices often entailed major reorganizations of firms, which aimed at cutting production costs by downsizing through massive layoffs and limiting labor compensation packages and wage growth. The threat of unemployment caused by downsizing further limited workers' ability to bargain for higher compensation because firms had an expanded pool of unemployed workers to hire at lower costs as a result of the increases in unemployment.

These labor market changes all contributed to the growing instability of labor market earnings and real wage declines. During the same period that labor market income became more insecure, the cost of many standard goods and services consumed by U.S. workers increased. Education, health care, housing, and transportation became more expensive for households as a result of two factors. First, the inflation-adjusted prices of these goods grew faster than the real wages of the majority of U.S. workers, meaning that the absolute cost of the goods rose. Second, public financing changed in fundamental ways that altered the systems of provision of these goods. Direct public expenditures that subsidized—and, in some cases, significantly lowered the cost of such goods—were replaced by tax expenditures.

Labor market income is the primary financial source for the majority of U.S. households. The downward pressure on wages and compensation stemming from labor market deregulation created new financial pressures for households trying to maintain their standard of living. Increased earnings instability makes it difficult to successfully plan consumption needs—both in the present and in the future. Households turned to credit markets in an attempt to meet their consumption needs.

RISING HOUSEHOLD INDEBTEDNESS

U.S. household indebtedness has risen during the era of financialization at an unprecedented pace. Growth has been both absolute and relative to gross domestic product (GDP) and the personal disposable income of the household sector. This section presents the data available about the growth in household indebtedness over the past 40 years, focusing on aggregate totals, such as ratios of debt to GDP and debt to disposable income, the composition of debt, and debt service burdens by income groups.

A standard measure of household indebtedness is total debt to GDP, the total output of the economy. It provides a measure of debt as a percentage of total economic activity. Debt as a percentage of GDP remained relatively stable throughout the 1960s and 1970s at around 45% (Figure 1). The total household debt to GDP ratio began its steady increase

FIGURE 1
Total Household Debt to GDP and Disposable Household Income

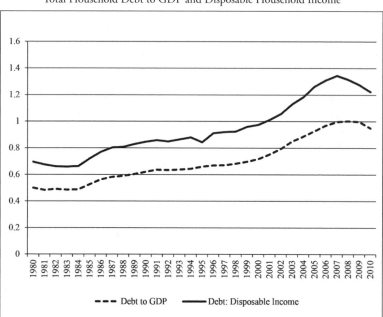

Source: Author's calculations from the National Income and Product Accounts (NIPA) from the U.S. Bureau of Economic Analysis.

in the 1980s, picking up pace throughout the early 2000s and reaching its historical peak of 100% in 2007. This means that the amount of debt households held in 2007 was equal to the total output of the U.S. economy.

While the ratio of total household debt to GDP provides a measure of the growing importance of debt in the U.S. economy, it doesn't provide much context about households' financial positions, which, in some instances, can provide a measure of financial stability and the sustainability of growing indebtedness. Figure 1 presents total household debt as a percentage of total disposable income. This measure represents the household sector's total indebtedness relative to their income each year. Income is the primary means that most households have to pay off their debt. As the ratio increases, households' ability to pay off their debt decreases. As was the case with total debt to GDP, total debt to disposable income was relatively stable throughout the 1960s and 1970s, hovering around 70%. Starting in the mid-1980s, the ratio began to steadily increase, picking up pace in the early 2000s and reaching its historical peak of 135% in 2007.

Another way to understand the debt of the household sector is the debt burden (i.e., the amount of income that households must use to make payments on their debt). It gives us an understanding of how rising indebtedness impacts the financial stability and financial freedom of households. Table 1 shows that the median debt burden for all households in the United States has been steadily rising since 1995, reaching its peak of 14% on the eve of the financial crisis and Great Recession. If we disaggregate this measure by income percentiles, it becomes clear that lower- and middle-income households have higher debt burdens than higher-income households. About 27% of households in the lowest 20th percentile of the income distribution had debt burdens greater than 40% in 2007, a measure of heavy indebtedness. This was higher than any other income percentile.

LABOR MARKET MOBILITY AND DEBT
Labor Market Mobility

In standard economic models, optimal levels of growth are achieved when resources are allocated efficiently throughout the economy (i.e., employing resources in the most productive manner, given the current state of technological and institutional development). Labor market efficiency can be assessed by examining the overall quality of job matches between employees and firms and by the level of labor market turnover. Factors that impede job mobility may lead to labor market inefficiencies because optimal employment matches may not occur (Rashad and Sarpong 2008).

Labor market turnover is an essential component of both the quality of job matches in the economy and the wage trajectory and job satisfaction of individual workers. Turnover improves the overall quality of job matches in an economy by reallocating workers to jobs that appropriately match their skills and abilities, thus increasing economic productivity and growth (Gruber and Madrian 2002; Jovanovic 1979; Lazear and Spletzer 2012; Monheit and Cooper 1994). Increased opportunities for job-to-job mobility also make it easier for workers to find job opportunities that offer either higher wages (Johnson and Corcoran 2003; Liu 2011); greater prospects for wage growth (Topel and Ward 1992); nonwage benefits such as job satisfaction (Connolly and Gottschalk 2004); or employer-provided health and retirement programs, or both. Job satisfaction is positively linked to worker productivity and is therefore another factor that contributes to labor market efficiency (Huysse-Gaytandjieva, Groot, and Pavlova 2013).

The level of turnover in the U.S. labor market can be estimated by using aggregate levels of hires, separations, job creation, and job destruction (Hyatt and Spletzer 2013). The U.S. Bureau of Labor Statistics (BLS) compiles the statistics of worker flows—the number of workers hired into jobs and the number of workers separating from a current job—in its

TABLE 1
Debt Service Burdens by Income Percentiles

	Median for debtors (%)								Debtors with ratio greater than 40% (%)							
	1989	1992	1995	1998	2001	2004	2007	2010	1989	1992	1995	1998	2001	2004	2007	2010
All families	15.3	15.9	16.3	17.9	16.7	18.1	18.6	18.2	10.0	11.4	11.7	13.8	11.7	12.4	14.7	13.9
Percentile of income																
< 20	15.3	13.5	13.1	17.2	19.6	19.5	18.8	16.0	25.9	27.0	27.1	29.5	29.7	27.3	26.7	26.2
20–39.9	16.0	15.7	17.9	17.8	16.5	17.5	16.7	17.5	14.7	15.4	19.1	19.5	16.0	18.5	19.7	18.6
40–59.9	15.2	15.8	15.7	19.6	17.8	19.5	20.4	20.1	11.1	11.5	8.9	15.9	12.8	13.9	14.5	15.3
60–79.9	17.8	17.6	19.0	19.4	18.1	20.6	21.9	20.4	5.4	7.8	7.8	9.6	6.1	7.3	12.8	11.1
80–89.9	15.1	16.7	17.0	17.8	17.2	18.2	19.1	19.3	2.3	3.6	4.9	3.4	3.7	2.7	8.1	5.3
90–100	11.9	14.0	12.3	13.6	11.2	12.8	12.6	13.1	2.3	2.4	2.9	3.0	2.0	1.6	3.8	2.9

Source: Bricker et al. (2012).

monthly Job Opening and Labor Turnover Survey (JOLTS). Hires are determined by the sum of new employment matches that include movements from nonemployment to employment, job-to-job mobility, or any additional jobs started (Hyatt and Spletzer 2013). Separations are composed of voluntary quits, layoffs, discharges, or other—such as retirement, death, or transfer to another location (Bruyere, Podgornik, and Spletzer 2011).

Labor market churn measures the movements of workers between jobs and is typically indicative of a healthy labor market because higher levels indicate that it is easier for workers to move between jobs, increasing the opportunity for efficient employment matches (Lazear and Spletzer 2012). It is important to note that labor market churn specifically refers to hires and separations that offset each other. This means that churn has no effect on net employment growth because it is a measure of the turnover of workers between existing jobs (Lazear and Spletzer 2012).

Labor market churn is procyclical because the dynamics between hirings and separations vary significantly throughout the business cycle (Bruyere, Podgornik, and Spletzer 2011; Lazear and Spletzer 2012). Churn drops during recessions as a result of changes in hiring, layoffs, and decisions to quit. Workers are more reluctant to quit during recessions because hiring rates drop and layoff rates rise (Lazear and Spletzer 2012). Involuntary employment separations account for a larger proportion of total separations during recessions than voluntary quits and are far less likely to be offset by a new hire (Lazear and Spletzer 2012).

That recessions decrease labor market churn should come as no surprise. But the longer-term economic consequences of reduced churn during recessions can be significant. Lazear and Spletzer (2012) estimate that reduced churn contributed to a $208 billion loss of GDP in the Great Recession and the immediate aftermath. This implies that the amount of churn in an economy is an important component of the level of output. Hyatt and Spletzer (2013) estimate that the rate of job-to-job flows in the U.S. economy fell by nearly half between 1998 and 2010. It is not clear what is driving this reduction or what the macroeconomic implications may be.

The decision to quit is determined by a variety of factors such as wages and benefits offered by other employers, job satisfaction and personal career ambitions, family situations, and retirement timing. As previously discussed, recent research has identified job lock (i.e., immobility caused by the nonportability of employment-based health insurance and uncertainty of alternative affordable health care coverage) as a significant factor in the decision to quit (Gruber and Madrian 2002).

Job lock has been on the front burner for quite some time in U.S. policy discussions, given the decade-long (or so) attempt to reform health insurance markets. Employer-sponsored insurance, in which employers cover a significant portion of plan premiums, has always been a crucial way for Americans to access affordable health care. In 2010, 55% of U.S. workers were covered by employer-sponsored health plans (U.S. Census Bureau 2011). Employees value subsidized health care as part of their compensation packages not only because it is much cheaper than purchasing individual plans in the market but also because employer-sponsored plans, unlike the private market alternative, cannot charge higher premiums or deny coverage based on health status (U.S. GAO 2011). Furthermore, health care costs have increased significantly throughout the past two decades, making access to affordable health care even more dependent on employer-sponsored plans (Adams 2004).

Research consistently finds evidence that health insurance coverage is an important factor in job mobility decisions.[5] The concern is that the health insurance factor significantly distorts the decision to quit a current job in order to find more satisfactory work in which a worker's productivity may increase. Job lock may therefore be limiting both individual welfare and overall macroeconomic efficiency and growth. While this hypothesis follows directly from economic theory, empirical studies have confirmed the magnitude of losses to neither individual welfare losses nor macroeconomic efficiency and growth (Gruber and Madrian 2002). All that can be said about job lock is that it exists as a constraint on job mobility for workers with employer-sponsored health coverage who would lose affordable access to health care if they quit.

The Cost of Job Loss and Debt Lock-In

High levels of household debt could also constrain voluntary turnover in ways similar to job lock. Because the amount of financial resources required to service debt burdens is tied directly to household debt levels, and given that the majority of households' financial resources come from employment, it is likely that increasing indebtedness will have important effects on individual labor market decisions. Larger financial commitments associated with increasing indebtedness may constrain a worker's ability to voluntarily quit a job to seek more gainful employment by increasing the cost of job loss.

The cost of job loss is a measurement that captures the post-displacement income loss associated with job separation. The formative cost of job loss models was used to calculate the employment rent (workers' expected cost of job loss) as a measure of both labor market tightness (Schor and Bowles 1987) and as a measure of optimal employee monitoring with equilibrium unemployment (Shapiro and Stiglitz 1984; Yellen 1984). These studies demonstrate that the cost of job loss influences the ability of workers to bargain for better employment conditions and compensation as well as the efficiency of overall employment outcomes in the economy.

Job lock is a clear expression of a contemporary cost of job loss measurement. The loss of employer-provided health insurance increases the post-displacement income loss associated with job mobility. Depending on the economic priorities of individual workers, otherwise productive job mobility will occur only if workers are confident that they can find affordable health insurance in alternative situations. Voluntary turnover will thus be limited based on the relative expense or limited coverage of alternative insurance programs.

The cost of job loss is also magnified by indebtedness. Debt service obligations—required interest, fees, and principal payments on outstanding debts—increase the amount of financial resources that are needed to meet economic responsibilities during a period of unemployment. As a result, the income loss associated with job separations increases the risk that households will be unable to finance their economic obligations. The consequences of not meeting economic obligations can be severe, ranging from decreased consumption (Browning and Crossley 2001) to home foreclosure (Herkenhoff and Ohanian 2012) and bankruptcy, which then leads to decreased access to credit markets in the future (Keys 2010). High debt service burdens may result in lower levels of voluntary quits among workers who would be more productive and satisfied in another job. Debt obligations may create a situation in which unsatisfied workers are "locked in" to their current job and are thus unable to make employment-enhancing mobility moves.

CONCLUSION

Financialization has significantly transformed the U.S. economy since the early 1970s. New financial market regulations have led to the creation of a new banking business model in which the interest and fee revenues generated by lending to individual households has become a primary profit source. The creation of new credit market instruments, coupled with the spreading practice of securitization, greatly expanded the supply of funds available for lending. Growing labor market insecurity during this period led many households to use equity and credit markets as a strategy to maintain consumption levels in the face of stagnating or declining employment incomes.

These supply- and demand-side factors led to a growth of household indebtedness, which is associated with higher financial market risk exposure (Debelle 2004). To the extent that financial market risk exposure is coupled with high debt service burdens, voluntary turnover will be limited as a consequence of the increased cost of job loss. This debt-induced labor market immobility, or what I have called "debt lock-in," further escalates labor market insecurity by constraining workers' ability to find other employment opportunities that could increase their job satisfaction and productivity.

This reinforcing cycle of labor market insecurity and financial risk exposure must be addressed in any policy attempt to deal with the economic consequences of increased household indebtedness. Policy programs that offer ways to re-regulate credit markets in order to decrease the level of fraudulent or unfair lending practices address only a small portion of the overall issue of household debt growth. A comprehensive policy program that addresses the full picture of the financialization-induced economic insecurities that U.S. households face is needed to effectively improve economic security. Such a program should, at a minimum, include measures to reduce the consequences workers experience from labor market insecurity.

Expanding access to and increasing benefit levels of income support programs during unemployment could enhance the ability of workers to search for better jobs. Despite the fact that many policy makers and workers support this kind of approach, such programs have been difficult to pass—especially in any meaningful monetary amount—in the wake of the Great Recession. A policy program that addresses the roots of economic insecurity (e.g., inadequate wage growth relative to the cost of living, increased job insecurity resulting from the practice of firms downsizing to increase shareholder value, and increased personal responsibility for managing retirement savings) would be even more difficult to pass, even though it could bring significant advances in the economic security of the mass of U.S. households.

ENDNOTES

[1] Author's calculations based on data from the Bureau of Economic Analysis 2010 National Income and Product Accounts (NIPA) and the Federal Reserve Board of Governors 2010 Flow of Funds Accounts.

[2] Productivity is the macro concern here. But, on an individual level, if we look at the factors that lead to higher productivity, skills matching and satisfaction are included.

[3] See Gindin and Panitch (2012), particularly page 171, for a full discussion of the dynamics of this policy shift.

[4] See Davis (2013) for a full theoretical and empirical treatment of the financialization of nonfinancial corporations.

[5] See U.S. GAO (2011) for an extensive coverage of the research.

REFERENCES

Bricker, Jesse, Arthur B. Kennickell, Kevin B. Moore, and John Sabelhaus, assisted by Samuel Ackerman, Robert Argento, Gerhard Fries, and Richard A. Windle. 2012 (Jun.). "Changes in US Family Finances from 2007 to 2010: Evidence from the Survey of Consumer Finances." *Federal Reserve Bulletin* (http://bit.ly/1Et2o55).

Adams, Scott J. 2004. "Employer-Provided Health Insurance and Job Change." *Contemporary Economic Policy*, Vol. 22, no. 3, pp. 357–369.

Blackburn, Robin. 2006. "The Global Pension Crisis: From Gray Capitalism to Responsible Accumulation." *Politics & Society*, Vol. 34, no. 2, pp. 135–186.

Brenner, Robert. 2006. *The Economics of Global Turbulence: The Advanced Capitalist Economies From Long Boom to Long Downturn, 1945–2005*. Brooklyn, NY: Verso Books.

Browning, Martin, and Thomas F. Crossley. 2001. "The Life-Cycle Model of Consumption and Saving." *Journal of Economic Perspectives*, Vol. 15, no. 3, pp. 3–22.

Bruyere, Caryn N., Guy L. Podgornik, and James R. Spletzer. 2011. "Employment Dynamics over the Last Decade." *Monthly Labor Review*, Vol. 134, no. 8, pp. 16–29.

Burhouse, Susan. 2003 (Sep. 17). "Evaluating the Consumer Lending Revolution." *FYI: An Update on Emerging Issues in Banking* (http://1.usa.gov/19DbTVL).

Cockshott, Paul, and Dave Zachariah. 2010. "Credit Crunch: Origins and Orientation." *Science & Society*, Vol. 74, no. 3, pp. 343–361.

Connolly, Helen, and Peter Gottschalk. 2004. *Wage Cuts as Investment in Future Wage Growth: Some Evidence*. Boston College Working Papers in Economics, No. 543.

Crouch, Colin. 2009. "Privatised Keynesianism: An Unacknowledged Policy Regime." *British Journal of Politics & International Relations*, Vol. 11, no. 3, pp. 382–399.

Cynamon, Barry Z., and Steven M. Fazzari. 2008. "Household Debt in the Consumer Age: Source of Growth—Risk of Collapse." *Capitalism and Society*, Vol. 3, no. 2, pp. 1–32.

Davis, Leila E. 2013. *Financialization and the Nonfinancial Corporation: An Investigation of Firm-Level Investment Behavior in the US, 1971–2011*. University of Massachusetts Amherst, Department of Economics Working Paper No. 2013-08.

Debelle, Guy. 2004. *Macroeconomic Implications of Rising Household Debt*. Bank for International Settlements Working Paper No. 153.

Dobos, Ned. 2012. "The Democratization of Credit." *Journal of Social Philosophy*, Vol. 43, no. 1, pp. 50–63.

dos Santos, Paulo L. 2009. "At the Heart of the Matter: Household Debt in Contemporary Banking and the International Crisis." *Ekonomiaz*, Vol. 72, no. 3, pp. 54–77.

Draut, Tamara. 2006. *Strapped: Why America's 20- and 30-Somethings Can't Get Ahead*. New York: Doubleday.

Dymski, Gary A. 2009. "Racial Exclusion and the Political Economy of the Subprime Crisis." *Historical Materialism*, Vol. 17, no. 2, pp. 149–179.

Epstein, Gerald. A. 2005. "Introduction: Financialization and the World Economy." In Gerald A. Epstein, ed., *Financialization and the World Economy*. Northampton, MA: Edward Elgar, pp. 1–16.

Epstein, Gerald A., and Arjun Jayadev. 2005. "The Rise of Rentier Incomes in OECD Countries: Financialization, Central Bank Policy and Labor Solidarity." In Gerald A. Epstein, ed., *Financialization and the World Economy*. Northampton, MA: Edward Elgar, pp. 46–74.

Fligstein, Neil. 1993. *The Transformation of Corporate Control*. Cambridge, MA: Harvard University Press.

Geisst, Charles R. 2009. *Collateral Damaged: The Marketing of Consumer Debt to America*. New York: Bloomberg Press.

Gindin, Sam, and Leo Panitch. 2012. *The Making of Global Capitalism*. Brooklyn, NY: Verso Books.

Glyn, Andrew. 2007. *Capitalism Unleashed: Finance, Globalization, and Welfare*. Oxford, UK: Oxford University Press.

Greenspan, Alan. 2004. "Testimony Before the Committee on Financial Services, House of Representatives," February 11.

Gruber, Jonathan, and Brigitte C. Madrian. 2002. *Health Insurance, Labor Supply, and Job Mobility: A Critical Review of the Literature.* National Bureau of Economic Research Working Paper No. 8817.

Guttmann, Robert, and Dominique Plihon. 2010. "Consumer Debt and Financial Fragility." *International Review of Applied Economics*, Vol. 24, no. 3, pp. 269–283.

Hacker, Jacob S. 2004. "Privatizing Risk without Privatizing the Welfare State: The Hidden Politics of Social Policy Retrenchment in the United States." *American Political Science Review*, Vol. 98, no. 2, pp. 243–260.

Herkenhoff, Kyle F., and Lee Ohanian. 2012. *Foreclosure Delay and US Unemployment.* Federal Reserve Bank of St. Louis Working Paper No. 2012-017.

Huysse-Gaytandjieva, Anna, Wim Groot, and Milena Pavlova. 2013. "A New Perspective on Job Lock." *Social Indicators Research*, Vol. 112, no. 3, pp. 587–610.

Hyatt, Henry R., and James R. Spletzer. 2013. *The Recent Decline in Employment Dynamics.* U.S. Census Bureau Center for Economic Studies Paper No. CES-WP-13-03.

Johnson, Rucker C., and Mary E. Corcoran. 2003. "The Road to Economic Self-Sufficiency: Job Quality and Job Transition Patterns after Welfare Reform." *Journal of Policy Analysis and Management*, Vol. 22, no. 4, pp. 615–639.

Jovanovic, Boyan. 1979. "Job Matching and the Theory of Turnover." *The Journal of Political Economy*, Vol. 87, no. 5, part 1, pp. 972–990.

Keys, Benjamin J. 2010. *The Credit Market Consequences of Job Displacement.* Board of Governors of the Federal Reserve System (U.S.) Working Paper No. 2010-24.

Krippner, Greta R. 2005. "The Financialization of the American Economy." *Socio-Economic Review*, Vol. 3, no. 2, pp. 173–208.

Krippner, Greta R. 2011. *Capitalizing on Crisis.* Cambridge, MA: Harvard University Press.

Langley, Paul. 2008. "Financialization and the Consumer Credit Boom." *Competition & Change*, Vol. 12, no. 2, pp. 133–147.

Lapavitsas, Costas. 2009. "Financialised Capitalism: Crisis and Financial Expropriation." *Historical Materialism*, Vol. 17, no. 2, pp. 114–148.

Lapavitsas, Costas. 2011. "Theorizing Financialization." *Work, Employment & Society*, Vol. 25, no. 4, pp. 611–626.

Lazear, Edward P., and James R. Spletzer. 2012. *Hiring, Churn and the Business Cycle.* National Bureau of Economic Research Working Paper No. 17910.

Lazonick, William, and Mary O'Sullivan. 2000. "Maximizing Shareholder Value: A New Ideology for Corporate Governance." *Economy and Society*, Vol. 29, no. 1, pp. 13–35.

Liu, Kai. 2011. "Wage Risk, On-the-job Search and the Value of Job Mobility." Unpublished manuscript.

McNally, David. 2010. *Global Slump: The Economics and Politics of Crisis and Resistance.* Oakland, CA: PM Press.

Monheit, Alan C., and Philip F. Cooper. 1994. "Health Insurance and Job Mobility: Theory and Evidence." *Industrial and Labor Relations Review*, Vol. 48, no. 1, pp. 68–85.

Montgomerie, Johnna. 2007. "Financialization and Consumption: An Alternative Account of Rising Consumer Debt Levels in Anglo-America." CRESC Working Paper Series, Vol. 43.

Montgomerie, Johnna. 2013. "America's Debt Safety-Net." *Public Administration*, Vol. 9, no. 4, pp. 871–888.

Moody, Kim. 1988. *An Injury to All: The Decline of American Unionism*. New York: Verso Books.

Onaran, Özlem, Engelbert Stockhammer, and Lucas Grafl. 2011. "Financialisation, Income Distribution and Aggregate Demand in the USA." *Cambridge Journal of Economics*, Vol. 35, no. 4, pp. 637–661.

Orhangazi, Özgür. 2008. "Financialisation and Capital Accumulation in the Non-Financial Corporate Sector: A Theoretical and Empirical Investigation on the US Economy: 1973–2003." *Cambridge Journal of Economics*, Vol. 32, no. 6, pp. 863–886.

Palley, Thomas I. 2007. *Financialization: What It Is and Why It Matters*. The Levy Economics Institute Working Paper No. 525.

Pollin, Robert. 1988. "The Growth of US Household Debt: Demand-Side Influences." *Journal of Macroeconomics*, Vol. 10, no. 2, pp. 231–248.

Rashad, Inas, and Eric Sarpong. 2008. "Employer-Provided Health Insurance and the Incidence of Job Lock: A Literature Review and Empirical Test." *Expert Review of Pharmacoeconomics & Outcomes Research*, Vol. 8, no. 6, pp. 583–591.

Schor, Juliet B., and Samuel Bowles. 1987. "Employment Rents and the Incidence of Strikes." *Review of Economics and Statistics*, Vol. 69, no. 4, pp. 584–593.

Shapiro, Carl, and Joseph E. Stiglitz. 1984. "Equilibrium Unemployment as a Worker Discipline Device." *The American Economic Review*, Vol. 74, no. 3, pp. 433–444.

Soederberg, Susanne. 2007. "Freedom, Ownership, and Social (in-)Security in the United States." *Cultural Critique*, Vol. 65, no. 1, pp. 92–114.

Soederberg, Susanne. 2009. *Corporate Power and Ownership in Contemporary Capitalism: The Politics of Resistance and Domination*. New York: Routledge.

Stockhammer, Engelbert. 2008. "Some Stylized Facts on the Finance-Dominated Accumulation Regime." *Competition & Change*, Vol. 12, no. 2, pp. 184–202.

Stockhammer, Engelbert. 2013. "Financialization and the Global Economy." In Wolfson, Martin H., and Gerald A. Epstein, eds., *The Handbook of the Political Economy of Financial Crises*. New York: Oxford University Press, pp. 512–525.

Sullivan, James X. 2008. "Borrowing During Unemployment: Unsecured Debt as a Safety Net." *Journal of Human Resources*, Vol. 43, no. 2, pp. 383–412.

Tomaskovic-Devey, Donald, and Ken-Hou Lin. 2011. "Income Dynamics, Economic Rents, and the Financialization of the US Economy." *American Sociological Review*, Vol. 76, no. 4, pp. 538–559.

Topel, Robert H., and Michael P. Ward. 1992. "Job Mobility and the Careers of Young Men." *The Quarterly Journal of Economics*, Vol. 107, no. 2, pp. 439–479.

U.S. Census Bureau. 2011. *Income, Poverty, and Health Insurance Coverage in the United States: 2010*. Washington, DC: U.S. Government Printing Office.

U.S. Government Accountability Office (U.S. GAO). 2011 (Dec. 15). *Health Care Coverage: Job Lock and the Potential Impact of the Patient Protection and Affordable Care Act*. GAO-12-166R. Washington, DC: U.S. Government Printing Office.

Van Arnum, Bradford M., and Michele I. Naples. 2013. "Financialization and Income Inequality in the United States, 1967–2010." *American Journal of Economics and Sociology*, Vol. 72, no. 5, pp. 1158–1182.

Weller, Christian E. 2009. "Credit Access, the Costs of Credit and Credit Market Discrimination." *The Review of Black Political Economy*, Vol. 36, no. 1, pp. 7–28.

Yellen, Janet L. 1984. "Efficiency Wage Models of Unemployment." *The American Economic Review*, pp. 200–205.

CHAPTER 11

Income Diversification as Insurance in an Increasingly Risky World: Identifying Policy Goals

CHRISTIAN E. WELLER
University of Massachusetts Boston
and
Center for American Progress

JEFFREY B. WENGER
University of Georgia
and
RAND Corporation

INTRODUCTION

Labor market risk exposure—the possibility of being harmed by high unemployment and earnings fluctuations—has grown for households over the past three decades, while labor market risks—the actual market ups and downs—have also increased. Households historically could rely on social insurance systems, mainly Social Security and unemployment insurance, and on private protections such as defined benefit (DB) pensions and unions to partially insulate them from the vagaries of the market. But these cash income protections have weakened over time just as risks have increased.

Both trends—greater market volatility and fewer protections—have been driven by the same underlying factor. The financial sectors' relentless pressure on companies to pursue short-term profits and the increasingly widespread focus on companies on their short profitability[1] has contributed to greater earnings volatility and higher levels of long-term unemployment. Companies have sought to reduce their risks and long-term liabilities as well as their costs. This risk and cost shifting has translated into fewer publicly and privately provided benefits and a shifting of economic risks onto individuals, who now face greater earnings fluctuations, fewer benefits, and more long-term unemployment.

Households are generally risk averse, and the loss of social and private insurance should lead them to seek out additional insurance elsewhere (e.g., by saving more) and to lower their risk exposure elsewhere (e.g., by diversifying their income). Greater economic uncertainty should lead households to save more on their own, especially in the era of increased financial innovation, where theoretically it should have become easier for households to save more and buy more insurance suited to their own financial needs. But the evidence indicates that households do not fully compensate for the greater risk exposure with additional savings (Browning and Lusardi 1996; Weller 2010a).

This leaves households with more risk exposure than in the past. Households could experience more economic insecurity during recessions, exacerbating economic downturns caused by declines in consumption, for instance. The increase in economic insecurity may be particularly large among those for whom risk exposure is especially pronounced, such as communities of color, single women, and those with less education (Weller 2013; Weller and Bernardo 2014a, 2014b), such that wealth inequality may also rise, exacerbating economic downturns.

Growing household labor market uncertainty increases the need for ways to address these increasing risk exposures (e.g., through income diversification). Left unaddressed, rising risk exposure can feed back into more widespread economic insecurity and slower economic growth. Lowering households' risk exposure requires a multi-pronged approach that could include more opportunities for income diversification so that household incomes fall less during downturns, as would be the case with less diversified incomes.[2] Households could diversify their incomes by drawing down savings[3] and through employment-related income diversification. Spouses, for example, could work in separate employment arrangements or individuals could combine part-time employment arrangements as salary and wage employees, independent contractors, and entrepreneurs.

There is also the possibility that greater income diversification could create a virtuous cycle of economic security for some households. Households with more diversified incomes could take a longer-term view of their future, save more, invest more for the long-term, start a business, and pursue different job opportunities than would be the case for households with less diversified incomes. These follow-on effects from income diversification could create new sources of future income diversification. Policy interventions to help households diversify their incomes may be efficient because of this virtuous cycle, assuming that such interventions can indeed do so.

This is a strong assumption. Diversification strategies—relying on savings, working in separate employment arrangements, and receiving annuities—are after all fraught with substantial challenges. Being able to draw down savings when other income sources decline requires that households accumulate sufficient funds before their income declines and that the savings are accessible without restrictions. The evidence suggests that households in fact save less than they otherwise would in nonhousing savings because of complex restrictions tied to federal savings incentives (Weller and Ungar 2014), leaving households with limited savings to diversify their income streams during a downturn—and to do so with savings that are not fully accessible when incomes decline. Households may also encounter substantial transaction costs and liquidity constraints if they want to draw on the equity in their houses to diversify their income. Moreover, households may face institutional obstacles when trying to work less than full-time in separate employment arrangements (e.g., a requirement to work full-time for one employer to maintain health insurance coverage). Finally, annuity incomes such as Social Security and DB pension benefits are generally available only to households above a certain age.

We argue in this chapter that income diversification deserves policy attention as a response to the growing labor market risks that households face as a consequence of increased financialization—the growing prioritization of short-term profits to satisfy financial investors and lenders. We further argue that past policy efforts hold lessons for future policy targets to help households diversify their incomes. Past policy efforts related to public transfer payments have increased the importance of these income streams as part of income diversification among wage and salary earners. And past policy changes have made it potentially more difficult for households to use withdrawals from private savings as income diversification. Households need more income diversification, and policy can make it easier for them to achieve it. There appears to be an especially large space for policy to intervene with respect to private income sources.

This chapter develops the background and goals for policy makers to consider in their efforts to help households diversify their income. We summarize the theoretical and empirical literature on income diversification and present some data on existing household income diversification and on the potential economic benefits for households from such income diversification. We then discuss possible obstacles to household income diversification in the labor market and through other means (e.g., through more capital, business, and annuity income). The chapter concludes by suggesting some policy goals to remove these obstacles to greater income diversification.

LITERATURE REVIEW

U.S. corporations have increasingly emphasized short-term profits over other goals during the past few decades (Weller 2014). This short-term profit prioritization has meant that, among other things, corporations have cut back on wages, benefits, and training (Lazonick 2007; also see chapter by Lazonick in this volume) and slowed hiring during expansions

(Bivens and Weller 2006). As a result, households have faced increasing labor market risks, both unemployment risk and compensation risk (i.e., the volatility of labor income) over the past three decades. Long-term unemployment, for instance, has been on the rise since the 1970s (Rothstein 2011), earnings volatility has grown as well (Dynan, Elmendorf, and Sichel 2007; Hacker 2006), and the share of jobs with employer-sponsored health insurance and retirement plans has eroded over time (Copeland 2013; EBRI 2010; Schmitt 2007; U.S. Census Bureau 2013).[4] Changes in corporate priorities in the name of shareholder value creation are one key factor that drives growing labor market risks.

Labor market risks tend to correlate with demographic characteristics, such that the rise in labor market risks has contributed to growing income inequality. African Americans and Latinos tend to experience higher unemployment rates, greater incidences of long-term unemployment, higher earnings fluctuations, and lower employer-sponsored benefits than is the case for whites (Hoynes 1999; Stratton 1993; Weller and Ahmad 2013). And there is some evidence that women typically have had higher earnings fluctuations than men (Hoynes 1999), while their unemployment fluctuations have increased over time to match those of men (Abraham and Shimer 2001; Goodman, Antczak, and Freeman 1993) . Finally, labor market risks have also grown for older workers as they have seen sharper increases in long-term unemployment than was the case for younger workers (Rix 2011, 2012).

Income diversification would help to stabilize household incomes, especially when labor market risks are high. Diversifying so that households receive income from uncorrelated sources should theoretically result in more stable incomes—that is, a household that receives income from wages, dividends and interest income from savings, royalties from a patent, and benefits from Social Security should experience fewer and smaller income fluctuations than a household that relies solely on wages, even if the average income is the same.

Income diversification then requires households to find income sources in addition to their primary source of income, which typically is wages and salary. One key argument of optimal portfolio strategies is that diversification requires households to invest in financial assets that have returns that are not correlated with each other (e.g., investing in two technology stocks is not diversification, but investing in stocks and in bonds is). Translated to labor market experiences, this implies that households can diversify labor market risks within limits only by taking another job. The part-time jobs a person can qualify for may all be in the same industry or occupation and thus offer earnings that are somewhat or are highly correlated. Households hence can theoretically address labor market risks within limits only by working several part-time jobs and thus need to consider diversifying their incomes with income from nonwage and salary sources, such as business income, capital income, and public assistance.

More stable incomes should, all else equal, offer households some additional benefits that could improve their economic security. Stability may result in lower internal discount rates, which may have a number of potential benefits. First, it would increase human capital and business investment. Second, by stabilizing income and lowering internal discount rates, households would have longer planning horizons, which tend to be positively related to more savings and a greater chance of successful entrepreneurship.

Income Diversification Through Separate Employment Arrangements

Most pre-retirement–age adults receive the overwhelming majority of their income from work; however, work-related income—wages and benefits—has become increasingly volatile in recent business cycles (Dynan, Elmendorf, and Sichel 2007). Wage and salary employment can also severely compromise household income in recessions because adverse business cycle fluctuations may be more severe for some wage and salary employees than for entrepreneurs and independent contractors (Baker and Nelson 2005; Bradley, Aldrich, Shepherd, and Wiklund 2011; Hipple 2004).

Self-employment, in comparison, may lead to smaller income losses during an economic downturn (Baker and Nelson 2005; Bradley, Aldrich, Shepherd, and Wiklund 2011; Hipple 2004). Independent contractors can diversify their income by working for several clients across economic sectors. Likewise, successful entrepreneurs may have the personal ingenuity and financial reserves to develop new offerings that can weather economic downturns, in contrast to those who are dependent on their employer's decisions and finances. It is thus possible that households could stabilize their incomes in part through engaging in separate employment arrangements.

This rosy scenario downplays entrepreneurial risk. First, self-employment also holds substantial income risks compared with wage and salary employment. Independent contractors and entrepreneurs may see substantial income fluctuations during a downturn if they have to cover the costs of maintaining office space, for instance, or of keeping employees and subcontractors. Second, a diversified strategy may mean they are unlikely to experience catastrophic reductions in income. But it may make it more probable that *some* reduction in income is likely. Wage and salary workers who keep their jobs may be wholly unaffected by a recession, but they may lose all of their income during a layoff, while those with diversified incomes may see only part of their incomes disappear—either from job loss or other income reductions during a recession. This suggests that combining separate employment arrangements—wage and salary employment, independent contracting, and entrepreneurship—could stabilize incomes. Rather than choosing one employment form over another, workers may be best served by combining multiple employment/entrepreneurial arrangements.

Households that can diversify their income sources within their primary employment arrangement should see less volatility. A household may simultaneously receive income from working for somebody else, from entrepreneurship, and from independent contracts. One or more people in the household may split their time between these options—that is, households with more diversified income sources should face less income volatility.[5]

One fundamental difficulty of this diversification technique, aside from the aforementioned correlation between one person's part-time jobs, is time—specifically the fact that time is limited. Workers cannot be expected to hold one and a half to two full-time jobs in order to attain income diversification. To make this option more feasible, high-quality part-time jobs need to be available. However, most part-time jobs are not high paying, nor do they provide benefits. These jobs tend to be focused in relatively low-paying occupations: cashiers, waiters, and sales clerks. Second, while businesses generated an unprecedented number of part-time jobs during the most recent recovery, unpredictable scheduling makes it nearly impossible for many part-time workers to diversify their income by holding multiple jobs. Pressure is now mounting to provide more normalized schedules for these part-time workers so that they may combine part-time work with other ways of earning income.[6,7]

Public policy can play some role in determining when and how households receive business income. Policy, for instance, can require employers to provide at least two weeks' notice of a worker's schedule. Policy can also encourage entrepreneurship through an array of measures that target, for instance, the availability of financial capital for a start-up or ongoing business venture, the education of entrepreneurs, and the market for a business' products (e.g., through procurement rules for government purchases). Tax policy can also influence whether business owners reinvest their earnings into their business or take distributions from their earnings.

Income Diversification Through Withdrawal from Savings

Receiving income from savings could also allow households to diversify their current income—if workers had significant savings. Households with working-age members could receive realized capital gains from all nonretirement savings as well as dividends and interest payments from nonretirement, nonhousing savings. However, given the small percentage of households that have capital gains income, this method is infeasible for the vast majority. More commonly, households have capital gains, interest, and dividend income in restricted savings, such as retirement savings accounts. This capital income can help households diversify their income only when they withdraw money from these accounts. Because these monies are typically earmarked for retirement, very few households with working-age members withdraw money from these accounts (Argento, Bryant, and Sabelhaus 2013). Consequently, we ignore retirement account withdrawals as a separate income diversification strategy in this discussion; it is likely that ignoring this income will have little influence on our overall conclusions.[8]

Households could also tap into their home equity through reverse mortgages or home equity lines of credit, but very few households of any age do so, in large part because of high transaction costs and other restrictions (AARP 2010; Redfoot 2011; Twomey and Jurgens 2009).

Finally, most nonhousing forms of savings face severe restrictions on withdrawals, limiting households' ability to use them as income diversification measures when other forms of income decline. Households can use retirement savings, for instance, for a limited number of purposes other than retirement—such as a down payment on a first residence, medical emergencies, and education—without incurring penalties. In other words, households will incur penalties if they withdraw money from their retirement savings as an income diversification strategy when those accepted reasons for pre-retirement withdrawals do not exist.

Income Diversification Through Annuity Income

Older households seeking to diversify their incomes may rely increasingly on Social Security as a buffer because earnings tests were reduced and eventually eliminated,[9] allowing older households to earn money without any penalties while also receiving Social Security benefits. The earnings limits for full-benefit Social Security recipients were removed in early 2000 (Burke 2000). This may have potentially incentivized older entrepreneurs to collect Social Security benefits earlier than they otherwise would have to grow and expand their businesses (Burke 2000). Again, public policy can play a direct role in determining when and how much income a household can receive from a source other than wages and salaries.

Older households may have access to annuity income, a DB pension, and, to a lesser degree, their defined contribution (DC) plans (e.g., 401(k), 403(b), 457). Households may receive annuity benefits while also continuing to receive some employment-based income, depending on their age and the details of their annuity benefits. Fry, Cohn, Livingston, and Taylor (2011) suggest that older adults may be economically advantaged relative to younger households by having inflation-indexed Social Security as the anchor of their annual income streams. Likewise, pensions and retirement accounts may have generated higher retirement incomes because of the strength of the financial market after 1983 (Phelps, Zoelga, Bentolila, and Scott 2001).

Obstacles to Income Diversification

Income diversification offers potential economic benefits to many households that have experienced labor market uncertainty, but households face serious obstacles employing the income diversification strategies discussed above—savings withdrawals, combining employment arrangements, and annuity income.

First, households need to have savings before they can use capital income as a diversification strategy. Many households have few liquid assets that they can use in an emergency (Brooks, Wiedrich, Sims, and Medina 2014) and thus have few opportunities to diversify their income with income from their liquid savings. Communities of color, single women, and younger households are less likely than whites, single men, and older households to have substantial savings (Brooks, Wiedrich, Sims, and Medina 2014; Wolff, this volume). Shapiro (2004) notes that in 1984, an African American household had between 5 and 10 cents in wealth for every dollar of wealth held by a white household. More recently, Shapiro, Meschede, and Osoro (2014) found by following a representative sample of households over time (using the Panel Study of Income Dynamics) that working-age African American households had a median wealth—net of home equity—of $6,500 compared with $113,000 for white households.

Second, households must be able to access savings with relative ease when they have them. Household members cannot access their savings in retirement accounts without restrictions until age 59-1/2. Otherwise, they can withdraw funds only within some limits or else pay excise taxes on their withdrawals (Argento, Bryant, and Sabelhaus 2013). Under certain circumstances, households can borrow against their retirement savings accounts at attractive interest rates. However, penalties and marginal tax rates apply in the case of default, and in the event of job separation (voluntary or involuntary), the loan is payable in full. This "feature" of DB loans effectively increases the risk associated with the job by bundling full repayment of the loan upon separation from the job (Wenger and Weller 2014).

Third, households may be locked into full-time wage and salary employment if they need access to certain employment-based benefits.

Typically, only full-time jobs offer employer-sponsored group health insurance, DB pensions, matches to retirement savings accounts, and disability insurance. Purchasing these benefits on their own can be cost prohibitive to part-time workers. Often, households will diversify by having work arrangements in which one household member's job provides health insurance and other benefits to the entire household (Wenger and Reynolds 2009). Communities of color, single women, and younger households are less likely than whites, single men, and older households to have employment-based benefits and thus are less likely to be locked into their current jobs.

The Affordable Care Act (ACA) provides lower-income households with significantly expanded access to health insurance and, consequently, to health care. The ACA does so in two important ways. First, it allows for continued health insurance coverage for young adults (up to age 26 via parents). Second, it provides subsidies for insurance coverage and created health care marketplaces with competitive pricing for low-income households. By partially decoupling health insurance access from employment, the ACA will foster opportunities for workers to diversify employment into work arrangements that have not typically provided health insurance, such as self-employment, independent contracting, and part-time hours (Blumberg, Corlette, and Lucia 2013). Health insurance, however, is only one employer-sponsored benefit that is tax advantaged. Pensions and disability insurance will still make full-time work an attractive option.

Fourth, a household member must be at least 62 years old to receive an annuity from Social Security and at least age 59-1/2 to receive penalty-free annuities from DB pensions. Occasionally, annuitants must meet certain other requirements—such as not working for their previous employer—if they want to use annuity income from Social Security and DB pensions as an income diversification strategy in addition to employment-based income. The vast majority of households have access to Social Security as they get older, but communities of color, single women, and more recent cohorts will be less likely than whites, single men, and older cohorts to have access to DB pensions (Wolff, this volume).

EMPIRICAL ANALYSIS

We now investigate the prevalence of household income diversification and examine which households pursue this strategy and which avoid it. We also examine the method and circumstances of income diversification and find that private savings and self-employment have played a declining role in income diversification. Public transfers and Social Security have gained in importance in creating diversified annual income streams for wage and salary earners—especially as labor income overall has become less stable. This implies a special role for policy in facilitating income diversification for wage and salary earners during a time of rising labor market risks.

Data

We use the Federal Reserve's triennial Survey of Consumer Finances (SCF) as our data source. The SCF is the main nationally representative household survey on household wealth, detailing substantial information on all types and amounts of household assets and debt (Bricker, Kennickell, Moore, and Sabelhaus 2012) in addition to household income.

The SCF allows us to study household income diversification in greater detail than many other publicly available data sources. We define income diversification as a household's reliance on more than one substantial source of income. A household has a substantial source of income by our definition if it receives $5,000 or more from that source in any given year. Households can report income from several sources in the SCF, which we combine into six separate sources for easier presentation:

- Wage and salary income
- Capital income (capital gains, dividend and interest income)
- Social Security and other retirement annuities
- Business and farm income
- Public transfers such as unemployment insurance and worker's compensation, the Supplemental Security Income (SSI) program, Temporary Assistance for Needy Families (TANF), and the Supplemental Nutrition Assistance Program (SNAP).
- Other income such as alimony payments and rental income from investment properties

Our main two interests in this chapter are to understand the potential for income diversification for salary earners and to discuss the implications for policy design to improve the prospects for future income diversification. We note that extreme care must be used in drawing conclusions from a heterogeneous category of income such as government transfers. Normatively, receiving low-income transfers represents a shortcoming of the labor market to provide wages sufficient to maintain an adequate standard of living and is not a measure of successful income diversification.

Capital income, Social Security and retirement annuities, business income, and public transfers are more or less directly subject to policy interventions. This is not the case for other incomes, which include alimony payments, income from personal trusts, charitable donations, family gifts, and rental income from investment properties[10]—although tax policy plays an important role in many of these.

The SCF also includes detailed data on households' economic situations—specifically, their sources and total amount of income, income sources, and employment status. The SCF allows us to classify households as being dependently employed or self-employed because it distinguishes between being formally employed, being self-employed, and holding multiple jobs. It also allows us to determine whether the self-employed have a significant financial interest in their business (i.e., they are entrepreneurs). The SCF also includes a range of household demographic characteristics such as age, marital status, household size, education, ethnicity, and race. Most SCF variables are available on a consistent basis dating back to 1989; the most recent survey data are available for 2010.

We focus on younger and older households in our analysis by splitting the sample at age 50—that is, households headed by someone younger than 50 years are included in the younger household group and everyone else is included in the older household group. We include retirees and nonretirees in order to investigate how households diversify their income sources over the life cycle, if at all. Many households self-identify as retired but continue receiving income from wage and salary employment and from self-employment. Including retiree households allows us to better understand the diversification strategies of older households. Our conclusions are generally not influenced by our sample definition.

Finally, we combine a number of years in our analysis to study income diversification over time. We combine years from 1989 through 1998 and denote them as early years; the years from 2001 through 2010 are denoted as later years. The recession of 2001 marked a break in labor market risks because longer-term trends in long-term unemployment, wage uncertainty, and benefit cuts accelerated after the recession—that is, labor market risks were higher in the later years than in the early years (Bivens and Weller 2006).

Income Diversification and Potentially Beneficial Economic Outcomes

Table 1 summarizes the link between income diversification and potentially beneficial economic outcomes for wage and salary earners. We specifically consider the link between income diversification and the probability of self-identifying as savers, as well as median household wealth, the chance of a household self-identifying as having a planning horizon of five years or more, and the probability of being an entrepreneur. These data are only suggestive of the possible benefits of income diversification because the causality between these economic outcomes and income diversification likely runs in both directions (i.e., income diversification makes it easier for households to be successful entrepreneurs and successful entrepreneurship increases household access to income diversification tools). In other words, income diversification could result in a virtuous circle of household income stability and growth, but only if households can initially diversify their incomes. Public policy can help provide households with some income diversification, and such policy interventions could be efficient if they jump-start a virtuous cycle.

TABLE 1
Correlation Between Income Diversification and
Economic Outcomes for Wage and Salary Earners

	Only one substantial income source	Two substantial income sources	More than two substantial income sources
Households younger than 50 years old			
Probability of self-identifying as saver	47.8%	48.2%	61.0%
Median wealth	$18,620	$58,500	$260,300
Probability of self-identifying as having a planning horizon of 5 years or more	37.8%	43.0%	52.6%
Probability of being an entrepreneur	5.1%	19.0%	34.8%
Households 50 years old and older			
Probability of self-identifying as saver	55.1%	53.5%	60.7%
Median wealth	$106,200	$162,780	$696,650
Probability of self-identifying as having a planning horizon of 5 years or more	47.2%	45.1%	52.9%
Probability of being an entrepreneur	7.0%	12.9%	32.9%

Sources: Authors' calculations based on Board of Governors, Federal Reserve System, Survey of Consumer Finances, various years. Washington, DC: BOG. Inflation adjustments are based on the Bureau of Labor Statistics, Consumer Price Index for Urban Consumers, Research Series (CPI-U-RS), 2012. Washington, DC: BLS.

Notes:
All dollars are in 2010 dollars. Income can come from five different sources: wages, Social Security and other retirement income, capital gains and interest and dividend income, business and farm income, and transfer payments and other income. We define substantial income as income greater than $5,000 (in 2010 dollars) from any of these five sources.

Savers are those who indicate they save irregular or regular amounts.

Entrepreneurs are households who own and manage their own business and the business is worth at least $5,000 (in 2010 dollars).

Sample includes all households with substantial wage and salary income.

Our summary data here highlight two economic channels by which a virtuous cycle could emerge. First, income diversification may lead households to save more and better plan for the long term, thus increasing household wealth that then could be used for future income diversification. Second, income diversification may improve households' long-term planning horizon, which is generally considered a key factor in helping them better manage their finances—save more, invest to avoid excessive risk taking, and build successful small businesses.

Table 1 shows that income diversification correlates with a number of positive economic outcomes for households with substantial wage and salary earnings. Households with more diversified incomes tend to be more likely to self-identify as savers, have substantially more wealth, have longer planning horizons, and to be more likely to be entrepreneurs than households with less diversified incomes. These results hold for younger and older households. Of older households with two substantial income sources, for instance, 60.7% self-identify as savers compared with 55.1% of older households with only one or no substantial source of income.

Table 1 also shows that older households with two substantial income sources have almost seven times the median wealth— $696,650 compared with $106,200—as older households with less income diversification. And older households with two substantial income sources have a 52.9% chance of having a planning horizon of five years or longer compared with a 47.2% chance for older households with less income diversification. Finally, older households with two substantial income sources have a 12.9% probability of being entrepreneurial compared with only 7% for older households with less income diversification. The summary data indicate that income diversification may be associated with some peace of mind in the present because households with diversified incomes have a longer planning horizon and are more likely to save, have more wealth, and be more likely to build a successful business than households without diversified incomes.

Income Diversification Trends by Age and Year

Considering the potential benefits from income diversification, the next question then is whether we can see a growing trend toward more income diversification because wage and salary employment has become more precarious in an age of increased financialization. The absence of a clear trend toward more income diversification could give rise to future policy interventions that make it easier for households to diversify their increasingly risky wage and salary incomes.

Table 2 summarizes the income diversification trends by year and by age for households with substantial wage and salary income. We separate households into two groups (50 years and older and those who are younger)

TABLE 2
Income Diversification Trends by Year and Age

Year	Households younger than 50 years			Households 50 years old and older		
	Not more than one substantial income source	Two substantial income sources	Three or more substantial income sources	Not more than one substantial income source	Two substantial income sources	Three or more substantial income sources
1989	74.0%	19.2%	6.8%	46.0%	34.4%	19.6%
1992	77.9%	16.0%	6.1%	48.3%	34.4%	17.3%
1995	78.3%	17.9%	3.8%	48.0%	34.1%	17.9%
1998	78.0%	16.9%	5.2%	53.5%	32.7%	13.8%
2001	79.3%	16.1%	4.5%	49.9%	33.6%	16.5%
2004	78.2%	17.0%	4.8%	49.1%	36.6%	14.3%
2007	75.6%	18.2%	6.2%	50.6%	33.7%	15.7%
2010	74.2%	19.7%	6.1%	45.5%	37.3%	17.2%

Sources: Authors' calculations based on Board of Governors, Federal Reserve System, Survey of Consumer Finances, various years. Washington, DC: BOG. Inflation adjustments are based on the Bureau of Labor Statistics, Consumer Price Index for Urban Consumers, Research Series (CPI-U-RS), 2012. Washington, DC: BLS.

Notes:
All dollars are in 2010 dollars. Income can come from five different sources: wages, Social Security and other retirement income, capital gains and interest and dividend income, business and farm income, and transfer payments and other income. We define substantial income as income greater than $5,000 (in 2010 dollars) from any of these five sources. The trends do not change if we put the threshold for substantial income at $3,000 (in 2010 dollars).

Shares calculated for respective populations of households, broken down by age.

Sample includes only households with substantial wage and salary income.

and consider the number of substantial income sources that households on average had in any survey year from 1989 through 2010.

Table 2 illustrates two important facts. First, income diversification substantially increases with wealth and wealth typically increases with age. More than half of older households typically have two or more substantial sources of income, while the share of younger households with two or more substantial income sources generally is at or below 25%. Older households in particular are generally more than three times as likely as younger households to have three or more substantial income sources.[11]

Second, Table 2 shows there is no clear trend toward more income diversification over time, even though labor market uncertainty has grown. The share of older households with more than one substantial income source has bounced between 49% and 55% from 1989 through 2010, while the comparable share of younger households fluctuated between 21% and 26%. The absence of a trend toward more income diversification among wage and salary earners may suggest that households encounter problems diversifying their incomes, even as wage and salary incomes have become less stable. This may give rise to policy interventions to stabilize household incomes through income diversification.

Combining the years from 1989 through 1998 and the years from 2001 through 2010 facilitates the presentation of summary statistics and ensures that we have sufficient sample sizes in all of our subsequent calculations. The absence of a trend toward more income diversification further justifies combining these data years.

Table 3 shows income diversification by demographic characteristics, age, and time period to highlight differences in income diversification across households. We specifically consider race, family status, and educational attainment as key household characteristics. We combine the data into two income diversification categories—one substantial source of income and more than one—to preserve observations and facilitate presentation. Remember, we include data only for households with wage and salary income, so households in the "one substantial source of income" category have substantial wage and salary incomes. We consequently report the share of households with substantial income in addition to wage and salary income in Table 3, broken down by race, family status, and education in addition to age and time period.

Three broad factors stand out from the data in Table 3. First, older households again tend to have more income diversification than younger households do. And second, we again see no trend toward more income diversification over time. Third, there are substantial differences in income diversification by age, mainly in expected ways. Whites, married couples, and households with college education have more income diversification

TABLE 3
Income Diversification* by Household Demographics, Age, and Time Period

	Households younger than 50 years		Households 50 years old and older	
	Early years (1989–1998)	Later years (2001–2010)	Early years (1989–1998)	Later years (2001–2010)
Whites	24.7%	25.1%	54.3%	54.9%
African Americans	18.9%	20.3%	35.6%	36.0%
Hispanics	13.0%	16.2%	31.8%	38.6%
Other	20.4%	22.6%	43.5%	42.4%
Married couples	24.4%	24.8%	53.8%	55.8%
Single men	16.6%	16.4%	48.6%	42.0%
Single women	22.6%	22.5%	41.7%	41.0%
Less than high school/GED	18.5%	16.7%	48.7%	47.0%
High school/GED	19.1%	21.6%	44.7%	48.9%
Some college	23.7%	20.9%	51.5%	47.0%
College graduate	26.9%	27.1%	57.6%	55.9%

*Diversification indicates substantial income in at least one category outside wage and salary income.

Sources: Authors' calculations based on Board of Governors, Federal Reserve System, Survey of Consumer Finances, various years. Washington, DC: BOG. Inflation adjustments are based on the Bureau of Labor Statistics, Consumer Price Index for Urban Consumers, Research Series (CPI-U-RS), 2012. Washington, DC: BLS.

Notes:
All dollars are in 2010 dollars. Income can come from five different sources: wages, Social Security and other retirement income, capital gains and interest and dividend income, business and farm income, and transfer payments and other income. We define substantial income as income greater than $5,000 (in 2010 dollars) from any of these five sources. The trends do not change if we put the threshold for substantial income at $3,000 (in 2010 dollars).

Shares calculated for respective populations of households, broken down by age.

Sample includes only households with substantial wage and salary income.

than do communities of color, single men and single women, and households with less education.[12] The bottom line, though, is that groups of households that generally experience greater labor market uncertainty and for whom labor market risks have especially grown tend to have less income diversification than their counterparts. Accordingly, policies to increase income diversification should ideally target population groups that generally face higher labor market risks than their counterparts.

Distribution of Income Sources for Households with Diversified Incomes

Table 4 highlights the importance of particular income sources for households with diversified incomes beyond wages and salaries.[13] We specifically report the shares of households with substantial income from capital income, business and self-employment income, Social Security and pension income, public transfer income, and other income in addition to wage and salary income.

Our summary data in Table 4 show widespread use of at least three additional sources of substantial incomes for working households. More than one fifth of young households and more than one fourth of older households had substantial capital income. Similarly, conditional on having employment income, more than one third of young households and more than one fourth of older households had substantial business and farm income. Finally, close to one fifth of younger households reported substantial transfer incomes, while more than half of older households indicated substantial Social Security and pension income. Households diversify beyond wage and salary incomes through a number of private and public sources. The use of private sources is comparable by age, but the use of public sources predictably varies with age, with older households relying more heavily than younger households on Social Security and younger households relying more heavily than older ones on public transfer programs.

Our data in Table 4 also show a few noteworthy and substantial changes from the early to the later years. Capital income declines in importance over time for younger and older households alike, Social Security and pension incomes gain in importance for older households, and public transfers gain in importance for younger households. These changes are all connected to policy changes, as we discuss in the next section.

We note that business and farm income fell slightly from the early to the later years. Starting a business is a comparatively easier way for households to diversify their incomes than relying, for instance, on savings withdrawals and public programs. Savings take time to build up, and income from public sources requires households to meet specific eligibility thresholds. Households wanting and needing to diversify their incomes amid rising labor market uncertainty should have turned increasingly to

TABLE 4

Substantial Income Sources for Households with Diversified Income
and Substantial Wage and Salary Income, by Age and Time Period

	Households younger than 50 years		Households 50 years old and older	
	Early years (1989–1998)	Later years (2001–2010)	Early years (1989–1998)	Later years (2001–2010)
Capital income	28.3%	21.2%	36.7%	27.2%
Business income	38.1%	35.7%	28.8%	28.2%
Social Security and pension income	14.1%	13.2%	55.3%	60.2%
Public transfer income	15.5%	21.8%	5.2%	8.1%
Other income	32.4%	35.5%	20.7%	20.9%

Sources: Authors' calculations based on Board of Governors, Federal Reserve System, Survey of Consumer Finances, various years. Washington, DC: BOG. Inflation adjustments are based on the Bureau of Labor Statistics, Consumer Price Index for Urban Consumers, Research Series (CPI-U-RS), 2012. Washington, DC: BLS.

Notes:
All dollars are in 2010 dollars. Income can come from five different sources: wages, Social Security and other retirement income, capital gains and interest and dividend income, business and farm income, and transfer payments and other income. We define substantial income as income greater than $5,000 (in 2010 dollars) from any of these five sources. The trends do not change if we put the threshold for substantial income at $3,000 (in 2010 dollars).

Shares calculated for respective populations of households, broken down by age.

The numbers add up to more than 100% because households can report more than one additional source of income in addition to substantial wage and salary income.

self-employment. The stable-to-declining importance of self-employment income then suggests that generating substantial self-employment income has not become easier for households over time. Policy changes may make it easier for households to become self-employed and thus diversify their incomes.

DRAWING POLICY IMPLICATIONS FROM THE DATA

Table 4 shows three key changes in the receipt of substantial income beyond wages and salaries: falling capital income for younger and older households, rising Social Security income for older households, and rising public transfer incomes for younger households. We discuss potential causes for these three changes to show that all of them are in part related to past policy changes. We also note that while diversifying income sources can be a way to stabilize income and consumption, some forms of diversification are unambiguously bad. Diversifying income by receiving SNAP (food stamps), TANF (welfare), or other means-tested programs is an indication that the workers and firms cannot jointly provide adequate income for maintaining consumption. Other nonmeans-tested programs such as unemployment insurance also indicate a failure in the labor market—either a short-term friction or a long-term structural problem. Again, this form of income diversification should not be considered a "healthy" form of diversifying.

Other forms of diversification are more ambiguous. First, realized capital income has become less relevant over time, in part because of growing incentives to save in tax-advantaged vehicles such as 401(k)s and individual retirement accounts (IRAs). These accounts restrict access to capital income until money is actually withdrawn, typically upon retirement. Thus, a policy-induced increase in savings incentives has limited the possibility for income diversification, thereby increasing the "lockbox" nature of retirement savings and providing an added hurdle to the temptation of using retirement savings for some other purpose.

Table 5 summarizes data on withdrawals from IRA/Keogh retirement accounts relative to capital income. A household member can usually withdraw funds from his or her IRA/Keogh at age 59-1/2 without penalty. We anticipate fewer withdrawals among younger households, along with a nontrivial share of households withdrawing funds in the later period. The SCF contains information on such withdrawals only for the years from 2004 through 2010. As shown in Table 5, adding withdrawals to capital income shows only minor changes to the share of younger households with expanded capital income compared with just capital income. But expanding the definition of capital income to include withdrawals raises the share of older households with capital income by about three percentage points compared with the narrower definition. This is a nontrivial increase in income diversification among older households. Restricting access to savings, in this case by limiting pre-retirement withdrawals, reduces households' use of capital income as an income diversification tool.

Second, the growing reliance on Social Security and pensions among older wage and salary households is not surprising. The gradual elimination of earnings limits for full retirees and the increases in earnings limits for early retirees have made it easier for older households to receive Social Security benefits in addition to wage and salary earnings—that is, older households have been able to diversify their incomes as a direct result of a policy change.

Third, the growth of public transfers income—unemployment insurance (UI), TANF, SSI, and SNAP—among younger households requires some additional explanation. The share of wage and salary households with substantial public transfers has grown particularly fast for younger single

TABLE 5
The Effect of IRA Withdrawals on Substantial Income

Year	Households younger than 50 years			Households 50 years old and older		
	With substantial capital income	With substantial capital income and IRA withdrawals	Difference	With substantial capital income	With substantial capital income and IRA withdrawals	Difference
2004	17.9%	18.3%	0.4%	26.5%	28.7%	2.3%
2007	21.6%	22.2%	0.7%	27.4%	31.8%	4.4%
2010	12.3%	13.0%	0.7%	21.1%	23.7%	2.6%

Sources: Authors' calculations based on Board of Governors, Federal Reserve System, Survey of Consumer Finances, various years. Washington, DC: BOG. Inflation adjustments are based on the Bureau of Labor Statistics, Consumer Price Index for Urban Consumers, Research Series (CPI-U-RS), 2012. Washington, DC: BLS.

Notes:
All dollars are in 2010 dollars. Income can come from five different sources: wages, Social Security and other retirement income, capital gains and interest and dividend income, business and farm income, and transfer payments and other income. We define substantial income as income greater than $5,000 (in 2010 dollars) from any of these five sources.

Shares calculated for respective populations of households, broken down by age.

Capital income refers to capital gains and to dividend and interest income; IRA withdrawals refer to withdrawals from individual retirement accounts and Keogh plans.

men, from 12.3% in the early years to 26.4% in the later years—an increase of 14.1 percentage points.[14] The comparable share for married couples has grown by 4.6 percentage points, from 16.2% to 20.8% and by 8.3 percentage points for younger single women, from 14.8% to 23.1%.

Table 6 shows that the growth of public transfers among younger single men is highly correlated with receipt of unemployment insurance. The SCF reports annual incomes (i.e., single men could have substantial earnings during part of the year and receive substantial UI benefits during the remaining years). The calculations show that more than 60% of younger households that had substantial wage and salary income and substantial transfer income also had substantial UI benefits in the early years. This share jumped to 85.8% in the later years. At the same time, the respective shares for married couples and single women declined—that is, the increase in public transfer income among younger men likely reflects growing labor market uncertainty, especially for that population. This finding is

TABLE 6

Share of Households with Substantial Unemployment Insurance Benefits Among Households Who Had Substantial Wage and Salary Income and Substantial Public Transfer Income, by Period, Age, and Family Status

	Households younger than 50 years		Households 50 years old and older	
	Early years (1989–1998)	Later years (2001–2010)	Early years (1989–1998)	Later years (2001–2010)
Married couples	71.2%	62.1%	36.7%	27.2%
Single men	63.5%	85.8%	28.8%	28.2%
Single women	39.6%	33.3%	55.3%	60.2%

Sources: Authors' calculations based on Board of Governors, Federal Reserve System, Survey of Consumer Finances, various years. Washington, DC: BOG. Inflation adjustments are based on the Bureau of Labor Statistics, Consumer Price Index for Urban Consumers, Research Series (CPI-U-RS), 2012. Washington, DC: BLS.

Notes:
All dollars are in 2010 dollars. Income can come from five different sources: wages, Social Security and other retirement income, capital gains and interest and dividend income, business and farm income, and transfer payments and other income. We define substantial income as income greater than $5,000 (in 2010 dollars) from any of these five sources.

Shares calculated for respective populations of households, broken down by age, period, and family status.

not surprising. Men have suffered more than women have from long-term unemployment in the aftermath of the two most recent recessions. And men often do not qualify for other cash transfer programs such as SSI and TANF.

One conclusion then is that unemployment insurance offered households access to income diversification when they needed it most (i.e., when the probability of becoming unemployed and the chance of being out of work for long periods of time increased).

Fourth, the small decline in business and farm income partly reflects the growth of single households. The share of married wage and salary households with substantial business income was much larger than among single households. And among older households, for instance, the respective share remained relatively stable over time, with 31.8% in the early years and 31.6% in the later years, although this share decreased from 43.7% to 40.9% for younger households.[15] Put differently, for single households, there appear to be severe obstacles to splitting their time between wage and salary employment and self-employment.

These obstacles, such as the tight linkages between full-time employment and benefit receipt, could become fruitful policy targets by making it easier for households to access key benefits when they are working less than full-time for a single employer.

PARAMETERS OF POSSIBLE POLICY REFORMS

Our discussion shows the need for, the possible benefits of, and the reality of income diversification. We conclude that private savings have played a declining role and self-employment has not increased, while public transfers and Social Security have gained in importance in creating diversified annual income streams for wage and salary earners as wage and salary income has become less stable. All of the changes in the relative importance of specific income streams for wage and salary earners can be traced to specific policy changes or lack thereof, as we discussed in the preceding section.

We now present a few basic parameters for future policy development to either strengthen or reverse existing trends, so that wage and salary earners can better diversify their household incomes in an era of growing uncertainty.

Private Savings

We note two important goals with respect to private savings: (1) a need for broad-based savings for lower- and middle-income households, and (2) a need to gain easier access to savings for households that have some.

Policy experts have long proposed a number of measures to increase household savings. These measures include automatic enrollment of participants into employer-sponsored retirement plans; automatic payroll deductions into IRAs; promoting low-cost, low-risk savings vehicles; and streamlining and more efficiently targeting federal savings incentives (Weller and Ungar 2014).

Similarly, public policy already facilitates reverse mortgages—and such efforts could be expanded. Making it easier for households to access their savings when they need them, such as by streamlining savings incentives, could help them diversify their incomes with capital income.

Self-Employment

A critical obstacle to self-employment as an income diversification strategy is that many households work full-time to secure crucial benefits such as health insurance, long-term disability, and employer-sponsored retirement savings. Public policy can make it easier for people to access these benefits in an affordable way, even if people do not work full-time for an employer. The Affordable Care Act of 2009 is one policy example whereby policy efforts have made it possible to decouple benefits from full-time employment (Blumberg, Corlette, and Lucia 2013). Employees who no longer receive health insurance benefits from their employers because they no longer work full-time can now purchase health insurance at terms similar to employer-sponsored insurance plans. Policy makers could theoretically model other publicly sponsored risk pools to make it easier for households to access affordable and critical benefits without working full-time for an employer.

It is possible, however, that faced with increasing quasi-fixed costs of employment, more employers may opt for creating part-time jobs (rather than full-time). The ACA has put in place a relatively low standard for full-time work (30 hours) and counts employees on a full-time equivalent basis—that is, two 15-hour-per-week employees constitute a full-time worker. It is unlikely that firms have much of an incentive from the ACA to create part-time work. It may be that workers are accepting part-time jobs and using the health care exchanges from the ACA to purchase group coverage. Current research is mixed on why part-time employment has increased in this recovery, but it seems clear that the ACA will be a boon for those who opt for self-employment.

Public Transfer Payments

Public transfer payments, especially unemployment insurance, have gained in importance as employment relations have become more precarious. However, many workers in vulnerable employment arrangements (i.e., involuntary part-time workers, low-wage workers, and workers with frequent bouts of unemployment) do not necessarily qualify for unemployment insurance benefits. States' differences in UI application rates vary dramatically, and there is little systematic research investigating this phenomenon. Policies that facilitate application and provide valuable job-search assistance, along with wage subsidies for workers who accept new jobs with significantly lower wages, would reduce the labor market volatility experienced by some workers.

Social Security

Past policy changes have made it easier for older workers to receive benefits while still earning a paycheck. Public policy can build on these efforts. It is also possible to make it easier for younger workers to access Social Security benefits, at least temporarily—for example, when a caregiving situation arises (Glynn and Farrell 2013), and Social Security modernization could improve benefits for vulnerable populations (Weller 2010b).

CONCLUSION

Income diversification as conceptualized in this chapter provides an important mechanism for households to maintain income and consumption during periods of economic hardship. Our conceptualization of income diversity differs from commonly accepted notions of diversification, such as those employed in portfolio management. Diversification here implies income from any and all sources, including those that are contingent—such as transfer programs and social insurance. While it seems clear that having these forms of income available to workers is beneficial, it is also the case that using them is indicative of labor markets gone awry.

We analyzed data from the Survey of Consumer Finance to show where public policy could intervene to improve income diversification for struggling workers. In theory, there is room for policy makers to build mechanisms that could make it easier for households to gain access to multiple substantial forms of income.

The data show that policy could make an important difference in helping households diversify their incomes. Public income sources already often serve as tools for income diversification either because people want to use them to stabilize their incomes or because they have to increasingly rely on public assistance in more volatile labor markets. Whether by choice or out of necessity, public transfer programs play a growing role in income diversification. One policy goal then is to give households more access to public transfer programs during periods of economic hardship, as long as well-known moral hazard problems with expanded social insurance access are addressed.

Moreover, the data show that policy has made it more difficult, or at least failed to facilitate, the use of private income diversification strategies (e.g., by restricting access to household savings). Calls for increased private savings are ubiquitous, while effective public policies have been rare. The United States continues to have historically, and internationally, low personal saving rates. In addition, retirement savings policy has effectively "bottled up" a considerable portion of the assets of the upper middle classes, making those assets difficult and costly to access.

In our analysis, we fully anticipated that entrepreneurs and the self-employed would play an important role in income diversification. It is the case that entrepreneurism and self-employment are important sources of income diversification, but they have not increased during the ensuing periods in which income insecurity has increased. The second policy goal then would be to make it easier for households to save and use their savings for income diversification when they so desire. Improving opportunities for households to diversify their incomes could create a virtuous cycle of income stability over time.

Much of our analysis investigated the relationship between income diversification and household wealth; however, it is unclear which way the causal arrow points. It seems intuitive that older, wealthier households would have income from a broad range of sources. Less clear is the effect of having multiple sources of income in leading to wealthier households, though we should not undersell this causal direction. Having the resources to maintain consumption, pay bills, avoid credit card default, and continue paying the mortgage may lead to higher overall wealth. So, too, will the managerial skills necessary for financial management that come from entrepreneurial activity. It seems likely that having a diverse income portfolio may lead to increases in wealth. Put more positively, income diversification could create a virtuous cycle so that more diversified incomes result in more income stability and wealth over time and more income stability and wealth result in more income diversification.

Diversifying risk, especially in a world of growing risks, through appropriate private sector and public policy tools is one of modern finance's most important contributions to economic well-being. Applying the lessons of diversification to a household's income can be an important tool in developing a more stable and healthier middle class amid rising labor market risks.

The mechanisms necessary for increasing income diversification are difficult but not impossible to build. Public policy can make important differences on the margins, often having the largest impacts on households who need assistance the most. Much work has already been done to show both the need and the potential for policy to provide more economic security over time with greater income diversification.

ENDNOTES

[1] There are some countervailing forces to this trend toward greater short-term profit orientation among U.S. companies and globally operating companies abroad (e.g., in Germany), but they only serve to slow, not change, the direction of this trend (Dörre, this volume; Lazonick this volume). Factors such as collective bargaining agreements and internal conflicts between managers and corporate owners appear to occasionally slow the prioritization of short-term profits over other corporate goals (Dörre, this volume; Lazonick, this volume).

[2] Public insurance strategies can include Social Security and unemployment insurance reforms as well as greater access to public health insurance. We focus only on income diversification in this chapter to illustrate the potential and limits of this approach.

[3] Savings refers to any store of wealth that the household could access when employment-related incomes decline. Private unemployment and disability insurance in addition to retirement savings would hence fall under this standard savings definition, as would home equity (see chapter by Wolff in this volume).

[4] The health insurance data ignore the declining quality of health insurance coverage. The insured face growing co-pays for health care services as well as rising shares of health insurance premiums (KFF 2013).

[5] The literature on households in developing countries discusses families diversifying income sources to decrease risk and increase stability. See, for instance, Reardon, Berdegue, Barrett, and Stamoulis (2006).

[6] See "A Push to Give Steadier Shifts to Part-Timers" (http://nyti.ms/1A21Ths).

[7] See "Part-Time Schedules, Full-Time Headaches" (http://nyti.ms/1B4erYA).

[8] We use data on withdrawals from IRAs as supplementary materials in our empirical discussion.

[9] For a complete history of Social Security earnings tests, see http://1.usa.gov/1A23fsp.

[10] Our treatment of rental income as other income requires additional explanation. Policy can encourage the purchase of investment properties, although this is the case only for particular circumstances (e.g., to encourage investment in low-income housing, in the United States). We therefore treat rental income as a nonpolicy-relevant income source.

[11] We checked to make sure that this is not just a spurious correlation between age and wealth. Specifically, we calculated the chance of having two or three (or more) substantial income sources by age and wealth levels. We still find lower probabilities of having more than one substantial source of income for younger households than among older households, even after controlling for wealth levels. For instance, 39.1% of younger households with wealth in the top third of all wealth holders had two or more substantial sources of income in the later years from 2001 through 2010 compared with 52.2% of older households. The conclusion that a larger share of older households had more substantial sources of income than was the case for younger households holds for all wealth levels in both the early and later time periods. Calculations are not shown here but are available from the authors upon request.

[12] We should note that single women are more likely than single men to have diversified incomes, which may be due to a better chance of receiving public assistance from programs that lend particular support to single mothers such as TANF, as we discuss later.

[13] We calculate that households with substantial wage and salary income are two to three times more likely to have diversified incomes as households without substantial wage and salary income, regardless of age and time period. Details are available from the authors upon request.

[14] Authors' calculations.

[15] Authors' calculations.

REFERENCES

AARP. 2010 (Oct. update). "Reverse Mortgage Loans: Borrowing Against Your Home." (http://bit.ly/17cpHVn).

Abraham, K., and R. Shimer. 2001. *Changes in Unemployment Duration and Labor Force Attachment.* NBER Working Paper No. 8513, Cambridge, MA: National Bureau of Economic Research.

Argento, R., V. Bryant, and J. Sabelhaus. 2013. *Early Withdrawals from Retirement Accounts During the Great Recession.* FEDS Working Paper No. 2013-22, Washington, DC: Board of Governors of the Federal Reserve System.

Baker, T., and R. Nelson. 2005. "Creating Something from Nothing: Resource Construction through Entrepreneurial Bricolage." *Administrative Science Quarterly*, Vol. 50, pp. 239–366.

Bivens, J., and C. Weller. 2006. "The 'Job-Loss' Recovery: Not New, Just Worse." *Journal of Economic Issues*, Vol. 40, no. 3, pp. 603–628.

Blumberg, L.J., S. Corlette, and K. Lucia. 2013. *The Affordable Care Act: Improving Incentives for Entrepreneurship and Self-Employment—Timely Analysis of Immediate Health Policy Issues.* Washington, DC: Urban Institute.

Bradley, S., H. Aldrich, D. Shepherd, and J. Wiklund. 2011. "Resources, Environmental Change, and Survival: Asymmetric Paths of Young Independent and Subsidiary Organizations." *Strategic Management Journal*, Vol. 32, no. 5, pp. 489–509.

Bricker, J., A.B. Kennickell, K.B. Moore, and J. Sabelhaus. 2012. "Changes in U.S. Family Finances from 2007 to 2010: Evidence from the Survey of Consumer Finances." *Federal Reserve Bulletin*, Vol. 98, no 2, pp. 1–80.

Brooks, J., K. Wiedrich, L. Sims, Jr., and J. Medina. 2014. *Treading Water in the Deep End: Findings from the 2014 Assets and Opportunity Score Card.* Washington, DC: Corporation for Enterprise Development.

Browning, M., and A. Lusardi. 1996. "Household Saving: Micro Theories and Micro Facts." *Journal of Economic Literature*, Vol. 34, no. 4, pp. 1797–1855.

Burke, T. 2000. "Social Security Earnings Limit Removed." *Compensation and Working Conditions*, Summer, pp. 44–46.

Copeland, C. 2013. "Retirement Plan Participation and Asset Allocation, 2010." *EBRI Notes*, Vol. 34, no. 4. Washington, DC: Employee Benefits Research Institute.

Dynan, K., D. Elmendorf, and D. Sichel. 2007. *The Evolution of Household Income Volatility.* Finance and Economics Discussion Series. Washington, DC: Federal Reserve Board.

Employee Benefits Research Institute (EBRI). 2010. *Retirement Plan Participation: Survey of Income and Program Participation, 2009 Data.* Washington, DC: EBRI.

Fry, R., D. Cohn, G. Livingston, and P. Taylor. 2011. "The Rising Age Gap in Economic Well-Being." Washington, DC: Pew Research Center (http://pewrsr.ch/1Bf6nnK).

Glynn, S.J., and J. Farrell. 2013. "What the FAMILY ACT Means for All Americans." Washington, DC: Center for American Progress (http://ampr.gs/1Bf6v6P).

Goodman, W., S. Antczak, and L. Freeman. 1993. "Women and Jobs in Recessions: 1969–92." *Monthly Labor Review*, Vol. 116, no. 7, pp. 26–35.

Hacker, J. 2006. *The Great Risk Shift: The New Economic Insecurity and the Decline of the American Dream.* New York: Oxford University Press.

Hipple, S. 2004. "Self-Employment in the United States: An Update." *Monthly Labor Review*, Vol. 127, no. 7, pp. 13–23.

Hoynes, H. 1999. *The Employment, Earnings, and Income of Less Skilled Workers Over the Business Cycle.* NBER Working Paper No. 7188, Cambridge, MA: National Bureau of Economic Research.

Kaiser Family Foundation (KFF). 2013. *Employer Health Benefits 2013 Annual Survey.* Washington, DC: KFF.

Lazonick, W. 2007. "Economic Institutional Change and Employer Pensions." In T. Ghilarducci and C. Weller, eds., *Employee Pensions: Policies, Problems and Possibilities.* LERA Research Volume. Champaign, IL: Labor and Employment Relations Association.

Phelps, E., G. Zoelga, S. Bentolila, and A. Scott. 2001. "Structural Booms." *Economic Policy*, Vol. 16, no. 32, pp. 83–106.

Reardon, T., J. Berdegue, C. Barrett, and H. Stamoulis. 2006. "Household Income Diversification into Rural Nonfarm Activities." In S. Haggblade, P. Hazell, and T. Reardon, eds., *Transforming the Rural Nonfarm Economy: Opportunities and Threats in the Developing World.* Baltimore: Johns Hopkins University Press.

Redfoot, D. 2011. *How Recent Changes in Reverse Mortgages Impact Older Homeowners.* AARP PPI Fact Sheet No. 211, Washington, DC: AARP Public Policy Institute.

Rix, S.E. 2011. *Recovering from the Great Recession: Long Struggle Ahead for Older Americans.* Washington, DC: AARP Public Policy Institute.

Rix, S.E. 2012. *The Employment Situation, March 2012: Unemployment Rises for Older Workers.* AARP PPI Fact Sheet. Washington, DC: AARP Public Policy Institute.

Rothstein, J. 2011. "Unemployment Insurance and Job Search in the Great Recession." *Brookings Papers on Economic Activity*, Fall, pp. 143–196.

Schmitt, J. 2007. *The Good, the Bad, and the Ugly: Job Quality in the United States Over the Three Most Recent Business Cycles.* Washington, DC: Center for Economic and Policy Research.

Shapiro, T.M. 2004. *The Hidden Cost of Being African American: How Wealth Perpetuates Inequality.* New York: Oxford University Press.

Shapiro, T., T. Meschede, and S. Osoro. 2014. "The Widening Racial Wealth Gap: Why Wealth Is Not Color Blind." In R. Cramer and T.R. Williams Shanks, eds., *The Assets Perspective: The Rise of Asset Building and Its Impact on Social Policy*. New York: Palgrave Macmillan.

Stratton, L.S. 1993. "Racial Differences in Men's Unemployment." *Industrial and Labor Relations Review*, Vol. 46, no. 3, pp. 451–463.

Twomey, T., and R. Jurgens. 2009. *Subprime Revisited: How Reverse Mortgage Lenders Put Older Homeowners' Equity at Risk*. Boston: National Consumer Law Center.

U.S. Census Bureau. 2013. *Income, Poverty, and Health Insurance Coverage in the United States: 2012*. Washington, DC: U.S. Government Printing Office.

Weller, C. 2010a. "Did Retirees Save Enough to Compensate for the Increase in Individual Risk Exposure?" *Journal of Aging and Social Policy*, Vol. 22, no. 2, pp. 152–171.

Weller, C. 2010b. *Building It Up, Not Tearing It Down: A Progressive Approach to Social Security*. CAP Report. Washington, DC: Center for American Progress.

Weller, C. 2013. *Making Sure Money Is Available When We Need It: Protecting Household Assets Must Become an Integral Part of U.S. Savings Policies*. Washington, DC: Center for American Progress.

Weller, C. 2014. "Sustainable Growth, Corporate Governance, and Fiduciary Duties." In J. Hawley, A. Hoepner, K. Johnson, J. Sandberg, and E. Waitzer, eds., *Handbook of Institutional Investment and Fiduciary Duty*. Cambridge, UK: Cambridge University Press.

Weller, C., and F. Ahmad. 2013. *The State of Communities of Color in the Economy*. CAP Report. Washington, DC: Center for American Progress.

Weller, C., and S. Bernardo. 2014a. "How Does Labor Market Risk Exposure Relate to Wealth Inequality?" Paper presented at the annual meeting of the Eastern Economic Association, Boston, March 2014.

Weller, C., and S. Bernardo. 2014b. *Putting Retirement at Risk: Has Financial Risk Exposure Grown Faster for Older Households Than Younger Ones?* Unpublished manuscript. Boston: University of Massachusetts Boston.

Weller, C., and S. Ungar. 2014 (Mar. 3). "Overhauling Federal Savings Incentives. Tax Notes Special Report." *Tax Notes*, pp. 1–9.

Wenger, J.B., and J. Reynolds. 2009. "Older Married Workers and Nonstandard Jobs: The Effects of Health and Health Insurance." *Industrial Relations: A Journal of Economy and Society*, Vol. 46, no. 3, pp. 411–431.

Wenger J.B., and C.E. Weller. 2014. "Boon or Bane: 401(k) Loans and Employee Contributions." *Research on Aging*, Vol. 36, no. 5, pp. 527–556. doi: 10.1177/0164027513507001

ABOUT THE CONTRIBUTORS

Eileen Appelbaum is senior economist at the Center for Economic Policy and Research and visiting professor at the University of Leicester in the United Kingdom. Previously, she was a professor at Rutgers University and director of the Center for Women and Work, research director at the Economic Policy Institute, and professor of economics at Temple University. Her research focuses on the implications of public policy and of ownership structures and company practices for organizational effectiveness and employee outcomes. She has written extensively about work and family policy and the implications of financialization for companies and workers. Her recent publications include *Unfinished Business: Paid Family Leave in California and the Future of U.S. Work–Family Policy* and *Good for Business? Connecticut's Paid Sick Leave Law* (both co-authored with Ruth Milkman), and *Private Equity at Work: When Wall Street Manages Main Street* (co-authored with Rosemary Batt). Appelbaum was president of LERA in 2010 and currently is on the board of the Industry Studies Association.

Rosemary Batt is the Alice Hanson Cook Professor of Women and Work at the ILR School, Cornell University. She is a professor in human resource studies and international and comparative labor and editor of the *ILR Review*. Her research focuses on comparative international studies of management and employment relations, with particular emphasis on financialization and globalization and their impact on industry restructuring and firm behavior. Batt has written extensively on human resource practices and their effect on firm performance, the quality of jobs, and wage and employment outcomes. Her work has appeared in such journals as the *Academy of Management Journal*, *British Journal of Industrial Relations*, *European Journal of Industrial Relations*, *Industrial and Labor Relations Review*, *Industrial Relations*, *International Journal of Human Resource Management*, and *Personnel Psychology*. She is co-author of *Private Equity at Work: When Wall Street Manages Main Street* and *The New American Workplace*, and co-editor of the *Oxford Handbook on Work and Organization*.

Rita Berlofa works for Santander Bank Brazil and is financial secretary for the São Paulo Osasco and Region's Bank Union. She coordinates negotiations for the Santander Bank Brazil workers' collective agreement on a national level. She also participates in the coordinating body of the Southern Region Union and coordinates the International Network of Santander Bank Workers for UNI Americas Finance. She is a member of the UNI Global Union and UNI Finanças Mundial's executive board. From 2005 through 2008, Berlofa was secretary of organization and administration for the bank union, and from 2003 through 2005, she served on the executive board for the Secretariat of Workers' Health in the same institution.

Sara M. Bernardo is a PhD candidate in the Department of Public Policy and Public Affairs at the University of Massachusetts Boston. Her research examines the relationships between U.S. household indebtedness, and financial and labor market developments and social policy, focusing on the transformations within economic and social security practices since the 1970s. Bernardo also is a lecturer in the Department of Economics at UMass Boston, teaching courses on money and financial institutions, the history of economic thought, and labor market economics. Her research and teaching objectives aim at bridging the gap between current economic policy issues and the standard theories taught in university economics curricula, with the goal of encouraging a deeper analysis of the policy-making process in order to develop more comprehensive economic security policies.

Joseph R. Blasi is author of *The Citizen's Share: Reducing Inequality in the 21st Century*, written with Richard Freeman and Douglas Kruse. Blasi is the J. Robert Beyster Distinguished Professor and a sociologist at the School of Management and Labor Relations at Rutgers University, where he teaches undergraduate and graduate courses on corporate governance. He also is a research associate at the National Bureau of Economic Research. Blasi's research interests include economic sociology, the social and economic history of the corporation, and public policy. He studies the relationship between the division of rewards, power, and prestige in organizations and performance using large datasets. His books and articles have addressed different systems of work and broad-based employee ownership, profit sharing, and stock options in corporations, countries, industry sectors (such as Silicon Valley), and historical periods. Another recent book, *Shared Capitalism at Work* (with Douglas Kruse and Richard Freeman), reported on a large study of employees with shares and was funded by the Russell Sage Foundation and the Rockefeller Foundation. Blasi also co-authored *In the Company of Owners: The Truth About Stock Options and Why Every Employee Should Have Them* (with Douglas Kruse and former *Business Week* associate editor Aaron Bernstein).

Janet Boguslaw is a senior scientist at the Heller School for Social Policy and Management at Brandeis University, associate director at the Institute on Assets and Social Policy, and associate director of the master's degree program in public policy. She previously worked at the Center for Corporate Citizenship at Boston College and for the Industrial Services Program, a quasi-public agency of the State of Massachusetts. Her work focuses on creating multisector innovations and partnerships to advance economic opportunity, security, and stability. Boguslaw has worked with corporate managers to advance community development initiatives; with state and federal agencies, unions, and nonprofits on workforce training, employment stabilization, and regional economic development; and with foundations and others on state and local asset-building initiatives. She is the author of *Social Partnerships and Social Relations: New Strategies in Workforce and Economic Development* and numerous other publications.

Dan Brooks retired in June 2010 as UAW assistant director of the UAW–Ford National Program Center, which handles all joint union–management programs on quality, safety, training, employee involvement, diversity, employee assistance, work–family matters, and other initiatives. As a trade unionist, Brooks is considered one of the nation's leading experts in high-performance work systems. He has participated in every national UAW–Ford negotiation since 1989. He is co-author (with Joel Cutcher-Gershenfeld and Martin Mulloy) of the forthcoming book *Inside the Ford–UAW Transformation: Pivotal Events in Valuing Work and Delivering Results.*

Noel M. Cowell is a senior lecturer in employment relations at the Mona School of Business and Management, University of the West Indies, Mona, Jamaica. His current research focuses on high-performance work systems in major Caribbean corporations. He also has carried out research on strategic human resource management responses to criminal violence and workplace misbehavior, and on sexuality and work.

Joel Cutcher-Gershenfeld is a professor and the former dean of the School of Labor and Employment Relations at the University of Illinois at Urbana-Champaign. He also is a senior research scientist at the National Center for Supercomputing Applications in Urbana and holds a fractional appointment at the University of Sydney. Beginning in January 2016, he will serve as a professor in the Heller School for Social Policy and Management at Brandeis University. He is co-author (with Dan Brooks and Martin Mulloy) of the forthcoming book *Inside the Ford–UAW Transformation: Pivotal Events in Valuing Work and Delivering Results.* Cutcher-Gershenfeld's current research focuses on the stakeholder alignment needed for agile institutions in the 21st century.

Klaus Dörre is a professor of sociology at Friedrich-Schiller-Universität Jena, Germany, where he chairs the Department of Labour, Industrial and Economic Sociology. He is the director of the German Research Foundation research group, Post-Growth Societies. His areas of research are financial market capitalism, labor relations, flexible and precarious employment, and the theory of capitalism, among others. He also is a research associate at the Society, Work and Development Institute at the University of the Witwatersrand, Johannesburg, South Africa, where he focuses on the politics of precarious society and decent work. Dörre's most recent book in English is *Sociology, Capitalism, Critique*, co-authored with Hartmut Rosa and Stephan Lessenich.

Richard B. Freeman is Ascherman Professor of Economics at Harvard University. He directs the Science and Engineering Workforce Project at the National Bureau of Economic Research, is faculty co-director of the Labor and Worklife Program at the Harvard Law School, and is co-director of the Harvard Center for Green Buildings and Cities. He is a Fellow of the American Academy of Arts and Science and in 2011 was appointed Frances Perkins Fellow of the American Academy of Political and Social Science. Freeman received the Mincer

Lifetime Achievement Prize from the Society of Labor Economics in 2006 and the IZA Prize in Labor Economics in 2007. His research interests include the job market for scientists and engineers, the transformation of scientific ideas into innovations, Chinese labor markets, income distribution and equity in the marketplace, and forms of labor market representation and shared capitalism. His most recent book, co-authored with Joseph Blasi and Douglas Kruse, is *The Citizen's Share: Reducing Inequality in the 21st Century*.

Teresa Ghilarducci is a nationally recognized expert in retirement security. She holds the Bernard L. and Irene Schwartz Chair in Economic Policy Analysis in the Department of Economics at The New School for Social Research and directs the Schwartz Center for Economic Policy Analysis, which focuses on economic policy research and outreach. She joined The New School in 2008 after 25 years as a professor of economics at the University of Notre Dame. Her most recent book, *When I'm Sixty Four: The Plot Against Pensions and the Plan to Save Them*, investigates the loss of pensions for older Americans and proposes a comprehensive system of reform. Ghilarducci's previous books include *Labor's Capital: The Economics and Politics of Employer Pensions*, winner of an Association of American Publishers award in 1992; and *Portable Pension Plans for Casual Labor Markets*, published in 1995.

Christos A. Ioannou, an economist, has served as deputy Greek ombudsman in charge of social protection, health, and welfare issues since 2013. He has also served as a mediator and arbitrator with the Organisation for Mediation and Arbitration in Greece since 1991. His research work has been in the areas of labor markets, human resources, collective bargaining, and wage and employment policies. His current research focuses on productive reforms in the Greek public sector and in the private economy.

Alexander B. Kaufman is a business consultant and research assistant whose work focuses on economics, political science, and finance. A graduate of Washington University, he earned his bachelor's degree in political science and was the student chair of the Investor Responsibility Advisory Committee. He was awarded the 2013 Grossman–Alexander prize for Outstanding Graduate in American Politics.

Douglas L. Kruse is a Distinguished Professor in the School of Management and Labor Relations at Rutgers University and a research associate at the National Bureau of Economic Research. He served as senior economist at the Council of Economic Advisers in 2013 and 2014. His research focuses on the employment and earnings effects of disability, and the causes, consequences, and implications of employee ownership and profit sharing. His most recent co-authored books are *The Citizen's Share: Reducing Inequality in the 21st Century*, *People with Disabilities: Sidelined or Mainstreamed?*, and *Shared Capitalism at Work*. He has published widely in peer-reviewed journals and is an editor of the *British Journal of Industrial Relations*. Kruse has testified four times before Congress on his economic research, authored or co-authored three U.S. Department of Labor studies, and served on the President's Committee on Employment of People with Disabilities.

William Lazonick is a professor of economics and director of the Center for Industrial Competitiveness at the University of Massachusetts Lowell. He is co-founder and president of The Academic–Industry Research Network. He also is a visiting professor at the University of Ljubljana, the Telecom School of Management (Paris), and the University of Toronto. Previously, Lazonick was assistant and associate professor of economics at Harvard University, professor of economics at Barnard College of Columbia University, and Distinguished Research Professor at INSEAD. His books include *Competitive Advantage on the Shop Floor*, *Business Organization and the Myth of the Market Economy*, and, which won the 2010 International Joseph A. Schumpeter Prize. His article, "Profits Without Prosperity: Stock Buybacks Manipulate the Market and Leave Most Americans Worse Off," received the HBR McKinsey Award for outstanding article in the *Harvard Business Review* in 2014. He currently is at work on a new book, *The Theory of Innovative Enterprise*.

Stephen Lerner is a labor and community organizer and architect of the groundbreaking Justice for Janitors campaign. Over the past three decades, he has organized hundreds of thousands of janitors, farmworkers, garment workers, and other low-wage workers into unions, resulting in increased wages, first-time health benefits, paid sick days, and other improvements on the job. A leading critic of Wall Street bankers and the increased financialization of the U.S. economy, Lerner argues that the growing power and influence of the finance industry has led to record income inequality and served as the primary driving force behind the creation of overwhelming debt obligations at the state and local levels. He advocates nonviolent civil disobedience as a tactic to challenge the influence of Wall Street and corporations. He is a frequent contributor on national television and radio programs and has published numerous articles charting a path for a 21st century labor movement focused on growth and meeting the challenges of a global economy. He currently is a Fellow at the Kalmonovitz Initiative for Labor and the Working Poor at Georgetown University.

Martin Mulloy is the former vice president of global labor affairs for Ford Motor Company. He handled Ford's global labor strategy, which encompassed approximately 200,000 employees worldwide. Mulloy led Ford's national negotiations in the United States with the UAW in 2007, 2009, and 2011—during which time Ford restructured to avoid bankruptcy and emerged as one of the most successful automakers in the world. He retired from Ford in January 2014 and is now president of Mulloy Consulting, LLC.

Danny Roberts is the head of the Hugh Lawson Shearer Trade Union Education Institution at the Consortium for Social Development and Research, Open Campus, University of the West Indies, Mona, Jamaica. He is a vice president of the Jamaica Confederation of Trade Union and previously held the positions of vice president of the National Workers Union; president of the Union of Clerical, Administrative and Supervisory Employees; and chairman of the Michael Manley Foundation. He is co-editor of *A Road Map for Trade Unions: Relevance and Sustainability* and a part-time lecturer in industrial relations at the University of the West Indies. Roberts is a published author and member of the board of National Integrity Action Limited.

Joelle Saad-Lessler is an economist with extensive experience in econometric modeling, statistical programming, and data analysis. She worked as an assistant professor of economics at Long Island University for nine years. She currently is an economist at the Schwartz Center for Economic Policy Analysis. Her research work is predominantly applied, with a focus on the economics of retirement. Her publications span a range of issues, including the impact of immigration on local wages, the economics of international child labor, the savings behaviors of Mexican Americans, and the automatic stabilization properties of various retirement savings vehicles.

Tanzia S. Saunders is a PhD candidate in the Public Sector Management Unit in the Department of Government and adjunct lecturer at the Mona School of Business and Management, University of the West Indies, Mona, Jamaica. She has published in the areas of employment relations, human resource management, sexuality and work, and sustainable development. Her research interests include employment corruption in the Jamaican public sector, employment governance, employment public policy, and sexuality and work.

Hina Sheikh currently serves as director of organizing at Community Coalition, a community organizing institution in South Los Angeles. She is a graduate of the University of Massachusetts Amherst, where she majored in political science. Sheikh did her graduate studies in urban and regional planning at University of California, Los Angeles.

Søren Viemose has worked as a neutral, independent advisor in numerous negotiations. He is part of the New European Industrial Relations research group, which covers 11 European countries and is looking into developing social dialogue in European organizations. He is the owner of The KALOVIG Center, which links theory and practice in negotiation, conflict management, and consensus building. This venue serves as a facility for labor negotiations, mediations, seminars, training, meetings, and research. Viemose also teaches in the Master of Conflict Mediation program at Copenhagen University.

Christian E. Weller is a professor of public policy at the University of Massachusetts Boston and a Senior Fellow at the Center for American Progress in Washington, D.C. Prior to coming to UMass Boston, he worked as the senior economist for the Center for American Progress and as a research economist with the Economic Policy Institute in Washington, D.C. He is an expert on retirement income security, wealth inequality, pensions, and Social Security but has also widely written on macroeconomics, corporate governance, and international financial stability. He has a prolific publications record spanning both academic and policy-oriented publications, including LERA's 2007 research volume, *Employee Pensions: Policies, Problems, and Possibilities*, co-edited with Teresa Ghilarducci. Weller was awarded LERA's Susan C. Eaton Outstanding Scholar–Practitioner Award in 2005, served as LERA co-editor in chief from 2010 through 2013, and was a member of LERA's executive board from 2008 through 2011.

Jeffrey B. Wenger is a senior policy researcher at the RAND Corporation. Before that, he was a professor of public policy at the University of Georgia's School of Public and International Affairs, Department of Public Administration and Policy. His research interests span several areas: unemployment insurance, health insurance, pension coverage, and entrepreneurism. His research has been published in the *Journal of Policy Analysis and Management, Journal of Aging and Social Policy, American Journal of Economics and Sociology,* and *Journal of Pension Economics and Finance.* Wenger is co-author of *Health Insurance Coverage in Retirement.*

Edward N. Wolff is a professor of economics at New York University, where he has taught since 1974. He also is a research associate at the National Bureau of Economic Research and is on the editorial board of *Economic Systems Research, Journal of Economic Inequality, Journal of Socio-Economics,* and *Review of Income and Wealth.* He served as managing editor of the *Review of Income and Wealth* from 1987 through 2004 and was a senior scholar at the Levy Economics Institute of Bard College (1999–2011), a visiting scholar at the Russell Sage Foundation (2003–2004), president of the Eastern Economics Association (2002–2003), a council member of the International Input–Output Association (1995–2003), and a council member of the International Association for Research in Income and Wealth (1987–2012). Wolff's most recent books are *Productivity Convergence: Theory and Evidence* and *Inheriting Wealth in America: Future Boom or Bust?*